UTB

UTB **2478**

W0224960

**Eine Arbeitsgemeinschaft der Verlage**

Beltz Verlag Weinheim · Basel · Berlin
Böhlau Verlag Köln · Weimar · Wien
Wilhelm Fink Verlag München
A. Francke Verlag Tübingen und Basel
Haupt Verlag Bern · Stuttgart · Wien
Verlag Leske + Budrich Opladen
Lucius & Lucius Verlagsgesellschaft Stuttgart
Mohr Siebeck Tübingen
C. F. Müller Verlag Heidelberg
Ernst Reinhardt Verlag München und Basel
Ferdinand Schöningh Verlag Paderborn · München · Wien · Zürich
Eugen Ulmer Verlag Stuttgart
UVK Verlagsgesellschaft Konstanz
Vandenhoeck & Ruprecht Göttingen
WUV Facultas · Wien

Barbara Korte

# The Short Story in Britain

A Historical Sketch and Anthology

A. Francke Verlag Tübingen und Basel

*Barbara Korte* ist Professorin für anglistische Literaturwissenschaft an der Albert-Ludwigs-Universität Freiburg i.Br.

Umschlagabbildung: Dora Carrington, Illustration zu "The Mark on the Wall" von Virginia Woolf.

Bibliografische Information der Deutschen Bibliothek

Die Deutsche Bibliothek verzeichnet diese Publikation in der Deutschen Nationalbibliografie; detaillierte bibliografische Daten sind im Internet über <http://dnb.ddb.de> abrufbar.

© 2003 · A. Francke Verlag Tübingen und Basel
Dischingerweg 5 · D-72070 Tübingen
ISBN 3-7720-3005-X

Das Werk einschließlich aller seiner Teile ist urheberrechtlich geschützt. Jede Verwertung außerhalb der engen Grenzen des Urheberrechtsgesetzes ist ohne Zustimmung des Verlages unzulässig und strafbar. Das gilt insbesondere für Vervielfältigungen, Übersetzungen, Mikroverfilmungen und die Einspeicherung und Verarbeitung in elektronischen Systemen.

Einbandgestaltung: Atelier Reichert, Stuttgart
Satz: Informationsdesign D. Fratzke, Kirchentellinsfurt
Druck und Bindung: Pustet, Regensburg
Printed in Germany

ISBN 3-8252-2478-3 (UTB Bestellnummer)

## Contents

**Part III: Anthology**

**Appendix**

## Preface

This book aims to provide a historical sketch of the short story in 'British' literature,[1] that is, writing produced in the cultural space now referred to as Britain and encompassing the cultural spaces of England, Scotland and Wales as opposed to Ireland. An ample amount of short fiction has been produced in this space and at a much earlier time than in the United States, yet the status which the genre has enjoyed in American literature has tended to overshadow critical opinion about the short story produced elsewhere. Despite a renewed interest in literary historiography over the last few decades, histories of English or British literature still curiously circumnavigate the short story.[2] Of course, the short story partakes in the major general developments of literary and cultural history, but its history also has specific traits that deserve to be investigated.

The present survey wishes to put the short story more visibly on the map of the literary landscapes of Britain. It will highlight important stages in its development, placing them in their wider cultural contexts, and cite important critical opinion about the nature of this development. The stories mentioned and discussed here represent some of the most significant tendencies. In a book of this scope it is impossible to consider all stories that have gained a 'classical' status because they have often been anthologized and discussed in collections of interpretations or critical studies. Neither can all 'famous' stories by 'famous' writers be mentioned. It has been attempted instead to present a balanced mixture of familiar (and easily accessible) stories and stories of a less familiar nature; most of the latter are of historical interest or of recent origin. For the authors included, it should be remembered that many have produced a far greater variety of story types than those discussed here. Stories are, where suitable, quoted extensively, and, to provide further illustration of how the short story has evolved in Britain over the centuries of print culture (from early modern to present post-

---

[1] On the problems of defining 'British' literature, see pp. 11–19 below.

[2] On the topicality of literary history and its practice, see the overview in Stierstorfer (2001, 451–470). Among the few histories which discuss the short story in Britain at least briefly are Fowler (1987) and Wagner (1988).

postmodern times), sixteen have been selected for the book's anthology section. As the first chapter will show, the telling of short stories long predates the age of print and has an oral tradition which still affects short-story writing today. It was in the medium of print, however, that short fiction in prose first gained 'literary' status, and it was a print medium, the periodical press, which helped the short story to shape itself into a genre in its own right. We have now entered a stage in literary history in which the computer-based hypertext is perceived as a challenge to established forms of printed literature; this book will end accordingly with a brief look at how short hyperfiction may imply a step beyond the current print-based notion of the 'short story'.

The book is primarily addressed at student readers on the undergraduate and graduate levels, but teachers may also find it useful as a guide to stories teachable in school, where the American short story still dominates the syllabus. Apart from providing an outline of major historical tendencies, the book is intended as a guide to major research, sources and research tools. Its bibliography, which is divided into five parts (Selected Anthologies – Reference Works – Collections of Interpretations – History, Theory and Criticism of the Short Story – Other Materials) is extensive and partly annotated. The bibliography is fairly complete in its listing of general and historical studies but gives only a selection of work on individual writers. For more information on writers and specific stories, readers are referred to a specialized journal, *Studies in Short Fiction*,[3] and the collections of interpretations listed in the bibliography. To minimize footnotes, studies on authors are acknowledged in the text only where they are directly quoted.

Stories are quoted, wherever possible, from an author's collection or, in some cases, their original place of publication in a periodical. In addition, the list of sources names selected anthologies in which the stories can also be located; these are either anthologies currently on the British and German market, or older anthologies accessible through university libraries. Note that stories are quoted without individual page references in order to reduce the amount of 'unreaderly' references in the text and reduce the number of footnotes. Since short stories are short and the respective quotations thus easy to identify, this practice has been found permissible here. Stories contained in the anthology section are identified in the text by bold print. The year given in parentheses for each story is, where possible, that of its first publication. However, dates for original periodical publication are difficult to ascertain, and, in some cases, only the first publication in an author's collection could be traced, indicated by 'first coll. in'.

[3] A cumulative index to volumes 1 to 32 is included in *Studies in Short Fiction*, 32.4 (1995).

For their help in locating stories and criticism, going through periodicals, catalogues and bibliographies, as well as checking the quotations, I should like to thank my Tübingen and Freiburg student assistants Katja Bay, Daniela Merz, Christine Pfeiler, Ulrike Pirker, Sandra Schaur, Christina Spittel (who also prepared the index), Christoph Schüly and Florian Zieger. For reading the manuscript and helpful comments, my thanks go to Dr Ralf Schneider and Dr Jochen Petzold, and for proofreading, to Neal O'Donoghue.

BK, Freiburg, May 2003

# Part I:

## Preliminaries to a History of the 'Short Story' in 'Britain'

An introduction to the short story in Britain and its most important developments raises questions that have to be asked *before* individual historical phases can be approached: How can the short story be defined as a 'genre' and when, depending on that definition, can it be said to have emerged? And how can a distinctively 'British' short story be demarcated? The following sections address these basic questions, starting with a sketch of dominant features that have defined the short story in the literary competence of the prime agents of the literary communicative system[1] since the end of the nineteenth century, when a notion of the short story as a distinct kind of literature, was, for the most part, firmly established.

## 1. Short Story Definitions

Short-story theory[2] and criticism agree upon the fact that the short story is a form of great elasticity and hence difficult to define. In the words of H.E.

---

1 These agents are text producers and receivers as well as mediators like publishers and post-processors like critics and academic interpreters. For the notion of 'literary competence', referring to the knowledge which authors, readers and other agents in the system of literary communication have, at a given time, of the constituents, conventions and norms that govern literary texts, see Culler (1975, 113–130). For an indepth discussion of the notion of the 'system of literary communicative interaction' and its participants, see S.J. Schmidt (1982).

2 For the purposes of a historical sketch, short-story theory forms a necessary background rather than an issue in itself. The most important theoretical studies by which this book is informed are listed in the bibliography. Susan Lohafer, in her "Introduction" to Lounsberry *et al.* (1998), distinguishes distinctive phases of short-story theorization: in the 1960s, the focus was on the history and aesthetic of the form, as well as the social dynamics of the genre; then structuralism became dominant until, in the course of the 1980s, "reception theory filtered in. The short story was defined in terms of the reading experience it generates, and that meant a return to Poe's emphasis on the imminence of endings." (x) Since, discussion has tended to be "genre-bending and interdisciplinary" (xi), but cognitive reception research is a prominent new branch (see for instance Lohafer 1998). Important theory collections include Lohafer and Clarey (1989) and May (1994); of the German publications, Goetsch (1978a) provides a most helpful introduction to basic issues.

Bates (1965, 15f.), a British short-story writer to whom we owe one of the most frequently-cited books about this kind of literature,

> the short story can be anything the author decides it shall be; [...] from the static sketch without plot to the swiftly moving machine of bold action and climax, from the prose poem, painted rather than written, to the piece of straight reportage in which style, colour, and elaboration have no place, from the piece which catches like a cobweb the light subtle iridescence of emotions that can never be really captured or measured to the solid tale in which all emotion, all action, all reaction is measured, fixed, puttied, glazed, and finished, like a well-built house, with three coats of shivering and enduring paint. In that infinite flexibility, indeed, lies the reason why the short story has never been adequately defined.

To Valerie Shaw (1983, vi), "[t]here are so many different kinds of short story that the genre as a whole seems constantly to resist universal definition", and to Clare Hanson (1985, 9), the short story "exhibits a protean variety". In this wide range of historical and typological variation, there seem to be few features that characterize all the different kinds of texts which readers nowadays will likely identify as short stories. Nevertheless, it is possible to come to a basic understanding of what kinds of literature are most *commonly* written, published and read as short stories today. These are texts of narrative prose[3] which report a minimal action or at least convey the sense of a passing of time. Their perusal can, as Edgar Allan Poe wrote in his review of Hawthorne's *Twice-Told Tales* of May 1842 (Poe 1984, 571f.), one of his famous *ur*-pieces of short-story theory, (ideally) be "completed at one sitting" of "a half-hour to one or two hours", and they thus tend not to exceed a limit of around 10,000 words.[4] If they do, classification seems to become a problem, and terms like 'long short story', 'novella', 'novelette' or even 'short novel' are employed for such instances as Charles Dickens's *A Christmas Carol* or Joseph Conrad's *Heart of Darkness*. That the brevity of a story also has a lower limit is indicated by the fact that '*short* short stories' (of approximately two hundred to a thousand words or less) and 'minimal stories' (consisting of just a few sentences) have been distinguished from the short story of a more extensive average length.[5]

The criterion of quantity is at the core of all attempts at definition.[6]

---

[3] See, however, anthologies of short stories in verse: Finn (1982) and Reid (2000).

[4] For this word count, see for example Beachcroft (1968, 2), who determines the "modern short story" as "the prose narrative of up to 10,000 words or so".

[5] For an introduction to the short short story, see Nischik (1993); the minimal(ist) story is discussed by Sodowsky (1996).

[6] On size as a factor generally influencing notions of genre, see Fowler (1982, 62f.): "differences of size have many repercussions on the nature of the reading experience."

However, as Norman Friedman (1972, 297) pointed out in a landmark article first published in 1958, there are many ways to make a short story short:

> a story may be short because its action is intrinsically small; or because its action, being large, is reduced in length by means of the devices of selection, scale, and/or point of view. No one can tell in advance that, if a story is short, it is short because it has a certain number of words, or because it has more unity, or because it focuses upon culmination rather than development. All we can do, upon recognizing its shortness, is to ask how and why.

The 'true' short story, according to most critics, is not just a story that is short. There is a special quality to its shortness, it has a calculated brevity and makes maximum use of its restricted scope.[7] Its elements of content have been carefully selected and shaped so as to give an impression of special unity, a particular economy of means, concentration and artfulness of composition. It has a particular suggestiveness, allusiveness and importance of ending and closure,[8] and it invites a degree of reader participation not – or at least less frequently – found in longer pieces of narrative, or in other forms of short prose.[9] In the words of H.E. Bates (1965, 220):

> A story must, so to speak, be weighed in the hands, to a fine and intuitive test. Its balance will collapse under a superfluous sentence, even a superfluous word. To see a writer building up his tale, piece by piece, as one builds up a toy tower of match-sticks, and to feel that he knows both instinctively and consciously which match-stick must be last and exactly when the tower will bear no more, is an experience which can become, also, a general critical test of form.

---

7 A special quality of shortness is also postulated for short films and short plays. See, for example, the contributions in Horstmann (1981), which emphasize that short narrative films are structurally different from long ones. Heinrich (1997, 52–58) discusses the brevity of the short film in terms of short-story theory; Cooper and Dancyger (1994) also explore the relationship between short story and short film. Raskin (2002) offers a close study of nine short-film 'classics'. For a brief introduction to short plays, see Kosok (1980).

8 The traditional plot story used to end on a climax, a point or a surprising turn. In an essay on "How to Tell a Story" (1895), Mark Twain speaks about "the snapper on the end" (in Weber and Greiner 1977, 54). While such endings are considered 'closed', the modern short story tends towards a more 'open' ending which leaves questions or problems unresolved. On techniques of ending (and beginning) short stories, see Bonheim (1982, chapters 6 to 8). The term 'closure' usually refers not to narrative technique but cognitive processes through which the reader constructs his or her sense of a story's 'completeness' (see, in particular, Lohafer 1983).

9 See Hardy (1993, 364): "It intensifies the normally participatory act of reading by insisting that we 'fill in the sketch' as we go along. Our degree of involvement is heightened, moreover, by the recalcitrance that comes from both density and brevity; we must hold several aspects of the story in our minds at once because the short narrative resists organizing them definitively under a single dominant mode."

H.E. Bates (1965, 24) claims that the short story proper could not emerge until readers had become competent enough to deal with its techniques of selection, compression, abridgement and implication: "Education, travel, wider social contact, the increased uniformity of life, dress, and manners have made us all familiar with things that were once remote enough to need to be described. [...] It is no longer necessary to describe; it is enough to suggest." The development of setting(s) and character(s) in short stories tends to be more restricted compared to the novel. In terms of subject, although short stories have been written about all kinds of themes imaginable, there emerges a certain preference for content-matter that tends to be intrinsically shorter or that lends itself to being treated in a shorter format. Short stories often render a single incident, an elemental human experience or a situation of crisis rather than developments over a long span of time; they tend to depict a "significant moment" (O'Connor 1963, 23), an instant of revelation or change in a character's life (hence the relatively frequent story of initiation), a comic or ironic reversal, an extraordinary event or liminal experience.

Since the days of Poe, the short story has undergone significant metamorphosis, especially under the treatment of modernists and postmodernists. Nevertheless, many of the criteria just mentioned can be traced back to Poe's postulate in his review of *Twice-Told Tales* that a successful "short prose narrative", like any piece of literature of the first order, should have a special "unity of effect or impression". Therefore, "[i]n the whole composition there should be no word written, of which the tendency, direct or indirect, is not to the one pre-established design". (Poe 1984, 571f.) Here and elsewhere, Poe himself never used the term 'short story'; in fact, this genre label was not coined until several decades after Poe, when the American professor of literature and critic Brander Matthews propagated Poe's ideas in his *Philosophy of the Short-story* (first published as an essay in 1885, and expanded into a book in 1901). Matthews magisterially proclaimed the distinctness of a kind of short narrative in prose which he termed 'Short-story', spelt with a hyphen to mark that this kind of narrative was essentially different from other kinds of stories that are merely short.

However, all criteria for defining the short story as a distinct genre with a distinct aesthetic are only relative.[10] Nevertheless, a basic understanding of the form rooted in Poe's notion of unity of effect has informed most critical studies until today. It has determined whether and where stories were and are published, has been shared by many of the form's practitioners, and has shaped the genre expectation of readers. But it is an understanding of

[10] See Goetsch (1978a, 23).

the short story which, in the English-speaking world, seems to be inextricably linked with the nineteenth-century work and theoretical reflection of *American* pioneers on the form and its criticism.

## 2. The Short Story in Britain – A Delayed Appearance?

In light of this prominent American contribution to genre definition and Poe's role as a genre *Übervater*, it is not surprising that the short story in Britain appears a stepchild of literary criticism and history when compared to its counterpart 'across the pond'. Studies and handbooks habitually observe that the short story 'proper' emerged in Britain with considerable delay, not until the *late* nineteenth century, and was overshadowed by the production and theorizing of the genre in the United States. Dean Baldwin (1993, 23), for instance, observes:

> One of the more curious anomalies of literary history is why the short story was so late to blossom in Britain. By the 1840s the genre was already established in America, and within two decades it had taken root in Germany, Russia, and France. I am speaking here, of course, of the modern short story, defined loosely as Poe's story of 'single effect', not simply of fiction shorter than the typical novel. This modern story did not achieve prominence in Britain until the 1880s, even though Britain would appear especially likely to develop the genre, since during the period of the story's 'invention', if we may call it that, Britain was a world leader in the writing and dissemination of fiction.

As in the United States, the short story has had a particular impact in colonial and postcolonial societies of the English-speaking world, both articulating cultural experiences on the 'margins' of the British Empire and of the subjects of colonization as well as playing an important role in the development of an independent literature.[11] The short story has been attributed with a special suitability for expressing marginalized positions (see below, p. 10), but the prime reason for its importance in the (former) 'colonies' is

[11] On the significance of the short story in colonial and postcolonial literatures, see Stilz (1980), Stummer (1986) and Bardolph (1989). The *Encyclopedia of Post-Colonial Literatures in English* (Benson and Conolly 1994) includes a long entry on "short fiction" which traces its role and special significance in the various postcolonial literatures in English: "Itself in flux, it provides glimpses of societies in the process of transformation and records shifts in linguistic practice, social theory, and critical expectation." (1455) See also the entry on the short story in the *Oxford Companion to Canadian Literature* (Benson and Toye 1997).

that it could be distributed in a medium – magazines and newspapers – producible within the respective regions themselves and thus a form of literary expression comparatively independent from the literary market in the 'mother country'.

By contrast, in the former centre of Empire, prominent practitioners themselves noted a backwardness in the evolution of the genre. W. Somerset Maugham is one of the most prolific and best-known writers of short stories from Britain, but found in the "Introduction" to his anthology *Teller of Tales* (1939) that

> English writers on the whole have not taken kindly to the art of the short story. They have felt the novel more congenial to their idiosyncrasy, for the English, though in conversation often tongue-tied, when they take a pen in their hands are inclined to prolixity. They have no natural instinct for succinctness, which is indispensable to the short story, nor a sense of form, which is essential to its significance. So the diffuseness of the national temper has found its most satisfactory literary expression in the long, unwieldy, shapeless novels of the Victorian Era which still remain the country's outstanding contribution to the world's fiction. English writers find it difficult to be brief without being trivial, and for the most part they have looked upon the short story as a thing of no great matter to be thrown off in their spare time in order to earn a few useful guineas without much expenditure of effort. I know only two English writers who have taken the short story as seriously as it must be taken if excellence is to be achieved, Rudyard Kipling, namely, and Katherine Mansfield. (Maugham 1963, 108f.)

Despite such depreciation, however, the short story has – at least during certain phases – played an important role in the literature(s) of Britain, and the culture(s) of Britain have produced some of the most internationally popular exemplars. Apart from Maugham, these include Sir Arthur Conan Doyle, 'Saki' [H.H. Munro], P.G. Wodehouse and Roald Dahl. Britain can also claim some of the applauded 'masters' of the form, such as Kipling and Mansfield (although she grew up in New Zealand), Robert Louis Stevenson, D.H. Lawrence, A.E. Coppard, H.E. Bates, V.S. Pritchett, or recently A.L. Kennedy, a female writer from Scotland whose first collections of stories have been widely praised. As Malcolm Bradbury observes in the introduction to his *Penguin Book of Modern British Short Stories* (1987, 12), "the short story has an importance and originality in the British line far greater than is often supposed", and

> there have been moments, specifically during the 1940s when the pressure of wartime experience and the shortage of paper brought us *Penguin New Writing* and *Horizon* and the talents to fill them, when general interest in the

> short story has enlarged. We seem to be living in another such moment now, with a new wave of interest in short fictional forms. [...] Ian McEwan and Clive Sinclair, Adam Mars-Jones and Rose Tremain have made special use of the short story, and in a number of cases established their reputations with them, much as Angus Wilson did in the 1940s.

Finally, when we look for 'beginnings' of the short story in English earlier than the days of Poe, it is Britain we have to look to.

Of course, the short story in this cultural space did not evolve in isolation from the ways in which the genre developed elsewhere. Influences from the United States have been noted widely, not least since America provided (and continues to provide) British writers with publishing opportunities in periodicals when such possibilities in Britain were scarce. There was also a considerable impact from the European continent, notably the 'realistic' stories of Guy de Maupassant (1850–93) and Anton Chekhov (1860–1904), who is considered of particular interest for the development of the modernist story in English. Inspiration for postmodernist practitioners of short fiction came, again, from the United States but also South America, especially the work of Jorge Luis Borges (1899–1986). Within the British Isles, it is difficult to discuss the short story in Britain in complete isolation from its tradition in Ireland. For reasons of political and cultural imperialism and the predominance of the English book and periodical market, the literatures of Ireland and Britain have long been intertwined. But just as it has become common today to discuss Irish literature as something culturally and linguistically distinguishable from an English 'mainstream', one can ask whether a distinctive 'British' literature exists and to what extent the short story produced in Britain has been marked by the specific cultural and social situations out of which it has been enunciated.

## 3. The Short Story in 'British' Society and Culture

As Malcolm Bradbury (1971, xiii) points out, literature is generally "an aspect of society. It coheres, structures and illuminates many of its most profound meanings. It is, in a particular sense, an institution of society." For the short story, however, it has been claimed that a 'sociological' relevance is less immediately obvious and that it relates to its social contexts in a manner different from that of the novel. Charles May (1994, 133), for instance, suggests, in somewhat simplified terms, that novel and short story embody different experiences and articulate different kinds of knowledge:

> whereas the novel is primarily a social and public form, the short story is mythic and spiritual. [...] The novel exists to reaffirm the world of 'everyday'

> reality; the short story exists to 'defamiliarize' the everyday. Storytelling does not spring from one's confrontation with the everyday world, but rather from one's encounter with the sacred [...] or with the absurd [...].

The short story is certainly not an ideal form for depicting a panorama of society, and the extraordinary event seems indeed a domain of the shorter form. But does that make the short story *per se* less apt to articulate cultural identities, desires and needs? Clare Hanson (1989) does not negate the short story's cultural relevance but locates it in other areas than that of the novel. She echoes Frank O'Connor's influential statement in *The Lonely Voice* (1963, 18–21) that the short story is about "submerged population groups", that "[a]lways in the short story there is this sense of outlawed figures wandering about the fringes of society" and that, while the novel adheres "to the classical concept of civilized society", the short story remains "remote from the community". To Clare Hanson (1989, 2 and 6), the short story is therefore "a form of the margins, a form which is in some sense ex-centric, not part of official or 'high' cultural hegemony", which has "offered itself to losers and loners, exiles, women, blacks – writers who for one reason or another have not been part of the ruling 'narrative' or epistemological/experiential framework of their society". It "gives us the other side of the 'official story' or narrative, or we might suggest that the short story suggests that which cannot normally be said". Mary Louise Pratt (1994, 98f. and 104) goes in the same direction when she claims that

> some of the narrative structures, subject matters, narrative traditions, and critical attitudes characteristically associated with the short story are associated with it (a) because the short story has been tacitly seen as incomplete or fragmentary with respect to the totality and completeness of the novel, and (b) because the short story has often redeployed materials that were dissociated by the novel, often because they were devalued in literary or social terms. The historical hypothesis that arises is that as the novel consolidated itself in the 19th century, the short story tended to shift around into positions of 'countergenre' to the novel. [...]
>
> Just as it is used for formal experimentation, the short story is often the genre used to introduce new (and possibly stigmatized) subject matters into the literary arena.

As our historical survey will show, such statements, like all generalizations in literary history, have to be qualified. In the course of its history in Britain, short fiction has often lent a voice to a wide range of marginalized experiences. However, just as novels have been used to express the marginal and 'submerged', it has equally been used to articulate central values and norms, for example during the eighteenth century. Even though the short story lacks the scope to investigate society and culture in breadth or in depth, it is certainly not dissociated from the society and cultural discourses out of which it is written. And it is strongly affected by specific circumstances of the *literary* subsystem of a society at a given time: the special make-up of the agents by whom literature is produced, materially distributed, read and processed in other ways of reception (criticism, adaptation, and so forth).[12]

But is the short story produced in the social and cultural space of Britain a 'British' story? Notions of Britishness and the issue of a British culture have been heavily contested since at least the 1980s.[13] Historically, 'Great Britain' did not come into existence until 1603 (with the union of the crowns of England and Scotland); 'Britain' is also used to refer to the United Kingdom (that is, Britain and Ireland from 1801 and, after Irish independence, Britain and Northern Ireland), and there are further past and present complexities of national political and cultural identity in Britain, many of which derive from external and internal colonization followed by processes of decolonization and devolution. One might therefore ask whether a discussion of 'British' literature or literature 'in Britain' is helpful at all – and how it is to be delimited from Irish literature and, in particular, regional and/or national literatures 'within': Scottish, Welsh and a more narrowly conceived 'English' literature. And is there a distinct Northern Irish short story (with writers like Jim Clarke or David Park) within 'British' literature, or should that be considered part of the Irish tradition?[14]

The literatures of Ireland and Britain have been closely related, and many Irish writers – of so different a cast as Sheridan LeFanu, George Moore, James Joyce or Elizabeth Bowen – have been considered part of a more widely conceived 'English' history of the short story. More recent writers like Julia O'Faolain and William Trevor also have an Irish background but are often included in anthologies of British writing. Despite such overlaps, it is now common to emphasize the special themes, forms and variety of the English language which the short story has developed in Ireland, as a form for which the Irish, with their long tradition of oral storytelling, have also been noted to have a particular propensity and which has acquired a particular vitality and importance in the Irish literary landscape.

---

[12] On the general significance of adopting a 'sociological' approach to the short story, including aspects of a specifically *literary* sociology, see Goetsch (1978a, 61).

[13] From a great number of relevant publications, see, for instance, Robbins (1998), Stratmann (1998), Easthope (1999) and Mergenthal (2002).

[14] For anthologies of Northern Irish stories, see, among others, Blair (1993) and Parker (1995).

Deborah Averill (1982, 3) notes in a standard study of the Irish short story that "the attitudes which Irish stories express are often deeply rooted in the national experience. The genre evolved in response to the peculiar frustrations and conflicts of Irish life."[15] Important Irish contributors to the short-story form, apart from those already mentioned, include, in the nineteenth century, William Carleton and Somerville and Ross, and in the twentieth Liam O'Flaherty, Sean O'Faolain, Frank O'Connor, Patrick Boyle, Michael McLaverty, Mary Lavin, Edna O'Brien, Brian Friel, John McGahern or Anne Devlin, to name only a few. Acknowledging that Irish writers have had considerable impact on the short-story writing in 'John Bull's Island', the present book will nevertheless set the Irish short story apart as belonging to a distinct national literature – conceding that many Irish writers have been residents in Britain for at least a certain period of their careers. Generally, consideration of the short story in Britain entails a number of writers who were not born in Britain but were or still are long-term residents there: Henry James, Katherine Mansfield, Olive Schreiner, Doris Lessing, or Salman Rushdie and William Boyd. Some of these writers will be considered where they are part of important developments of the short story in Britain.

Writers from Scotland and Wales pose a greater challenge to notions of 'British' culture. In the wake of the recent moves towards political and cultural independence in these areas, their special traditions of story-telling, varieties of English and thematic preoccupations have gained increased attention. Short stories by writers with a Scottish and Welsh background have been collected in programmatically 'separate' anthologies. John J. Stinson (1985, 20), for example, tries to demarcate the 'Welsh' short story thus:

> The term *Welsh regional writers* must be defined somewhat arbitrarily, but it should include Caradoc Evans, Gwyn Jones, Glyn Jones, Margiad Evans, Gwyn Thomas, Rhys Davies, Alun Lewis, Kate Roberts, and D.J. Williams (the latter of whom write in Welsh). The work of other Welsh writers such as Dylan Thomas, Richard Hughes, and Roald Dahl has been assimilated into the English mainstream.[16]

With writers from Scotland, we encounter the same oscillation between cultural distinctiveness and assimilation into an 'English' mainstream. Sir Walter Scott's "The Two Drovers", one of the stories in his *Chronicles of the Canongate* (1827), deals with contrasts between Highland and Lowland cul-

[15] For related statements, see Rafroidi and Brown (1979), Kilroy (1984) and Thompson (1989).

[16] On Welsh writers, see also Baldwin (1985, 53–56) and Evans (1985, 128).

tures, yet addresses English readers at the same time. Robert Louis Stevenson, too, is certainly part of a literature that can be identified as 'Scottish' – especially with stories written in Scots such as "Thrawn Janet" (1881) – but, having published in periodicals with a nation-wide distribution, Stevenson was also a highly influential figure for the general development and popularization of the short story in Britain as a whole. In the mid-1980s, Dean Baldwin (1985, 52f.) found the work of most Scottish writers after the Second World War only weakly distinctive. The short stories of Fred Urquhart, Neil Gunn, Eric Linklater, Naomi Mitchison, Ian Hamilton Finlay or Muriel Spark seemed to betray little that

> one could define as an essential 'Scottish' quality. [...] The Scots, unlike the Irish, have rarely used political weapons to insist on a separate identity, and perhaps for this reason have been treated most often as English writers, without a regional identity. Like the Irish, the Scots frequently capitalize on their colorful language, Celtic heritage, and traditional ways to convey what is unique about Scotland, but rarely is there any insistence that the Scottish character is radically different from the English, at least in the stories analyzed here.

Such an assessment has to be revised today in light of the recent work of writers like Alasdair Gray or James Kelman, work which is marked by an explicit Scottishness. For earlier writers from Scotland it is also certainly possible to claim a cultural distinctiveness in the sense that Alun Richards does in his *Second Penguin Book of Welsh Short Stories* (1994, x): "The place is Wales, and the time is this century. They reflect Wales as it is, or has been, and collectively form part of the Welsh experience as it belongs to these writers." It is beyond the scope of this book to do justice to the cultural distinctiveness of Welsh and Scottish short-story writing, but writers from Wales and Scotland will be considered where they have taken part in developments that characterize short-story writing in 'Britain' as opposed to developments in other parts of the English-speaking world.

This leaves us to consider the 'English' component of the cultures of Britain. Since it was England that dominated cultural developments in Britain for so long, not least because London was the centre of the literary market, it is understandable, though perhaps not justifiable, that many short stories have been anthologized as 'English', even though they were written by writers with a Welsh, Scottish or Irish background. Christopher Dolley's two well-known *Penguin Books of English Short Stories* (1967 and 1972), still widely used for teaching purposes, include works by Joyce, Mansfield and Spark. Derek Hudson's *Classic English Short Stories 1930–1955* (1972) takes 'English' to mean 'not American' and 'not Commonwealth' and comprises stories by writers of Anglo-Irish and Scottish descent like Bowen, Spark, Linklater and Urquhart, at the same time acknowledging, however, that it excludes "the many admirable indigenous short stories of Ireland, Scotland, and Wales, which are properly the subject of collections in their own right". (Editor's note) Only recently and in light of a new understanding of Englishness as *one* of the cultural identities within the British context, has A.S. Byatt, in her *Oxford Book of English Short Stories,* made an effort *not* to equate English with British and deliberately excluded writers of Scottish or Welsh (or Irish) origin. Her "Introduction" indicates, however, how difficult the Englishness of English stories still is to define:

> There is a reluctance to think about Englishness. [...] It is not quite nice to think about being English. When I was asked to put together an Oxford Book of English Short Stories, I hesitated. It meant looking very narrowly for writers with pure English national credentials, or there was no point. [...] I was very carefully *not* looking for stories that would give images of England, or of the Empire; I very carefully tried to have no preconceptions of any 'English' styles or subject-matter. (Byatt 1998, xv)

While Byatt rejects stories which openly advertise an English identity, another recent anthology of new short stories was assembled deliberately to trace how a new sense of English identity is currently in formation. As the editors of *England Calling,* first published in 2001, write in their introduction:

> At the start of a new millennium we live in a country which is restless, uneasy, questioning and devolving. English politics is showing signs of breaking free from Westminster following the devolution of power to Scotland and Wales, but what is happening to the cultural life of the country in the wake of these developments? [...]
>
> *England Calling* is an attempt to mark out some of this ground, both geographically and socially. We wanted to gather together writers from every corner of the country and from a broad cross-section of society. These writers are not only telling stories of the landscapes of England, but peeling back the layers of Englishness in the process – Englishness as it is now: multicultural, messy, survivalist. Writing about landscape inevitably raises political and social questions, because social change is writ large in the topography of England. Here we have history jostling with industry, towerblocks and cob-walled cottages, pubs and Euro wine-bars, claustrophobic suburbia, the weather, the sea, the moors, the roads and nuclear reactors. Cities and whole swathes of countryside are modified and reconstructed so quickly that they become unrecognisable almost overnight.
>
> The stories in this book illustrate a nation questioning its identity in the face of these changes; and they suggest that one way of orientating ourselves in new times is through fiction. (Bell and Gay 2002, ix, xi)

The present book is aware of the cultural pluralism within Britain and will use 'English' with the same restrictive- and distinctiveness as 'Welsh' or 'Scottish'. But in the face of cultural pluralization, when may we speak of a 'British' short story? The denomination 'British' has been rejected as too broad a generalization, especially by proponents of cultural nationalism. Thus Douglas Dunn writes in the introduction to his *Oxford Book of Scottish Short Stories* (1995, xxiv): "Within the British Isles the survival (and resurgence) of deviant or oppositional national and regional cultures can look like proof of the failure of the 'British' political system. Without the opportunism or happenstances of Empire, there was little to bind the various parts of 'Britain' together." Nevertheless, there still are reasons for using 'British' as an umbrella term. After all, as Alfred E. Ward pointed out as early as 1924, 'British' provides a framework under which it is possible to consider the very *difference* of voices that went into the making of the short story in Britain: "it is necessary to particularize *British* rather than *English* writers, since it was the Scottish mind and the Anglo-Indian [Robert Louis Stevenson and Rudyard Kipling] that first found expression in the short story on the eastern side of the Atlantic." (Ward 1924, 102) And there are, as the following chapters will show, tendencies in the development of the short story in Britain that straddle the island's internal cultural divisions. Thus for the twentieth century in particular, several anthologies have been published for the 'British' rather than the 'English' short story. Ashley and Astor (1968, vi) write in the preface to their anthology *British Short Stories: Classics and Criticism*:

> The stories in this collection show a sense of national identity too often obscured in anthologies that offer only a miscellany of stories regardless of origin. Works of art are created within and are integral with their social and historical background, and in subject matter, theme, setting, and allusion, as well as aesthetic theory, these chronologically arranged narratives mirror the changing values and concerns of the British people from the age of imperialism to the present.

Esmor Jones's *British Short Stories of Today* (1987), which encompasses a significant number of writers with a Welsh or Scottish background, is specifically advertised in the blurb as a collection "ideal for the serious student of life in Britain today". Finally, today's inheritance of the British Empire provides a particular reason as to why it makes sense to look at the literature of 'Britain' since this framework seems the most appropriate way to refer to the cultural contributions of migrants from former colonies and their descendants since the Second World War. The latter tend to see themselves as 'Black British' or 'Asian British', that is, identify themselves through citizenship rather than feeling rooted in a region with an English, Scottish or Welsh historical identity.

A point of view that is sensitive to cultural context yields a historical map that shows how the short story in Britain has manifested itself in culturally distinctive forms; it should not be blind to the concomitant fact, however, that the cultures of Britain have also brought forth many stories that are *not* culturally distinctive, which appear 'international' or 'universal' rather than 'British'. If some preference is given here to the first viewpoint, this is because such an angle has not yet been pursued systematically for the short story in Britain to date.

Perhaps the most obvious markers of cultural distinctiveness are settings and subject matters associated with Britain and its internal cultures. Like in the United States, for instance, these cultures have produced a range of local-colour stories. Such stories are anchored in and descriptive of a specific region. They emerged in Britain with the Romantic interest in native landscapes, local ways of life and social milieus aroused by the massive social restructurings of industrialization and urbanization. This interest comprised not only regions in the so-called Celtic Fringe, but also regions in England. In 1819, Mary Russell Mitford began to publish the stories and sketches later collected as *Our Village* (see p. 69f. below), and in the late nineteenth century, rural 'Englishness' dominates many stories of Thomas Hardy; the tradition was continued in the twentieth century by writers like A.E. Coppard and H.E. Bates. The special significance of the countryside for a sense of English identity was emphasized a few years after the end of the Second World War by the editor of an anthology of *English Country Short Stories* (Lewin 1949, 9):

> We are a people which is traditionally even more country-loving than seafaring; but the industrial revolution has progressively diminished our available areas of unspoilt countryside [...]. The myth, therefore, of the countryside as The Great Good Place, the Earthly Paradise from which we have been expelled, the region to which we return in our day-dreams and wishful thinking, prevails among more and more of us as society is increasingly urbanised and industrialised. [...] To the Earthly Paradise of the countryside the Englishman will always try to return [...].

The anthology contains a piece by Stacy Aumonier, a writer once famous for his stories about the Great War, a piece in which the myth of the countryside is particularly obvious. "The Match" (1916) depicts a cricket match in the village of Celminster. During the match, the narrator has an epiphanic experience in which the beauty of his country seems to reveal itself to him: "The birds and little insects in solemn unison praised God, or, rather, to my mind, at that moment they praised England, the land that gave them such a glorious setting." Love for the country will soon make the cricketers fight and die for it in the theatres of the First World War.[17] During the 1990s, the new sense of diversification within British society and culture has led to a renewed interest in stories specifically linked with certain regions – even the publication of several *series* of regional anthologies.[18]

A distinctive subject matter associated with *Britain* rather than its regions and internal cultures is the Empire, which provides an opportunity to explore Britishness in its relationship with foreign- or otherness. As far as the short story is concerned, Rudyard Kipling is the most famous writer associated with this thematic area since the publication of his first collection, *Plain Tales from the Hills*. It was published in Britain in 1890, but the stories were originally written for a provincial Anglo-Indian newspaper, *The Civil and Military Gazette*, for which Kipling was engaged as a reporter in 1886, and were first collected for readers in India in 1888. Kipling made the Anglo-Indian short story – the short story written by and for British colonials – known first to a British and then a world-wide audience, but he was not the only writer to be successful with stories about Anglo-India. Flora Annie Steel was a woman writer well-known for stories in which she rendered turn-of-the century colonial life from the point of view of British women in India. In "The Doll-Maker", for example, a woman is shown to have suffered for many years after her children were sent back 'home' to Britain to be educated. Stories from and about other colonies enjoyed similar popularity during the final decades of the nineteenth and in the early twentieth century. As late as 1941, a twelve-volume selection of stories located in the Empire was extracted from the popular *Blackwood's Magazine* and published as *'Blackwood' Tales from the Outposts*. To Gerhard Stilz (1980, 1), the colonial short story, and the Anglo-Indian specifically, exemplifies how a literary

[17] As a matter of fact, stories about the experience of both the First and the Second World War are found with relative frequency in anthologies. This is not surprising when one considers that both wars have played an important role in defining English and British collective identity. Examples include, about the First World War, Arthur Machen's "The Bowmen" (1914) and Rudyard Kipling's "Mary Postgate" (1915). Well-known stories about the Second World War were written by William Sansom (based on his experience as a fireman in London during the Blitz), H.E. Bates (who wrote about the Royal Air Force under the pseudonym 'Flying Officer X'), and Roald Dahl (whose first stories also deal with the experience of flying in the war). The civilian experience is captured, for example, in Elizabeth Bowen's "Mysterious Kôr" (1944) and V.S. Pritchett's "The Voice" (1943).

[18] See, for example, the series of (inexpensively produced) anthologies devoted to specific regions of Britain published during the 1990s under the title *Shorts from ...*; individual volumes were edited by Sheila Ashwood, Suzi Blair and Tracey Walton; Suzi Blair is also the editor of a similar series entitled *Paper Clips ...*.

genre intersects with specific political and social circumstances. The colonial writers' intention was to depict colonial life realistically and thus to depart from patterns of a romantic exoticism, which their readers back home may still have expected nonetheless. (For a more detailed discussion of Empire stories, see pp. 95–99 below.)

When W. Somerset Maugham wrote his stories set in the South Seas and the Far East in the early twentieth century, the Empire was already in progressive decline. Britons, however, were still abroad in the service of the Empire and exposed to an irritatingly 'strange' world in which the dominant value systems of the mother country were undermined. Maugham explored this theme in a number of stories (see p. 123f. below), and he coined the term "exotic story" in his "Introduction" to *Teller of Tales* for a type of story "the scene of which is set in some country little known to the majority of readers, and which deals with the reactions upon the white man of his sojourn in an alien land and the effect which contact with peoples of another race has upon him". (Maugham 1963, 110) This definition fits stories that take Empire as their theme, but also stories covering other forms of intercultural encounter. After all, the British were widely-travelled in foreign countries inside and outside their Empire. The resulting encounters reveal as much about British as they do about 'other' cultures. The 'exotic' story became, according to Robert Gish (1985), an important variety of the short story in Britain during the late nineteenth and early twentieth centuries, its representatives including, apart from the writers already mentioned and among many others, Robert Louis Stevenson, E.M. Forster and Graham Greene.

Another subject area considered to be of typical relevance to British culture is the specific manifestation of a class society at home, a subject which short stories have treated both in the mode of comedy of manners and more serious moods. Examples discussed later in this book include work by H.G. Wells around the turn of the twentieth, and Saki, P.G. Wodehouse, Aldous Huxley and Evelyn Waugh in the early twentieth century. Dennis Vannatta (1985, ixf.) diagnoses the British short story after the Second World War as "the product of a society in often painful flux", a society haunted by the decline of its status of a former world power and economic problems during the long period of reconstruction after the war. This is the social climate in which the stories of Angus Wilson are set. They present us, as John Stinson (1985, 14f.) writes, with "an array of vulgar or eccentric people" whose grotesqueries, pretenses and delusions are relentlessly exposed; among his targets are, in particular, the middle classes: "people who cannot, or will not, fairly assess themselves, people who cannot come to honest terms with themselves or the reality of their social situation." During the 1960s, harsh criticism of the developments in post-war British society came from a number of writers who have been called 'angry' and 'young' and whose prime focus of attention was on the working classes: John Wain, Kingsley Amis, Alan Sillitoe and Nell Dunn (see below, p. 147f.).

Having approached the issue of a 'British' short story, we must now reexamine the second essential question of our historical survey: Where should a beginning of the short story (in Britain) be posited? A closer look at genre theory will justify why the historical chapters in Part II set in well before the days of Poe.

## 4. Where to really begin a History of the Short Story in Britain?

As we have seen, the short story in Britain is often claimed to have got off to a later start than in the United States. But is it possible at all to say when the short story as a distinct genre 'began'? Instead of the nineteenth century, many handbooks, critical studies and writers' statements claim an even later emergence of the short story proper which they consider as a distinctly 'modern' phenomenon. Elizabeth Bowen, in her preface to *The Faber Book of Modern Short Stories* (1936), called the short story "a young art: as we now know it, it is the child of this [the twentieth] century". (Bowen 1994, 256) Short forms have been attributed a specific suitability for rendering the 'fragmented' experience and velocity which allegedly characterize modernity. V.S. Pritchett, for instance, claimed in an essay on "Short Stories" in *Harper's Bazaar* (1953) that the short story owes "everything to the restlessness, the alert nerve, the scientific eye and the short breath of contemporary life". (in Weber and Greiner 1977, 162)

While such statements appear plausible but somewhat speculative, the sociology of literature provides harder evidence for the claim that the short story as we understand it today emerged within a specific system of literary communication which did not come into being until the later nineteenth century. The 'rise' of the short story depended on specific genre constellations and hierarchies, circumstances of literary production, reception and especially distribution in which pieces of short narrative prose functioned to serve specific demands and achieved a status and reputation which they had not enjoyed before. This system was characterized by a bigger and more differentiated literary market than in any former period, which catered to a greater number of literate people than ever before. An audience with heterogeneous social backgrounds and tastes caused the literary market to be diversified into a great variety of publication forms – books and periodicals – which were able to co-exist and sustain an increasing number of professional writers.

Since a short story, like other short literary forms, is rarely published on its own (to the regret of at least some writers[19]), it depends on being published as part of an assemblage of texts: in collections of individual authors, in anthologies (that is, collections from the work of several writers), and, particularly, in newspapers and magazines. The latter, which H.E. Bates (1965, 31) considers a platform without which "the short story could never, I think, have been what it is to-day", burst into a flourish in the nineteenth century as the readership increased and periodicals became increasingly cheaper to produce. This significant development within the constellation of print media established a market for short stories – at least potentially. It was in the US-American periodical market that a great demand for short fiction arose, while magazines in Britain were dominated, from the 1830s to the final decades of the nineteenth century, by the serialized novel. This is a frequently-made point first observed by Brander Matthews: "The Short-story is of very great importance to the American magazine. But in the British magazine the serial Novel is the one thing of consequence." (Matthews 1901, 56) Outside the magazines, too, the fiction market in Britain was overshadowed by the novel, whose most usual mode of publication in book form was for many decades the edition in three volumes – or 'three-decker' – which the circulating libraries demanded. When books were still expensive even for upper-middle-class readers to purchase, these commercial libraries influenced not only what kinds of literature were to be published, but also how they were to be published. Matthews (1901, 58–60) claims that the three-decker so dominated the market that it checked British writers' efforts in shorter forms:

[19] H.G. Wells, for example, wrote in his "Introduction" to *The Country of the Blind and Other Stories* (1911): "Each [story] is intended to be a thing by itself; and if it is not too ungrateful to kindly and enterprising publishers, I would confess I would much prefer to see each printed expensively alone, and left in a little brown-paper cover to lie about a room against the needs of a quite casual curiosity." (in Weber and Greiner 1977, 86) See also Shaw (1983, 8): "the plain fact that the short story is composed as a single entity but frequently published as one item among many [...] has scarcely been to the advantage of any writer dependent on the periodical market. Instances of short stories published by themselves are rare; Virginia Woolf was fortunate in having her own press and so being able to produce 'Kew Gardens' (1918) as an aesthetic object with its own atmospheric integrity, enhanced by her sister Vanessa's woodcut illustrations." Even in a periodical, however, an individual story has greater prominence than in a story collection or anthology where, according to William Sansom – in a *London Magazine* essay in 1966 – stories, "like pictures in galleries", tend to "cancel themselves out. It is best for a short story to be found in a magazine, as a picture is best isolated on a wall of its own." (in Weber and Greiner 1977, 194)

> The three-volume system is peculiar to Great Britain: it does not obtain either in France or the United States. As a consequence, the French or American writer of fiction is left free to treat his subject at the length it demands, – no more and no less. [...] I do not say, of course, that the good and genuine Short-story is not written in England now and then, [...] but this is merely an accidental growth, and not a staple of production. [...] It is the three-volume Novel which has killed the Short-story in England.

Not until the end of the nineteenth century were writers' protests against the tyranny of the circulating libraries successful and did the leading of these libraries, Mudie's and W.H. Smith's, announce in 1894 that they would no longer buy three-deckers; the serial novel soon became unpopular in the wake of this decision. Only then did British periodicals also develop a major demand for stories and did the genre gain in prestige, especially when it was practiced by renowned writers.

There seems to be good reason, then, to claim that the short story we have become used to and which can be 'defined' in the terms outlined above emerged in the course of the nineteenth century, under specific conditions of the literary market and, arguably, as a form particularly suited to capture the experience of modern life. On the other hand, however, "[t]here is no such phenomenon as a totally new genre. Genres that appear to be new [...] are the results of reactions against and integration of preexisting literary forms." (May 1981, 178) The art of telling short narratives is ancient, long pre-dating the time when the first of these narratives were written down or even printed,[20] and when the telling of stories in print had become the established mode, oral narration survived in written guise. The beginning of Sir Walter Scott's ghost story "The Tapestried Chamber" (1828), for example, explicitly discusses the differences between oral and written story-telling and pretends that the story it conveys was originally *told* rather than written:

> the particular class of stories which turns on the marvellous, possesses a stronger influence when told, than when committed to print. The volume taken up at noonday, though rehearsing the same incident, conveys a much more feeble impression, than is achieved by the voice of the speaker on a circle of fireside auditors, who hang upon the narrative as the narrator details the minute incidents which serve to give it authenticity, and lowers his voice with an affectation of mystery while he approaches the fearful and wonderful part. It was with such advantages that the present writer heard

[20] For a general introduction to the relationship between oral and written literatures, see Ong (1982).

> the following events related [...]. In its present form the tale must necessarily lose all the interest which was attached to it, by the flexible voice and intelligent features of the gifted narrator. Yet still, read aloud, to an undoubting audience by the doubtful light of the closing evening, or, in silence, by a decaying taper, and amidst the solitude of a half-lighted apartment, it may redeem its character as a good ghost story.

Stories with frames which pretend that an embedded story is rendered orally are still found frequently. Characteristically, such stories are referred to as 'tales', thus etymologically indicating the connection with 'telling', for example in Graham Greene's "Across the Bridge" (1938): "Any man [...] is better fitted by long observation to tell Mr Calloway's tale than I am."[21]

The link between the modern short story and traditional – originally oral – so-called 'simple forms'[22] of narrative (like anecdotes, fables, parables, fairy tales, legends, jokes, proverbs or riddles) has repeatedly been observed. Mary Louise Pratt (1994, 108f.) even claims that the short story's ongoing relationship with traditional forms of narrative differentiates it from the novel:

> the novel does hark back to history and document, while everywhere in the short story we see revivals and remains of oral, folk, and biblical narrative traditions [...]. In mainstream literature, there are [...] indications that the old oral traditions are 'relegated' to the short story, that because of their orality, their associations with folk culture, their didacticism and/or antirealism, the traditions were incompatible with the literary values of early bourgeois novelists and were left behind by the prestige genre, to reappear in the lesser one.[23]

This might again be an exaggeration and oversimplification of the differences between short and long forms of fiction, but references to and adaptations of traditional forms are frequently found in the 'modern' short story. Warren S. Walker (1982, 19–22), for instance, notes fairy-tale and legend elements in E.M. Forster's "The Story of a Siren" (1904) and "The

21 However, as Goetsch (1978a, 71) points out, older forms are never simply adapted in modern stories since the latter are produced and read under different conditions, above all by an anonymous and heterogeneous audience.

22 For a discussion of these forms, see Jolles (1982, first publ. 1930).

23 See also May (1994, "Introduction", xxvi): "In their very shortness, short stories have remained close to the original source of narrative in myth, folktale, fable, and fairy tale. They, therefore, are more apt to focus on basic desires, dreams, anxieties, and fears than novels are and thus are more aligned with the original religious nature of narrative. Short stories are therefore apt to embody a timeless theme and are thus less dependent on a social context than novels."

Celestial Omnibus" (1908), D.H. Lawrence's "The Rocking-Horse Winner" (1926), or Arthur Machen's "The Bowmen" (1914). One could add Eric Linklater's "Sealskin Trousers" (first coll. 1947), in which a twentieth-century woman is seduced by a selkie, a seal in human shape, and follows him into the sea. The use of the fairy tale in the more recent work of women writers, like in Angela Carter's collection *The Bloody Chamber* (1979), is perhaps the best-known case of the survival or re-emergence of traditional forms in the modern story (see also pp. 159–161 below). Old didactic forms, like fables and parables, can be traced in H.G. Wells's "The Country of the Blind" (1904) and "The Door in the Wall" (1906), D.H. Lawrence's "The Man Who Loved Islands" (1927), or many stories by T.F. Powys, like "Mr Pim and the Holy Crumb", one of the *Fables* he published in 1929.

The *written* tradition of short fiction begins in the middle ages. It comprises a variety of forms which have been named as antecedents of the modern short story – if not as short stories proper. As Edgar Hill Duncan (1972, 1) points out: "It is highly unlikely that a concept inclusive of several genres of narrative, all brief, ever occurred to a medieval thinker. But pieces that can be subsumed, with more or less assurance, under this label do survive from both the Old and the Middle English periods – roughly from the mid-seventh through the fourteenth centuries."[24]

The majority of late-medieval short narratives were still composed in verse rather than prose. Many were intended to be used for edification, often religious instruction, like *exempla* (originally used as parts of sermons and collected, for instance, in Robert Mannyng of Brunne's *Handlynge Synne*, c. 1303), fables, legends and saints' lives (as in the *South English Legendary*, c. 1280–1350). There was also a secular tradition which included shorter romances of the courtly tradition (deriving from the French *lai*, like the late-thirteenth-century "Sir Orfeo") or, for a lower-class audience, the comic, more realistic and often bawdy stories of the *fabliau* type (like "Dame Siriz", the oldest surviving *fabliau* in English, c. 1285). Medieval verse narrative culminated in the late fourteenth century, with John Gower's *Confessio Amantis* (1390–93) and, in particular, Geoffrey Chaucer's *Canterbury Tales* (c. 1387). The latter have been widely praised as the climax of the medieval tradition of story-telling and in fact an *omnium-gatherum* of (almost) the entire spectrum of medieval narrative popular at the time of their inception. (Canby 1909, 64) "The Miller's Tale", for example, renders a *fabliau*, "The Wife of Bath's Tale" a *lai*, and "The Nun's Priest Tale" an animal tale.

---

[24] Duncan (1972 and 1974) discusses a range of Old English and Middle English examples. For a survey of medieval antecedents of the short story, see also Canby (1909, parts 1 and 2), and Beachcroft (1968, chapters 3 to 5).

Compared to Chaucer's *Tales*, medieval stories in prose appear rather artless. Perhaps the most famous collection of prose stories derived from the middle ages are the *Gesta Romanorum*, a collection of stories written originally in Latin and probably compiled in England in the late thirteenth century. Thomas O. Beachcroft (1968, 52) cites them as "the best known and most long lasting collection of anecdotal short stories of medieval times. Wynkyn de Worde produced the first printed English edition between 1510 and 1515, and new editions went on well into the eighteenth century." In one of the early-modern versions (dated 1595), the fifth story gives an account of the Emperor Betoldus who ordained that women committing adultery should be severely punished. The argument which precedes the story proper (the 'History') announces the moral purpose:

*The Argument.*

> The fornication of wicked worldly men is here detected by the prouidence of God, and by his gratious fauour delivered out of the thraldom of sinne vnto the libertie of life euerlasting.

*The History.*

> There raigned sometime in Rome a mightie Emperour and a wyse named Betolde, which ordained a law that what woman were taken in aduoutry hir husband beeing a liue, she should bee cast into perpetuall prison. There was that time a knight that had a fayre lady to his wife, which committed aduoutry hir husband being a live, and was with childe, therefore by the law shee was put in prison, wher within short tyme after shee was deliuered of a fayre sonne. This childe grew vp till hee was seuen yeeres old, his mother dayly wept hartely. And when the child hard this hee said to his mother. O mother why weepe yee thus, and for what cause are you thus perplexed. Then saide his mother. O my sweete sonne, I have great cause to mourne, and thou also, for aboue our heads is people walking, and the sunne shineth in cleerenes, and great solace haue all men that are aboue vs, and wee bee heere continually in such darknes that I may not see thee, ne thou me, alas that euer I conceived thee. Then sayd the sonne, such ioye, ne such light as yee spake of, sawe I neuer, for I was borne here in this darknes, therefore if I had meate and drink enough, heere would I liue all the dayes of my life, therefore mother weepe yee not, but show mee solace. This lamentation that was betweene the mother and the sonne, heard the Emperours Stewarde that stoode aboue their heads, wherof he had great compassion, and wept vnto the Emperour, and kneeling, beesought him of his grace, that the mother and the sonne might bee deliuered out of prison. The Emperour as a mercifull Lord graunted that they should bee deliuered. Neverthelesse if

they trespassed so in time to come, they should bee punished with double paine, and after that they were deliuered, this woman ended hir life in that Citie.

*The Morall.*

Deere friends, this Emperour is the Father of heauen that made this law, that what wedded woman, that is to saye, what soule that is wedded to our Lord, and doth commit aduoutry, that is to say, doth worship strange gods, should be cast in the prison of hell, therefore a sinfull soule hath great cause to weepe, for shee is departed from light, that is to saie, from the ioys of heauen. Hir sonne that desired meate and drinck, are the wealthie wicked worldlings of this wolde, that say to the prelates of the Church, and to the preachers that preach vnto them the ioyes of Heauen, that while wee may liue and haue all the solace of the world, wee desire none other heauen. The Steward that heard their lamentation is our Lord Jesu, that knoweth all the priuities of our sorowful and repentant harts for our sinners, beesought the Father of heauen for us, that wee might bee deliuered from the prison of sinne, and that wee might come to euerlasting life, to that which bring vs all our Lord Jesus. Amen.

The narrative part of this *gestum* is plain: there is no attempt to embellish character, setting, atmosphere or mood, and the characters' direct speech is reduced to bare essentials. In the *exemplum* tradition, the prime function of the 'history' is to serve as an illustration for the comprehensive explication attached to it. Nevertheless, however remote such a narrative-cum-comment is from prevalent ideas of a short story today, it undoubtedly *is* an example of short narrative in prose. So if claims can be made both for a medieval and nineteenth-century provenance of the short story, what does this imply about our notion of the short-story *genre*?

## 5. The History of the Short Story and Genre Theory

Genre theory went through a spell of unpopularity before it was revived in the 1980s.[25] One reason for its temporary unpopularity was the fact that the criteria employed to define 'genre' were considered too vague and inconsistent and therefore of little use: "The fuzziness of the term arises not

[25] For important work other than that specifically mentioned, see Hernadi (1972), Todorov (1974), Rosmarin (1985), Fowler (1989) and Fishelov (1993). Vosskamp (1977) and Wenzel (2001) provide outlines of genre as a sociocultural phenomenon. On the discus-

just from its being applied at different levels, but also from its being applied according to different criteria. Genre distinctions are based variously on subject matter [...], narrative situation [...], surface linguistic form [...], effect sought in audience [...], mode of execution of text [...] and so on." (Pratt 1994, 92) Nevertheless, notions of genre or sub-genre, fuzzy though they may be, have an important influence on how the agents within the literary system behave: they determine the way in which literature is written (for example consciously within or against usual notions), published (for instance because a text conforms to a type popular at a certain time) and, last but not least, how it is read. The ability to identify a text as belonging to a certain 'kind of literature' is part of a reader's literary competence, part of the acquired schemata which he or she activates when a text is cognitively elaborated. As Allan Pasco (1994, 127) notes: "However impressed one might be by those who would avoid the problem of literary genres by denying them, it is indisputable that most readers are firmly conscious of genre and use their preconception to guide their reading."

The gist of current insights – some of the most influential of which we owe to Alastair Fowler – is that genres cannot be defined in essentialist terms but should be considered as historical, dynamic constructs, "continuously undergoing metamorphosis" (Fowler 1982, 23) and definable only within certain social and cultural contexts. Genres can be delimited in fairly stable terms for a certain context and time, but genre notions may then dissolve again, surviving only in a more loosely defined form. To Fowler, who draws on Ludwig Wittgenstein's concept of family resemblance[26] to provide a flexible model of genre, texts which can be assigned to the same genre need not display a complete set of defining features, but resemblance in a certain number of essential features is sufficient: "In literature, the basis of resemblance lies in literary tradition [...] a sequence of influence and imitation and inherited codes connecting works in the genre. As kinship makes a family, so literary relations of this sort form a genre. [...] Both historically and within a single period, the family grouping allows for wide variation in the type." (42f.) Variation is caused not only by alteration of features within a certain kind of literature, but also through shifts in the relationship in

sion of genre in cognitive literary theory see, among others, Olson *et al.* (1981), Fishelov (1991 and 1995) as well as Lázló and Viehoff (1993). Cognitive theory explains that cognitive schemata for genre notions are activated in a top-down process when a reader constructs an understanding of a text, but it also explains how genre notions are changed when, in a bottom-up process, the encounter with specific texts causes a modification or expansion of existing cognitive schemata.

[26] Developed in Wittgenstein's *Philosophic Investigations/Philosophische Untersuchungen* (1933).

which different kinds of literature stand to each other within the genre system. There are diachronic and synchronic "intergeneric relations" (251), and labels for genres can change as well: "Not only do generic labels change with time, but also (and this is far more confusing) the same labels come to be used in different ways." (130) Relatively fixed kinds of literature may 'die', that is, no longer be active, but even then they will not disappear entirely but may survive within other genres in the form of a more loosely defined mode – like elements of legend, fairy tale, etc., noted in the modern stories above.[27]

For a definition of a notoriously elusive genre like the short story, such considerations are particularly helpful, and it is hardly surprising that Fowler has inspired the more recent discussions in short-story theory.[28] To Allan Pasco (1994, 116), "[t]he hope of contriving a definition of short story which will remain useful until the end of time will be possible only when the short story dies as a genre". Charles May (1996, 464 and 470) urges "a pluralistic approach to genre" and argues that

> the short story is a mixed form whose development has been anything but organic. The short story demands a formal generic theory that should be judged on its explanatory power in understanding the form's historical changes, without assuming that the short story is a 'pure' form or that its history has been 'evolutionary.' [...] A genre theory must deal with the form both diachronically and synchronically. [...] The important thing is that one moves back and forth within the dialogistic tensions between the theoretical and the historical. I simply accept the fact that the short story is diachronic and thus always in the process of forming, yet at any one time is completely formed.

If we take as the most general modern notion of the short story a short piece of narrative prose with a certain unity of composition, then the mid-nineteenth century seems a reasonable point to begin a history of the short story in English. It was on the basis of texts of that period, first of American, but later also of British provenance, that our prevalent idea of the short story was formed. And it was that period in which the first theorizing of the short story took place in a context that encouraged the occurrence of exactly this kind of literature. Characteristically, it was only in the late nineteenth century that the genre 'label' was coined, reflecting the fact that there was now an awareness of the short story as a kind of narrative literature in prose distinct, among others, from the novel.

---

[27] See Fowler (1982, 167) and Pratt (1994, 93).

[28] See, in particular, May (1994 [1984]), Pasco (1994) and Pratt (1994).

The novel, in fact, is the genre against which the short story is most frequently defined. Brander Matthews (1901, 15) claimed that "the difference between a Novel and a Short-story is a difference of kind". John Wain pronounced in the *Kenyon Review* in 1969 that, "within the area of modern fiction, the short-story writer does those things that the novelist does not do". (in Weber and Greiner 1977, 197) However, such definitions require a relatively clear understanding of what a 'novel' is, and for those periods in which this notion did not yet exist, distinctions between longer and shorter forms of prose fiction are porous, as we shall see for the sixteenth to eighteenth centuries. It has also been observed, with some justification, that many of the characteristics now associated with the short story can also be found in earlier examples of short narrative, and old forms of telling short stories have survived as a mode in the more modern examples. Antecedents of the short story may not have been called or been recognized as 'stories'; their contemporary readers may have identified them – out of *their* knowledge of genre systems – as essays, pieces of reportage, sketches or tales, but they can, in retrospection, be re-classified as short stories. In the words of Ian Reid (1977, 15), "any generic definitions which aim to be precise and complete ought not to be formulated without a long historical perspective in mind". And since, synchronically, no genre stands alone in a genre landscape, it seems natural that the short story has, through its history or prehistory, always been defined in relation to neighbouring kinds of literature with which it has shared or from which it has even borrowed certain features.

The short story's crossing-over into non-narrative forms, like the essay (with its focus on discussion and exposition) and the sketch (with its focus on description), have been frequently discussed. Local-colour stories, for instance, with their extensive description of landscapes, milieus and characters, have a strong sketch-like quality, and in the context of modernism, sketch-like stories like Virginia Woolf's "Kew Gardens" (1919) gained seminal importance as a reaction against the plot story and its focus on external events. The sketch character of Arthur C. Clarke's "Nightfall" (1947), a piece of science-fiction writing, is motivated by the nature of the world which this 'short story' depicts:

> A church had stood here by the river's edge, and though no trace of the building remained, the gravestones that the years had gathered round it still marked its place. Now the stone slabs lay in parallel rows, snapped off at their bases and pointing mutely along the line of the blast. Some were half flattened into the ground, others had been cracked and blistered by terrific heat, but many still bore the messages they had carried down the centuries in vain. [...]

> Timidly the waters touched the worn gravestone that for more than three hundred years had lain before the vanished altar. The church that had sheltered it so long had given it some protection at the last, and only a slight discoloration of the rock told of the fires that had passed this way.

The cemetery described here is one formerly surrounding a shrine of English culture, the parish church of Stratford-upon-Avon, which houses Shakespeare's grave. But in Clarke's story the famous site is envisaged in a future in which all human life has been destroyed by a nuclear strike. After this strike, 'events' have become impossible. The story's extreme use of the mode of description is determined by the simple fact that there are no agents any more who might be responsible for any kind of narratable action – it is a world about which stories in the narrower sense of *narratives* can no longer be told.

The short story has also been observed to have a particular relationship with journalism, which seems natural since, in periodical publications, it shares a platform with journalistic writing. However, this connection has also been claimed to be harmful to the short story's literary prestige:

> The short story's continued involvement with journalism has damaged its standing while ensuring its popularity, creating a dilemma for writers and critics who are anxious to preserve standards. Despite the fact that so many of the best short-story writers, including Chekhov, Kipling and Hemingway, began their careers as newspapermen, there is a suspicion that a storyteller's artistry may be far too closely tied up with external considerations like space limitations, restrictive house-styles and editorial stipulations. The size of a *Tatler* sheet, not artistic choice, was what set 2,000 words as a maximum for short fiction in that periodical; it was available space that determined features like the amount of dialogue or the use of a first-person narrator who could compress information and provide retrospective summaries of narrative action. Later, the daily 'turnover' of exactly one column and a quarter in the *Civil and Military Gazette*, where Kipling began publishing stories in 1886, provides a comparable case of implacable word-restriction disciplining short-story form, irrespective of who was employing it. These exigencies, however, are not to be regretted if they are seen as the spurs which chafe the art of the short story into existence. (Shaw 1983, 7)[29]

[29] In Kipling's stories, we often find references to journalistic practice: for example in "The Man Who Would be King" (see below, p. 98), or in "A Matter of Fact" (1892). Here three journalists meet on a steamer that takes them from Cape Town back to Britain; they are committed to facts, but during their voyage they experience a strange event: an unknown creature of the deep sea is brought to the surface and dies, mourned by its partner. The journalists wonder what to make of the event. The American, Keller, wants to tell it in journalistic terms, but no one will believe that the story is factual. As the British

Furthermore, the short story has been seen not only in relation to neighbouring forms in fictional and expository prose, but also in relation to poetry – because of its formal concision – and drama. H.E. Bates (1965, 215) notes, for example, that the short story,

> not so rigidly confined as a sonnet yet superficially more restricted than a novel, stands nearer the drama than either. It is at once restricted, yet free; its range of time, place, and movement is necessarily limited, and like the drama it is forced back on the use of suggestion, implied action, indirect narration, and symbolism to convey what might otherwise be conveyed by a plain catalogue of solid words.[30]

W. Somerset Maugham claimed, in the preface to the American edition of his *Complete Short Stories* (1952), that he "did not take to writing stories seriously till [he] had had much experience as a dramatist" – an experience which taught him "to leave out everything that did not serve the dramatic value" of a story. "It taught me to make incident follow incident in such a manner as to lead up to the climax I had in mind." (Maugham 1963, 60) In Graham Greene's story "Across the Bridge", the text itself openly refers not only to oral story-telling (see above, p. 22), but also repeatedly to drama: "it was a tragedy for Mr Calloway"; "And the next act again was pure comedy"; "Somebody ought to write a play about it"; "They all watched the drama proceed with immense interest, sympathy and respect".

Other parallels have been observed between the short story and art forms in other media, such as painting, photography and the cinema.[31] Like a painting and a photograph, which freeze an instant in time and thus can

---

journalist realizes, the story can thus only be conveyed in the form of a fictional tale: "'What are you going to do?' 'Tell it as a lie.' 'Fiction?' This with the full-blooded disgust of a journalist for the illegitimate branch of the profession."

[30] See also the following statements, all of which are excerpted in Weber and Greiner (1977): Henry James in the "Preface to The Author of Beltraffio" (1909): "the innumerable repeated chemical reductions and condensations that tend to make of the very short story [...] one of the costliest, even if, like the hard, shining sonnet, one of the most indestructible, forms of composition in general use" (77); Arthur Ransome in *A History of Story-Telling* (1909): "The short story proper is in narrative prose what the short lyric is in poetry" (78); Elizabeth Bowen in her preface to *The Faber Book of Modern Short Stories* (1936): "Poetic tautness and clarity are so essential to it that it may be said to stand at the edge of prose; in its use of action it is nearer to drama than to the novel" (124); Angus Wilson in a *Paris Review* interview (1957): "Short stories and plays go together in my mind" (173); and Frank O'Connor in an interview in the same journal (1957): "the nearest thing I know to lyric poetry" (168).

[31] On the short story and the cinema, painting and photography, see also Shaw (1983, 12 and 14).

only suggest a wider context of events, the short story, too, depends on such suggestion.[32] To V.S. Pritchett, the short story is a typical "hybrid" which, among others, "owes much to the quickness, the objectivity and cutting of the cinema", as he observed in his essay on "Short Stories" in *Harper's Bazaar* (1953). (in Weber and Greiner 1977, 162) Elizabeth Bowen has remarked in a similar vein, in her preface to *The Faber Book of Modern Short Stories* (1936):

> The cinema, itself busy with a technique, is of the same generation: in the last thirty years the two arts have been accelerating together. They have affinities – neither is sponsored by a tradition; both are, accordingly, free; both, still, are self-conscious, show a self-imposed discipline and regard for form; both have, to work on, immense matter – the disorientated romanticism of the age. The new literature, whether written or visual, is an affair of reflexes, of immediate susceptibility, of associations not examined by reason: it does not attempt a synthesis. (Bowen 1994, 256)

In light of all these considerations concerning the short story's generic status, the following sketch of its history in Britain will not limit itself to a definition which views the short story as a 'modern' phenomenon. Adopting a diachronic and flexible notion of the short story as genre, the present book extends its scope backward into traditions of short prose fiction in print which antedate Poe's and later notions of the short story. It is committed (without being able to actually fulfil it) to an ideal which Paul Goetsch (1978a, 118) has outlined for a genre history of the short story:

> Ideally, the history of the genre must do justice to the [short story's] literary and social conditions and be aware of its parallels to the history of other genres, general changes of style, as well as the complex relationship between literary and extra-literary developments. Neither can it assume that there is a causal connection between individual works, nor must it imply that developments can be understood as organic or teleological evolution. Rather, it will have to restrict itself to pointing out how genres and conventions

[32] Brown (1997) emphasizes the parallel between the short story's tendency to highlight significant moments and Gotthold Ephraim Lessing's notion, proposed in his *Laokoon*, of the 'pregnant moment' in visual art which permits the spectator to conjecture an action from the static work of art. Rabb's *The Short Story and Photography 1880's–1980's* (1998) is an anthology reflecting the affinity, through accentuating the moment rather than temporal developments, of short story and photography since the 1880s. British nineteenth-century examples include E.W. Hornung, "A Spoilt Negative", Rudyard Kipling, "At the End of the Passage", Arthur Conan Doyle, "A Scandal in Bohemia" and Thomas Hardy, "An Imaginative Woman". For an explicit intermedial and ekphrastic (that is, word-painting) relationship with painting, see also A.S. Byatt's *Matisse Stories* (1993).

change, how they are established, popularized, exhausted, parodied, renewed and reformed, and how there is always a contemporaneity of the non-contemperaneous. [my translation]

# Part II:

## The Historical Overview

## 1. The Sixteenth and Seventeenth Centuries

### *Early-Modern Diversity*

In the early-modern period, the course of literary history in English was significantly determined by the new print culture (the technology of printing with movable type) and a concurrent proliferation of literary prose into which older forms of oral narrative were partly transferred. In the final quarter of the sixteenth century, a commercial book market was established and the professional writer emerged who was able to earn his living with his pen (rather than being rewarded by a patron at court) because there was now a readership capable and willing to buy literature on an open market for print products. By 1600, about fifty per cent of the population were literate, a notable acceleration of the spread of literacy having taken place in the last quarter of the sixteenth century. The sixteenth century was yet uncertain about the literariness of prose fiction and its place in the established genre system, but there was now a notable increase of that kind of literature in both longer and shorter forms. These were not neatly distinguished from each other, and in terms of our modern notions of genre, neither the novel nor the short story were yet in existence. As Paul Salzman (1986, 342) notes, "prose fiction sparked off very little critical debate or theorizing" between the mid-sixteenth and the end of the seventeenth century. The readership for early-modern fiction in print included the court but also the expanding and increasingly literate new middle classes of the towns. Salzman (1986, 1f.) draws attention to the "great variety of approaches to prose narrative which were taken by the Elizabethans". This variety reflects not only the mixed audience but also the great interest which writers took in the possibilities of the new language for literature and the opportunities it offered for experiments in genre and style.

As pointed out before, short forms of literature strongly depend for publication on text compilations and the periodical press. The latter did not emerge properly until the eighteenth century; from the fifteenth through the seventeenth centuries, many examples of short fiction in print are therefore found in collections. Short fiction was also distributed, however, through the unbound pamphlet, and it may be presumed that a considerable amount of examples published in this medium were lost.

Margaret Schlauch (1966) provides a concise survey of English short fiction in the fifteenth and sixteenth centuries.[1] For the decades before the reign of Elizabeth I, she notes that various kinds of late-medieval short narrative – in romantic, edifying and comic modes – survived into Tudor England, but there were also important elements of change:

> First of all, the medium of verse was very widely, though by no means exclusively, replaced by prose. The shift was no doubt connected with the technological innovation represented by printing and the consequent increase in the habit of silent reading instead of listening to public deliveries in verse. [...] A second important change was to be seen in the fact that collections of short tales and anecdotes began to appear without attached *moralitates*. [...]
>
> The result of this latter change was the appearance of Tudor jest books [...]. The jest books did not usually pretend to be edifying. [...] the later collections are clearly devoted to entertainment alone. In contents the collections range from the simplest of jokes based on puns, malapropisms, dialect forms, and mispronunciations, to expanded anecdotes and to genuine short tales of a humorous character. The line of demarcation between narrative and non-narrative is thus hard to draw. But the more expansive of the jests may claim to represent short fiction. As such, they offer interesting material for the study of techniques anticipating in miniature those of modern realistic writing, for instance in the use of dialogue, ironical comment by the narrator, and above all colloquial as opposed to formal literary English. [...]
>
> The pioneer collection of this type, *A Hundred Mery Talys* (1526), is also the least derivative insofar as it does not rely on translation or paraphrase from foreign sources, and it is also very native in style. (Schlauch 1966, 404f.)

The *Hundred Merry Tales* are composed in a style marked by simple syntax and diction, and many poke fun at members of contemporary professions, like lawyers, the clergy, scholars, but also merchants. In the eighth tale, which is quoted here in full and in modern spelling, an Oxford scholar's pretentious use of learned inkhorn terms makes it hard for him to cope with everyday life and the representative of a more ordinary profession:

> In the University of Oxenford there was a scholar that delighted much to speak eloquent English and curious terms, and came to the cobbler with his

[1] For other surveys, see also Canby (1909, part III), Beachcroft (1968, chapter 6) and Waller (1981).

> shoes which were peaked before – as they used that season – to have them clouted [cleated] and said this wise: 'Cobbler, I pray thee set me two triangles and two semicircles upon my subpeditals and I shall give thee for thy labor.' This cobbler because he understood him not half well answered shortly and said: 'Sir, your eloquence passeth mine intelligence but I promise you if ye meddle with me, the clouting of your shoon shall cost you three pence.'
>
> By this tale men may learn that it is folly to study to speak eloquently before them that be rude and unlearned.

Another favourite subject matter of the jest books are the strains of married life and the battle of the sexes so frequently found in Tudor and Elizabethan literature. The sixty-sixth of the *Hundred Merry Tales* is a fairly typical example:

> A young man lately married to a wife thought it was good policy to get the mastery of her in the beginning, and came to her when the pot was seething over the fire. Although the meat therin were not [cooked] enough, he suddenly commanded her to take the pot from the fire – which answered and said that the meat was not ready to eat. And he said again: 'I will have it taken off for my pleasure.'
>
> This good woman, loath yet to offend him, set the pot beside the fire as he bad. And, anon after, he commanded her to set the pot behind the door. And she said thereto again: 'Ye be not wise therin.'
>
> But he precisely said it should be so as he bad, and she genteely again did his commandment. This man yet not satisfied, commanded her to set the pot ahigh upon the hen roost. 'What!' quod the wife again, 'I trow ye be mad.'
>
> And he fiercely then commanded her to set it there or else, he said, she should repent. She somewhat afraid to move his patience, took a ladder and set it to the roost, and went herself up the ladder, and took the pot in her hand – praying her husband then to hold the ladder fast for sliding, which he so did.
>
> And when the husband looked up and saw the pot stand there on high, he said thus: 'Lo, now standeth the pot there as I would have it.' This wife, hearing that, suddenly poured the hot pottage on his head and said thus: 'And now been the pottage there as I would have them.'
>
> By this tale men may see it is no wisdom for a man to attempt a meek woman's patience too far, lest it turn to his own hurt and damage.

Both stories centre on witty action rather than character. The characters are not developed as individuals but typify certain roles in contemporary society. The two stories are also characteristic of the jest books in that they are enlivened by passages of dialogue. They still have an explicit moral attached to them, but this moral appears as a mere tag and clearly pokes fun at those to whom it seems to be directed. The main interest is in a good story, far less in what can be seriously learned from it. Some later jest books were collected around characters like Howleglass or the Parson of Kalenborowe.[2] They all aimed at a relatively low kind of entertainment and simple characterization of society and appealed to an audience that included a significant number of merchants and craftsmen.

They were also the prime readership of the cony-catching pamphlets, a variety of rogue literature which, during the reign of Elizabeth, depicted the dangers posed by contemporary criminals who lured their victims like 'conies' (that is, rabbits) into traps. This kind of literature about low life appealed to readers whose affluence had to be protected against a conspicuous amount of thieves, beggars and confidence men in contemporary society and for whom it was a vital interest to be informed about the tricks that might be used against themselves. Examples include John Awdeley's *Fraternity of Vagabonds* (c. 1561) and Thomas Harman's *A Caveat for Common Cursetors* (1566), but in terms of *story*-telling and literary quality, Robert Greene's cony-catching pamphlets of the early 1590s are more noteworthy.

Greene was one of the late-Elizabethan professional writers with a great talent for writing for all kinds of tastes and demands. The 1590s were a period of major change in the English social structure; counter-discourses to the court became increasingly important – also in literature, where attempts at social realism and social satire became conspicuous on a scale wider than ever before. As well as writing pastoral romances in the courtly mode, Greene also contributed to the realistic and satirical mode addressed at an audience outside the court. His cony-catching pamphlets expose the dangers emanating from the Elizabethan underworld (and thus exemplify an early focus on a 'submerged population group'), but they also entertain through their inclusion of stories in the jest-book tradition. An example is "**How a cunning knave got a trunk** *well-stuffed with linen and certain parcels of plate out of a citizen's house, and how the master of the house holp the deceiver to carry away his own goods*". An element of instruction is obvious at the end of the story; the narrator emphasizes that the merchant has been punished for his own lack of suspicion and care – but, at the same time, the victim of the thief is also the victim of the author's satire:

> When the trunk was missed, I leave to your conceits what household grief there was on all sides, especially the goodman himself, who, remembering how he helped the fellow up with a trunk, perceived that hereby he had beguiled himself, and lost more than in haste he should recover again. How this may admonish others I leave to the judgment of the indifferent opinion,

[2] Several of which are included in Zall (1963), see bibliography of quoted sources.

> that see when honest meaning is so craftily beleaguered as good foresight must be used to prevent such dangers.

Apart from this (mock) didacticism, however, this is, above all, a lively story, developing from panoramic narrative to a short dialogue scene, with an element of suspense (when the thief appears to have been caught), followed by an antithetical surprise ending. The story has a significant amount of circumstantial detail which contributes to an effect of realism.

All of these elements have also been noted for the work of Thomas Deloney, which is set in the recent past but also rooted firmly in realities of middle-class life during the final years of Elizabeth's reign. Deloney's works of fiction published between 1597 and 1600, *Jack of Newberie, The Gentle Craft* and *Thomas of Reading,* celebrate the social success and the value system of craftsmen, shoemakers and cloth traders. As Paul Salzman (1986, 102f.) notes, Deloney's fiction indicates "the arrival of a reading public which appreciated literature written about their own lives (or lives to which they aspired)". Deloney's prose works have been seen as highly episodic antecedents of the novel, but they can also each be seen as series of connected tales, thus indicating the extent to which long and shorter forms of fiction were still linked. It is not surprising that episodes from *The Gentle Craft* and *Thomas of Reading* have been included in later short-story anthologies, like the narrative about the career of Sir Simon Eyre, who rises from shoemaker's apprentice to Lord Mayor of London in *The Gentle Craft,* or the murder of Thomas Cole from *Thomas of Reading.*[3]

The great diversity of Elizabethan fiction also comprised an artistically more ambitious line of short narrative in prose which was able to satisfy the aesthetic demands of the court and associated circles and, as a consequence, carried other cultural interests than the jest books: those of courtly life and humanist learning. In courtly literature, the status of print was still contested. Famously, Sir Philip Sidney's *Arcadia,* a long piece of prose fiction in the courtly mode of the pastoral romance, was initially only circulated in manuscript form. But at least some prose literature with a court appeal was also available in print, such as the collections of *novelle.*[4] The novella (the term translates literally as 'a little new thing') was imported, around the mid-sixteenth century, from Italy, the frequently travelled model of humanist culture, and from France as an intermediary of Italian culture. Giovanni Boccaccio had developed the prose novella in the mid-fourtheenth century; his

---

[3] "Sir Simon Eyre" is included in Wilson (1921) and "How Thomas of Reading Was Murdered" in Melville and Hargreaves (1931).

[4] For a more detailed discussion of this form of short Elizabethan narrative, see Salzman (1986, chapter 2).

*Decameron* (c. 1349–51) – which already influenced Chaucer – is the prototypical collection of this type of stories (which are, in this collection, united by a frame narrative). The work of a famous sixteenth-century Italian writer, Matteo Bandello (who died in 1561), was translated into French by Belleforest, who in turn was an important source for English writers. The novella is a type of vivid, action-focussed story; it tends to restrict itself to a central event or situation and can serve a variety of serious, romantic, comic or satirical effects. The Elizabethan versions of these narratives soon became popular during the 1560s and 70s. According to Henry Seidel Canby (1909, 107), it is in the novella type that a real innovation in the telling of short fiction in England occurred: "With the interest in a fresh ideal of life, and only with it, came in the new short story. [...] An elixir of new courtesy, new philosophy, new civilization came in with the *novelle* [...]."

The famous Elizabethan compilations of novella-type stories, some composed by writers with a university education, consisted for the most part of translations, or rather adaptations, of Italian and French sources like Boccaccio, as well as *novelle* of Cinthio, Matteo Bandello, Marguerite de Navarre, and others. The 'translators' also drew on the stories of classical antiquity such as those found in Herodotus or Livy, which they then retold in the manner of the novella. The modern reputation of the Elizabethan story books rests mainly on the fact that they were the sources from which the Elizabethan and Jacobean dramatists extracted many of their plots. However, as Thomas O. Beachcroft (1968, 59) reminds us, they "were a great deal more than 'compost', as C.S. Lewis aptly called them, for the dramatists, and were read eagerly for a generation or so before they were turned into plays". The *novelle* in these collections are predominantly of the romantic type, with a focus on love plots, but merry tales are also found.[5] While the element of heavy didacticism was disappearing from the jest books, its presence became most conspicuously felt in the *novelle*, at least in the more serious varieties. Another element in which the courtly story books differed from those of the middle class was their more elegant, rhetorically conscious style meant to enhance the literariness of prose. With such elements, the *novelle* collections were at the height of fashionable taste, and short fiction became a prime literary form for catering to the cultural interests of the upper echelons of society. As Henry Seidel Canby (1909, 107f. and 111) observes:

[5] *The Palace of Pleasure*, for instance, ends with a jest-type story of how a lawyer is conned by two criminal merchants, "A Doctor of the Laws".

> In England the short story had to bear the whole burden of the renaissance. Erudition, discourses upon various subjects quite foreign to the plot, a highly rhetorical style certainly never learned from *The Decameron* or from Bandello. [...] the Elizabethan short story owed its extra-narrative features to the humanist literature which sprang from the peculiar interests of the renaissance.

One of the first and most highly acclaimed collections is William Painter's *The Palace of Pleasure* (first edition 1566/7, third edition 1575). It was dedicated to a courtly patron, the Earl of Warwick, and contains about a hundred stories, two thirds deriving from the novella genre, and one third retelling classical authors. Painter himself referred to the stories as 'novels' in the extended title of the collection: *The Palace of Pleasure: beautified, adorned and well furnished with pleasant histories and excellent novelles selected out of divers good and commendable authors.* His dedication "To the Reader" indicates that he was well aware of the original meaning of 'novel' and used it to advertise the newness of the type of stories he was offering: "these newes or Novelles here presented". While *The Palace of Pleasure* had the capability to appeal to courtly readers and express values of their circles, it was also clearly a commodity on a more democratic book market. This emerges from the outrage with which Roger Ascham, one of the leading educators and proponents of humanist learning of the time, speaks of this kind of literature, presumably having Painter at the top of his mind. In his treatise on genteel education, *The Scholemaster* (1570), he complains about "the enchantments of Circe brought out of Italy to mar men's manners in England":

> much by example of ill life but more by precepts of fond books, of late translated out of Italian into English, sold in every shop in London, commended by honest titles the sooner to corrupt honest manners, dedicated overboldly to virtuous and honourable personages, the easilier [sic] to beguile simple and innocent wits. It is pity that those which have authority and charge to allow and disallow books to be printed be no more circumspect herein than they are. (Ascham 1967, 67)

Henry Seidel Canby (1909, 123) praises the "dramatic value" of Painter's "realistic, vivid, admirably plotted narratives", but such elements, to a modern audience at least, appear somewhat repressed by the layers of narratorial comment typically found in the stories as well, like in "The Duchess of Malfy", a source for John Webster's tragedy of the same title. This narrative is about a widowed duchess secretly married to the gentleman who acts as master of her household; as a consequence of family intrigues, the relationship ends disastrously for both. The dramatic nature of the material is emphasized in the narrative itself: "Behold the first act of this tragedy, and the provision of the fare which afterwards sent them both to their grave [...]." This quality is, however, undermined throughout by intrusive narratorial comment and explanation. A two-page exposition indicates right from the start how readers are to interpret the story and draw a lesson from it. Elements of the courtesy book, a contemporary text type giving advice of proper courtly behaviour, are also apparent, as is the fact that, in comparison with stories for the middle classes, the style register is marked by a more difficult, latinate vocabulary, a complex, hypotactical syntax and a firework of rhetorical devices (parallelisms, alliterations, similes, antitheses and many others):

> The great honour and authority men have in this world, and the greater their estimation is, the more sensible and notorious are the faults by them committed, and the greater is their slander. In like manner more difficult it is for that man to tolerate and sustain fortune, which all the days of his life hath lived at his ease, if by chance he fall into any great necessity than for him which never felt but woe, mishap and adversity. Dionysius the Tyrant of Sicily, felt greater pain when he was expelled his kingdom, than Milo did, being banished from Rome: for so much as the one was a sovereign lord, the son of a king, a justiciary on earth, and the other but a simple citizen of a city, wherein the people had laws, and the laws of magistrates were had in reverence. So likewise the fall of a high and lofty tree, maketh greater noise, than that which is low and little. High towers, and stately palaces of princes be seen further off, than the poor cabins, and homely shepherds' sheepcotes: the walls of lofty cities more aloof do salute the viewers of the same, than the simple caves, which the poor do dig below the mountain rocks. Wherefore it behoveth the noble, and such as have charge of commonwealth, to live an honest life, and bear their port upright, that none have cause to discourse upon their wicked deeds and naughty life. And above all modesty ought to be kept by women, whom as their race, noble birth, authority and name, maketh them more famous, even so their virtue, honesty, chastity, and continency more praiseworthy. [...] I will not here endeavour myself to seek for examples of Samson, Solomon or other, which suffered themselves fondly to be abused by women: and who by means of them be tumbled into great faults, and have incurred greater perils: contenting myself to recite a right pitiful history done almost in our time, [...]. In the very time then lived a gentleman of Naples called Antonio Bologna [...].

Only with this reference to one of the main characters, the master of the duchess's household, does the story proper set in. The long non-narrative beginning, which locates the story in contexts of classical and Biblical learning and the codes of courteous behaviour, seems 'superfluous' in light of our dominant understanding of the short story as a tightly constructed unity, but for a courtly audience in Elizabethan times, it was precisely these elements which linked the story with the leading discourses of their culture.[6] Henry Seidel Canby (1909, 154) wonders why the stories included in the courtly collections, which were widely popular with their audience, did not lead to a further blossoming of the art of *short* story-telling, and suggests that this might be due to an over-burdening of the format:

> It has performed all the services of the modern novel without its capability for such service – and has been ruined in the process. Throughout all the period it has been slipping from beneath our hands into something progenitory of this novel, and, at the end, the narratives that are still professedly short are neither excellent in themselves, nor suggestive of better to come. An age in which this form of fiction was more widely read, more widely practised than all other literary narrative has not left us one short story of the first rank!

Around the 1590s longer forms of fiction became the new vogue, and outside the more popular traditions,[7] short fiction, although still produced in great numbers and in a great variety of forms through which writers explored the possibilities of prose narrative, went, according to some critics, into a period of decline that lasted until the second half of the seventeenth century. Charles Mish (1968/69, 233) observes that

[6] Other Elizabethan story collections include George Pettie's *A Petite Palace of Pettie his Pleasure* (1576), which is notorious for its euphuistic, extremely elaborate style, or Barnaby Rich's *Rich His Farewell to Military Profession* (1581), which includes the story from which Shakespeare took the plot for *Twelfth Night*, "Of Apolonius and Silla" (included in Melville and Hargreave 1931).

[7] Here the chapbooks are noteworthy because they took old stories into later centuries. These were publications in pamphlet form, simply illustrated and containing popular tales, ballads, tracts and other texts, usually sold by itinerant dealers at a relatively cheap price. "Most of the horde of chapbooks that were hawked around England during the eighteenth century [...] had ancestors which were born before 1700, some of them leaving a permanent impress on children's literature. It is noteworthy that the first prose redactions of several well known stories, such as those of Robin Hood, Guy of Warwick, and Bevis of Hampton, appear in these years. [...] We may cite as examples of chapbook material a couple of the texts associated with the name of John Shirley. [...] his stories are aptly characterized as 'ghosts of the Middle Ages and of the sixteenth century'; they seem deliberately contrived by virtue of their typography (black letter, with woodcuts), content, and syntax to give the impression that they are of considerable antiquity. Motifs from romances of chivalry abound, and the punctuation is that old-fashioned sort that hooks strings of sentences together (one presumes they are sentences) with semicolons and colons." (Mish 1968/69, 316f.) Selections of the popular tradition are included in Mish's anthology *Short Fiction of the Seventeenth Century* (1963). Of the courtly tradition, this anthology presents a selection of romances, anti-romances, moral tales and sentimental love stories; most of them are far longer than modern short stories.

> [a] change occurred after the Restoration. Under the influence of French models, short fiction underwent a revitalization that resulted in a great upsurge in both quantity and quality. [...] By 1700 short fiction had more than regained the ground lost during the first part of the century; it had gone ahead and, again, though this time in actuality, seemed on the threshold of a significant future.[8]

*Short Fiction of the Restoration*

Much of the Restoration fiction Mish here has in mind was written under the influence of the French *nouvelle* (from the pen of writers such as Paul Scarron and Madame de Lafayette) and its narratives of gallantry and intrigue, or the more action-orientated Spanish novella (as written, for example, by Cervantes). It became common now for English writers to refer to shorter forms of fiction as 'novels'. In the preface to his *Incognita* (1692), for instance, a narrative based on the Spanish model, William Congreve explicitly distinguished the 'novel' from the longer and traditional romance, not only in terms of length, but also in terms of structure. Congreve intended to "imitate Dramatick writing" and strive for a unity of action – or rather a "Unity of Contrivance" – greater than in the rambling romance. (Congreve 1966, 33f.)[9] The Restoration 'novel' is on average considerably shorter than the romance but longer than what qualifies as a short story today (Mish considers narratives up to 25,000 words). And despite such examples as Congreve's *Incognita*, it does not always meet modern criteria of unity and concision: "seventeenth-century fiction tends to be very diffuse; the story begins before it should and ends after it should, dialogue is usually orotund and long-winded, characterization is hesitant and piecemeal, plots are repe-

[8] Shorter Fiction of the seventeenth century is also discussed by Beachcroft (1968, chapter 7) and Salzman (1986, 308 *passim*). The list of Restoration novels in Salzman's bibliography (374-378) includes fairly short examples like those collected in *Delightful and Ingenious Novells* (1685). For a collection of women's shorter fiction of the Restoration and early eighteenth century see also the anthology by Backscheider and Richetti (1996), which includes, among others, work by Aphra Behn, Mary Delarivière Manley, Penelope Aubin and Eliza Haywood.

[9] For a sense that the new shorter kind of fiction deviated significantly from the romance, see also the following statement by the novelist Mary Delarivière Manley in the preface to her *Secret History of Queen Zarah* (1705): "These little Pieces which have banish'd *Romances* are much more agreeable to the Brisk and Impetuous Humour of the *English*, who have naturally no Taste for longwinded Performances, for they have no sooner begun a Book but they desire to see the end of it." (in Weber and Greiner 1977, 7)

titious and sprawling." (Mish 1968/69, 233) But this kind of narrative displayed a new direction in that it went

> toward the interiorization of fiction, toward psychological analysis and verisimilitude in action and setting [...]. Various devices were used to achieve these aims: interest in a definite historical milieu, for instance, to achieve a realistic setting, the disappearance of the older romantic hero whose excessive gallantry and feats of arms had come to seem ludicrously hyperbolic, and (especially in Mrs. Behn) the development of the eye-witness narrator. It should again be pointed out, however, that these realistic elements must be evaluated in comparative terms; they may not seem very strong in the light of today's writing, but they do represent a marked change from earlier writing. (*ibid.*, 330)

An instance of a relatively short example of the Restoration 'novel' is Aphra Behn's *The Unfortunate Happy Lady: A True History* (probably written 1684, published 1698), which is set in contemporary England and offered as an authentic depiction of contemporary manners.[10] It tells the story of a woman, Philadelphia, whose life takes an unhappy course when her own brother behaves most treacherously towards her, and it begins with the following comment by the narrator:

> I cannot omit giving the world an account, of the uncommon villany of a Gentleman of a good Family in England, practic'd upon his Sister, which was attested to me by one who liv'd in the Family, and from whom I had the whole truth of the Story. I shall conceal the unhappy Gentleman's own, under the borrow'd names of Sir William Wilding, who succeeded his father, Sir Edward, in an estate of near 4,000 l. a year, inheriting all that belong'd to him except his Virtues. 'Tis true, he was obliged to pay his only Sister a Portion of 6,000 l., which he might very easily have done of his Patrimony in a little time, the Estate being not in the least incumbered. But the death of his good Father gave a loose to the extravagance of his Inclinations, which till then was hardly observable.

The brother sells Philadelphia to a procuress, but the gentleman to whom she is to be prostituted, aptly named Gracelove, proves virtuous. He takes her with him, falls in love with her and leaves her in the care of a kind elderly gentleman when he has to go abroad on business. Unfortunately, his ship sinks and he is believed dead. After a certain time, the old man takes Philadelphia as his wife to provide for her. After his death, this leaves Philadelphia a wealthy woman, and when Gracelove returns unexpectedly,

[10] For a brief discussion, see also Salzman (1986, 316f.).

a wearied and impoverished traveller, she is empowered to restore him to a gentlemanly state and chooses him as her new husband, also forgiving her brother, who has meanwhile come down in the world. With a course of action that stretches over several years, the narrative conveys no sense of unity of action, and to us the text reads like a short novel rather than a short story in the modern sense.

Apart from its production of shorter forms of fiction, the late seventeenth century seems most notable for the further history of the short story because it cultivated the forms of the essay and the character sketch – forms with which the short story is closely related in the eighteenth century – and gave rise to the first magazines: that form of publication which was to flourish in the next century with a considerable impact on the short story. The *Gentleman's Journal* appeared monthly between 1692 and 1694, attracting its readers not only with recent news but also with literary pieces, including short 'novels' that were probably written by the periodical's editor, Peter Anthony Motteux. According to Charles Mish (1968/69, 314f.), these stories are "[s]ophisticated and urbane", and they

> seem intended more for a masculine than a feminine audience, which is to say they are sex-stories rather than love-stories. The relations between men and women are looked at in a way that is, if not cynical, at least unromantic. In a word, these are fabliaux for those with some taste and education, and they necessarily involve some depiction of manners and a realistic viewpoint.
>
> The second story in the first issue, 'The Noble Statuary' [...] offers a good case in point. Hippolita, thought the model spouse in her husband's lifetime, rather overdid her grief after his death; but her sorrow was quickly assuaged by the appearance of the stone-cutter she sent for to do the monument for her dead spouse. [...]
>
> In 'The Friendly Cheat' [...], we have a sexually irregular incident prevented by a moral friend. Two gentlemen wish to swap wives for a night; a friend to both offers to make the arrangements for them, and manages things so that each man gets his own wife in the dark.

During the period discussed in this section, we are still remote from the short story as generally understood today. In the genre systems of the Renaissance and Restoration, the area of prose fiction had a different status and a different internal division from the system in which the 'short story' was first fully defined and named as a genre of its own. Prose fiction in general was not yet a particularly prestigious kind of literature, and lines of demarcation between longer and shorter forms of short fiction were fuzzy. The relative novelty of prose fiction in print gave rise to a lot of experiment and thus a great diversity of forms. But in this very diversity it is also possible to find examples that approximate later notions of the short story. Generally, however, not only was there no short story; there was no novel in the sense that we understand these kinds of literature today as well. In the eighteenth century, as the following section will show, prose fiction still configures differently in the genre system than from the nineteenth century onwards. What emerges now, however, is a new publication platform that encourages short fiction and eventually leads to its manifestation in forms from which Poe's theorization could take hold.

## 2. The Eighteenth and Early Nineteenth Centuries

The increase in literary periodicals makes the eighteenth century more significant for the evolution of the short story than the preceding ones. Throughout the eighteenth century, shorter forms of fiction are also found in other publication contexts. Short novels, for instance, which were in some instances very short,[11] continued to be published individually (like those of Mary Delarivière Manley and Eliza Haywood[12]) or were collected in such series as Samuel Croxall's *A Select Collection of Novels and Histories* (1720–29). What would today be identified as a short story was even occasionally attached to a treatise or part of a treatise itself – like a famous 'ghost story' by Daniel Defoe, "The True Relation of the Apparition of one Mrs Veal", which was published in association with a religious tract, Drelincourt's *Consolations against the Fears of Death* in 1705. The story re-tells a then current story about the apparition of a woman after her death to one of her neighbours, but it is not a ghost story in a post-Romantic understanding. It

---

[11] That it is still difficult for the eighteenth century to draw a clear dividing line between 'novels' and 'short stories' emerges not only from Dr Johnson's definition, in his *Dictionary* (1755), of a *novel* as "a small tale, generally of love", which would also fit many short *stories* of the period. It is also evident from the fact that pieces of fiction with rather complex plots, spanning many years and involving a great number of characters, could actually be very short. Robert Mayo, in his *The English Novel in the Magazines 1740–1815* (1962), lists a great number of such works of a length of 5,000 words upwards and notes that "many of the so-called novelettes of the magazines are merely short stories that have strayed, so to speak, into a higher bracket". (4) To Mayo, "[t]here were no established orders of magnitude in eighteenth-century magazine fiction, which ranged unmethodically and by imperceptible degrees from fables and anecdotes of less than one hundred words to full-length novels of over two hundred thousand". (5) For a critical discussion of Mayo's categorizations, see Pitcher (1977).

[12] For examples, see Paula R. Backscheider's edition of Haywood's selected fiction and drama (Haywood 1999) and the anthology of women's shorter fiction by Backscheider and Richetti (1996).

does not hinge on mystery and suspense, but its prime intent is to present factual evidence for the uncanny event. Defoe was a prolific journalist, and his shorter fiction is often associated with the themes with which his daily journalism – for example in his own periodical of political commentary, the *Review* (1704–13) – was occupied or the concerns he pursued in his longer nonfiction. Another story about an apparition included in later short-story anthologies, "In Defence of His Right", is originally part of Defoe's book-length treatise about *The History and Reality of Apparitions* (1727), where it is printed without a separate title. Like the story about Mrs Veal, the story has no purpose to create suspense, but its prime intention is to establish the plausibility of apparitions in a down-to-earth, middle-class English milieu. Defoe's historical account of the Great Plague and succeeding Great Fire in London, *A Journal of the Plague Year* (1722), includes not only statistics and other information but stories of human suffering as well, and his episodic long fiction often reads like a string of stories rather than a carefully plotted novel and provides further evidence that neat genre divisions between short and long fiction were not yet extant in the early eighteenth century. Throughout the eighteenth century, stories were also embedded in novels, for example the works of Henry Fielding, Sarah Fielding or Tobias Smollett. In addition, a small number of collections of original short stories were on the market, but generally, as Robert Mayo (1962, 253) observes, "the short story in the eighteenth century enjoyed a meager existence, and attracted no major talent" outside the periodicals. Significantly, when Leigh Hunt compiled his popular collection *Classic Tales* in 1806/7, which was "intended to contain the best short fiction of the previous age" (Mayo 1962, 255), periodicals were among his chief English sources.[13]

*Periodicals and the 'Age of Reason'*

In the new types of periodicals, the short story found a congenial medium and was put to systematic use by important writers – although neither the writers of short pieces of fiction nor the critics "seem to have formed [a] clear conception of such a genre". (Boyce 1968, 96) It was the essay, in par-

[13] It is Hunt's five volumes, in fact, from which many later anthologists seem to have drawn their selection of eighteenth-century stories and thus preserved them in literary history. The *Classic Tales* not only contain tales, but also "Critical Essays on the Merits and reputation of the Authors"; of the stories mentioned in this chapter, the following are found in Hunt's collection: Mackenzie's "Louisa Venoni", Goldsmith's "The Disabled Soldier", "The Man in Black" and "The Man-Hater", Dr Johnson's "Story of Misella" [*sic*] and Hawkesworth's "History of Melissa".

ticular the more personal and informal 'familiar' essay, which dominated the periodicals, and it is in an essayistic framework that short narratives are usually interspersed. That the eighteenth century still lacked a distinctive label for short stories emerges from John Hawkesworth's comment in an essay which he wrote for his *Adventurer* (no. 4, Saturday, November 18, 1752), dealing with "the different kinds of narrative, and why they are universally read". Here Hawkesworth clearly has genre labels for certain kinds of narrative literature at his disposal: 'History', 'Voyages and Travels', 'Epic Poem', 'Old Romance' and 'Novel'. But he has no special term yet for the kind of "short pieces" which the *Adventurer* published regularly and of which he composed quite a number himself.[14] Even though he lacks a label, however, Hawkesworth already notes that limited incident and brevity characterize the short periodical narrative:

> From a dramatic poem to those short pieces which may be contained in such a periodical paper as the *Adventurer*, is a bold transition. And yet such pieces although formed upon a single incident, if that incident be sufficiently interesting to engage the passions, may afford an entertainment which, if it is not lasting, is yet of the highest kind. Of such, therefore, this paper will frequently consist; but it should be remembered, that it is much more difficult and laborious, to invent a story however simple and however short, than to recollect topicks of instruction, or to remark the scenes of life as they are shifted before us. (Hawkesworth 1771, 18)

Eighteenth-century periodicals took various forms; their frequency of publication ranged from daily to monthly appearance.[15] As far as literary history is concerned, the 'periodical essay' (or 'essay serial') and the 'miscellany' are of prime importance. The former was developed in Richard Steele and Joseph Addison's *Tatler* (1709–11), whose individual numbers each contained a single 'essay' on various themes presented by a fictional editor. The *Tatler*'s editor persona was Bickerstaff, and its essays often integrated narratives or consisted entirely of a story. The model was successfully followed in Addison and Steele's *Spectator* (1711–15), Elizabeth Haywood's *Female Spectator* (1744–46), Dr Samuel Johnson's *Rambler* (1750–52) or John Hawkesworth's *Adventurer* (1752–54). The editor's voice was occasionally varied by (invented) letters to the editor.[16] The magazine miscellany, by contrast, was

[14] See, for example, Hawkesworth's "History of Melissa" (in nos. 7 and 8 of the *Adventurer*, 1752), about the misfortunes of a young woman who loses her parents and later a benevolent friend, but eventually becomes an heiress.

[15] For a survey of the eighteenth-century periodical market, see Sullivan (1983a), with an introduction by Morris Golden followed by profiles for individual periodicals.

[16] On the "Single-Essay Periodical", see also Mayo (1962, chapter 2).

composed of consciously multi-voiced material; this was the type of periodical already introduced by Motteux and followed in the influential and long-lived *Gentleman's Magazine* (from 1731), which was the first English periodical to use the image of the storehouse, the 'magazine', in its title to indicate the provenance of its contents from a number of different sources. Other important magazines which regularly printed short narratives included the *London Magazine* (1732–85), the *Ladies Magazine* (1749–53), the *Connoisseur* (1754–56), or the *Lady's Magazine* (1770–1819), to name only a few. These periodicals still had fairly small editions of only a few thousand copies per issue. As Richard Altick (1957, 47) notes, their great influence "upon the eighteenth-century reading habit was due not to large circulations but to the increase in the number of individual magazines [...] and to their presence in the coffeehouses, where they found most of their readers. The number of coffee-drinkers who pored over a single copy of the *Gentleman's Magazine* [...] in the course of a month ran into many scores." Furthermore, the most popular of the periodicals were also issued in the form of bound volumes and thus remained familiar to readers long after their original appearance.

Malcolm Bradbury (1971, 182) has pointed out that "the periodical as a form of cultural communication, grew up in the eighteenth century in response to a new technology and a new readership". This new readership was composed significantly of the middle classes alongside the more traditional gentry audience and included many female readers. It was an audience to be initiated into the workings of contemporary society. James Leheny (in Sullivan 1983a, 309) points out how the *Spectator*, for instance, was the product of, and suited to, a culture in change: "The old social order, based largely upon wealth derived from inherited land in the country, was being challenged and undermined by [...] newly prosperous entrepreneurs in London." In the political scene of the day, Addison and Steele were associated with the Whigs, the political faction which sympathized with the urban middle classes, and their periodicals "helped to support these relatively new social forces, sometimes by celebrating new institutions, social groups, and ideas, and sometimes by applying the balm of good humour to the wounds which the political divisions of the preceding decades had created". (*ibid.*) Typically, periodicals of the eighteenth century intended to depict and criticize the manners and morals, personal and social relations of contemporary society. Although the fictional pieces certainly served to entertain the readers,[17] they were, as Edward W. Pitcher (1975a, 200) notes, clearly subjugated "to an unwritten code of socio-moral utilitarianism":

---

[17] See the statement of John Hawkesworth quoted above (p. 49), which explicitly mentions entertainment.

> In the early eighteenth century, authors deliberately sought to fuse a new narrative style and fictional content with an ancient narrative purpose: there was a marriage of realism to didacticism. The prolific outcome of that marriage was a distinctly eighteenth-century form of moral tale. The characteristics of this new kind of moral fiction were, in general, the overt use of plot, character, and scene to illustrate a moral thesis, the statement of that thesis in prefactory or otherwise intrusive authorial commentary, the tendency to use autobiographical narrative techniques and structure, the tendency to affect a direct communication between narrator and reader, and the tendency to use contemporary, familiar, and typical situations and scenes.[18]

A delightful story in the *Tatler* (no. 61, October 11, 1709), for example, renders a lively account of a marriage that ends in irreconcilable separation because of a most trivial quarrel between Sir Henry Willit and his wife: "Sir Harry was reading a grave author; she runs into his study, and in a playing humour, claps the squirrel upon the folio. He threw the animal in a rage on the floor; she snatches it up again, calls Sir Harry a sour pedant, without good nature or good manners." The vivid narrative is not presented *per se*, however, but told by the *Tatler's* editor as an admonition to his sister Jenny Distaff on the evening of her wedding. It is preceded by serious advice:

> and I take it to be the first maxim in a married condition, that you are to be above trifles. When two persons have so good an opinion of each other as to come together for life, they will not differ in matters of importance, because they think of each other with respect in regard to all things of consideration that may affect them, and are prepared for mutual assistance and relief in such occurrences; but for less occasions, they have formed no resolutions, but leave their minds unprepared.

Central to the periodicals' narratives was an effect of authentic contemporaneity, and since so many of them were meant to portray and criticize social types, they also often come close to the character sketch. As Benjamin Boyce (1968, 98) notes, "[a]ll through the century in the periodicals descriptions of representative creatures pass before one's eyes", and many stories "are examples of successful short fictions that expand a single quirk of character into graphic scenes of recognizable behavior".

The didactic purpose of the stories in the *Spectator* is obvious, for instance, in the narrative written by Addison for number 123 (July 21,

[18] See also Canby (1909, 182): "one finds in these periodical short stories a mixed art, part story, part character sketch, part criticism, a true art for its place and for its purposes. [...] They embody, not dead in essays, but alive in narrative, the criticism of manners so characteristic of their age." On the "Commitment to Contemporaneity" which expressed itself in the new journalism, see also Hunter (1990, chapter 7).

1711).[19] The *Spectator* is supposed to be written by Mr Spectator, a learned and travelled man who acts as an observer of London society. He is the member of a fictional club in which different segments of polite society (the merchantile, the army, the country gentry, the town) are each represented by other characters. Sir Andrew Freeport, as his name already indicates, represents the eighteenth-century merchant, the member of an increasingly important class in contemporary society, while Sir Roger de Coverley stands for the gentry and the old social order. To Leheny (in Sullivan 1983a, 309), "Addison's portrayal of this ineffectual and quixotic country squire can be read as a covert attack on conservative men of property and the inordinate proportion of power they wielded in the nation". Sir Roger is therefore the perfect hinge for a story about the lack of education among those who still have the rule of the land. When Sir Roger and Mr Spectator are once "taking the air", they are overtaken, at extreme speed, by a young gentleman on horseback. This act of eighteenth-century rowdyism gives rise to a discussion of the lack of education of young gentlemen, who are thus unfit both to perform the social role they claim and fulfil their social responsibility:

> The Truth of it is, since my residing in these Parts I have seen and heard innumerable Instances of young Heirs and elder Brothers, who either from their own reflecting upon the Estates they are born to, and therefore thinking all other Accomplishments unnecessary, or from hearing these Notions frequently inculcated to them by the Flattery of their Servants and Domesticks, or from the same foolish Thought prevailing in those who have the Care of their Education, are of no manner of use but to keep up their Families, and transmit their Lands and Houses in a Line to Posterity.

Only after this analysis is the story about Eudoxus and Leontine introduced, two gentlemen who have made their way in the world and decide to exchange their children, a daughter and a son, to provide them with the best education possible. The experiment is successful. Son and daughter grow up to become models of virtue and end as a happy couple. Their fathers receive "in the dutiful and affectionate Behaviour of *Florio* and *Leonilla* the just Recompense, as well as the natural Effects, of that Care which they had bestowed upon them in their Education". The strong presence of the narrative voice and its close relationship with the readers gives support to the story's didactic intent,[20] which is just as obvious as the lesson at the end of Dr

[19] For a discussion specifically of the types of short fiction found in the *Spectator*, see Kay (1975).

[20] On the significance of overt narrators in this kind of fiction, see also Pitcher (1975a, 203,

Samuel Johnson's **"The History of Melissa"**. This story about a rich heiress who loses many 'friends' when her fortunes change is composed in the form of a letter written to the editor persona of Johnson's *Rambler*, Mr Rambler (*The Rambler*, December 4, 1750) and concludes with the following explicit and disillusioned statement about human nature:

> This, Mr. Rambler, is 'to see the world'. It is impossible for those that have only known affluence and prosperity, to judge rightly of themselves or others. The rich and the powerful live in a perpetual masquerade, in which all about them wear borrowed characters; and we only discover in what estimation we are held, when we can no longer give hopes or fears.

The extent to which the didactic narrative still dominated the mid- and later eighteenth century is exemplified by a story included in many short-story anthologies. Oliver Goldsmith's narrative about a disabled soldier (originally published in *The British Magazine*, 1760) starts with a passage of direct narratorial comment:

> The misfortunes of the great, my friend, are held up to engage our attention, are enlarged upon in tones of declamation, and the world is called upon to gaze at the noble sufferers; they have at once the comfort of admiration and pity.
>
> Yet where is the magnanimity of bearing misfortunes when the whole world is looking on? Men in such circumstances can act bravely even from motives of vanity. He only who, in the vale of obscurity, can brave adversity, who without friends to encourage, acquaintances to pity, or even without hope to alleviate his distresses, can behave with tranquillity and indifference, is truly great: whether peasant or courtier he deserves admiration, and should be held up for our imitation and respect.

This opinion is illustrated by the story about a simple soldier and his misfortunes. Although he ends up poor and crippled, he still seems to enjoy life and has even remained a patriot. The story was later included (as Letter

205): "Preparing the reader to hear these moral 'histories' was the essential, if limited art of the authors of the didactic fiction of this period. The emphasis was placed upon the creation of a viable relationship between narrator and reader, rather than upon the creation of a plausible relationship between narrator and story. One may fairly argue that this emphasis was a consequence of the emergence of the didactic tale out of the essay proper. It seems probable, however, that whatever the original relatedness of discursive essays and exemplary short tales, authors who wrote in the period after *The Spectator* normally conceived a story first, and appended commentary as part of a conventional presentational technique. [...] The conventional 'public' narrator was a paragon of reliability, not merely on matters of fact, but most emphatically so on matters of importance to the correctly and justly organized society."

CXIX) in Goldsmith's collection of essays and stories, *The Citizen of the World* (1762). Most of this volume consists of the 'Chinese Letters' which Goldsmith originally published in the *Public Ledger* in 1760 and 1761. For these letters, Goldsmith created a foreign character to depict the follies and morals of contemporary society, a fictional Chinese traveller-philosopher staying in London. The 'Man in Black' portrayed in Letter XXXI is one of the Chinaman's London friends and serves as an example of natural philanthropy in a narrative which also remained fairly well-known through its inclusion in later anthologies.

While the stories considered up to now have an English and specifically London setting, the eighteenth century also discovered the attractions of exotic locations. The 'oriental' tale was, as Benjamin Boyce (1968, 100f.) notes,

> inaugurated soon after readers for the first time had access to English translations of *The Arabian Nights* (beginning in 1704), of *Turkish Tales* (1708), and of *Persian Tales or the Thousand and One Nights* (1714–1715). *The Spectator* and, forty years later, *The Adventurer* offered many stories of this sort – vaguely biblical in manner and often solemn in tone, with magic rings, wildly improbable shifts of good and evil fortune, visions of supernatural places, contrasts of simple peasants and luxurious palaces to make up for the lack of serious characterization. [...]
>
> Addison and Hawkesworth succeeded in establishing the oriental apparatus for developing what *The Arabian Nights* did not include – strong lessons in morality and even in religion.

Addison's "The Vision of Mirzah" appeared in the *Spectator*, no. 159 (September 1, 1711). It is introduced by the remark that Mr Spectator has, during his travels, picked up several Oriental manuscripts in Cairo, from which he will "translate" excerpts for his readers "when I have no other entertainment for them". The first-person narrator of the manuscript, Mirzah, describes a vision of the fate of mankind which a Genius has revealed to him on a hill near Bagdad. Mirzah falls into despair when he witnesses scenes of man "given away to Misery and Mortality! tortured in Life, and swallowed up in Death!". However, the Genius then makes him realize that paradise can only be reached "through the Gates of Death". Goldsmith's narrative of Asem, the Man-Hater, was written later in the century (and originally published in the *Royal Magazine* in December 1759), but follows the same pattern. Asem has withdrawn from human society because he is disappointed by its vices. Just as he is about to commit suicide, a Genius takes him deep under the surface of a lake, into an alternative world which is "wholly inhabited by men who never do wrong". However, this world proves less perfect than Asem expects it to be: its inhabitants never do wrong, but they also lack determination and wisdom. They therefore cannot control the animal world around them, have never developed a complex civilization, and are unhappy because they have not achieved anything. After these revelations, Asem is reconciled to the imperfections of his own world, engages with it again and becomes a success in it – thus fulfilling a social ideal of the age of reason.[21] Didactic tales continued to be written in great numbers during the later eighteenth and early nineteenth centuries, but their dominant note began to change under the impact of Sentimentalism, Romanticism and political radicalism.

*Sentimentalism and Romanticism: The New Story of Social Critique and Education*

Sentimentalism, the (re-)discovery of the heart and individual sensibility, was a reaction to the emphasis which the earlier eighteenth century had given to rationality and sociability. True moral behaviour now came to be seen as a matter of feeling rather than reasoning. Feeling was perceived as the basis for moral action. The emphasis on sentiment was one element in an emerging Romanticism which also began to affect the telling of short stories in other respects: short narratives around the turn of the century reflect the Romantic 'discovery' of rural settings and characters from the margins of society, as well as a fascination with the irrational. With respect to form, one observes a new appreciation of description, but also a new attention to tight plots capable of creating suspense.

Unlike the earlier moral tales, sentimental tales of the late eighteenth century did not aim at their reader's cognitive response but, as Edward W. Pitcher (1975b, 327) observes,

> the appeal was to the reader's emotions, or sensibility, and the example was an exaggeration, a larger-than-life representation of emotions presumed to be common among men. The distance between the reader and the fictional subject, between the public norm and the exaggerated example, was bridged by desire, by a willing identification of reader with fictional character.

[21] Other oriental tales include Addison's "Alnaschar" (*The Spectator*, no. 535), Dr Johnson's "The History of Almamoulin" (*The Rambler*, no. 120) and "The History of Abouzaid" (*The Rambler*, no. 190), and John Hawkesworth's "Amurath an Eastern Story" (*The Adventurer*, nos. 20–22). Beachcroft (1968, 84) points out that the oriental tale survived into the nineteenth and twentieth centuries, for example in the oriental fantasies which George Meredith published under the title *The Shaving of Shagpat* in 1856; one of the stories collected here is "The Punishment of Shahpesh, the Persian, on Khipil, the Builder". Several volumes of Ernest Bramah's *Kay Lung* stories were published in the first three decades of the twentieth century. A related but ideologically different type of Eastern story is found in Salman Rushdie's collection *East, West* (1994).

A sentimental story that enjoyed long popularity – not least because it was the first story reprinted in Leigh Hunt's *Classic Tales* – is "Louisa Venoni", which the Scotsman Henry Mackenzie first published in his periodical *The Mirror* in 1780. In this story, a young man from Britain is touring Italy where he meets Louisa, the daughter of a peasant. Her father intends to marry his daughter to a neighbour who is "coarse, vulgar, and ignorant" and for whom she accordingly has little affection. Since Louisa and Edward have meanwhile fallen in love, Louisa develops a deep melancholy which the story takes time to depict in a natural setting perfectly suited to highlight the character's mood:

> In the evening she wandered forth to indulge her sorrows alone. She had reached a sequestered spot, where some poplars formed a thicket, on the banks of a little stream that watered the valley. A nightingale was perched on one of them, and had already begun his accustomed song. Louisa sat down on a withered stump, leaning her cheek upon her hand. After a little while, the bird was scared from its perch, and flitted from the thicket. Louisa rose from the ground, and burst into tears! She turned – and beheld Sir Edward.

Louisa elopes with Edward and lives with him in England, where she is deeply unhappy since her "virtue [...] was vanquished; but her sense of virtue was not overcome". While she is pining away, Edward starts to discover the virtue of Louisa and in particular her natural sensibility, while he himself becomes increasingly disenchanted with his London circle and their artificial manners: "In their conversation fantastic, not refined, their ideas were frivolous, and their knowledge shallow; and with all the pride of birth and insolence of station, their principles were mean, and their minds ignoble." He deeply regrets having led the "artless", trusting girl astray and becomes a reformed character. The story has a happy ending: disguised as a musician, old Venoni finds his daughter, and Edward marries Louisa.

This story's critique of the manners of London's fashionable society appears as a relatively weak form of social criticism when compared to a new type of tale that was inspired by turn-of-the-century radical political and social ideals in the context of the French Revolution. It described and demanded sympathy for the plights of the poorer parts of the population – victims of society or, to use Frank O'Connor's term, submerged population groups. To Edward W. Pitcher (1976, 331), this type of 'philosophic' tale was "a deliberate assault upon the mind and conscience of the reader". It "usually did hold out an image of society as it might be and should be if corruption and inequalities could be expelled from society, or controlled in it by just laws and enlightened citizens". An example which Pitcher discusses at length is James Montgomery's "The Cottage", published in *The Whisperer* in 1798. Here the narrator finds a starved family in a cottage who are beyond help and who represent

> a host of other sufferers who were perishing in the midst of a potential paradise. In sentimental fiction, the emphasis normally fell upon the goodness of the giver of charity, and such charity was almost always sufficient to relieve distress in time. The 'philosophic' tale turned from this kind of self-congratulation in sentimental fiction, and had the courage to be self-critical, or, at least, to admit the limitations of sympathy when faced with acute, or widespread, distress and need. (*ibid.*, 334)

Another example of this line of story is Mary Wollstonecraft's "Story of Crazy Robin" published in her *Original Stories from Real Life* (1788). Mary Wollstonecraft was a prominent social critic of her time, and the stories, produced fairly early in her career as a writer, reflect this attitude as well as the fact that Wollstonecraft had formerly earned her living as a teacher and governess. The *Original Stories* were intended for the moral education of children; they are told by Mrs Mason, whose audience within the stories are two girls, twelve and fourteen years old. Apart from the stories proper, the volume contains conversations among the characters about the issues treated in the narratives. In "Crazy Robin", Mrs Mason tells the girls about a man who has become mentally deranged after he has lost his entire family to poverty, hunger and illness. His grief is depicted in a sentimental tableau apt to arouse the listeners' – and readers' – pity:

> The poor father, who was now bereft of all his children, hung over their bed in speechless anguish; not a groan or a tear escaped from him, whilst he stood, two or three hours, in the same attitude, looking at the dead bodies of his little darlings. The dog licked his hands, and strove to attract his attention; but for awhile he seemed not to observe his caresses; when he did, he said, mournfully, thou wilt not leave me – and then he began to laugh.

However, the man is unfortunate enough to also lose his only remaining companion; the dog is shot by a gentleman because it has disturbed his horse. The poor man, although surrounded by sympathetic characters such as Mrs Mason, then starves himself to death.

That the story of "Crazy Robin" is told to children, whose natural morality is appealed to and whose moral judgement the story is meant to further educate, is another feature of Romantic sensibilities. Romantic interest in the child and its education was inspired by the work of the French philosopher Jean Jacques Rousseau. Around the turn of the century, short tales were regularly written for a young audience. Maria Edgeworth, for instance, the Anglo-Irish writer who, with her father, had written an influential treatise on *Practical Education* (1798), composed her *Moral Tales* (1801) "to illustrate the opinions delivered in *Practical Education*". She meant them to be "suited to the early years of youth, and, at the same time, conformable to the complicate relations of modern society"; they were intended to "display examples of virtue, without initiating the young reader into the ways of vice". To make sure that the stories were also read as intended, Edgeworth's preface spelled out what the individual tales could teach: "Forester", for example, is about an "eccentric character" who might, "by improper management [...] have become a fanatic and a criminal", and "Angelina" warns against "the nonsense of *sentimentality*".

Charles Lamb and his sister Mary Lamb co-wrote a collection of stories entitled *Mrs Leicester's School* (1809). The uniting frame for the stories is that they are all supposed to be told by girls newly arrived at a boarding school in order to introduce themselves to each other. Although many have a sad content, none is exaggeratedly dramatic and each renders events from a point of view that is believably that of a child. The didactic impetus is more subdued than, for example, in Edgeworth's tales for young readers, although most of the Lambs' stories tell how crises can be survived or character weaknesses remedied. The girls have learned to cope with the loss of one or both parents ("The Sailor Uncle", "The Father's Wedding-Day"), the fascinations of a 'wrong' religion ("The Young Mahometan") or the unwholesome effects of reading too many stories about witches ("The Witch Aunt"). But they also relate positive experiences like the pleasures, for a four-year-old, of first visiting her grandmother's farm ("The Farmhouse") and enjoying country life. The following excerpt from the latter story illustrates the attempt to approximate a young child's style and perception, and to render the love for a life in nature which the girl develops naturally through her visit to the country:

> There was no end to the curiosities that Sarah had to show me. There was the pond where the ducks were swimming, and the little wooden houses where the hands slept at night. The hens were feeding all over the yard, and the prettiest little chicks, they were feeding too, and little yellow ducklings that had a hen for their mamma. She was so frightened if they went near the water! Grandmamma says a hen is not esteemed a very wise bird.
>
> We went out of the farmyard into the orchard. Oh, what a sweet place grandmamma's orchard is! There were pear-trees, and apple-trees, and cherry-trees, all in blossom. These blossoms were the prettiest flowers that ever were seen; and among the grass under the trees there grew buttercups, and cowslips, and daffodils, and blue-bells. Sarah told me all their names, and she said I might pick as many of them as ever I pleased.
>
> I filled my lap with flowers, I filled my bosom with flowers, and I carried as many flowers as I could in both my hands; but as I was going into the par-

> lour to show them to my mamma, I stumbled over a threshold which was placed across the parlour, and down I fell with all my treasure.
>
> Nothing could have so well pacified me for the misfortune of my fallen flowers as the sight of a delicious syllabub which happened at that moment to be brought in. Grandmamma said it was a present from the red cow to me because it was my birthday [...][22]

Educational stories of the period were not only directed at the young, but also at adult readers from the poorer circles of society. To a considerable extent, the new literacy of these circles was the product of the educational efforts of various religious groupings, in particular the Evangelicals. In an atmosphere of political radicalism, this literacy was perceived as a threat by those in power. After all, it was not only the Bible which poor people were now able to read. Richard Altick (1957, 72) notes the explosive nature of reading during the 1790s:

> The major result of the surge of popular interest in reading during the 1790's [...] was not so much any permanent expansion of the reading audience as the reaction of the ruling class. Suddenly, in the supercharged atmosphere of a nature plunged, unprepared and bewildered, into a general war, the potentialities inherent in the press spread alarm among the people who prized above all the settled stability of the nation. The widespread belief that printed exhortations to 'sedition' and 'atheism' found their way into every calloused hand in the kingdom was nothing short of a nightmare. Compared with the threat of internal subversion, that of military subversion was small.

It is not surprising that the writer Helen Maria Williams felt obliged to defend herself against the reproach of being a supporter of French radicalism in the preface to her *Sketches of the State of Manners and Opinions in the French Republic Towards the Close of the Eighteenth Century in a Series of Letters* (1800). This volume contained a story that remained popular for many decades, the "History of Perourou, or the Bellows-Mender". Here a man of humble origins is asked to take part in a plot of revenge against a woman who has rejected a bourgeois engraver because she feels above him. Perourou poses as

[22] Charles Lamb is also important as a representative of a new type of essay that emerged alongside new types of story-telling. This essay is notably less didactic and expository than the examples of the earlier eighteenth century. Rather, it pays attention to irrational states of mind, like dreamlike states, or focusses on 'trivial' details rather than giving a wider image of society. Some of Lamb's essays verge on stories and are occasionally found in anthologies of short stories today, like Charles Lamb's "Dream Children" (1822) and "Old China" (1823) (both from the *Essays of Elia* which he published originally in the *London Magazine*). On these essays and their impact on the evolution of the short story, see Beachcroft (1968, 86).

a wealthy man and gets married to her; the woman is shamed and retires into a convent rather than living with the man who has thus tricked her. Years later, when Perourou has become a truly wealthy merchant, he manages to win the woman's hand and heart in an honest manner. The story has a political message in that it depicts a transcending of class barriers that was at the core of the French Revolution, and Williams's preface to the *Sketches*, although it emphatically dissociates its author from sympathies with the Reign of Terror, suggests at the same time that the original intentions of the French Revolution were worth supporting: "however deeply I may lament the calamities and the crimes which have sullied the French Revolution, I shall not cease to hope, that it will yet ultimately terminate in the establishment of a perfect Government in the country where it originated, and the extension of liberty even in states still more despotic."

In a climate highly suspicious of any traces of radicalism, writers who had contributed to the instruction of the lower levels of society found themselves under attack and felt obliged "to repair the damage they and others had inadvertently done by their failure to foresee the coming of Tom Paine". (Altick 1957, 73) From different political positions, writers set out to teach the poor a virtuous, that is, humble and peaceful way of life, or proclaimed the necessity of a commitment to the poor, if only to detract them from the aims of the French Revolution. This tendency resulted, among others, in one of the most popular collections of stories of the early nineteenth century. Between 1795 and 1798, the Evangelical Hannah More published and partly wrote herself a series of Cheap Repository Tracts in pamphlet form. These were moral treatises which made frequent use of ballads and prose narrative and had a clear anti-seditious and Christian message.[23] When a selection of her tracts were included in a collected edition of her works in 1801, that is for readers of a higher social level than the original addressees, More wrote the following advertisement which emphasizes the growing readership for this kind of literature:

> To improve the habits, and raise the principles of the common people, at a time when their dangers and temptations, moral and political, were multiplied beyond the example of any former period, was the motive which im-

[23] On the Cheap Repository, see also Harris (1979, 32): "The evangelical movement, which had founded Sunday morning schools to teach the poor to read, felt it necessary to provide cheap, simple, and edifying material for the new class of readers they were creating. [...] Primarily as a result of the foresight which caused the Cheap Repository to set up its own system of publication and distribution, these moral tales soon formed a chief portion of the reading matter in many a small library open to the poorer classes, and the demand apparently justified the many nineteenth-century reprintings."

pelled the Author of these volumes to devise and prosecute the institution of the Cheap Repository. [...] as an appetite for reading had, from a variety of causes, been increasing among the inferior ranks in this country, it was judged expedient, at this critical period, to supply such wholesome aliment as might give a new direction to their taste, and abate their relish for those corrupt and inflammatory publications which the consequences of the French Revolution have so fatally pouring in upon us. The success of the plan exceeded the most sanguine expectation of its projector. Above two million of the Tracts were sold within the first year, besides very large numbers in Ireland; and they continue to be very extensively circulated, in their original form of single Tracts [...]. As these stories, though *principally*, are not calculated *exclusively* for the middle and lower classes of society, the Author has, at the desire of her friends, selected those which were written by herself, and presented them to the public in this collection of her works, in an enlarged and improved form.

These stories betray their didactic intention clearly. The amount of plot is fairly low compared to the high amount of dialogue between 'common' and socially superior characters, dialogue being the mode in which the issue of virtuous behaviour in the poor is primarily discussed. In "The Shepherd of Salisbury Plain" (1795), a shepherd who leads a pious, humble and industrious way of life is presented as an example of "honest poverty" and deeply impresses his upper-middle-class visitor Mr Johnson. "Betty Brown, The St. Giles's Orange Girl" presents a naive and parentless young girl who works as a street-seller of oranges but is shamelessly exploited by a female usurer who robs her of all her profits. A lady from the higher ranks of society helps Betty to free herself from the woman's harmful influence, to set up her own business and, in particular, to become a virtuous woman who will be able to resist the temptations of the street. Sam Pickering (1975, 18) characterizes the stories in the Cheap Repository and other tracts as "relentlessly didactic and psychologically simplistic", but since they enjoyed such a wide distribution – because of their use in the Sunday schools and reprintings in book editions – they helped to create "a vogue for the short story". Not less frequently read, Maria Edgeworth's *Popular Tales* (1804) were addressed at young *and* adult readers, explicitly those of the newly literate class, as Edgeworth's father explained in his preface to an edition of 1832:

Burke supposes that there are eighty thousand readers in Great Britain, nearly one hundredth part of its inhabitants! Out of these we may calculate that ten thousand are nobility, clergy, or gentlemen of the learned professions. Of seventy thousand readers which remain, there are many who might be amused and instructed by books, which were not professedly adapted to the classes that have been enumerated. With this view the fol-

> lowing volumes have been composed. The title of *Popular Tales* has been chosen [...] from the wish that they may be current beyond circles which are sometimes exclusively considered as polite.

A story like "The Lottery", for instance, teaches readers from the lower ranks of society that material possession is not everything: "that a good character, and domestic happiness, which cannot be won in any lottery, are worth more than the five thousand, or even the ten thousand pounds prize". The message is thus very similar to that of the Cheap Repository – one can be poor and yet content.

It is with the emergence of Romantic sentiment that short forms of fiction begin to be notably concerned with segments of society outside the dominant discourses of power, in particular with the poorer circles of contemporary society. Of course, this tendency is also reflected in other genres of the day, including longer fiction, but it has been claimed that short fiction, with a yet 'undefined' status within the literary system, offered the Romantics a particular potential to express their major political and aesthetic interests. After all, they also rediscovered traditional forms of storytelling that had been preserved in folk rather than upper- and middle-class cultures. As Marie-Antoinette Manz-Kunz (1981, 458f.) observes:

> Such vaguely defined short prose forms as the anecdote, the fable, the sketch, and the short novel appealed to the Romantics because they had preserved a certain natural freshness while having been left by the wayside of the main literary currents of the classical period. In the hands of the Romantics these short fictional forms were infused with new life and luminosity. They seemed most yielding to the theme of the individual at odds with circumstance when seeking fulfillment of his nature against ethical, political, or social imperatives and strokes of fate, a theme cherished by many a Romantic author. Also, they offered the writer a great measure of freedom by their lack of formal rigidity. By abandoning the classical precepts of form, epic prose opened to innovation and experimentation with various techniques, from which arose the grave danger of overwriting and shapelessness.

### *Romanticism: The Emergence of the Gothic Tale*

The kind of short fiction which most radically departs from age-of-reason standards of theme and style is the Gothic tale, a type of story which flourished from the 1790s onwards[24] and which became an important catalyst

[24] Anna L. Aikin (later Mrs Barbauld) wrote an early example in this form, "Sir Bertrand,

for the kind of story which Edgar Allan Poe was to practice and theorize on a few decades later. In the words of Elizabeth MacAndrew (1981, 469),

> [t]he Gothic authors had found techniques for evoking dream states and nightmares, which the short fiction writers of the nineteenth century used to full effect in their tales of terror and their mystery and ghost stories. Above all, Gothic authors had developed means of creating suspense, which is so necessary for the sustained effects of short fiction, in general, as well as for horror stories.

The Gothic tales of the late eighteenth century, like the contemporary longer fictions in the Gothic mode, offer a counter-world to the age of reason. They "speak the socially unspeakable", articulate the "psychological and social dilemmas" of bourgeois society, as David Punter (1980, 417) writes. He argues further (424f.):

> If one accepts that the images of terror [...] are historically specific, then there seems to be only one conclusion to be drawn, and that is that there is some inner social and cultural dynamic which makes it necessary for those images to be kept alive. The most likely hypothesis is an extension of Freud's comments on the ambiguity of the civilising process: that, as far as the development of capitalism is concerned, the Industrial Revolution constituted some kind of birth trauma, and that it remains necessary for those who rule a world based on industry to come to terms with their antecedents. [...]
>
> Seen from this angle, Gothic fiction becomes a process of cultural self-analysis, and the images which it throws up become the dream-figures of a troubled social group.

Short Gothic fiction displays all the predilections for certain settings (like those medieval ones which gave the Gothic mode its name, but also Catholic Italy or Romantic Germany), character types (the lady in distress, villains and heroes) and themes that also mark the Gothic novel. It also works with supernatural effects, like the apparition of ghosts and the return of the dead, or other liminal figures like monsters and vampires. John Polidori's "The Vampyre" (1819) introduced the figure of the vampire into English literature; it was allegedly composed in 1816 on the shores of Lake Geneva, during the legendary gathering of the Shelleys, Byron and Polidori

---

a Fragment", published in her *Miscellaneous Pieces in Prose* (1773) and included in many later collections and anthologies; see Pitcher (1975b, 339). Leigh Hunt's "A Tale for a Chimney Corner" (1819) takes up the vogue not only by telling a ghost story itself, but also by reflecting about this type of story in the first third of the text. Peter Haining's anthology (1973) gives a broad survey of stories by anonymous and lesser-known writers as well as the famous names of Gothic fiction.

which also gave birth to Mary Shelley's novel *Frankenstein*.[25] The story narrates the tragic encounter between the evil vampire, Lord Ruthven, and the Englishman Aubrey. The latter soon discovers that all is not well with Ruthven and tries to separate from him, but Ruthven manages to bite and kill the woman whom Aubrey loves and, while Aubrey is losing his mind, to acquaint and get married to the latter's sister to boot. The narrative ends in tragedy. Aubrey dies, a rescue party alerted by him comes too late: "Lord Ruthven had disappeared, and Aubrey's sister had glutted the thirst of a Vampire!" "The Vampyre" develops its narrative over a rather long period of time and makes use of various settings across Europe. Although the plot reaches a definite climax when Aubrey's sister is in danger, tension is not necessarily built throughout.

In this respect, **"Raymond"** comes closer to modern notions of the unified and climactic short story since, in the form of the 'fragment', it produces a Gothic effect within the span of just a momentary experience. Typically, the Gothic fragment centres on one incident, opens and closes abruptly, has a definite climax and is therefore capable of eliciting a strong emotional response.[26] "Raymond" has all these features and is also exemplary in its intensive use of atmosphere. The story, by the pseudonymous author 'Juvenis', was originally published in *The Lady's Magazine* in 1799.[27] It opens with an atmospheric nature scene and ends in an equally atmospheric indoor scene when its dreadful climax is reached. The story begins with a depiction of Raymond, a melancholy recluse, who thinks about his beloved lost wife, Miranda. Although the story is conspicuously vague in

---

[25] Haining's anthology (1973) includes not only "The Vampyre", but also other work engendered during the meeting at Lake Geneva, like Percy Bysshe Shelley's "The Assassins", Mary Shelley's "The Dream" and Byron's "The Burial".

[26] On the increasing popularity of the Gothic fragment at the end of the nineteenth century, see also Pitcher (1975b, 339).

[27] Pitcher (1976, 351f.) discusses another version of this story which is identical except for the characters' names. He points out that the story has elements of the Romantic dream vision and can thus be read as a manifestation of the male protagonist's unconscious. In a later essay, Pitcher (1996) elaborates this idea, linking it specifically to a male concern with female chastity which causes a psychological dilemma during the wedding night when the husband violates that which he has so far valued in his bride. That the story can be read as "a Gothicizing of the bridal night of a virtuous couple" (39) is validated by the story's abundant use of phallic symbols (the tower, Raymond's sword and the murderer's dagger) as well as its imagery of penetration. Grove (1997) generally discusses the Gothic fragment in gender terms; its disorientating "fragmentation can be used to expose the restrictive gender politic characteristic of the ancient romance" (3f.) and it can therefore serve as a counter-text to the more fully closed male adventure story, that is, "call into question the biases, elitism, and violence inherent to narratives of male adventure" (10).

this respect, Miranda seems not to be dead but merely abducted, and Raymond longs to have her back, though only in the state of virginity in which he has apparently lost her. An idyllic night scene soon turns frightful when, during a dreadful thunderstorm, Raymond hears a shriek uttered by a female voice. His knightly instincts are aroused and he hurries to "an ancient tower, whose walls were tottering under the decay of time". Here, Raymond enters "a large Gothic chamber" (the typically confined space of Gothic fiction) from which the woman's shrieks have reached his ear – only to find, as the culmination of the plot, that the woman, who has just been stabbed by another man, is his missing wife. The story breaks off abruptly with this nightmarish surprise:

> He beheld a man, brandishing, exultingly, a dagger, reeking with blood, over the body of a female, who had fallen a victim to his barbarity. His savage triumph was not long lived; for Raymond soon gave him that reward he so justly deserved, and thus, revenging the death of the murdered female, sent his loaded soul to expiate his mortal crimes in the regions of eternal misery.
>
> He now approached the corpse of the unfortunate fair. On beholding her distorted countenance, a sudden shivering seized him, his strength failed him; he tottered a few paces back, and fell senseless to the floor. – It was Miranda.

With its focus on one extraordinary moment in an atmosphere of intense fear and suspense, this story takes a significant step towards the "unity of effect and impression" which Poe and Brander Matthews would later promulate. Poe parodied the type of story which *Blackwood's Magazine* preferred to publish,[28] but this Edinburgh periodical, established in 1817, was in fact a primary distributor of Gothic fiction in the earlier nineteenth century – and a periodical of great influence for the further development of the short story. As Wendell V. Harris (1979, 22) notes, it "provided the century's first steady and respectable market for short fiction. From its first issue, which included a tale by James Hogg, short fiction appeared regularly, the editors happily maintaining a preference for the tale which could be published entirely in a single issue."

In 1832, *Blackwood's* published William Mudford's "The Iron Shroud", a story noted for its similarity to the tales of terror which Poe was beginning to write around this time. It exemplifies a unity of effect to as high a degree

[28] See his "How to Write a Blackwood Article" (1845; published earlier as "The Psyche Zenobia" in 1838). However, Poe appreciated at least the "earlier numbers of Blackwood" since they contained "many fine examples" of "tales of effect". See his review of *Twice-Told Tales* (Poe 1984, 573).

as the stories praised and written by Poe himself. The story is restricted to a single setting capable of arousing a strong emotional response and written from the perspective of a single consciousness – that of a man imprisoned in a dungeon. The readers are thus enabled to share the character's experiences and his growing panic as he watches the walls of his prison contract each day. The diminution of space around him is the sole action in this story, whose main focus is clearly on the impact of this action on the character's mind. The story underlines the growing urgency of his existential fears by occasionally switching from the use of the past to the present tense: "His brain already feels the descending horror, – his bones seem to crack and crumble in the mighty grasp of the iron walls! Unknowing what it is he does, he fumbles in his garment for some weapon of self-destruction." Suspense grows as the prison shrinks. When the story culminates, the utter horror of the prisoner's final hours in a space which is now extremely confined and still narrowing is orchestrated by the knelling of his death bell:

> As he lay gathered up in lessened bulk, the bell beat loud and frequent – crash succeeded crash – and on, and on, and on came the mysterious engine of death, till Vivenzio's smothered groans were heard no more! He was horribly crushed by the ponderous roof and collapsing sides – and the flattened bier was his *Iron Shroud.*

Apart from magazines,[29] gift books or annuals, which published poems, extracts, and tales once a year and in a single volume, were an important distributor for short fiction in the early nineteenth century. As Bradford Allen Booth (1938, 1) notes in the introduction to his anthology of stories from the annuals, a "spectacular rise of annual gift books" can be observed during the second quarter of the nineteenth century. These books, sold in particular during the Christmas season, were expensively produced but nevertheless intended to be "of wide, popular appeal" (*ibid.*) – at least in those strata of society who could afford them. Despite this restriction to readers from the middle and upper classes, Booth emphasizes that "[t]here have been few such successful attempts to interest the great mass of the people in literature". (2)[30]

---

[29] For a survey of the periodical scene in the early nineteenth century, see Sullivan (1983b).

[30] Booth's anthology includes work by W.H. Ainsworth, John Galt, James Hogg, Mary Russell Mitford, Mary Shelley and others. See also Polsgrove (1974, 420): "In 1823 another market opened up with the publication of the first British annual, *The Forget-Me-Not.* Although the vogue for annuals [...] began to decline in 1832, [...] the annuals were for a time enormously popular. In the 1828 season, 100,000 copies of annuals were sold all together, usually at twelve shillings each for a total of more than 70,000 pounds." One

The gift books offered many women an opportunity to publish and earn money by their pen with short fiction in a variety of modes and on a range of themes apart from the Gothic. Mary Shelley, for instance, wrote many of her shorter narratives for the gift-book market. Although most of these are not written in the Gothic mode but more usually constitute "tales of passionate love and hate set in medieval Italy, sixteenth-century France, or contemporary Europe",[31] Shelley did write a number of supernatural tales such as "Transformation" (first publ. in *The Keepsake* in 1831). Here an arrogant and reckless young man encounters an uncanny creature, a "misshapen dwarf, with squinting eyes, distorted features, and body deformed, till it became a horror to behold". This dwarf makes the man change bodies with him, promising him great riches. However, suspecting something terrible, the man, in his new shape, follows the evil creature and at the last minute prevents him from getting married to the woman whom he loves himself. He manages to regain his own body and becomes a reformed character.

One of the many writers who contributed to Gothic fiction in the early nineteenth century was Sir Walter Scott. Well-known examples found in many short-story anthologies include "The Two Drovers" (1827), "Wandering Willie's Tale" (originally part of the novel *Redgauntlet*, 1824) and "The Tapestried Chamber" (1828 in *The Keepsake*). The latter story is already marked as being part of a tradition and plays with genre conventions of the Gothic tale when the main character's experience of horror is told only in retrospect, and not while he is actually experiencing it. A general sojourns in a castle and is given a certain chamber to sleep in. The next morning, he is obviously disturbed. His host makes him admit that he has seen the ghost of an extremely evil-looking woman. In turn, his host confesses that he has

---

of the most popular was *The Keepsake* (1828–57). Nevertheless, as Harris (1979, 24f.) emphasizes, this medium of publication did little to enhance the literary *reputation* of the short story: "Dealing heavily in sentimentality, the annuals offered little which demanded more of the reader than a ready sigh, and they were accordingly held in contempt by writers of reputation – who nevertheless often found their principles melted by the promise of good payment. The attractiveness of the offers made by the annuals was increased by the ease with which the writing could be done: the editors did not desire pieces of much over 10,000 words and were happy to use shorter – the briefer the stories the longer and more impressive the table of contents. Under these circumstances there is little cause for wonder that such writers as Harrison Ainsworth, John Galt, Mary Russell Mitford, Mrs. S.C. Hall, and G.P.R. James – along with many now almost forgotten writers whose names carried assurance to contemporary buyers – gave little thought to their contributions to the gaudy gift books."

[31] Thus Shelley's editor Charles E. Robinson in the introduction to the quoted edition (1976, xv).

used the general for an experiment, namely for testing an old rumour that the chamber is haunted, for which reason it had been walled up and only recently, under its new owner, been opened again. When the general identifies a woman in the house's gallery of ancestral portraits as the ghost that has appeared to him, the chamber is sealed up again. In this story, Scott works not only with the conventions of Gothic fiction. His description of the story's external locations also has a strong regionalist flavour. Placing his stories in landscapes that are distinctly English or Scottish, Scott generally exemplifies qualities of a new local-colour movement within Britain.

*Romanticism: The Rise of Local-Colour Stories*

The location of regionalist local-colour stories in Romantic sensibility is outlined by Marie-Antoinette Manz-Kunz (1981, 462):

> Dialects, details of the toils and hardship of the frugal existence of peasants and artisans in surroundings barely in touch with civilization, and rugged rustic types became the subject matter of regional tales, whereas the confines of provincialism and philistine quaintness made admirable themes for longer prose forms. Realist writing with a regionalist flavor attracted writers for several different reasons. Some returned to their native soil to seek revival for the creative sensibility both in the domain of the senses and in the domain of the spirit, thus following the train of thought of Jean-Jacques Rousseau; others hoped to restore their souls in bounteous nature and the peasant world which they believed to be sound and firmly rooted in its environment and which would thus soothe the confusion in their hearts and minds; yet another group merely satisfied their taste for pastoral idylls and put local color and idealized rusticality to use for stylistic effects.[32]

A large section of local-colour or regionalist short fiction was produced by Irish writers like John and Michael Banim, William Carleton, Samuel Lover or Anna Maria Hall. They wrote primarily for an audience in England whose interest in the 'other' British Isle had increased with the Act of Union that incorporated Ireland politically into Great Britain in 1801. Scottish writers like Sir Walter Scott, John Galt and James Hogg were also renowned for their regionalist writing.[33]

---

[32] On the local-colour story in Britain, see also Ferguson (1997, 6f.).

[33] John Galt's *Annals of the Parish* (1821), told from the point of view of a country minister, is often referred to as a novel, but was not written as such. Hogg's subject matter, according to Harris (1979, 37f.), is "emphatically Scottish; taken together, his fiction and related prose constitute a compendium of Scottish superstitions, historical legends,

An English local colourist is Mary Russell Mitford, whose series of stories later entitled *Our Village: Sketches of Rural Life and Scenery* began in *The Lady's Magazine* in 1819. "The Village Schoolmistress", for instance, like its companion stories, depicts ordinary human life in a small Berkshire village and contains long descriptive passages which establish the physical environment and the various characters. The narrative voice betrays a Romantic feeling for nature, and it is often communal, creating a sense of the rural community through frequent use of the personal pronoun in the first-person plural. That Mitford herself referred to her pieces as 'sketches' reflects the extent to which the mode of description, rather than the report of events, dominates the texts. In "The Village Schoolmistress", the narrative impetus is also comparatively minimal and the focus of interest lies on the two main characters and the life they lead. The schoolmistress, Mrs Allen, has cared for an orphan girl, Jane. Jane grows up an excellent young woman who becomes the schoolmistress's assistant and is beloved by the whole village. Since Jane has no family or fortune, she will have to earn her living as a governess, but shortly before her departure, she is spared this typical fate of the educated spinster when a wealthy uncle from India seeks her out and she ends as the wife of a rich heir. "The Fresh Water Fisherman" sets in with a long passage of description in which the note of regionalism is established in precise topographical terms and references to local myth:

> This pretty Berkshire of ours, renowned for its pastoral villages, and its picturesque interchange of common and woodland, and small enclosures divided by deep lanes, to which thick borders of hedgerow timber give a character of deep and forest-like richness, seldom seen in counties of more ambitious pretension; – this beautiful Berkshire is for nothing more distinguished than for the number and variety of its rivers. I do not mean, in this catalogue, to include the large proportion of bright, shallow, trouting streams, for the most part unchristened and unregistered even by a parish historian, or the compiler of a county map, and known only as 'the brook' by the very people whose meadows they dance through. To confine myself to rivers of state and name, we have, first of all, the rapid, changeful, beautiful Loddon, a frisky, tricksy water-sprite, much addicted to wandering out of bounds, and as different from the timid, fearful nymph Lodona, whom Pope, in a metamorphosing strain, was pleased to assign as the source of those clear waters, as anything well can be. Next we have the Kennet [...]

supernatural tales, and sketches of rural Scottish life. The twenty-one pieces in *The Shepherd's Calendar*, most published in *Blackwood's* before being collected as a volume (1829), provide an excellent sampling of Hogg's briefer exercises in these modes."

> which, in our part at least, has, generally speaking, a fine pastoral character, now sweeping along through broad valleys of meadow-land, rich and green, and finely dappled by trees, chiefly oak and elm, in park-like groups; now confined within a narrower channel, and spanned by some lofty bridge as it passes the quiet village or small country town, enlivening every scene which it approaches by the pleasant flow of its clear waters, cool and glittering as a moonbeam. Lastly and chiefly, we possess, for the whole length of the county, and for the most part forming its sinuous boundary, the deep majestic Thames, gliding in tranquil grandeur, with a motion so slow as to be almost imperceptible; [...]. And what a course it is! The classic domes of Oxford; the sunny plains of Berkshire; the Buckinghamshire beechwoods; Windsor, with its royal towers; Richmond, and its world of gardens; then London – mighty London; and then the sea – only rival in riches and in fame. [...] Our business, however, is not with the mighty Thames [...] but with the pleasant and pastoral Kennet.

The humorous narrative which then unfolds is about Adam Stokes, a Kennet fisherman and English patriot, who gets married to a Frenchwoman. The bliss of their married state is threatened – though in the end happily restored – through the intrigues of another woman whom he has rejected.

### *The 'Dramatic' Story*

Not all stories of the late eighteenth and early nineteenth centuries are as directly affected by Romanticism as the Gothic tale and the local-colour story, and Romanticism was certainly not the only factor to influence the course of short-story writing. What one can also observe during the early decades of the nineteenth century, for example, is a distinct sense that the tight structure of drama can be a model for short fiction (see p. 30 above for general remarks on the affinity of the modern short story to drama).[34] One may read this as an indication that here there is a growing demand for stories, at least stories of 'effect', to be tectonically sound, that is concisely built, rather than haphazardly crafted.

In one instance, the dramatic impetus even gave rise to a story which, in its contemporary context, verges on the experimental and genre-bending: Matthew Gregory Lewis, whose claim to fame was a Gothic novel, *The Monk*, published "My Uncle's Garret Window" in his *Romantic Tales* in 1808.

---

[34] For the occasional relationship between earlier short fiction and dramatic writing, see Canby's observations on Painter and Congreve's preface to *Incognita* (pp. 41 and 44 above).

This 'tale' strikes readers today with its theatrical – and one might say even filmic – quality. From his uncle's attic window, the first-person narrator observes events within a well-to-do family who live in the house opposite. With this point of view, the readers learn about the events only what the narrator is able to observe through his telescope and the conclusions he draws from his observations. What happens, what the characters feel and what they possibly say is only surmised, constructed from what can be visibly perceived from a fixed perspective. The father, apparently married to a young second wife, seems to discover that his son from his first marriage has a secret relationship and throws him out of his house. For a while, the young wife also seems to have something to hide, and one suspects that she might be her stepson's lover. However, as far as the narrator interprets the ending, she only supports the young man who has secretly got married to the woman he loves. In a theatrical climax during the final scene at night, all characters are united and there seems to be a happy ending. Through its unusual and strictly monoperspectival handling of point of view, the story makes for a high degree of unity of effect and impression and, what is more, manages to approximate drama without giving us a single piece of authentic characters' speech.

More explicitly, the dramatic quality of short-story writing was also emphasized by Harriet Lee in 1832 when she wrote the preface for a highly popular collection of stories that she had started to write with her sister Sophia in 1797 and which spanned a diversity of themes like love and marriage, but also revolution and war. The Lee sisters named their stories after a 'classical' model, Chaucer's *Canterbury Tales*. But Harriet Lee, at least, had a strong sense that she and her sister had embarked on a new sense of 'telling' tales. She ends her preface with the observation that

> when these volumes first appeared, a work bearing distinctly the title of 'Tales', professedly adapted to different countries, and either abruptly commencing with, or breaking suddenly into, a sort of dramatic dialogue, was a novelty in the fictions of the day. Innumerable 'Tales' of the same stamp, and adapted in the same manner to all classes and all countries, have since appeared; with many of which I presume not to compete in merit, though I think I may fairly claim priority of design and style.

### *Summary*

By the early nineteenth century, short fiction was produced in a variety of modes and in growing numbers. Statements like Harriet Lee's indicate that in Britain too an awareness of the specificity of telling 'tales' rather than novels had emerged, and there were publication platforms like periodicals and annuals that encouraged the writing of short fiction. In fact, short-story writing could even be profitable to its practitioners, particularly during the 1820s and 1830s, as Carol Polsgrove (1974, 417 and 420f.) has pointed out:

> by the time the American and French short-fiction masters – Poe and Hawthorne, Balzac, Mérimée, and Stendhal – began writing short stories in the 1830's, short fiction was already a clearly recognizable and popular genre in Great Britain, not only in the magazines but also in annuals and book collections. [...]
>
> The sheer number of such book collections, many of which went through several series and editions, underlines the difference between the status of short fiction in the early nineteenth century and its status in the eighteenth century. [...] True, very few of the writers who published short fiction during these years achieved lasting fame. Yet the publication of their stories in book form suggests the strength of readers' new interest in short fiction.

Developmental lines from early-nineteenth century short fiction, in particular the tradition of the ghost story, were continued during the Victorian decades of the nineteenth century with an output that is certainly not negligible. Nevertheless, the predominant note in most short-story criticism and history for the nineteenth century is that of regret about Britain's backwardness in short-story production in comparison with the United States.

## 3. The Victorian Nineteenth Century

### *The Short Story in Competition with the Novel*

Deprecatory remarks about the short story in Victorian Britain before the 1880s are legion. To Henry Seidel Canby (1909, 265), Victorian writers produced, at best, "short stories *manqués*", and Wendell V. Harris (1979, 12) concludes from his survey that "by far the greater portion of the short fiction written in the first three-quarters of the nineteenth century, even by well-known writers, is careless, formless, and repetitive". Like other critics and literary historians, Harold Orel (1986, 2f.) identifies the novel as the Victorians' central prose genre and literary commodity, while the short story was "a by-product, filler material", which "did not pay well" for either its authors or distributors and roused little theoretical interest: "neither writers of fiction nor literary critics were interested in debating the aesthetics of the short story as a genre." With characteristic outspokenness, H.E. Bates (1965, 36) hails Elizabeth Gaskell as "the only potentially important English short-story writer", while Dickens "could well have saved his ink" (14) and "in hands such as Hardy's", the story was "choked crudely to death, like a baby fed on a diet of two-inch steaks and porter" (41). To Lionel Stevenson (1972, 268), as to many others, only the long format was congenial to the interests of contemporary writers of fiction to depict a wide historical and contemporary social spectrum. This is also noted by Wendell V. Harris (1979, 18–20):

> The rise of the novel coincided with the rise of a more self-critical, self-conscious style of writing history as well as with the rise of the middle class. The genre grew, flourished, and prospered through the nineteenth century, a period when the historical consciousness was so great that it has been said, not altogether facetiously, that the nineteenth century discovered history. The great prophet-essayists of the century certainly gave themselves to the tracing of chains of causes and effects and to the analysis of the subtle interweaving of relations throughout society and across time. [...] Ruskin, Arnold, Morris, and even Mill found themselves constantly expanding the temporal and intellectual contexts in which basic social questions should be considered; each conducted his own survey of the network of human interaction, seeking to discover the point of leverage from which the interlinked structure of society could be altered. The novelists conducted similar surveys of the great nexus in their fictive histories. The worlds of the great Victorian novels depend on the shaping of each individual by the interaction between the pressures of the socioeconomic world and the choices made by the individual.

Occasionally, regrets about the neglect of short-story writing in Britain were voiced already by Victorians themselves, for instance an anonymous commentator on "The Art of Story-Telling" in the June issue of *Fraser's Magazine* of the year 1856. His comment is also remarkable because it tries to locate the short story's potential in the spirit of a *modernizing* age and thus to claim for it a specific social relevance other than that of the contemporary novel:

> Of all countries in the world, England ought to be the country in which stories should enjoy the widest range of popularity. In no other country is time of so much value. [...]
>
> This should be the country for stories which condense into a few pages the essence of volumes; which realize in fiction the great economical maxim, by packing the largest quantity into the smallest space; and which, as pabulum for minds in a great hurry, that must travel light, and cannot afford to carry much provision with them, may be compared to the pemmican supplied to Arctic voyagers, a single grain of which is equal to many pounds'

> weight of bread and meat. Yet, inconsistent as it may appear with our wants and habits, there is no country in which stories are held in such low estimation. [...] The English [...] will have nothing to do with a story unless it is in three volumes. (in Weber and Greiner 1977, 40f.)

This dominance of the novel in the literary system of Victorian Britain was supported by the importance which the long novel, publishable in three volumes, had for the circulating libraries. These commercial libraries were a prime distributor for original fiction for whom novels were a valuable commodity while short stories were not.[35] Not even the fact that the periodical press – the ideal publication platform for short stories – played an ever-increasing role during the first decades of Victoria's reign helped the short story to acquire a standing comparable to that in the United States. The Victorian periodical market addressed a wide range of readers' tastes and educational backgrounds (although the prime audience of the major magazines were respectable middle-class families), and it offered products that were far more affordable than books, even for the more affluent levels of the middle classes. The magazine boom of the mid-Victorian decades was helped by the removal of taxes and a more effective printing technology (the web rotary press was introduced in 1856), which led to price reductions. A certain amount of short fiction *was* published in some of the magazines – but the preferred mode of fiction found in the Victorian periodicals until the very end of the century was the serial novel, which was, after all, a more reliable means to bind readers to a magazine in a highly competitive market than stories that could be finished in a single issue. As Wendell V. Harris (1979, 24) observes:

> By mid-century, when Dickens launched *Household Words*, followed in 1859 by *Macmillan's Magazine* and in 1860 by *Temple Bar* and the *Cornhill*, the demand for short fiction began to become brisk. However, a great many periodicals stood out until the end of the century against the inclusion of fiction. The appearance of a short story in each issue of the weekly *Black and White* was advertised as an unusual feature; the *New Review* began including short stories only with volume 10 (1894); the *Athenaeum* did not begin publishing its weekly story until 1905.

[35] One of the most authoritative surveys of the Victorian book and periodical market and library system still is Richard Altick's *The English Common Reader* (1957); in our context, see especially chapters 12 to 15. Sullivan (1984) gives a survey of the Victorian periodical scene; the introduction by Christopher Kent states that "of no time or place can it be said that periodicals had greater cultural impact than they had on Victorian Britain". (xiii) The growing status of magazines in Britain during the first half of the nineteenth century is discussed by Baldwin (1993, 24–26).

These findings are confirmed by Dean Baldwin (1993, 27):

> An analysis of the *London Journal* for 1848 shows that in one quarter, it devoted under 5% of its space to short fiction, while a serial novel occupied almost 27%. [...] A similar study of four 'highbrow' magazines in 1872 and 1878 – *Contemporary Review, Fortnightly Review, Fraser's*, and *Macmillan's* – shows that among them they published four serialized novels in these two years, but not a single piece of short fiction.

As a result of this limited market, it took time until the short story became profitable for writers in Victorian Britain, both in terms of payment and reputation. As Baldwin (1993, 29–31) observes:

> Tracing the careers of the great Victorian writers like Dickens, Trollope, and Eliot, as well as the lesser-known figures like William Carleton and Joseph Sheridan LeFanu, reveals that none of them made substantial sums through their short fiction. Of course, they did publish short fiction, or at least fiction shorter than full-length novels, in periodicals, but the amount of money received for any given story, and the relative proportion of their income that could be derived from stories, was comparatively small. [...]
>
> What retarded the development of the British short story, then, could be called a problem of 'the market' in that editors and readers did not insist upon relatively brief, self-contained, single-effect stories but were content with short fiction that was in essence a condensed novel or that took the form of a joke, fantasy, or thriller. But more accurately it was an aesthetic problem – one that American and Continental authors had solved, but not one that interested British writers. Dickens is a case in point: as an author, he defined the short story as anything told orally by a narrator within the story; as an editor, he regarded it as anything shorter than four serial installments. Similarly, Trollope concentrated his writing of short fiction on the decade of the 1860s when he was editor of *St. Paul's*. He earned most of his considerable lifetime income from novels and regarded stories as brief novels whose purpose was to report on the social world.

Conditions and practice were not very favourable to a rise of the 'true' short story in Britain until the two final decades of the nineteenth century, when these conditions markedly changed. Nevertheless, as Wendell V. Harris (1979, 12) also points out, "to consider only those earlier works which anticipated the genre of the short story as it emerged in the 1880s and 1890s is to undervalue the intentions of many of the earlier writers and to ignore large tracts of fictional endeavor which were once under intense cultivation". And there was, after all, "a limited number of narratives in the previous eighty years which fit perfectly well into the yet-to-be-recognized genre". (*ibid.*)

*Modes and Themes of the Victorian Short Story*

To Harris (1979, 83), "the chief merit of many of the best tales of the first seventy-five years of the century is a kind of richness of character, situation, or narrative style possible only in more leisurely storytelling". An example of this more leisurely story-telling which enjoyed wide popularity (and was even distributed in individually printed and illustrated pamphlets) is Dr John Brown's "Rab and His Friends" (1859). The story's first-person narrator, a Scottish doctor, begins with his childhood acquaintance with a huge mastiff, Rab. The dog, which is muzzled, is attacked by a smaller but vicious dog. In order to help the mastiff, the narrator and his friends cut his muzzle and Rab, in self-defence, kills his attacker. The narrator's next major experience with the dog takes place years later, when he assists the surgeon who operates on a woman's breast cancer. She is the wife of Rab's owner. Her brave death, after having been nursed by her husband and watched over by Rab, forms the story's main part. It reaches its sentimental ending when Rab's owner also dies soon after his wife's funeral and Rab is killed by his new owner. This quiet, loosely-structured tale does not aim at effecting an exciting climax, but focusses on the dignity of its simple human characters as well as the friendly and loyal nature of the powerful dog.

The sentimental mode is one of many in which the telling of short fiction was practised before the 1880s. Stories were also set in historical periods (catering to the Victorians' interest in the past), they offered melodramatic and sensational plots (as did many novels and plays of the time), provided sketches of rural and urban life, thus continuing the earlier local-colour tradition,[36] or they were exercises in the humorous and mildly satirical mode, caricaturing types of contemporary society. Among the latter were the popular sporting stories and sketches by Robert S. Surtees (published from 1831 in *The New Sporting Magazine*), the stories of Mark Lemon (one of the founders, in 1841, and first editors of *Punch*) and the stories of Douglas Jerrold (a frequent contributor to *Punch*, who pursued a more radical social agenda).[37] *Punch* was also the periodical for which William Make-

[36] See, for example, Charles Dickens's *Sketches by 'Boz', Illustrative of Every-Day Life and Every-Day People* (first book collection 1836/37); Elizabeth Gaskell's series of linked sketches of village life later collected under the title *Cranford* (1851–53 in *Household Words*), or Margaret Oliphant's *Chronicles of Carlington* series (which consisted of both novels and stories) about a small country town in the mid-nineteenth century (begun in *Blackwood's Magazine* in 1861).

[37] Melville and Hargreaves (1931) reprint Surtees's "The Cheltenham Dandy", Lemon's "The Adventures of a Christmas Turkey", and Jerrold's "The Preacher Parrot", about the fate of a parrot who is maltreated by his various owners because he speaks the truth. In

peace Thackeray frequently wrote. His *Comic Tales and Sketches* appeared in 1841, and the *Book of Snobs* (1846), also in the sketch tradition, investigated the manifestations of pretense in Victorian life. Throwing spotlights at certain types and phenomena, these stories served their original readers' interest in contemporary society, though in a different manner than in the novel.

Anthony Trollope, too, did not lose his eye for the weaknesses of his contemporaries when he tried his hand at the shorter modes of fiction rather than the many volumes of his Barchester chronicles. To Harold Orel (1986, 79), Trollope used short fiction for the same purposes to which he also wrote his many novels, namely to "observe the world around him, and record, in fiction, what he had seen and heard". This is most obvious in the stories in which he employed material assembled during his many travels into all parts of the world. After their first appearance in various magazines, they were collected as *Tales of All Countries* (1861, second series 1863). "Relics of General Chassé: A Tale of Antwerp" (1860) narrates the plight of an English gentleman in Belgium whose trousers fall prey to a group of female English souvenir hunters who mistake these garments for the trousers of a famous general. "An Unprotected Female at the Pyramids" (1860) caricatures a fairly new phenomenon – the figure of the woman travelling on her own. Miss Dawkins is just as eager and intrepid a tourist as the men in her tourist group, in contrast to the latters' more conventional wives and daughters:

> This entrance into the Pyramids is a terrible task, which should be undertaken by no lady. Those who perform it have to creep down, and then to be dragged up, through infinite dirt, foul smells, and bad air; and when they have done it, they see nothing. But they do earn the gratification of saying that they have been inside a Pyramid.
>
> 'Well, I've done that once', said Mr. Damer, coming out, 'and I do not think that any one will catch me doing it again. I never was in such a filthy place in my life.'
>
> 'Oh, Fanny! I am so glad you did not go; I am sure it is not fit for ladies', said poor Mrs. Damer, forgetful of her friend Miss Dawkins.
>
> 'I should have been ashamed of myself', said Miss Dawkins, bristling up, and throwing back her head as she stood, 'if I had allowed any consideration to have prevented my visiting such a spot. If it be not improper for men to go there, how can it be improper for women?'

---

general, this anthology provides a good overview of the variety of Victorian short fiction, also including work by R.H. Barham, Thomas Hood, G.P.R. James, George Borrow, Benjamin Disraeli, George Eliot, Charles Reade, 'Ouida' and others.

> 'I did not say improper, my dear', said Mrs. Damer, apologetically.
>
> 'And as for the fatigue, what can a woman be worth who is afraid to encounter as much as I have now gone through for the sake of visiting the last resting-place of such a king as Cheops?' And Miss Dawkins, as she pronounced the last words, looked round her with disdain upon poor Fanny Damer.
>
> 'But I meant the dirt', said Mrs. Damer.
>
> 'Dirt!' ejaculated Miss Dawkins, and then walked away. Why should she now submit her high tone of feeling to the Damers, or why care longer for their good opinion? Therefore she scattered contempt around her as she ejaculated the last word, 'dirt'.

The story is loosely composed of several such anecdotes and interspersed with much narratorial comment on the follies of tourism and tourists; it does not have a unifying plot line. Trollope's stories about contemporary literary life, based on his own experiences as editor for the *Fortnightly Review* and *St Paul's* in the late 1860s, were collected in *An Editor's Tales* (1870). Of these, as Harold Orel (1986, 87) mentions, Trollope considered "The Spotted Dog" (1870) as his best story. It deals with the tragedy of a man of great learning who is reduced to writing for the cheap Penny Dreadfuls – the cheapest item on the periodical market addressed to a working-class readership. The other 'tales' in this volume are also comic and tragicomic stories about people with hopeless literary ambitions and allow their narrator, the literary editor, much space to unfold his opinions. It is not surprising in light of the later preference for a tectonically refined story that the Trollope story still most frequently anthologized is a more tightly structured one: "Malachi's Cove" (1864) traces the emerging relationship between a rather wild young woman, a collector of sea-weed in Cornwall, and a young man whom she first hates but then falls in love with when he has an accident during a weed-collecting competition.

Love, courtship and marriage are, in fact, themes in which the Victorians had a particular interest and which they treated in short as well as long forms of fiction, and in a range of modes from the sentimental to the sensational to the realistic. Marriage became particularly topical from the mid-century onwards when there was a considerable increase in volume in the debate about women's role in society, their role in the home, their right for education and a profession, and their right to be divorced.[38] "For the Victorians", Kate Flint notes in the introduction to her anthology of the period's love stories (1997, vii), "to write of love almost always meant offering some

[38] For a concise survey, see the introduction to Orel's anthology (1990).

kind of reflection on the position of women within society". As will be seen later in this chapter (p. 110), stories from the final decades of the century tended to present a bleak view of the matrimonial lot, for women as well as for men. But this was not the only view offered. A story by Elizabeth Gaskell, "The Manchester Marriage" (1858), has obvious sentimental traits but also represents a marital relationship in which a husband is truly caring for his wife and children. This story centres on the marriage of the Openshaws, who have come to London from Manchester where the husband works as a salesman for a large firm. The family have two children, of whom the elder sibling, a girl, suffers from a deformed spine. She is Mrs Openshaw's daughter by her first husband, who was declared dead at sea. Her stepfather is devoted to her, evidenced by the fact that even before his proposal to her mother, who earns her meagre living by running a boarding-house in which Openshaw has taken lodgings, "he was perpetually devising small new pleasures for the child. [...] One time, it was a little chair for drawing the little sufferer along the streets; and, many an evening that following summer, Mr Openshaw drew her along himself, regardless of the remarks of his acquaintances." Although Openshaw is rough and practical in his manners (he delivers his proposal "in as indifferent a voice as he could assume" and gives the woman five minutes to make up her mind), he is a most responsible husband and father. The couple's marriage is a happy one, guided by Openshaw's "strong sense, warm heart, and powerful will". Mrs Openshaw is lucky in having chosen a *pater familias* who exerts his authority with kindness and does not misuse the power which society has granted him. This happiness is threatened when, after many years, the first husband comes back and learns about his wife's second marriage. In despair, and possibly to spare his former wife and daughter misery, he drowns himself in the Thames. Mr Openshaw, to whom the tragedy is revealed, feels responsible for the man's fate, gives him a decent burial and hides everything from his wife.

Even before the 1880s, then, we encounter a wide spectrum of Victorian short stories, many of which have an explicit social relevance, dealing with issues that were of central concern in Victorian social discourse. As with the stories of the age of reason, many stories confront core social values and ideals directly rather than devoting themselves to what was marginalized and submerged in Victorian culture. This explicit social concern of the Victorian short story has only recently been reflected in criticism and anthologies. The prevailing impression conveyed about the Victorian short story is, by contrast, that it was only successful where it *did* address the submerged and the marginal and formed a continuation of the Gothic tradition inherited from Romanticism.

*Victorian Gothic*

The short story is suited better than the novel to create a concentrated effect of intense fear, as Julia Briggs (1977, 13) also emphasizes: "A horror that is effective for thirty pages can seldom be sustained for three hundred, and there is no danger of confusing the bare scaffolding of the ghost story with the rambling mansion of the Gothic novel." Whenever Charles Dickens is praised for his story production, it is for his ghost stories. It should be noted, however, that apart from his own production, Dickens is of significance for the genre in mid-Victorian times in his role as editor of enormously popular magazines: *Household Words* (1859–59) and *All the Year Round* (1859–70[39]). Serial novels were the prime attraction in these periodicals, but Dickens also regularly commissioned stories by reputed authors of the time, like Elizabeth Gaskell (whose "Manchester Marriage" appeared in *Household Words*) and Wilkie Collins. Self-contained stories (rather than instalments of a novel) were suited especially for the separate Christmas issues, and *ghost* stories, which generally filled the Victorian periodicals in great quantities,[40] enjoyed particular popularity in the seasonal supplements.[41] In the wake of the established mode of the Romantic Gothic tale, Victorian stories of the supernatural are the kind of short narrative that comes closest to the short story à la Poe and thus the evolving notion of the 'modern' short story. Thus Suzanne Ferguson (1989, 187) argues that

> the sensational element developed in the best of the nineteenth-century and early twentieth-century English ghost story writers [...] contributed in a significant way to the rise of the highbrow, 'mainstream' short story in the twentieth century. The techniques of description used to create the realistic setting in which the outré events take place, the symbolic character of the

[39] After Dickens's death, the magazine continued to publish until 1895.

[40] See Orel (1986, 195, n. 6): "More than two thousand short stories designed to shock, terrify, or thrill readers with the activities or influence of forces beyond human comprehension were printed in Victorian periodicals."

[41] See Briggs (1977, 40) for the special link between the Christmas season and ghost stories, which dates back to oral traditions. Christmas had been for some decades the time of year when printed matter was given as a gift, and the special Christmas issues of the Victorian magazines can be seen as a more affordable continuation of the earlier gift annuals like the *Keepsake*. As Altick (1957, 362f.) notes: "with the coming of mass-circulation periodicals, the gift annual was transformed into the special Christmas number or supplement, bulging with verse, stories, and pictures. From about 1860 to the end of the century, activity in the periodical trade reached its feverish peak in December. The sales of some of these annual supplements were tremendous, eclipsing even the records set by the Christmas numbers of *All the Year Round* under Dickens' editorship. [...] their presence in English homes had a powerful effect on the spread of reading interest."

setting, and the psychological involvement of the protagonist were important in the development of significant settings and psychological plots in the twentieth-century short story.

That the Victorians in Britain developed a particular talent and appreciation for precisely this kind of short story has been related to wider issues in their culture. It is the Gothic mode in which many mid-Victorian stories elaborate alternatives to the master discourses of their culture. The story of the *super*natural – with its focus on the experience of the liminal in everyday experience – permitted Victorian writers and their readers to explore the threats and dangers which the major developments in their society entailed. Mid-Victorian Britain was the most progressive society in the world in terms of technological and scientific advancement and general economic prosperity. Under Queen Victoria, the British Empire came to reach its greatest expansion. Politically, Britain was the world's leading nation. Behind the self-confident façade, however, Victoria's subjects were also troubled by these very developments. Technology created a world that offered modern comforts and speedy transport but was also disconcerting in its very modernity. Ruling the Empire took its toll on those who ruled. Economic prosperity and the advance of science coinciding with a crisis of established religious belief gave rise to a growing materialism, which in turn caused a strong interest in all kinds of 'spiritual' phenomena. This is the main reason which Julia Briggs gives for the ghost story's unprecedented standing in the second half of the nineteenth and early decades of the twentieth century. To Briggs (1977, 17 and 19), the story of the supernatural provides a "reassertion of older and more spiritual values"; it evokes a past that has been lost because modern advances have "displaced the older continuities, cutting the individual off from his past". In a disturbing cultural situation, "the ghost story set up counter-suggestions that provided reassurance, beneath its more obvious terrors: undermining the apparent predictability of the material world, it gave comforting proof that there *was* something beyond". (*ibid.*, 24)[42] This analysis is supported by the fact that in many Victorian stories of the supernatural the tension between contemporary scepticism, science, materialism on the one hand and a belief in spirits on the other is explicitly addressed. Significantly, a great number of these stories are set not in remote times and countries (like in the earlier Romantic Gothic) but take place in the recognizable present, the familiar, everyday world.

A story by Edward George Bulwer, Lord Lytton, "The Haunted and the Haunters: Or, The House and the Brain" (1859 in *Blackwell's Magazine*), is set

[42] For a helpful discussion of the Gothic mode and its evocation of worlds of the past during the Victorian and later periods, see also Punter (1980) and Mighall (1999).

right in the middle of contemporary London. A house is said to be haunted, and the sceptical first-person narrator spends a night there in order to disprove this superstition. However, he then witnesses the most horrible apparitions which enact events that had happened to past inhabitants of the house. One ghost even breaks the neck of the narrator's dog. The narrator believes that the apparitions must be the outcome of a powerful brain and tries to explain his reasoning with analogies from science: "these are but agencies conveyed, as by electric wires, to my own brain from the brain of another." But the phenomenon he is concerned with is clearly beyond the grasp of science and the spell on the house is broken only when occult devices found in a secret room are destroyed and the haunted part of the house is demolished. We find the same mixture of the supernatural and a (pseudo-)scientific approach in a story often named as one of the best by an Irish master of the story of the supernatural, Joseph Sheridan LeFanu. His collection *In a Glass Darkly* (1872) – which also contains the vampire story "Carmilla" (1871) – includes "Green Tea". In this story, the narrator, a German physician, finds a 'scientific' explanation for the fact that a man of the clergy with a strong un-Christian interest in the spirit world is haunted by the apparition of a diabolic monkey (which situates the story in the then-current debate around Darwinism and its implications for Christian belief): during his studies, the Reverend has consumed great quantities of green tea which, according to the German physician, has affected a fluid in the nerves "which we have in common with spirits" and thus opened an "inner eye" which makes people susceptible to the spirit world.

"Green Tea" was first published in 1869, in Dickens's *All the Year Round*. Of Dickens's own ghost stories, "The Signal-Man" (written for the 1866 Christmas number of *All the Year Round*), is often singled out as his most effective one. It takes place at a site which exemplifies the achievements of nineteenth-century engineering – a tunnel where a signalman operates railway signals. When the first-person narrator first meets this signalman, the latter is troubled because ghosts have appeared to him three times, and after each of the first two visions a dreadful accident has taken place. Nothing happens after the third apparition, but the signalman is certain that the third ghost has tried to warn him of something. However, he is unable to decipher the ghost's gesture. In the end it turns out that the ghost has tried to warn him of his own death: the signalman himself is killed during a third railway accident. But the most uncanny aspect about the story is that the narrator seems to be mysteriously implicated in what has happened; in a somewhat understated manner, this final point is narrated as a coda to the main plot:

> Without prolonging the narrative to dwell on any of its curious circumstances more than on any other, I may, in closing it, point out the coincidence that the warning of the Engine-Driver included, not only the words which the unfortunate Signal-man had repeated to me as haunting him, but also the words which I myself – not he – had attached, and that only in my own mind, to the gesticulation he had imitated.

That the ghost story reacts to a modernized, materialist and rational world is even more outspoken in a story by Amelia Edwards which Dickens commissioned for the Christmas issue of *All the Year Round* for 1864, **"The Phantom Coach"**. Its main character and first-person narrator is a barrister, a man of the law whom one expects to be capable of making clear judgements. However, what he experiences makes him realize that there are phenomena beyond reason. Significantly, the events begin when the narrator loses his way – both literally and metaphorically. From his well-ordered life he trespasses onto territory where his accustomed ways of approaching reality are seriously questioned and shaken for the rest of his life. The lonely house on a moor where he finds refuge stands for another kind of trespass, that from science into occult knowledge. Its strange owner has become an outsider of society because, as a scientist, he has discredited himself through his belief in "ghosts, spectres, and supernatural appearances". What then happens to the barrister is proof of the old man's conviction that science provides too narrow an approach. The phantom coach, which the narrator mistakes for the regular service, is a relic from the past, a less sceptical world in which the supernatural was still acknowledged. How the narrator gradually notices what kind of vehicle he has entered and what his ghostly fellow passengers really are, is a masterpiece of carefully built horror and suspense.

Amelia Edwards belongs to an impressive number of Victorian women writers who wrote effective and popular stories of the supernatural. Others include, among many women no longer known, Elizabeth Gaskell, Margaret Oliphant[43] and Mary Elizabeth Braddon; they were followed, in Edwardian times, by writers like Vernon Lee [Violet Paget] and E[dith] Nesbit. Of course, the percentage of female writers of ghost stories is proportional to the generally increased number of women writers during the nineteenth

---

[43] Oliphant's stories of the supernatural frequently have a Scottish setting. In "The Secret Chamber" (first publ. in *Blackwood's Magazine* in 1876), a young man is initiated into the secret of a horrible ghost who inhabits his ancestral home and has haunted his family for centuries. In "The Library Window" (first publ. in *Blackwood's* in 1896), a young girl with the gift of second sight is one of the few people who can see a window in the wall of a library building and the spirit of an unhappy scholar who was killed there years ago.

century and in particular during Victoria's reign.[44] But a special affinity between women and ghost-story writing has also been noted. Cox and Gilbert (1986, xiii), in the introduction to their anthology, suggest that women, "being on the margins of society – politically speaking – during the nineteenth century, were especially impelled to write about the margins of the visible, for the ghost story [...] deals with power and thus might be expected to appeal to those who felt the absence of self-determination in their own lives". In a story by Mary Elizabeth Braddon, "The Shadow in the Corner" (1879 in *All the Year Round*), a servant girl hangs herself in a room haunted by an earlier suicide after her fears have not been taken seriously enough by the rational men living in her household. She thus appears as a victim to misguided male authority. In a famous story by Elizabeth Gaskell set in a woman-dominated environment, the prime agent of the past crime which haunts the present is also an authoritarian male. In "The Old Nurse's Story" (first publ. in the Christmas number of *Household Words*, 1852), a young woman, the first-person narrator, is nurse to an orphaned girl, Rosamond, whom she takes to an elderly relative to live with. Miss Furnival, her companion Mrs Stark and three servants are the only people living in an old manor house. The house is uncanny; one wing has not been opened for many decades, and one can occasionally hear the sounds of an organ although the instrument has been completely destroyed inside. One winter night, Rosamond disappears; she is found outside, almost frozen to death, and claims that she was taken there by another girl, whose mother she has also met. Her nurse does not believe her until she sees the ghost girl herself. Only then is she told about the household's secret. Miss Furnival's strict father, when discovering that his eldest daughter was secretly married to an Italian musician and had a child by him, hit the child and chased his daughter out of the house; in a freezing night, the child died and the mother went mad. The surviving Miss Furnival experiences pangs of conscience with regard to her sister: she was also in love with her sister's husband and was the one who betrayed her secret. The story climaxes in a suspenseful scene in which this drama of the past is re-enacted by apparitions of all its protagonists, including the still-living one. The father figure clearly dominates the tableau of phantoms: "All at once, the east door gave way with a thundering crash, as if torn open in a violent passion, and there came into that broad and mysterious light, the figure of a tall old man, with grey hair and gleaming eyes." Deeply shocked by the unbrooked flow of the past into the present, Miss Furnival dies, muttering "what is done in youth can never be undone in age!". An editor of Gaskell's Gothic tales, Laura Kranzler, notes

[44] For an anthology, see Jump (1998).

their special concern with female life and female writing (Gaskell 2000, xxviii):

> The stories and novellas collected here suggest the subtlety and variety of Gaskell's own forms of empowerment, both as a means of expressing problems of domesticity otherwise repressed in her novels, and as a means, perhaps, of speaking for all of the silenced women represented within these tales. Her stories could thus be seen to explore the Gothic underside of female identity, domestic relations and the authority of the spoken and written word.[45]

*Excursus: Fin-de-Siècle and Later Gothic*

Counter-discourses gained in importance as the nineteenth century drew to a close. In the *fin-de-siècle* decade, with its general preoccupation with deconstructing the tenets of high Victorianism and fascination with decay and decadence, interest in the supernatural became particularly intense and lasted until about the 1920s.[46] To Julia Briggs (1977, 76) the nineties story of the supernatural "reflects the age's growing spiritual unease, alienation, melancholy, soul-sickness or *Weltschmerz*" and "provides an early expression of that sense of displacement, of disorientation in the face of rapid change which characterizes so much modern literature". Not only writers with a deliberate counter-cultural stance – like Oscar Wilde – now wrote about the supernatural, but also writers more closely associated with a traditional system of values. Rudyard Kipling, for instance, used the ghost story in "The Phantom Rickshaw" (1885) to express anxieties related to the imperialist project.

Arthur Machen's stories of evil, horror and the supernatural began to be published in the 1890s, as were stories of supernatural horror by Bram Stoker, Arthur Conan Doyle, Arthur Quiller-Couch, Henry James and H.G. Wells. Many of them are clearly marked by a decadently morbid trait. Co-

[45] On Gaskell's general concern with patriarchy and the woman as writer, expressed with greater freedom in her shorter fiction, see also Watson (1996), who discusses, in particular, Gaskell's collection *Round the Sofa* (1859). This volume also contains melodramatic stories like "The Poor Clare" and "The Half-Brothers". On Gaskell's use of the supernatural, see also Shelston (1995).

[46] "There has been occasional speculation about why ghost stories proliferated during this period, most of it an appendage of the larger question of the Edwardian obsession with ghostly societies, experiments, and manifestoes. The apocalyptic quality of these stories [...] is part of a spirit of dissonance and restlessness [...]. Like so much art of the transitional period between the late nineteenth century and World War I, the tale of terror was symptomatic of a cultural malaise which some historians view as a premonition of the Great War." (Sullivan 1978, 3)

nan Doyle's "The Ring of Thoth" (1890), for example, is about an ancient, immortal Egyptian priest who visits the Egyptian department of the late-nineteenth-century Louvre in search of the mummy of a beloved woman and the antidote that will help him to fulfil his death wish. Contributors to the Edwardian ghost story include Algernon Blackwood, E.F. Benson (who continued to produce ghost stories until the 1940s), W.W. Jacobs, and M.R. James. In Jacobs's "The Monkey's Paw" (1902), the charm to which the title refers permits its owner to fulfil himself three wishes, but the magic has the most evil consequences. M.R. James was a medievalist at Cambridge, and many of his *Ghost Stories of an Antiquary* (1904) arise from an encounter with relics of the past or antiquarian research.

Around the turn of the century, new insights in psychology – above all the 'discovery' of the unconscious – gave an obvious impetus to the genre, but so did further discoveries in the natural sciences, in particular physics and chemistry, which destabilized established concepts of time and space and drew attention to invisible substances and forces. The latter were of particular significance for the rise of science fiction (see below under H.G. Wells, p. 102), but the uncanny aspect of the new knowledge was also negotiated in the more traditional Gothic mode. In Rudyard Kipling's "Wireless" (1902), for instance, an experiment with a radio transmission is parallelled with another, clearly *meta*physical transmission; while one man tries to receive radio waves, a drugged apothecary, who is normally completely ignorant of poetry, appears to 'receive' the spirit of John Keats.

The nineteenth century, then, established a strong tradition in British ghost-story writing, which has remained an important sub-genre throughout the twentieth century, with examples such as T.H. White's "The Troll" (written in the early 1930s), in which a man is pursued by a dangerous, man-eating troll who disguises as a respectable professor, or Robert Grossmith's "Company" (1989), in which the ghost of a man killed in the First World War wants to make contact with a little girl but tragically causes her death.

### *Crime and Detective Stories*

Detective stories form another popular sub-genre of short-story writing in Britain today[47] whose origins can be traced to Victorian times. Detective stories seem a rational complement to stories of the supernatural, and like

---

[47] For the years 1980 to 2000, the amount of genre-specific anthologies listed in the British Library Catalogue is highest for detective and crime fiction, ghost and horror stories, and science fiction and horror – all of these being sub-genres which originated in the nineteenth century.

the latter, they are particularly effective in the short format. Edgar Allan Poe, after all, wrote 'tales of ratiocination' alongside his Gothic stories of effect. Both types of story are concerned with mysteries, but in the detective story, reason remains in control. Detective stories thus seem more in accord with the acknowledged aspects of a culture rather than its dark underside. But they, too, are reminders that such an underside exists, and that order is always potentially endangered.

As Richard Altick (1972) has shown, the Victorians were fascinated by crime just as much as by the supernatural, and reading about crime, whether in journalism or fiction, was a favourite entertainment. Patricia Craig (1990, iv), in her anthology of the English detective story, dates the beginning of this type of story as a sub-genre proper with the emergence of Arthur Conan Doyle's Sherlock Holmes in the final decade of the nineteenth century:

> It was Poe, with his 'Murders in the Rue Morgue', who inaugurated fictional detecting in the 1840s; but it was not until the advent of Sherlock Holmes that the genre, as we know it, came into being. Between 1841 and the first appearance of Sherlock Holmes over forty years later, there was no shortage of detective writers in either England or America, but they tended not to differentiate between the 'sensation' mode then prevalent, and plain detection (without gothic or picturesque embellishments, that is). They were drawn to the theatrical assignation and the bated breath. The emotional effects of a crime were played up rather than being subdued. Conan Doyle changed all that by devising a pattern in which the puzzle was paramount, the detective memorable, and the investigative procedure riveting.

Nevertheless, stories about crime and its detection were written before Conan Doyle and permit glimpses of the Victorians' insecurities and fears. A frequent contributor to Dickens's magazines, Wilkie Collins, for example, is a writer specially known for his writing of mystery, suspense and crime fiction. "A Terribly Strange Bed" (1852 in *Household Words*) involves an intricate machinery for murdering guests in a gambling house; the story is highly disconcerting even though the strange bed's inventors are arrested in the end. Collins is also the first writer of a detective story in Britain. "The Lawyer's Story of a Stolen Letter" is one of the pieces which Collins and Dickens wrote, under the title *The Seven Poor Travellers*, for the 1854 Christmas supplement of *Household Words*; like "A Terribly Strange Bed", it was later included in Collins's collection *After Dark* (1856). In a plot strongly reminiscent of Poe's "The Purloined Letter" (1845), the story depicts how the first-person narrator, a lawyer, manages to retrieve a compromising letter from the man who has stolen it.

That the detective story, like the story of the supernatural, had a "golden age" (Symons 1972, chapter 6) between the 1890s and the First World War, can again be traced to the *fin-de-siècle* tendency to question Victorian certainties. Conan Doyle's Sherlock Holmes is a gentleman who hunts down criminals and helps to restore order; he is frequently employed by the representatives of the old order, the ruling houses of Europe and even Queen Victoria, but he is also clearly an outsider with traits that locate him beyond respectable middle-class culture: he is an aesthete with a cocaine addiction and has no family ties (except his equally strange brother Mycroft). Conan Doyle also wrote two Sherlock Holmes novels, but it is in his many short stories about the charismatic detective that his successful formula is most effective: at the beginning of each of these stories, the client arrives at 22B Baker Street and Holmes baffles him and Watson, who also serves as the admiring first-person narrator, with his powers of detection. In the main part of the story, the case is investigated and Holmes identifies the criminal. In the final part, Holmes presents the solution in retrospect. The first stories by Conan Doyle with this pattern were "A Scandal in Bohemia" and "The Red-Headed League", both published in 1891 and, like all other Holmes stories, in the *Strand Magazine*. Not only was the short story more congenial to the type of story which Conan Doyle had to tell than the novel, it also permitted him to fulfil his readers' voracious appetite for ever more stories about Holmes.[48]

This enormous success sparked other series around detective figures in the 1890s and the first decades of the twentieth century: Arthur Morrison's Martin Hewitt stories (which also appeared in the *Strand*), R. Austin Freeman's stories about a forensic scientist, Dr Thorndyke, and J.K. Chesterton's Father Brown Stories, in which crime is also explored from a metaphysical point of view (from 1911). Baroness Orczy's 'Old Man in the Corner' stories originally appeared in the *Royal Magazine* between 1901 and 1905; from 1910, Orczy also wrote stories about a female investigator, Lady Molly of Scotland Yard. **"The Mysterious Death on the Underground Railway"** is one of Orczy's 'Old Man' stories. Like most Holmes stories, it is set in contemporary London; here, the crime even takes place in a means of public transport which exemplifies the progressive modernity of London's metropolitan space. Orczy's detective differs from the hound-like Holmes, however, in that he never leaves his favourite seat in an ABC teashop, a circumstance which emphasizes his capacity to solve crimes by pure reasoning alone – solutions which he then discloses to another modern phenomenon,

[48] For a discussion of the Sherlock Holmes stories, see Symons (1972, chapter 5).

the girl reporter.[49] A second 'golden age' of the detective story in Britain, with writers like Agatha Christie and Dorothy Sayers, began in the 1920s, and writers like Ruth Rendell have taken the successful model right into the present.

The ghost story and the detective story have taken us from 'high' Victorianism into the 1890s and even further into the twentieth century, which suggests important lines of continuity. These lines reach back into the earlier decades of Victoria's reign (and, in the case of the Gothic story, even further), and the output of Victorian writers of short fiction is impressive. Nevertheless, many overviews of the short story in Britain claim that it was not until the 1880s and 1890s that the short story began to flourish.

### *New Conditions for the Short Story?*

An important reason usually given for this blossoming is the appearance of more favourable conditions for publishing short fiction, conditions which were closely linked with the demise of the three-volume novel. It is no coincidence that Kipling, a writer to whom the long novel was not congenial but the short story most obviously was, wrote a poem about "The Three-Decker" in 1894, celebrating its 'extinction' and the extinction of the kind of novel which this form of publication had encouraged.[50] As pointed out before (p. 21), once the three-decker was 'killed' in the second half of the 1890s, the novel also lost its dominance in the magazines. It became less and less common to serialize novels in the periodical press, which had more

---

[49] An interesting because subversive phenomenon of the nineties and Edwardian crime story are E.W. Hornung's Raffles stories, in which the criminal is the hero. Symons (1972, 91f.) writes about them: "Raffles is on the surface an image of a perfect English gentleman. He is captain of the school cricket team and later becomes the finest slow bowler of his decade (an amateur, naturally). Apart from playing cricket all the summer he leads a life of apparent idleness. Apparent: for he really makes a living as a burglar, and *Raffles, the Amateur Cracksman* (1899) records his adventures in collaboration with Bunny, who has worshipped Raffles since fagging for him at school. [...] The series, which includes the later *Raffles* (1901) and *A Thief in the Night* (1905), shows the public school ethos turned round, with the traditional virtues of sticking to your chums and doing the decent thing used in the service of theft. [...] Hornung never sees Raffles as an enemy of the class in which he had been brought up, as an earlier writer would have done, but as a man who adheres to the standards of this class even though he is a crook. For him, as for Bunny, Raffles's sins are cancelled out by his heroic death in the Boer War."

[50] Quadflieg (1988, 128f.) refers to a story by Rudolf Dircks, "A Ghost of an Experience" (*Versimilitudes*, 1897), in which two characters discuss the three-decker novel and explicitly compare it to short forms of fiction.

space for short fiction as a result – not least because the periodical market was booming and now served a readership that had grown significantly after the education reforms of the 1870s. Only now did a market develop for short stories in which stories were well-paid for, and a new type of 'commercial' story emerged; the success of detective fiction, for instance, following the phenomenal response to Conan Doyle's stories about Sherlock Holmes, has been mentioned above.

The periodical market of the 1890s spanned a wide spectrum, from the penny press for lower-class readers to the popular middle-class *Strand Magazine* and its comparatively huge distribution (of 500,000), to small literary magazines. When the *Strand* was launched by George Newnes in January 1891 (it would eventually run until 1950), the introduction to the first number did not mention serial novels any more but announced that this new publication (among "the immense number of existing Monthlies") would "contain stories and articles by the best British writers, and special translations from the first foreign authors".[51] Harold Orel (1986, 188) points out that the *Strand* "enjoyed the largest circulation of any English or American periodical during the years before the Great War, and influenced greatly the development of a mass-market interest in shorter fiction".[52] Another important forum for the literary story were the periodicals published by W.E. Henley, in particular the *National Observer* (1888–94). Henley was known for his political conservatism, patriotism and counter-decadent attitude, but the stories he published in his magazines do not necessarily reflect this. They include work by writers so diverse as Thomas Hardy, Rudyard Kipling, Robert Louis Stevenson, Henry James and H.G. Wells.

After all, while the deliberately commercial and popular story emerged, the genre also gained a new reputation as a form of *artistic* expression, and 'little' magazines even encouraged the avant-garde *art story*. The *Yellow Book* (1894–97), for instance, and its short-lived imitator, the *Savoy* (1896), edited by Henry Harland and Arthur Symons respectively, are famous for promoting aestheticism (see below, p. 104). Even in its outward appearance, the *Yellow Book* aimed to be different from the mainstream magazines; each

---

[51] See also Richardson (2002, xlv), who points out in the introduction to her anthology that in 1891 another journal, *Black and White*, declared explicitly that it would print "'no serial stories: but a complete short story by an eminent writer, English or foreign, will appear in each number'".

[52] Adrian (1991a and b) collects mystery stories from the *Strand*. In its long history, however, the *Strand* also published 'serious' work by writers such as Rudyard Kipling, H.G. Wells, Jerome K. Jerome, Joseph Conrad, D.H. Lawrence, Aldous Huxley, Arnold Bennett and Graham Greene. They are included in the collection of *Strand* stories edited by Beare (1992).

issue came in the form of an expensively and beautifully produced hardcover book.

In a changing genre system, the short story began to be appreciated as a form of fiction that represented a serious alternative to the novel – in particular since the late nineteenth century began to seriously question the possibilities of the novel, and, in some cases, reject it in its established forms. This debate about the role of fiction (and the functions of literature generally) was part of the wide-scale *fin-de-siècle* scepticism towards Victorian values and institutions. The need for a new aesthetics in fiction was felt as alleged Victorian certainties crumbled rapidly and the master narratives of the Victorians came under increasing attack. Faced with the consequences of massive urbanization and industrialization, challenges to traditional class structures, political and social reforms, the new imperialism, and an increasing secularism, late-nineteenth-century Britain was undergoing a rapid and disconcerting transformation. The belief in progress which had marked the mid-Victorian decades gave way to a sense of decline and degeneration (ideas also nourished by Darwinism) as well as scepticism regarding the consequences of modernization for society and the individual. 'Reality', which the Victorian novel had aspired to unveil to its readers, was now perceived to be complicated and multi-facetted, evading single and reliable interpretation. The traditional understanding of the novel, with its emphasis on mimeticism and didacticism and authoritative narrators, found itself in a state of crisis. The debate about the 'art of fiction',[53] as Henry James entitled an influential essay in 1884, accentuated new perspectives for longer fiction, but the short story, with its capacity to focus on minor, fragmentary and momentary experiences, was now also perceived as an adequate mode of rendering the idiosyncracies of contemporary life, as Wendell V. Harris (1979, 108–110) points out:

> The short story as it developed in the 1880s and 1890s [...] created a role for itself partly by becoming the vehicle for the expression of discontinuity and isolation. [...] the essence of the short story is to isolate, to portray the individual person, or moment, or scene in isolation, detached from the great social and historical continuum which it had been the business of the English novel, and the great concern of nineteenth-century essayists, to insist upon. [...] Whereas in the traditional novel the significance of events was defined only over time, in the short story the significance could be, implicitly or explicitly, immediate. Whereas in the novel each character or event was un-

[53] For surveys of this debate, which involved many important writers and critics like Leslie Stephen, Edmund Gosse, Henry James and Robert Louis Stevenson, to name only a few, see the collections of essays by Olmsted (1979) and Eigner and Worth (1985).

derstood only as part of a far-reaching web (the warp of that web being the flow of time, the weft the social structure), the short story could designedly restrict itself to the illumination of only a small portion of the web – though of course it might imply the nature of the rest.[54]

Walter Pache (1990, 222) observes that many of "the iconoclasts amongst the young writers [...] regarded the new short story as a protest against the novel, the established form of prose narrative". Valerie Shaw (1983, 4) also sees the "rise of the short story in England" as "closely linked with the emergence of the characteristic figure of the modern artist, and with anti-Victorianism in its widest sense" and claims that "in the atmosphere of the 1880s and 1890s it was simply inconceivable that short fiction should *not* have been talked about". Looking back to the 1890s in 1911, when he wrote the introduction to a collection of his stories (*The Country of the Blind and Other Stories*), H.G. Wells linked the decade's extraordinary flourishing of the short story in Britain explicitly to its encouragement through the contemporary periodical scene, which offered not only pay but also acclaim:

> The 'nineties was a good and stimulating period for a short-story writer. Mr. Kipling had made his astonishing advent with a series of little blue-grey books, whose covers opened like window-shutters to reveal the dusty sunglare and blazing colours of the East; Mr. Barrie had demonstrated what could be done in a little space through the panes of his *Window in Thrums*. The *National Observer* was at the climax of its career of heroic insistence upon lyrical brevity and a vivid finish, and Mr. Frank Harris was not only printing good short stories by other people, but writing still better ones himself in the dignified pages of the *Fortnightly Review. Longman's Magazine*, too, represented a *clientèle* of appreciative short-story readers that is now scattered. Then came the generous opportunities of the *Yellow Book*, and the *National Observer* died only to give birth to the *New Review*. No short story of the slightest distinction went for long unrecognised. [...] Every sort of artist demands human responses, and few men can contrive to write merely for a publisher's cheque and silence, however reassuring that cheque may be. [...] Scarcely any artist will hesitate in the choice between money and attention; and it was primarily for that last and better sort of pay that the short stories of the 'nineties were written. People talked about them tremendously, compared them, and ranked them. That was the thing that mattered. (in Weber and Greiner 1977, 84f.)

[54] For a discussion of the short story in the final decades of the nineteenth century, see also Hönig (1971).

Not only were writers encouraged by the genre's new prestige, but criticism also contributed to the shaping of a new genre awareness. This awareness was significantly influenced by America, notably by the ideas of Brander Matthews, which were first published in a British magazine. As Wendell V. Harris (1979, 91f.) notes, Matthews's distinction of the Short-story from the story which is merely short

> provided the key for almost all serious discussion of the short story for at least the next twenty years. The most important word was 'unity', 'unity as a Novel cannot have it.' [...] As Frederic [*sic*] Wedmore developed the point later, [...] 'But one thing it can never be – it can never be a 'novel in a nutshell'. Suggestions for achieving unity varied from Matthews's prescription of 'a single character, a single event, a single emotion, or the series of emotions called forth by a single situation' to Henry Harland's 'You begin by taking not what they call an "idea" in the trade; not an incident, nor a coincidence; above all not an invention. You begin by taking an impression.' Actually, Harland's view developed naturally enough out of Matthews's phrase 'unity of impression', for though Matthews referred to the effect on the reader, it was easy enough to use the same term to refer to the author's inspiration, especially since 'impressionism' as an aesthetic term was in the air.

Frederick Wedmore's article "The Short Story", which is referred to here, was published in *The Nineteenth Century* in March 1898. He explicitly discusses the short story "not as a ready means of hitting the big public, but as a medium for the exercise of the finer art" and emphasizes that the short story "admits of greater variety of form than does the long novel". (in Weber and Greiner 1977, 60f.) Henry Harland's "Concerning the Short Story" appeared in the *Academy* in 1897, and an influential article by the American writer Bret Harte about "The Rise of the American Short Story" was published in 1899 in the *Cornhill Magazine* (in Weber and Greiner 1977, 65f.). Anne M. Windholz (1990, 156) summarizes the critical reception of American short stories in Britain between 1880 and 1900, pointing out how this reception also increased attention in short-story production at home and helped to define the contours of the short-story genre:

> a study of short story reviews in the *Athenaeum* between 1880 and 1900 reveals that English critics were indeed reading, considering, and commenting on American work with the same vigor and interest they brought to the examination of English short fiction. The reviews consciously articulate theories of the successful short story in response to features identified as distinctively American – native humor, local color, dialect, and a technical emphasis on conciseness and unity of effect. Reacting to (and sometimes against) these features, *Athenaeum* reviewers developed during the last two

decades of the 19th century a common rhetoric of criticism that was applied to English as well as American short stories.[55]

With Henry James, an American voice managed to aquire a permanent audience in the British literary scene, and he was to be of particular importance for the aestheticist writers of the 1890s (see below, p. 105).

*Stevenson and Kipling: Figureheads of the New Beginning*

It is a commonplace of criticism on the British short story to name two writers as figureheads of the genre's renewed status during the final decades of the nineteenth century. Robert Louis Stevenson and Rudyard Kipling both achieved great popularity with their audience *and* marked the history of the short story by a particular skill in the short mode. Through their international success, they helped to give the genre a prestige it had not enjoyed before and made a type of story popular which focussed more strongly than the majority of earlier Victorian stories – apart from the ghost story – on unity of event, form and effect. To Henry Seidel Canby (1909, 322), "not until 1877, and Robert Louis Stevenson's first published narrative, does any Englishman of real caliber show both desire and ability to do something *new* with the short story" or, as Joseph M. Flora (1985, xvi) writes, "the first major writer in the British Isles to specialize in the short story was Robert Louis Stevenson. His 'A Lodging for the Night', first published in the October 1877 *Temple Bar,* is generally recognized as the first modern British short story."

In light of the successful short stories pointed out earlier in this chapter, such claims seem exaggerated. It cannot be denied, however, that stories like "A Lodging for the Night", which deals with an episode from the life of the French poet and vagabond of the fifteenth century, François Villon, show Stevenson's highly developed sense of form. In her chapter on Stevenson, Valerie Shaw (1983, 42) notes that, at the same time, Stevenson was still a traditional story-teller, with a strong interest in adventure as well as moral issues, often setting his stories in exotic places or otherwise exploiting a 'strange' atmosphere: "his contribution to the evolution of the short story lay more in his fiction's reminiscent cast than in any clear advance towards 'modernity'". Harold Orel (1986, 127) observes similarly that Stevenson was so successful because he had studied a market which "flourished when the literary commodity sold by the periodical was es-

[55] On the importance of American critics for the short story in Britain, see also Beachcroft (1968, chapter 11).

capist, highly colored, and unobtrusively moral in its implications". Stevenson's particular attraction to moralism and romance (as opposed to realism) is reflected, for instance, in one of his stories of the supernatural, "Markheim" (1885). Its eponymous protagonist, the story's first-person narrator, is confronted with an uncanny *doppelgänger* who one might interpret as the mirror held up to a reckless materialist. The double appears when the narrator, a gambler, has killed the owner of a pawnshop because he urgently needs money. In quite obvious terms, the *doppelgänger* appears as a manifestation of the narrator's conscience. "'I know you', replied the visitant, with a sort of kind severity or rather firmness. 'I know you to the soul.'"

Stevenson's story material is not as immediately contemporary as that found in Kipling, and while Stevenson composed around thirty stories in all, Kipling was far more prolific in this genre, writing stories until after the First World War and on a wide range of subjects: Anglo-India, the life of soldiers, the world of children, life in (rural) England, the experience of the Great War, or modern technology like the radio (in "Wireless") and the cinematograph (in "Mrs Bathurst", 1904). Kipling was so popular that even his hard-bound collections sold well, as Harold Orel (1986, 143f.) points out. He rose to popularity with his very first collection of stories, *Plain Tales from the Hills* (1890). That his first readers perceived Kipling's stories as something distinctly new is explained by Wendell V. Harris (1979, 98) in their obvious contrast to the dominant type of story on the market:

> All one need do is read through a volume or two of *Tales from Blackwood* – still the standard of short fiction at the time – and then open the pages of *Plain Tales*. In the latter are none of the tedious and often irrelevant introductions in which earlier writers seemed so often to be circling around their material while trying to find a way to approach it, none of those awkward, digressive, and complicated explanations of the background which must be got out of the way before the story could be launched. [...] the control of the structure which still can be felt in practically every one of them must have seemed dazzling at the time.

As has been noted in chapter 1 (p. 17), the *Plain Tales* were originally written for an Anglo-Indian newspaper, the *Civil and Military Gazette*, and Kipling's experience in journalistic writing and the space at his disposal in the *Gazette* is at least partly responsible for the stories' concision. His style, too, shows traces of his work as a newspaperman. Walter Allen (1981, 64) characterizes Kipling's prose as "based on the vernacular, on speed and directness of narration, on an unerring eye and economy of means". Thomas O. Beachcroft (1968, 143f.) names the following as characteristics of Kipling's short stories:

> the highly dramatic vision; the intense interest in men at work together; the gift for absorbing information about jobs and crafts; the conception of men as parts of a vast work to be achieved, while the human stuff is hardened or broken in the process; the theories of a harsh punitive justice and the recurrence of personal revenge; the outcroppings of sheer magic; the near absence of women, of home and married life; and present throughout it all, the personalized narrator, the man who is in the know, the narrating 'I', who impresses on the reader that he has it all 'from the horse's mouth', whether that means simple private soldiers or archangels.

However, Kipling also aroused massive criticism for the obtrusiveness of his narrators, criticism which was as strong as the dislike he provoked with his conservative ideology and, in particular, his alleged imperialism.[56]

Despite the wide thematic range of his story oeuvre, Kipling is best known as a representative of the colonial short story, depicting settings, manners and types of Indian colonial society. The stories in *Plain Tales*, whether about comic or tragic incidents, do not indulge in a picturesque exoticism. Rather, the enthusiasm of their original reception is due to the new type of local colour which Kipling offered his contemporary British readers. Instead of romanticizing India, the stories portray the dilemma with which British colonials were faced in countries which they ruled but were inadequately equipped to physically and mentally cope with. At the same time, the stories clearly hold up values such as white authority and superiority and occasionally use a vocabulary of racialist discourse. This is prominent, for instance, in "His Chance in Life" (1887), where Michele, a young telegraph operator of mixed race, manages a crisis during a riot. In a situation where he is the only person present with at least some 'white' blood in his veins, he becomes a natural authority for the other natives ("the old race-instinct which recognises a drop of White blood as far as it can be diluted") – until an Englishman arrives on the scene and "Michele felt himself slipping back more and more into the native". The very opening of the story is race-conscious:

> If you go straight away from Levées and Government House Lists, past Trades' Balls – far beyond everything and everybody you ever knew in your respectable life – you cross, in time, the Borderline where the last drop of White blood ends and the full tide of Black sets in. [...] The Black and the White mix very quaintly in their ways. Sometimes the White shows in spurts of fierce, childish pride – which is Pride of Race run crooked – and sometimes the Black in still fiercer abasement and humility, half-heathenish customs and strange, unaccountable impulses to crime.

[56] For a vehement attack of Kipling's imperialism, see the chapter on Kipling in Ward (1924, 116–119). For a summary of the Kipling debate, see also Beachcroft (1968, chapter 12). Gilbert (1972), by contrast, aims at a rehabilitation of Kipling.

Similar in tone, the beginning of **"Beyond the Pale"** (1888) proclaims that "[a] man should, whatever happens, keep to his own caste, race and breed" and illustrates what may happen when the "safe limits of decent everyday society" are overstepped. In this story, a white man with "too deep an interest in native life" falls in love with an Indian widow who is punished terribly by her own people for her violation of the racial borderline: her hands are hacked off.

However, the *Plain Tales* are also critical of the whites and their value systems and betray a sympathy for those who are violated by white supremacy. In "Lispeth" (1886), the protagonist is a young Indian woman educated by a Christian chaplain and his wife; she falls in love with a young Englishman whom she has literally found during one of her 'constitutionals' and whom she is determined to marry. The chaplain couple and the young man find this idea ridiculous, but when the man decides to take his leave, they pretend that he will soon come back and marry her. When he does not return, Lispeth, in protest, gives up Christianity and goes back to a native way of life. She may be naive, but the narrator's irony makes it clear that the white people's condescension and their lies are the real things to be condemned. "Kidnapped" (1887), too, raises doubts as to the colonizer's alleged superior judgement. The beginning still seems to assert this superiority but already hints at the fact that the behaviour of the 'enlightened' race might not always be so different from that of a people who practice arranged marriage: "We are a high-caste and enlightened race, and infant-marriage is very shocking, and the consequences are sometimes peculiar; but, nevertheless, the Hindu notion [...] of arranging marriages irrespective of the personal inclinations of the married is sound." In this story, a white man is abducted by his well-meaning friends to 'protect' him from a love marriage with a woman whom they suspect of not being purely white.

Many of the British characters in Kipling's colonial stories are disorientated and occasionally demoralized by the foreign world by which they are challenged; they tend to forget 'civilized' norms – for example when male characters choose the 'wrong', that is native, female partner. In the worst case, characters who cannot cope commit suicide, like the overprotected 'boy' in "Thrown Away" (1888) who comes to India as a young subaltern, believes that he is a failure and shoots himself. "The Man Who Would Be King" (1888) has been read as a parable about the imperial enterprise; it is certainly a cynical one since those who want to be kings in this story are badly educated loafers who misuse the infrastructures of the British Empire to make their own personal fortune. They are far from the positive type which Kipling draws elsewhere of the British colonial: the man who knows his responsibility and bears difficulties stoically. Peachey Carnehan and

Daniel Dravot impersonate journalists who want to expose corrupt governments but then blackmail the rulers of several native Indian states. When this scheme is no longer successful, they decide to go to Kafiristan (a remote part of Afghanistan) and take the country over. This wild scheme actually succeeds; Dravot is crowned king and worshipped as a God with Carnehan as his co-ruler; but when Dravot desires a woman he proves he is only human and the natives rise up against the two foreign kings. Dravot dies, Carnehan survives a crucifixion and is sent away with Dravot's severed but crowned head in his luggage. He arrives back in India a broken man and dies after a short while. This story far from idealizes imperialism; rather, it indicts selfish exploitation of the colonies.

With the disorientation they depict, Kipling's stories deal with a phenomenon of life under the circumstances of evolving modernity. Despite their author's political conservatism, his colonial stories – as well as many of his later stories – show a "breakdown of the self" (Hanson, 1985, 32) and present characters who are outsiders. This is even more extreme in Joseph Conrad's stories about men who are destroyed in the name of the imperialist cause. *Heart of Darkness* (1899, 1902) is the obvious text that comes to mind here, but it is too long to qualify as a short story. The briefer "An Outpost of Progress" (1898) also tells of a tragedy which takes place between two white men in charge of a trading station in the Congo, "in the centre of Africa". Kayerts and his assistant Carlier are obviously displaced and disorientated in a world which they perceive as the opposite of the civilized world to which they are accommodated: "a wilderness rendered more strange, more incomprehensible by the mysterious glimpses of the vigorous life it contained. [...] the contact with pure unmitigated savagery, with primitive nature and primitive man, brings sudden and profound trouble into the heart." The two Europeans are thus unfit to represent 'progress' as one of the key legitimizing ideas of imperialism; their station deteriorates while the men eagerly await the arrival of the steamer which will take them back to the civilized world. Meanwhile, they are unable to resist their employee Makola, who sells the station hands to slave dealers in exchange for ivory. The two white men feel that they are complicit in this inhuman act and fall into further physical and moral decay. Their crisis culminates when the steamer is late and they run out of provisions. In the end, they struggle desperately over a lump of sugar. Makola kills Carlier, and Kayerts commits suicide. To Robert Gish (1985, 2), such stories of the age of imperialism and its decline are "inseparable from both the causes and the results of the *angst* and alienation associated with modernity". One can also find this aspect of modernity in some of Stevenson's stories. "Markheim", with its *doppelgänger* motif, for instance, can be read as a treatment of identity crisis, of a self alienated in an increasingly materialist world. Although Stevenson and Kipling, like most writers of their time, were still "interested in 'traditional' story forms rather than in experimentation as such", as Clare Hanson (1985, 19) observes, they used such forms to articulate an anxiety about the world in which they were living; the mystery tale, among other traditional forms, offered them "a means by which they could structure and organise their common preoccupation with disorder, transgression and the breaking of limits". Other prominent writers of the time who addressed issues of modernity – in quite different types of story – were Thomas Hardy and H.G. Wells. And again, we have writers here who use the form of the short story to articulate central concerns of their culture.

### *Thomas Hardy and H.G. Wells*

Critical opinion about Thomas Hardy as a writer of short stories is divided. Kristin Brady (1982, 198f.) quotes a selection of negative criticism but then qualifies:

> The discrepancy between the allegations of critics who claim that Hardy had no sense of the short story as form, and his own stated concern for 'beauty of shape' in all narratives may be attributed to the rigid definition which the term 'short story' has gradually acquired since Edgar Allan Poe's famous essay on Hawthorne declared the importance of the *'single effect'*. While Poe's standard can help to illuminate his own work, as well as that of several 'modern' writers, it fails to isolate either the weaknesses or the strengths of an artist such as Hardy, whose sense of form developed from a different tradition altogether, and who was more concerned with 'story' than with 'effect'.

The tradition from which Hardy writes his stories is by and large an oral one, as Harold Orel (1986, 108) emphasizes, one which "contravened currently fashionable doctrine about documentation of fictional setting, the need for verifiable detail in the depiction of manners and social behavior, and analogies between the technique of a story-teller and that of a scientist". Hardy's reliance on oral traditions is most apparent in his regionalist *Wessex Tales* (1888), which present a rural western England and its ways of life to modern urban readers no longer familiar with these ways of life. To Kristin Brady (1982, 2), the tales "are all firmly grounded in Dorset life and folklore during the mid-nineteenth century and are drawn together by a unique narrative perspective, the pastoral voice". Set a few decades in the past, they suggest a sense of tradition, of memories associated with the region, and the stories all convey the impression that they "present history as it has come down through oral sources". (*ibid.*, 46) In "The Three Strangers" (1883), which Wendell V. Harris (1979, 89) considers Hardy's "finest short story", the action is set in the 1820s; the beginning emphasizes the lapse of time and vanished life-style:

> Among the few features of agricultural England which retain an appearance but little modified by the lapse of centuries, may be reckoned the high, grassy and furzy downs, coombs, or ewe-leases, as they are indifferently called, that fill a large area of certain counties in the south and south-west. If any mark of human occupation is met with hereon, it usually takes the form of the solitary cottage of some shepherd.
>
> Fifty years ago such a lonely cottage stood on such a down, and may possibly be standing there now. In spite of its loneliness, however, the spot, by actual measurement, was not more than five miles from a county-town. Yet that affected it little.

Three strangers come to this region, to a farmer's house where the first child's christening is just being celebrated according to local custom. The first stranger is an escaped convict, a village's poor clockmaker who has been condemned to death because he has stolen a sheep for his starving family. The second is the hangman on his way to the execution; he does not know that the other stranger was to be his victim; a third stranger arrives, who is later revealed to be the convict's brother. To Kristin Brady (1982, 8), the man sentenced to be hanged and his executioner "provide the most dramatic opposition in the story between the rural and the urban worlds". The hangman is an outsider from the city and has no sensitivity to the country people's way of life. The convicted man can escape because the rurals are unwilling to help the executioner. The story ends with a hint that the story just told has become part of the local tradition:

> The grass has long been green on the graves of Shepherd Fennel and his frugal wife; the guests who made up the christening party have mainly followed their entertainers to the tomb; the baby in whose honour they all had met is matron in the sere and yellow leaf. But the arrival of the three strangers at the shepherd's that night, and the details connected therewith, is a story as well known as ever in the country about Higher Crowstairs.[57]

Another well-known volume of Hardy's short fiction is *Life's Little Ironies* (1894), in which the mode of narration is, again, traditional, with a well-defined narrative voice, but where Hardy's focus is on conventions of con-

[57] Other well-known stories included in the *Wessex Tales*, with the same features as the ones discussed here, are "The Distracted Preacher" (1879) and "The Withered Arm" (1888).

temporary middle-class society rather than vanishing rural life. A theme prominently explored is that of the unhappy marriage and unhappy relationships between men and women generally. "For Conscience' Sake", first published in 1891 in the *Fortnightly Review*, tells the story of a man who marries the woman he abandoned many years earlier. That this act of belated respectability might not be a source of happiness for those concerned is indicated in the narrator's ironic comment right at the story's beginning:

> Whether the utilitarian or the intuitive theory of the moral sense be upheld, it is beyond question that there are a few subtle-souled persons with whom the absolute gratuitousness of an act of reparation is an inducement to perform it; while exhortation as to its necessity would breed excuses for leaving it undone. The case of Mr. Millborne and Mrs. Frankland particularly illustrated this, and perhaps something more.

Millborne is middle-aged when he remembers the woman whom he has left pregnant because he thought she was below him. When he falls ill, he is plagued by his conscience and decides that he wants to undo this act of injustice. He finds the woman in a country town in a relatively prosperous and respectable condition. Posing as a widow, she has become "quite a recognized townswoman" who conducts a music and dancing school together with her now adult daughter. Although the woman does not want to get married, Millborne insists. Mother and daughter have to give up their school and live unhappily with Millborne in London. By accident, the daughter's fiancé discovers that Mr Millborne is not her adopted, but her real father and threatens that he will end a relationship which is not respectable enough for him. In one of 'life's little ironies', Millborne's attempt to restore respectability has turned into its opposite, and he is reproached by his wife: "Why did you show yourself in my world again, and raise this scandal upon my hard-won respectability – won by such weary years of labour as none will ever know!" Millborne then has no alternative but to provide his wife with a fortune and go abroad so that his daughter may still get married. Thanks to his conscience and sense of conventional propriety, Millborne ends in an unhappy and morally doubtful condition:

> As he formerly had been weighted with a bad conscience, so now was he burdened with the heavy thought which oppressed Antigone, that by honourable observance of a rite he had obtained for himself the reward of dishonourable laxity. Occasionally he had to be helped to his lodgings by his servant from the *Cercle* he frequented, through having imbibed a little too much liquor to be able to take care of himself. But he was harmless, and even when he had been drinking said little.

In a more popular mode than Hardy, the stories of H.G. Wells also deal with urgent concerns of the late nineteenth century. As J.R. Hammond (1992, 22) observes, Wells "arrived on the literary scene at a time of deep questioning in human affairs", and the characteristic themes of his stories "are *change*; the *precariousness of man*; the *frontier* dividing the world of reality from that of the imagination; and *new perspectives* on life. [...] from the outset metamorphosis was the leading motif of his fiction". But Wells wrote in a style and form notably distinct from Hardy's and particularly shaped to appeal to the mass audience of the contemporary periodicals. Harold Orel (1986, 173) notes that Wells used the new short-story market expertly and with great commercial success: "The mass-circulation market existed, and no writer of the 1890s understood better than Wells how to appeal to its imagination, its interest in science, its fears and hopes for the future – or how to make it pay." Like Kipling's, Wells's stories are quite short, and he often uses a structural pattern that is in line with Poe's idea of a unity of impression and effect – in particular an effect located at the story's very end. Many of his stories end with a surprise or at least a poignant sting, according to his own conviction expressed in "The Contemporary Novel" (1911) that

> [a] short story is, or should be, a simple thing; it aims at producing one single, vivid effect; it has to seize the attention at the outset, and never relaxing, gather it together more and more until the climax is reached. [...] it must explode and finish before interruption occurs or fatigue sets in. [...] A short story should go to its point as a man flies from a pursuing tiger: he pauses not for the daisies in his path, or to note the pretty moss on the tree he climbs for safety. (Wells 1925, 361f. and 365)

Many of Wells's stories are of the type which he himself referred to as 'scientific romance' and which are today referred to as 'science fiction', investigating problems which the progress of human science was likely to cause. In "The Lord of the Dynamos" (1894), an electric machine appears as a deity to the Asian assistant at a railway station, and in "The Plattner Story" (1896), the protagonist is a man "who has moved out of space into what is called the Fourth Dimension, and [...] has returned again to our world".

As a writer with socialist sympathies, Wells was also interested in the pressing social and political issues of his time: **"The Stolen Bacillus"** (1894) is about an anarchist who steals what he believes are dangerous bacilli that will kill the inhabitants of London but what in fact are only bacilli that will turn him blue. Wells also wrote in more serious modes, however. In "A Slip under the Microscope" (1896), Hill, a talented student of biology with a lower-middle-class background (his father is a cobbler), falls in love with a female fellow student from a more affluent family. Hill's rival, both for the woman and the best exam result, is Wedderburn, a man from the same class as the woman. This situation makes Hill take advantage of an accident – a slip of mind, actually – during his final exams. The task is to identify a slip (in the sense of specimen) under a microscope, and it is not supposed to be moved by the candidates. However, on reflex Hill does exactly this and is thus able to perform the task, not being observed by anybody. His love for the girl makes him use his advantage, but he suffers from his bad conscience and confesses his breach of honour to his professor, hoping that the latter will only set his mark down a grade. The professor, however, is a bureaucrat who will see that Hill is severely punished; Hill's career and his family's hopes for better life are ended therewith.

Many of Wells's stories, like Stevenson's, belong to the romance type in that they go beyond the experiences of everyday reality – like the stories of adventure, detection or the supernatural which were also particularly popular during the final decades of the nineteenth century.[58] In their special mode of reaction to contemporary society and culture, such romance-type stories bear a certain affinity to the 'aestheticist' short story of the 1890s, which was, in turn, complemented by a radical 'new realism'.[59]

### *The Aestheticist Story*

In simple terms, aestheticism was a movement which expressed criticism of contemporary life and the Victorian value system by setting art against it. It is significant that the fairy tale, with its penchant for the anti-mimetic, was revived by the aesthetes in general and Oscar Wilde in particular. In his dialogue-essay about the relationship between nature and art, "The Decay of Lying" (1891), Wilde has Vivian, one of his speakers, identify "the proper aim of Art" as "the telling of beautiful untrue things" (Wilde 1948, 992). It would be too simple, however, to consider the aestheticist short story – and aestheticism generally – as a reaction to contemporary reality which completely ignores this reality. Wilde's fairy tales, like the title story of *The Happy Prince and Other Tales* (1888), express a critique of contemporary society in their own terms. "The Happy Prince", for instance, rejects a hedonistic pose in favour of an active sympathy with the poor – treating the problem

---

[58] See Harris (1979, chapter 7) about 'romanticism'. See also the *Dictionary of Literary Biography*, 159 (1996), especially the introduction by William F. Naufftus.

[59] For more extensive discussions of the short-story types of the 1890s, to which the following sections are indebted, see Seiler-Franklin (1977), Harris (1979, chapter 6), Ahrends (1983) and Quadflieg (1988).

of poverty in a manner very different from the contemporary East End stories (see below, p. 113f.). A fairy tale by Kenneth Grahame, "The Reluctant Dragon" (one of the stories in his *Dream Days*, 1898), conveys a clear anti-war message while British imperialist engagement was at its height: a polite and tame dragon wishes to live in an English village and is eventually permitted to do so after the English national patron, Saint George – the dragon slayer – agrees to have a mock fight with him instead of a real one.

Furthermore, it is difficult to completely separate the aestheticist story and another, 'new-realist' type of story of the nineties. Both types were published in the *Yellow Book*, the publication most frequently associated with aestheticism; both have traits in common (as will become obvious below, pp. 108–110) and are usually collected side by side in period anthologies like Gerber (1967) and Stanford (1968). Short-story writers primarily associated with aestheticism include Arthur Symons, Henry Harland, Richard La Gallienne and Ernest Dowson.

Aestheticism gained significant inspiration from Walter Pater, in particular the programmatic "Conclusion" to his *Studies in the History of the Renaissance* (1868). Here Pater postulated that, since there is no longer a stable approach to reality, no longer any uncontested transcendental order, subjective impression is the central category for experiencing reality:

> At first sight experience seems to bury us under a flood of external objects [...] But when reflexion begins to act upon those objects they are dissipated under its influence; the cohesive force seems suspended like a trick of magic: each object is loosed into a group of impressions – colour, odour, texture – in the mind of the observer. [...] Every one of those impressions is the impression of the individual in his isolation, each mind keeping as a solitary prisoner its own dream of a world. (Pater 1982, 59f.)

The "Conclusion" ends with the phrase, "art comes to you professing frankly to give nothing but the highest quality to your moments as they pass, and simply for those moments' sake". (*ibid.*, 62) Art, according to this position, does not have to fulfil a direct social function, it does not express a 'moral' or reflect an objectively given reality. Instead, it devotes itself to the momentary, short-lived experience. Wendell V. Harris (1979, 110f.) notes to what use the short story could be put in the framework of such an aesthetic:

> Many writers of the 1880s and 1890s [...] turned with relief to the isolable, the detachable. The incompatibility of their views with those which supported the great nineteenth-century tradition of the novel is manifested in their frequent inability to master the longer form. But they were clear that quite another sort of vision had value, that the expression of that vision was the task of the short story, and that the legitimacy of that aim and that form was

still largely unrecognized. As Lena Milman wrote in an essay on Henry James published in the *Yellow Book* in 1895:

> 'It is not yet ours to realize how the most exquisite in life are just those passing emotions, those elusive impressions which it behoves the artist to go seeking; over them so cunningly to cast his net of words or colour as to preserve that emotion, that impression, for the delight of mankind forever. We are too apt to regard the short story as the cartoon for a possible novel, whereas any elaboration of it is as thankless a process as the development of a fresco from an easel-painting. The treatment, the pigment, the medium, the palette are other from the very beginning.'

As Harris (1979, 86) further points out, Henry James was of particular significance for the nineties writers because he provided a model

> not only in the careful adjustment of every portion of a story to the atmosphere, theme, and total effect of the work, but also in the tasteful but telling use of the language. To the extent that there was one figure toward which all the conscientious coterie around the *Yellow Book* looked for inspiration, it was James. In writing of the delights James offered to that privileged group, Ethel Coburn Mayne speaks of 'pages that shone and shimmered and sparkled, that spread and spilt and built before our eyes the grass and flowers and trees, the streams and brooks, the old grey churches and old rose-red houses making up the English landscape', and Lena Milman's 'Appreciation' of James for the *Yellow Book* in 1895 similarly comes back to the style again and again. Third, as everyone knows, James thought deeply about the precise point of view from which each story should be told, and the control of point of view is at least as, and probably more, important in the short story than in the novel.[60]

For the aestheticists, the main purpose of the work of art lies in its perfection *per se*. The short story with its brevity seemed a perfect medium for achieving the highly controlled form, expression through symbolism and the beauty of language to which they aspired in prose fiction as well as in poetry. It also seemed ideal for capturing the experience of the isolated moment. Pater's "Conclusion" underlines the singularity of each individual consciousness's reaction to the world. The aesthetes of the nineties paid special attention to the workings of consciousness, the individual's heterogeneous thoughts and sense impressions, thus developing a story that deviated from the traditionally 'closed' and homogeneous story and paving

---

[60] Milman's "A Few Notes upon Mr. James" first appeared in the *Yellow Book*, 7 (October 1895), 71–83. On James's importance for the aestheticist short story, see also Quadflieg (1988, 58f.) and Shaw (1983, chapter 3).

the way for the modernist story of the early twentieth century. The new aesthetic of the aesthetes is most apparent where their stories break away from plot and, in a cultural environment in which the discipline of psychology was undergoing significant renewal,[61] focus instead on states of consciousness and emotion, moments of subjective experience and subjective sense impression (hence also the transfer to this literature of the term 'impressionism' from art history).[62]

Since the relationship between art and reality was a prominent concern of the nineties aesthetes, it is natural that artist figures feature prominently in their stories:[63] writers, painters and musicians, music being, for the aesthetes, the purest form of art. Many nineties stories draw the artist as a tragic figure who fails to cope with life. Their artists are outsiders of society and the stories provide sketches of their complex psychology, making high use of the various techniques for presenting consciousness in fiction.

Arthur Symons's "Christian Trevalga" (first coll. 1905), for instance, presents the reflections of a pianist who has had a mental breakdown at the age of thirty-six and now waits for a doctor to tell him whether he will recover. While he waits, he ponders about his development as an artist, which went hand in hand with his growing isolation from society and human

---

[61] See, for example, the work of William James, whose *The Principles of Psychology* appeared in 1890. The *Principles* were the first publication to use the term 'stream of consciousness', referring to the flow of all kinds of impressions that impinge on an individual's consciousness along with his or her rational thoughts. Freud's psychoanalytical method – using free association – was developed in the course of the 1890s. *The Interpretation of Dreams* (*Die Traumdeutung*) appeared in 1899, but it took time until his ideas were popularized.

[62] Ferguson (1994, 219f.) notes that the short story exemplifies the new aesthetic more clearly than longer works: "the short story, because it has fewer 'optional' narrative elements in its structural 'slots', manifests its formal allegiances to impressionism even more obviously than does the novel and, consequently, seems more radically different from earlier short fiction than the impressionist novel seems different from the realistic novel that preceded it."

[63] Quadflieg (1988) devotes her entire chapter 4 to the theme of art in the nineties short story. The nineties art(ist) stories had predecessors among the Pre-Raphaelites, as Harris (1979, 72) also notes. Artist figures are central, for example, in D.G. Rossetti's "Hand and Soul" (1850) and William Morris's "The Story of the Unknown Church" (1856). "Hand and Soul" is about a Renaissance artist, the painter Chiaro, with a coda on how his masterpiece strikes a visitor of Florence in 1847; Morris's "The Story of the Unknown Church" is narrated by a voice from the past: the master-mason of a medieval abbey that has long disappeared. Walter Pater provided another model for the nineties writers of artist stories with his *Imaginary Portraits* (1887). In "The Child in the House" (first publ. in *Macmillan's Magazine*, 1878), a man remembers his childhood experience of a house; the sense of security he then felt, but also his first experience of *Weltschmerz*, his growing sense of beauty and fear of death.

company. With its high amount of free indirect discourse for rendering the character's consciousness, the beginning is characteristic of the story as a whole:

> He had never known what it was to feel the earth solid under his feet. And now, while he waited for the doctor who was to decide whether he might still keep his place in the world, and make what he could of all that remained to him of his life, the past began to come back to him, blurred a little in his memory, and with whole spaces blotted out of it, but in a steady return upon himself, as the past, it is said, comes back to a drowning man at the instant before death. There was that next step to take, the step that frightened him; was it into another, more painful, kind of oblivion? He was still an artist, his fingers were still his own; but had the man all gone out of him, the power to live for himself, when his fingers were no longer on the keyboard? That was to be decided; and the past was trying to make its own comment on the situation.

Trevalga's withdrawal from the world is particularly painful where he rejects the woman he loves; the attitude towards marriage expressed in the following passage clearly violates the prevalent Victorian notion of marriage as a happy haven:

> To live with a woman, thought Christian, in the same house, the same room with her, is as if the keeper were condemned to live by day and sleep by night in the wild beast's cage. It is to be on one's guard at every minute, to apprehend always the claws behind the caressing softness of their padded coverings, to be continually ready to amuse one's dangerous slave, with one's life for a forfeit. The strain of it, the trial to the nerves, the temper!

Living exclusively for his art, Christian finally suffers the breakdown during which his identity seems to dissolve and he seems to entirely lose connection with material reality. Five years after the consultation for which Trevalga is waiting, he dies in an asylum; he has gone mad. The story ends with what seems an exuberant rejection of plot: a loose collection of Trevalga's notes about music, which are also a tribute to art. The story's concern with illness and death marks it as a product of a period fascinated with decadence.

The same can be said of a story by Ernest Dowson, "The Dying of Frances Donne: A Study" (first publ. in the *Savoy*, 1896), which violates a taboo in that it attempts to depict the very moment of death itself. In this story, a thirty-five-year-old surgeon who has long been fascinated by death notices that he suffers from an illness which will soon end his own life. He goes to France – the country paradigmatically associated with *décadence* – so that he can die alone: "Since Death is coming to me, said Francis

Donne to himself, let me meet it, a stranger in a strange land, with only strange faces round me and the kind indifference of strangers, instead of the intolerable pity of friends." As a man who has exiled himself thus, Donne experiences his approaching end with great intensity. This experience, especially during his sleepless nights, is again presented in long passages of free indirect discourse:

> He had been all his life absorbed in science; he had dissected, how many bodies? and in what anatomy had he ever found a soul? Yet if his avocations, his absorbing interest in physical phenomena had made him somewhat a materialist, it had been almost without his consciousness. The sensible, visible world of matter had loomed so large to him, that merely to know that had seemed to him sufficient. All that might conceivably lie outside it, he had, without negation, been content to regard as outside his province.
>
> And now, in his weakness, in the imminence of approaching dissolution, his purely physical knowledge seemed but a vain possession, and he turned with a passionate interest to what had been said and believed from time immemorial by those who had concentrated their intelligence on that strange essence, which might after all be the essence of one's personality, which might be that sublimated consciousness – the Soul – actually surviving the infamy of the grave?

The *fin-de-siècle* reaction against Victorian materialism could hardly be expressed more explicitly than in this passage. As has been pointed out above (p. 85), the nineties were a period when stories of the supernatural, about life after death, enjoyed particular popularity. Dowson's story, however, stops short of suggestions of the transcendental when it renders Donne's moment of dying, that is, an absolute threshold experience. Behind the threshold, the story suggests, there seems to be nothing, and this makes its ending even more provocative than through the depiction of dying *per se*:

> All that was distorted in life was adjusted and justified in the light of his sudden knowledge. *Beati mortui* ... and then the great tiredness swept over him once more, and a fainter consciousness, in which he could yet just dimly hear, as in a dream, the sound of Latin prayers, and feel the application of the oils upon all the issues and approaches of his wearied sense; then utter unconsciousness, while pulse and heart gradually grew fainter until both ceased. And that was all.

The aesthetes frequently challenged established norms and decorum. The violation of taboos is an aspect which their stories share with the work of writers predominantly associated with the so-called 'new' realism, like Arthur Morrison, Henry Nevinson, Arthur St John Adcock, Hubert Crackanthorpe, George Gissing or Ella D'Arcy and 'George Egerton'. However, as mentioned before, dividing lines between the two groups are porous. The new-realist writers also explored their characters' states of mind, and the very titles of collections of stories by D'Arcy – *Monochromes* (1895) – and Egerton – *Keynotes* (1893) and *Discords* (1894) – suggest impressionism and a relationship with the neighbouring arts. Many of Gissing's stories are distinguished by a naturalist attention to the seedy and ugly side of life, but their protagonists are often characters with artistic ambitions. In "The House of Cobwebs" (1900), for example, a young writer without money desperately struggles to finish a manuscript; when he has completed it under many sacrifices, he cannot at first find a publisher.

*The New-Realist Story*

The 'new realism' was inspired by naturalism, a literary programme nourished by post-Darwinist thought, proposing that human beings are essentially *animal* creatures guided not by a higher spirit but by natural forces: by heredity and by their respective environment. The most influential proponent of naturalist fiction was the French novelist Emile Zola, who had prominent followers among American writers whose fiction provided a close and notoriously frank 'documentation' of all aspects of human nature and life, including taboo areas. British writers did not adopt this programme with the same radicalism, so that the notion of a 'new', more outspoken realism has been found more adequate to describe their work than naturalism. As Wendell V. Harris (1979, 112f.) notes for the short story specifically, the 'new realism' did not exist as an explicit programme and notions about it were vague:

> There was no common agreement as to the definition of realism, nor was there agreement among the many opponents of its more startling forms as to whether the new movement was to be regarded as an offense against aesthetics, morality, religion, or metaphysics. On the broadest level, writers were simply trying to expand the subject matter of the short story to include a wider spectrum of contemporary human life. This quite naturally led to the treatment of subjects hitherto taboo. Since these had a novel fascination, adultery, seduction, and the sordid in general were certainly unrealistically prominent; the unfortunate result was that most critics and reviewers writing for the popular papers and magazines equated the new realism with daring subject matter, overlooking the realists' attempts to find fiction-worthy ways of treating commonplace situations and events.

Critique of the new realists' over-explicitness was voiced not only in the popular magazines. In the first volume of the *Yellow Book* (1894), the publisher and critic Arthur Waugh (1894, 204) attacked this manner of writing as too gross and demanded greater restraint: he conceded that the "truest fiction of any given century [...] must be a criticism of life, must reflect its surroundings", but that there was also "a sort of middle point, a centre of equilibrium, to pass which is to disturb and overset the entire fabric of his labours. Midway between liberty and licence, in literature as in morals, stands the pivot of good taste, the centre-point of art". To Waugh, contemporary realists were overstepping limits, allowing freedom of speech, a national virtue of the English, to degenerate into "a licence which some of us cannot but view with regret and apprehension". (212) His position gained him a sharp reply from the writer Hubert Crackanthorpe in the next volume of the *Yellow Book*. Crackanthorpe proclaimed the essential non-morality of art: "Theoretically, Art is non-moral. She is not interested in any ethical code of any age or any nation, except in so far as the breach or observance of that code may furnish her with material on which to work." (Crackanthorpe 1894, 265) A position prominent in the aestheticist programme is used here to defend the outspokenness of the new realism.

Prominent in the new-realist stories is the theme of the problematic marriage and failed relationships between the sexes generally – that is, a theme also found, as we have seen, in the work of Hardy and addressed by Kipling in the colonial context, while earlier in the century Elizabeth Gaskell had still been able to write about marriage in more positive terms (see above, p. 79). Marriage, with its prescribed gender roles, was one of the hallowed Victorian institutions – praised, for instance, in John Ruskin's essay "Of Queen's Gardens" (in *Sesame and Lilies*, 1865) – which had come under increasingly critical inquiry and become a subject of public debate as social and legislative changes (in particular the Married Women's Property Acts of 1870 and 1882) granted married women greater independence from their husbands. Portraying failed marriages was an effective way of criticizing not only this particular institution but also Victorianism in general.

Nineties marriage stories include Ella D'Arcy's "Irremediable" (1894, in the *Yellow Book*) and "A Marriage" (1896, in the *Yellow Book*), or Hubert Crackanthorpe's "Embers" (first coll. in *Wreckage*, 1893). In "Irremediable", a young man gets married to a woman from the lower classes, a seamstress, and the unsuitable relationship ruins his life. The story ends with the young man in a posture of despair: "But when he understood the terror of his Hatred, he laid his head upon his arms and wept, not facile tears like Esther's, but tears wrung out from his agonising unavailing regret." In "A Marriage", D'Arcy writes about another misalliance; a woman of lower social standing than her middle-class husband uses him for her own social advancement. The development of this union is narrated by the husband's sympathetic friend, who strongly dislikes the woman. Love between the partners soon dies, and when the husband is terminally ill, his cold-hearted wife seems to look forward to widowhood. In Crackanthorpe's "Embers", an occasional writer lives a lonely life after his wife has deserted him. She has become an alcoholic and possibly a prostitute, and when on meeting him again by chance she starts to ruin him. The story ends with a scene in which both are in despair.

A considerable number of these stories about marriage relationships were written by women[64] – though not necessarily by women sympathizing with women. In D'Arcy's stories, the women who ruin their husbands' lives are characterized in obviously negative terms. Other women writers of the nineties, however, were so-called New Women with a feminist interest; their fiction often depicts the new type of middle- and upper-class femininity and the reaction it provoked.[65] 'Victoria Cross' [Annie Sophie Cory], for example, portrays an unconventional woman in "Theodora: A Fragment", which first appeared in the *Yellow Book* in 1895. Theodora is a wealthy and independent heiress who will lose her fortune should she get married; it is indicated, however, that this will not prevent her from having the sexual experiences she is obviously interested in: "A girl like that, if she can't marry, will probably forego nothing but the ceremony." Theodora openly signals her sympathy and desire to the male narrator of the story:

> That impulse towards some physical demonstration, that craving for physical contact, which attacks us suddenly with its terrific impetus, and chokes and stifles us, ourselves, beneath it, blinding us to all except itself, rushed upon me then, walking beside her in the dark passage; and at that instant Theodora sighed.
>
> 'I am tired', she said languidly. 'May I take your arm?' and her hand touched me.
>
> I did not offer her my arm, I flung it round her neck, bending back her head upon it, so that her lips were just beneath my own as I leant over her, and I pressed mine on them in a delirium of passion. [...]
>
> [...] I sought her eyes in the dusk.
>
> [...] There was no confusion nor embarrassment in them, they were full of the hot, clear, blinding light of passion; and I knew there would be no need to crave forgiveness.

---

64 For an anthology of women's marriage stories of the 1890s see Bennett (1996). Women's stories of the period are also collected in Showalter (1993).

65 For an anthology of stories about the New Woman, by female and male writers, see Richardson (2002).

To Valerie Shaw (1983, 223), the New Women's use of the short story "to urge social change" is an example of the genre's "disposition towards 'frontier subjects'. When women as a class saw themselves reaching a threshold, so it might be argued, they turned to a form which allowed them to combine 'greater artistic stringency, and a broader moral permissiveness'." Elaine Showalter, in the introduction to her anthology *Daughters of Decadence* (1993, viiif.), observes that "[f]or late-nineteenth-century women writers in particular, the short story offered flexibility and freedom from the traditional plots of the three-decker Victorian novel, plots which invariably ended in the heroine's marriage or her death. In contrast to the sprawling three-decker, the short story emphasised psychological intensity and formal innovation."[66] A story by the feminist writer 'George Egerton' [Mary Chavelita Dunne Bright] is typical of the nineties story with its urban London setting and focus on moods and impressions. At the same time, it also exemplifies the hostility that existed between the feminist writers and the 'decadents'. As Showalter (1993, x) notes, "the decadent artist was invariably male, and decadence, as a hyper-aesthetic movement, defined itself against the feminine and biological creativity of women", so that many New Women writers wrote against this misogyny. Egerton's **"A Lost Masterpiece: A City Mood, Aug. '93"**, first published in the *Yellow Book* in 1894, renders an impression of London street life from the perspective of a decadent artist who believes that he has the inspiration for a masterpiece but then is disturbed by the appearance of an energetic woman in modern, unfeminine attire. The story is remarkable for its subversive point of view: at first, from the artist's perspective, the woman is described in highly negative terms, she appears as a caricature of the unfeminine New Woman. But it then becomes obvious that the artists's view is distorted and that it is he who is caricatured in the story – as an aestheticist dandy too convinced of

[66] Showalter also points out, however, that it was precisely because of their writing of short stories rather than novels, that the women writers of the 1890s have tended to be overlooked in literary histories of that period. (viii) Her anthology includes a story by Charlotte Mew, "A White Night" (first publ. 1903 in *The Temple Bar*), which uses the popular ghost-story genre to subvert the conventional presentation of femininity. In this story set in the year 1876, a woman is confronted, during her honeymoon trip, with a highly disturbing vision of a 'medieval' women's fate, but it is unclear whether what she sees is an apparition from the past or something still occurring in the present – though a present that is alienated by a foreign, Spanish and thus Catholic setting. In a convent church in Andalusia, the woman, her husband and her brother witness how a woman is buried alive by priests and monks. The horror is increased by the fact that the male spectators do not interfere but appear to be voyeuristically fascinated by the spectacle, while the woman is petrified by fear. As Showalter comments in her introduction (xviif.), "[t]he ritual scene seems like a warning of female destiny in the contexts of patriarchy".

his artistic qualities which are, in fact, so slight that his inspiration vanishes at the mere sight of the allegedly ugly woman. The aestheticist pose devalidates itself, while the New Woman is clearly marked as a presence in London streets that is visible enough to disturb traditional perceptions of gender.

With its treatment of taboo subjects – failed marriages, 'illegitimate' relationships, (female) sexual desire, female emancipation – the stories of the nineties exemplify the short story's particular suitability for "dealing with the unconventional, in relationships, in attitudes, in behaviour" (Shaw 1983, 223), and its status as "the mode preferred by those writers who are not writing from within a fixed and stable cultural frame work [...,] who find themselves to be personally opposed to the society in which they live and for whom the idea of society and shared values is problematic" (Hanson 1985, 12). This is also obvious in the new-realist stories which engage with lower-class life.

The 1890s were a period when the urban working class, the London East End and its social problems were discovered as a literary subject, also by writers of short stories. Many of these stories deal with adultery, alcoholism, wife-beating, illegitimate children and other subjects transgressing the limits of conventional respectability. The stories in Arthur Morrison's *Tales of Mean Streets* (1894), for example, were written to present the East End to middle-class readers for whom this was a foreign part of London about which they had many misconceptions. The sketch of "A Street", first published 1891 in *Macmillan's Magazine* and later used as the introduction to *Mean Streets*,[67] directly addresses these misconceptions:

> This street is in the East End. There is no need to say in the East End of what. The East End is a vast city, as famous in its way as any the hand of man has made. But who knows the East End? It is down through Cornhill and out beyond Leadenhall Street and Aldgate Pump, one will say: a shocking place, where he once went with a curate; an evil plexus of slums that hide human creeping things; where filthy men and women live on penn'orths of gin, where collars and clean shirts are decencies unknown, where every citizen wears a black eye, and none ever combs his hair. [...] Many and misty are the people's notions of the East End; and each is commonly but the distorted shadow of a minor feature. Foul slums there are in the East End, of course, as there are in the West; want and misery there are, as wherever a host is gathered together to fight for food. But they are not often spectacular in kind.

[67] The other stories were originally published in Henley's *National Observer* between December 1892 and early 1894.

Although written against stereotypical conceptions, Morrison's East End stories too portray dismal living conditions. "Behind the Shade" depicts how, in a house aspiring to respectability, a mother and her daughter starve to death. In "Lizerunt", a young worker at a pickle factory gets married to a man by whom she is regularly abused. When all their money is used up, he sends her into the street to prostitute herself:

> It was more than Billy could bear: so that, ''Ere', he said one night, 'I've 'ad enough o' this. You go and get some money; go on.'
>
> 'Go an' git it?' replied Lizer. 'O yus. That's easy, ain't it? "Go an' git it", says you. 'Ow?'
>
> 'Any'ow – I don' care. Go on.'
>
> 'Wy', replied Lizer, looking up with wide eyes, 'd'ye think I can go an' pick it up in the street?'
>
> 'Course you can. Plenty others does, don't they?'
>
> 'Gawd, Billy ... wot d'ye mean?'
>
> 'Wot I say; plenty others does it. Go on – you ain't so bleed'n' innocent as all that. Go an' see Sam Cardew. Go on – 'ook it.'
>
> Lizer, who had been kneeling at the child's floor-bed, rose to her feet, pale faced and bright of eye.
>
> 'Stow kiddin', Billy', she said. 'You don't mean that. I'll go round to the fact'ry in the mornin'; p'raps they'll take me on temp'ry.'
>
> 'Dam the fact'ry.'
>
> He pushed her into the passage. 'Go on – you git me some money, if ye don't want yer bleed'n' 'ead knocked auf.'
>
> There was a scuffle in the dark passage, with certain blows, a few broken words, and a sob. Then, the door slammed and Lizer Chope was in the windy street.

This excerpt illustrates the extensive use which Morrison makes of the East End's sociolect; other writers, like Henry Nevinson in *Neighbours of Ours* (1894), even use it in the narrator's speech.[68]

---

[68] Nevinson is included in an anthology of working-class stories of the 1890s, Keating (1971), alongside Morrison, Kipling, Gissing, Edwin Pugh, Arthur St John Adcock and Clarence Rook. A writer of another kind of East End story was Israel Zangwill, whose main topic was the East End's Jewish community. "A Rose of the Ghetto" (first publ. in *The Idler*, 1894) is a humorous story involving problems with a matchmaker. W.W. Jacobs wrote stories set in the milieu of the London waterfront, which were collected as *Many Cargoes* (1896).

*Summary*

By the 1890s, the short story had come a long way from a genre which in the early and mid-Victorian years had still been dominated by the novel. During the final decades of the nineteenth century, a more favourable market helped the short story to secure itself a more prominent position within the contemporary literary landscape. It manifested itself in consciously 'literary' forms which explored new ways of writing fiction, but was, at the same time, a popular genre attractive to a new mass readership of a new mass form of publication. It addressed central issues of contemporary culture and was, at the same time, used to express that which was not yet acceptable in the culture's dominant discourse structure: whether a concern with working-class life or the new positions of emancipated women. With its variety of modes and themes, the short story in nineties Britain paved the way for the genre's great success during the early twentieth century when the market for short stories was, as Harold Orel (1986, 191) writes, "enormous, and apparently insatiable".

## 4. The Short Story in the Twentieth Century

*A Modern Genre for Modern Times?*

That the short story increased its standing in the literary system and its popularity with the audience even further during the first decades of the twentieth century has been related to the great demand for it on the periodical market. It has also been explained by the short story's suitability for capturing the *condition moderne* with its sense of hurry, fragmentation and uncertainty and the feeling that only in brief moments can significance be looked for and found. Valerie Shaw (1983, 17) quotes G.K. Chesterton, who in his book *Charles Dickens* (1906) considered the "modern attraction to the short story" to be "a sign of a real sense of fleetingness and fragility; it means that existence is only an impression, and, perhaps, only an illusion. [...] We have no instinct of anything ultimate and enduring beyond the episode." An anonymous author in the *Times Literary Supplement* wrote on "The Modern Short Story" in 1925:

> The present age is frequently, and with some justice, stigmatized as the misbegotten child of superficiality and hustle. [...] We can no longer with any confidence hope for long leisurely novels of such solid build and ample scope as the older masters delighted in; the spirit of the times is not friendly

> to epic poetry [...]. This is the age of Snap, a brisk little deity with a squint, who manifests himself ubiquitously in short sentences, short gossiping paragraphs, and short stories. [...]
>
> The short story, whether we like it or not, has come to stay; the man in the street is a man in a hurry; he has a train to catch, business letters to write, and probably a garden that demands his attention. Until he is supplied with something better, but equally brief, he will continue to corrode his brains with the scandalously bad fiction to be found in our monthly magazines. And until the most characteristic literary form of the age is taken seriously, by writers and critics alike, its artistic advance will remain imperceptible. [...]
>
> If we examine those tales which yield us most potent aesthetic pleasure, we shall find that each of them exists for the sake of this illuminated and illuminating moment, of beauty or of terror, of wonder or of sheer surprise [...]. This moment, which may do its work in us even though itself remain undetected, is what the short story writer gives us; it is this that we retain. (in Weber and Greiner 1977, 106f. and 109)

Later critics have repeated such observations. To H.E. Bates (1965, 222f.), the short story belongs to an age marked by the dislocations caused by two world wars: "The war of 1914–18 prepared the ground for a new story; the intermediate period of distrust and dislocation fostered it; and it would not surprise me very much if the literature of the second war, and its inevitable aftermath of still more distrustful dislocation, found in the short story the essential medium for whatever it has to say." John Bayley (1988, 182f.) believes that the short story came into its own only in

> an age in which God has disappeared and solutions have ceased to be expected. From being [...] a miniature novel, with a point and meaning commensurate with its concentration, the short story becomes the vehicle for the sense of life's unfulfilment, the momentariness of its experiences. It can preserve only short significances, temporary enlightenment. And indeed novels themselves, like Virginia Woolf's, may begin to resemble the short story.[69]

As a matter of fact, not only did novels come to resemble short stories, but in the early twentieth century the cycle of linked stories – like Joyce's *Dubliners* – gained importance as an alternative to the novel. Susan Garland Mann (1989, 19), in her discussion of the twentieth-century story cycle,

---

[69] For similar statements, see – among many others – Elizabeth Bowen's "Preface" to *The Faber Book of Modern Short Stories* (Bowen 1994); Nadine Gordimer's essay "The Flash of Fireflies" (in May 1994, 263-267); Kilchenmann (1967, 194) and Ferguson (1989, 191).

emphasizes the "tension between the separateness and interdependence of stories" as a characteristic that makes it particularly suitable for expressing modern disruptedness.[70]

As we shall see (pp. 127–130), it was the modernists, with their special and experimental use of the genre, who most radically explored its affinity with modern life. More traditional ways of story-telling also persisted, however, and enjoyed wide popularity. After all, many writers who had begun their careers in the 1880s and 90s – with Kipling and Wells in the forefront – continued their careers as writers of short stories during the early decades of the twentieth century, and sub-genres like the ghost story and the detective story continued to flourish during Edwardian times.

The big and popular magazines encouraged types of stories which had proved successful with the mass readership, and the 'commercial', market-orientated story emerged on a grand scale. It was written to schemes recommended in many manuals for aspiring authors,[71] and it was usually of the strongly plot-based variety. As Richard Harter Fogle (1985, 101) notes: "In the 1920's and 30's there were many illustrated magazines on both sides of the Atlantic paying high for good humorous short stories, five-to-eight-thousand-word episodes, complete with sunny plot, a beginning, middle and end, and the young happily paired off in the fade-out." In 1936, a commentator in the *Times Literary Supplement* on "The Short Story To-Day" lamented the commercial writer's prime interest in

> amusing without perturbing, and dealing therefore with essentially standardized situations, characters and emotions, seeking not like the artist to explore life but instead to reduce it to a series of familiar and accepted attitudes. The demand of art for a total fidelity to one's vision admits of no such conformity; its very life is in the new, the unique, the unpredictable. It is not suggested, of course, that the mass of successful writers of the commercial short story do not write often, perhaps generally, with a perfect honesty; what must be doubted is whether they can be, or can remain, under such conditions, authentic artists, more than trivially originative minds. (in Weber and Greiner 1977, 123f.)

---

[70] Dunn and Morris (1995) prefer the term 'composite novel' but also emphasize the structural tension between the cycle's wholeness and the autonomy of its individual stories as a compositional principle of this mode of publication. They trace a number of composite novels in the nineteenth century but identify the twentieth as the heyday of the form: "Only in the twentieth century did the composite novel become a mature genre." (1)

[71] Manuals for commercial stories appeared not only in the United States, but also in Britain. See, for example, R.F. Foster, *How to Write and Sell Short Stories* (London 1926) or Michael Joseph, *Short Story Writing for Profit* (London 1932).

However, writers with more originative minds also found encouraging outlets – particularly in the little magazines which flourished in the 1920s and especially the 1930s, like John Lehmann's *New Writing*, the first series of which appeared 1936–1938. As Thomas O. Beachcroft (1968, 192) observes: "*The Criterion*, edited by T.S. Eliot, *The London Mercury*, edited by J.C. Squire, and afterwards by R.A. Scott-James, *The Adelphi*, edited by Middleton Murry, and later by Richard Rees; these and other monthlies and quarterlies were all taking short stories and providing in themselves a variety of critical selection."[72] The short story between the wars was also significantly supported by influential anthologies, like Elizabeth Bowen's *Faber Book of Modern Short Stories* (1936), and, in particular, annual anthologies which preserved the 'best' stories drawn from the periodicals. Of the latter, Edward J. O'Brien and John Cournos's *Best British Short Stories* (established in 1923 with a collection of stories that had been published during the previous year) became a landmark. As Cournos wrote in his introduction to *The Best British Short Stories of 1922*, the series' programme was to "gather and save from obscurity every year those tales by English authors which are published in English and American periodicals and are worth preserving in permanent form. It is well known that short-story writers in Anglo-Saxon countries have not the same chance of publishing their wares in book form as their more fortunate colleagues, the novelists." (xviii) It was not only the little magazines from which the series was drawn. The stories in the first volume, for example, were originally published in a range of periodicals that included the *Strand Magazine, Cornhill Magazine, The Graphic, The Dial, English Review, Story-Teller, Ladies' Home Journal*, among others. Each issue of *Best British Short Stories* also incorporated the *Yearbook of the British Short Story*, with listings of the periodicals publishing short stories, of articles on the short story in British periodicals, of individual short story volumes and of distinctive short stories. These supplements indicate the extent to which a genre awareness had by then been established.

The first decades of the twentieth century were essential, then, for stabilizing the genre and strengthening its status in the literary system in various respects. Masses of more traditionally narrated stories were produced for – and found – a mass readership. At the same time, a modernist aesthetic tested and expanded the established notion of the short story. As the following sections will point out, both the 'traditionalists' and the 'modernists' employed the genre to react to the social and cultural issues which Britain experienced from Edwardian days to the years of the Second World War.

---

[72] On the twentieth-century magazine scene in Britain before the Second World War, see also Sullivan (1986), in particular the introduction by Muriel Mellown.

*Traditionalists I: Humorists and Satirists*

The most obviously traditional form of story-telling in the early twentieth century was the story that was still clearly plot-orientated and employed an explicit narrator figure. A type of story which enjoyed particular popularity (and hence dominated the 'commercial' story) was the kind whose plot worked its way up to a point, to a clever surprise ending, to a twist of circumstance for which the American writer O. Henry had become famous. In Britain, this story type was often used for social critique in the humorous or more harshly satirical mode (and thus continued earlier traditions found in the eighteenth-century's *Spectator* stories or, more recently, the humorous stories and sketches of Victorian times; see above pp. 76–78).

'Saki' and P.G. Wodehouse were the prime (and enormously prolific) practitioners of the short 'comedy of manners' in prose during the 1910s and 1920s. Their principal target was British class society, especially the fashionable circles. Their great success can be explained not only with a skilled use of the short form, but also the topicality of their themes in a society whose traditional class structure was upset by the continuing rise of the middle classes and increasing radicalism among the working classes (a topic also addressed, as we have already seen, by H.G. Wells).

Saki is another short-story writer experienced in journalism (he worked for the *Daily Express* and the *Morning Post*). Many of his stories first appeared in the *Westminster Gazette*. His early 'Reginald' stories, published from 1901 onwards, centre around a young London dandy and satirize types of Edwardian society. "Reginald", the first story collected in *Reginald* (1904), is told from the perspective of an older female relative and presents its protagonist in the context of a garden party during which he manages to provoke the more conservative characters present – like the representative of the Empire and a paragon of Puritan morality in the excerpt quoted below. At the same time, however, Reginald is also part of the social setting and not exempt from critique. Implicitly, the story suggests that Reginald provokes his elders not from a position of social critique or even outright class consciousness but because he enjoys the pose of the *enfant terrible*:

> It must have been ten minutes later [...] when I perceived, out of the corner of my eye, that Reginald was not where I had left him, and that the *marrons glacés* were untasted. At the same moment I became aware that old Colonel Mendoza was essaying to tell his classic story of how he introduced golf into India, and that Reginald was in dangerous proximity. There are occasions when Reginald is caviare to the Colonel.
>
> 'When I was at Poona in '76 –'

> 'My dear Colonel,' purred Reginald, 'fancy admitting such a thing! Such a give-away for one's age! I wouldn't admit being on this planet in '76.' [...] The colonel went to the colour of a fig that has attained great ripeness, and Reginald, ignoring my efforts to intercept him, glided away to another part of the lawn. I found him a few minutes later happily engaged in teaching the youngest Rampage boy the approved theory of mixing absinthe, within full earshot of his mother. Mrs. Rampage occupies a prominent place in local Temperance movements.

Saki's "Tobermory" (1909) is a more fantastic story in which the cat Tobermory has been taught to understand and speak human language. This causes dismay in the upper-class family to whom the cat belongs and their guests, especially when Toby starts to uncover their secrets and hypocrisy: "The panic had indeed become general. A narrow ornamental balustrade ran in front of most of the bedroom windows at the Towers, and it was recalled with dismay that this had formed a favourite promenade for Tobermory at all hours, whence he could watch the pigeons – and heaven knew what else besides." To save their reputation, the party are prepared to poison Tobermory, but he is eventually granted a more natural death when he is killed by a rival tom-cat. **"Esmé"** (1911) also effectively contrasts animal and human behaviour when it raises the question which is the worse hyena: the animal that kills a gipsy child because it is in its nature to kill, or two pitiless society women.

One of Saki's most frequently anthologized stories is "Sredni Vashtar" (1910). The story is less openly satirical than others, but it also relentlessly exposes the human shortcomings of a certain class of people and relates human to animal life – although here the animal seems to be on the victim's side. An orphaned ten-year old boy, Conradin, lives unhappily in his guardian's household. Mrs De Ropp is unsympathetic, strict and stiflingly overprotective. Conradin hates the 'Woman' and escapes into a fantasy world in which a ferret he secretly keeps in a tool-shed becomes a powerful god: "Every Thursday, in the dim and musty silence of the tool-shed, he worshipped with mystic and elaborate ceremonial before the wooden hutch where dwelt Sredni Vashtar, the great ferret." The boy prays that Sredni Vashtar will do "one thing" for him, that is, rid him of the Woman, and eventually, this fantasy seems to come true. When Mrs De Ropp enters the shed to find out what the boy might be hiding there, she does not leave it alive. Instead, the ferret comes out, with "dark wet stains around the fur of jaws and throat". While the maid who finds the body wonders how to break the news of her mistress's death to the boy, Conradin, in the story's pointed ending, revengefully indulges in the buttered toast which his guardian has so often denied him.

During the 1920s and 1930s, P.G. Wodehouse enjoyed great popularity; many of his collections of stories still remain on the British market even at the beginning of the twenty-first century. Wodehouse is particularly famous for his stories around the characters of Bertie Wooster, a somewhat silly young man-about-town and his reliable valet, Jeeves. Jeeves rescues Bertie from all kinds of absurd situations which usually involve his aunts and young women. Wodehouse characters are typically rooted in the British upper-class milieu of the inter-war period. The criticism which the stories convey of this milieu is mild compared to Saki's, and usually found between the lines, like in the following example. The first story in the collection *The Inimitable Jeeves* (1923) begins with an exchange between Bertie and Jeeves:

> 'Morning, Jeeves,' I said.
> 'Good morning, sir,' said Jeeves.
> He put the good old cup of tea softly on the table by my bed, and I took a refreshing sip. Just right, as usual. [...] A most amazing cove, Jeeves. So dashed competent in every respect. [...] Every other valet I've ever had used to barge into my room in the morning while I was still asleep, causing much misery: but Jeeves seems to know when I'm awake by a sort of telepathy. He always floats in with the cup exactly two minutes after I come to life. Makes a deuce of a lot of difference to a fellow's day.
> 'How's the weather, Jeeves?'
> 'Exceptionally clement, sir.'
> 'Anything in the papers?'
> 'Some slight friction threatening in the Balkans, sir. Otherwise, nothing.'
> 'I say, Jeeves, a man I met at the club last night told me to put my shirt on Privateer for the two o'clock race this afternoon. How about it?'
> 'I should not advocate it, sir. The stable is not sanguine.'

Such passages with direct speech thrive on a style highly typical of the characters' social environment. Bertie speaks in the jargon adopted by the young gentleman of the twenties, and Jeeves's speech is marked not only by professional politeness but also by a hyper-refined vocabulary which clashes with the deliberately casual diction Bertie prefers. Bertie is mocked even though he is the first-person narrator. He may be a likable and harmless representative of his class, but he is clearly more interested in his lifestyle and trivial pursuits like horse racing than in serious affairs. He is therefore unaware of the irony with which Jeeves refers, in deliberate understatement, to world politics: "some slight friction threatening in the Balkans". To the story's original readers, any 'friction' in the Balkans would have roused alarming memories of the causes of the First World War.

More bitingly critical of the upper classes and contemporary manners are the cynical stories which Aldous Huxley and Evelyn Waugh wrote before the Second World War. In Huxley's "The Gioconda Smile" (first coll. 1922), for instance, the male protagonist, Mr Hutton, is a careless womanizer with an ailing wife. He has an affair with a woman with a Cockney background and has also casually flirted with an unmarried neighbour, Miss Spence, who cultivates a mysterious smile like that of the Mona Lisa. Miss Spence mistakenly believes that Hutton has recognized her as a soul-mate, but when Mrs Hutton dies suddenly after a lunch to which Miss Spence was invited, Mr Hutton gets married to his lover and rejects Miss Spence. In revenge for this humiliation, the latter spreads the rumour that Hutton has killed his wife, who is, upon exhumation, indeed found to have been poisoned with arsenic. Hutton is convicted and executed, but the surprise ending reveals that it was really Miss Spence, with her mysterious smile, who committed the deed. Society's 'better' circles are satirized for their egotism and lack of human compassion. This theme is also taken up in Huxley's "Fard" (1922), where a hedonistic upper-class woman shows no concern for her worn-out servant and even asks her impetuously and inconsiderately to put on some of her make-up to hide her exhaustion – the 'fard' which can also be read symbolically as the facade of respectability which masks human deficiencies.

Evelyn Waugh's "An Englishman's Home" (1939) is set among a community of respectable people residing in the Cotswolds, a landscape of stereotypic English beauty perfectly suited for a stylish country life. The community is conned by two brothers who know how to exploit people's desire to preserve the traditional "cult of the countryside" with "its agricultural processes, its social structures, its vocabulary, its recreation" and the strict social ranking among the inhabitants. With its underdeveloped sense of sympathy for the victims, the story reminds one of Robert Greene's Elizabethan cony-catching tales, though without the pretense of giving serious advice. In Waugh's "Mr Loveday's Little Outing" (first coll. 1936) the class system is observed even in a lunatic asylum. Angela, daughter of the inmate Lord Moping, feels pity with one of the "lower-class lunatics", Mr Loveday. The latter has murdered a young woman and been institutionalized for thirty-five years; he acts as secretary and valet to Mr Moping and since he seems perfectly harmless and sane, Angela manages to get him released. The story ends, however, with an unpleasant twist: the murder of another young woman, after which Mr Loveday returns to the institution for good. The upper-class woman's 'social' concern for an alleged victim of an institution – while she makes no attempt to free her own father – has been clearly misguided.

W. Somerset Maugham is arguably the most prominent writer of short stories of the early twentieth century (his career continued, in fact, until after the Second World War). He was a writer who explicitly related himself both to older – notably oral – traditions of story-telling and the new short-story 'industry'. He liked best, as he wrote in *Points of View* (1958, 152f.), "the sort of story I can write myself", that is, an anecdotal kind of story with an interest in curious incident and "a beginning, a middle and an end" – a type of story that can be told "over the dinner table or in a ship's smoking room" and hold the listeners' attention. Maugham's awareness of the power of the literary market (which gained him a lot of criticism) emerges from another passage in *Points of View*: "The possibility of publication, the exigences of editors, that is to say their notions of what their readers want, have a great influence on the kind of work that at a particular time is produced. So, when magazines flourish which have room for stories of considerable length, stories of that length are written; when, on the other hand, newspapers publish fiction, but can give it no more than a small space, stories to fill that space are supplied." (*ibid.*, 149)

Some of Maugham's stories are set in the haunts of and satirize fashionable society. In "The Facts of Life" (first coll. 1940), a young man who goes on a tennis tournament in Monte Carlo manages to prove all his father's advice wrong: he gambles, lends money, has a short love affair (with a woman who tries to steal his money) and yet comes out the lucky winner. The story is told by the perplexed father himself, to a circle of his friends. **"Louise"** (first coll. 1936) sketches an egotistical woman who pretends that she has a weak heart whenever it suits her. The first-person narrator believes that he has prevented her from destroying her daughter's happiness. In the story's ironical twist at the end, however, Louise *does* have a heart attack on the day of her daughter's wedding, thus making the daughter feel guilty for the rest of her life.

Maugham is best known for his 'exotic' stories, many of which cast a critical and less humorous light on the English abroad, whether in service of the Empire, the Christian mission or simply as travellers. "The Force of Circumstance" (first coll. 1926) is set in the Malayan archipelago. A husband has to explain to his newly wedded wife from England that before his marriage he had lived together with a 'native' wife and had three children with her. The Englishwoman cannot cope with this knowledge and after a few months leaves her husband; the man, faced once more with the unbearable loneliness of life in the colony, permits the native wife to return to him. The earlier "Rain" (1919) is set in the South Sea Islands. Davidson and his wife, fanatically Puritan and self-righteous missionaries, are forced by heavy tropical rain to spend some time in the company of a prostitute, Sadie Thompson, whom they despise for her immorality. The Davidsons are proud to have converted 'their' South Sea island and to have instilled "into the natives the sense of sin": "We had to make sins out of what they thought were natural actions." That their mission is literally misplaced is indicated by the tropical rain which, as the narrator points out, is "not like our soft English rain that drops gently on the earth" but "unmerciful and somehow terrible; you felt in it the malignancy of the primitive powers of nature". Despite this reminder that their notions of English respectability might not fit everywhere and that nature may be more powerful than what they take for 'civilization', the Davidsons exert their moral outrage at Sadie and have her extradited. To Sadie, this means that she will have to take the next steamer to San Francisco, where the penitentiary is waiting for her. Sadie is desperate, but Davidson insists that she must suffer for her sins. He is, however, willing to pray with her for her soul, and the ending reveals that during their prayer session, Davidson must have succumbed to nature and Sadie's attractiveness. Having sinned against his own principles and civilizing mission, Davidson cuts his own throat with a razor: a bigotry rooted in a feeling of cultural superiority that has been nourished by decades of imperialism and missionary work has finally judged itself. The humorously critical and more darkly satirical mode was a prominent line in British short-story telling during the early twentieth century. But of course, there were other varieties.

*Traditionalists II: Supernaturalists and Materialists*

It has been mentioned before that the 'classical' story of the supernatural enjoyed a particular spell of popularity in the early twentieth century. Walter de la Mare, who was also an important poet, developed his own variety of the supernatural and mystical in which the transcendence of everyday experience is essential, but without the thrill of suspense which characterized the established ghost story. De la Mare's stories are not of the hair-raising kind; they open up glimpses into 'another', irrational world that seems to co-exist with – and determine life in – the ordinary world. In "Seaton's Aunt" (first coll. 1923), the orphaned friend of the story's first-person narrator is traumatized through the inexplicable power which his aunt has over him. The woman is rather unspectrelike, but the young Seaton demonizes her and even as an adult he seems unable to free himself from her negative influence over his life. Like the narrator, one might suspect that Seaton himself is responsible for his unhappiness – that, after his parents' death, he has projected fears and negative emotions upon his aunt and that her uncanniness is thus only a creation of his own psyche. The story ends, however, with the experience of the narrator who himself, after Seaton's early death, feels the woman's haunting presence. "The Creatures" (first coll. 1923) is a parabolic story with a lost-world motif: a man seems to enter a dreamlike, paradisical world inhabited by 'creatures' of another, supernatural world.[73]

Alongside such otherworldly tales, there is also a continuation of short-story writing in the realist mode: stories that relate comparatively unspectacular incidents set in an everyday, contemporary world which is depicted with circumstantial detail. Although primarily a novelist, Arnold Bennett wrote a number of stories in this manner, and like his novels, they are often set in the milieu of the Five Towns (pottery towns in Staffordshire, the best-known of which is Stoke-upon-Trent) or centre on middle-class characters with a background in this environment, like the stories in Bennett's *The Matador of the Five Towns* (1912). In this collection, "Mimi" deals with the complications that arise during a couple's honeymoon in Brighton. They have married secretly because of old feelings of jealousy between the bride and her sister. Ironically, however, the sister and her family (which includes the girl Mimi) also spend their holiday in Brighton, and the story focusses on how the husband and Mimi cope with the embarrassment that arises from the situation. The story's focus is not on plot, then, but on human behaviour and psychology, and its beginning exemplifies the care with which Bennett develops the external details which characterize his protagonists and setting, as well as the culture clash between the English North and South of which at least the male protagonist is keenly aware:

> On a Saturday afternoon in late October Edward Coe, a satisfactory average successful man of thirty-five, was walking slowly along the King's Road, Brighton. A native and inhabitant of the Five Towns in the Midlands, he had the brusque and energetic mien of the Midlands. It could be seen that he was a stranger to the south; and, in fact, he was now viewing for the first time the vast and glittering spectacle of the southern pleasure city in the unique glory of her autumn season. A spectacle to enliven any man by its mere splendour! And yet Edward Coe was gloomy. One reason for his gloom was that he had just left a bicycle, with a deflated back tyre, to be repaired at a shop in Preston Street. Not perhaps an adequate reason for gloom! ... Well, that depends. He had been informed by the blue-clad repairer, after due inspection, that the trouble was not a common puncture, but a malady of the valve mysterious.
>
> And the deflation was not the sole cause of his gloom. There was another. He was on his honeymoon. Understand me – not a honeymoon of romance, but a real honeymoon.

[73] On de la Mare's form of supernaturalism, see also Briggs (1977, chapter 9).

This is a 'slow' beginning which, through its excursus about the bike, suggests how the man appears to suppress the problem that he has just discovered the presence of his in-laws. We are thus able to share in the impressions of the character's mind; at the same time, however, the narrator also makes his presence felt by his ironic comments.

Similar features mark the stories of John Galsworthy, another writer better known for his novels than his stories. In a foreword to a collected edition of his short stories, *Caravan* (1925, vii), he explicitly emphasized that his stories were certainly not of the "sting in the tale" variety. And indeed his stories take time to quietly depict characters in situations into which they have been cast. Galsworthy's "Told by the Schoolmaster" (1927) is marked by a strong element of oral narration. A schoolmaster tells the story of two of his pupils who get married when the boy joins the First World War. Their love comes to a tragic end when the boy is shot as a deserter only because he wants to be present when his wife gives birth to their first child.

Bennett and Galsworthy – along with H.G. Wells – are the writers whom Virginia Woolf identified as old-fashioned novelists in an essay which is now considered one of the important British statements about the modernist aesthetic, "Modern Fiction" (1919):

> If we tried to formulate our meaning in one word we should say that these three writers are materialists. It is because they are concerned not with the spirit but with the body that they have disappointed us, and left us with the feeling that the sooner English fiction turns its back upon them, as politely as may be, and marches, if only into the desert, the better for its soul.
>
> [...] for us at this moment the form of fiction most in vogue more often misses than secures the thing we seek. Whether we call it life or spirit, truth or reality, this, the essential thing, has moved off, or on, and refuses to be contained any longer in such ill-fitting vestments as we provide. [...]
>
> Examine for a moment an ordinary mind on an ordinary day. The mind receives a myriad impressions – trivial, fantastic, evanescent, or engraved with the sharpness of steel. From all sides they come, an incessant shower of innumerable atoms; and as they fall, as they shape themselves into the life of Monday or Tuesday, the accent falls differently from of old [...].
>
> Let us record the atoms as they fall upon the mind in the order in which they fall, let us trace the pattern, however disconnected and incoherent in appearance, which each sight or incident scores upon the consciousness. Let us not take it for granted that life exists more fully in what is commonly thought big than in what is commonly thought small. (Woolf 1994, 158–161)

Woolf here writes about the novel, not the short story, demanding that the novel depict not external action but subjective consciousness, not coherent plot but the fragmentary experience of "the atoms as they fall upon the mind". It is, however, precisely the insight into the atomic nature of experience, the insight that *moments* are the units to which human subjects ascribe significance, which gives the short story a particular standing in the modernist aesthetic of fiction. As the preceding sections have indicated, short stories can deal with modernity without adopting modern*ist* principles of form. It is through innovative formal expression, a style that deliberately violated continuities, however, that art reacted to modernity *as art*.[74]

*The Modernist Story*

Key elements of the new avant-garde aesthetic were anticipated, as we have seen, in the aestheticist story of the 1890s: a rejection of established modes of narrative, in particular the neatly plotted narrative with a strong interest in external action, and a focus instead on the experience of the moment, on subjectivism and impressionism. These tendencies were strengthened in the early twentieth century as the world and above all world *views* appeared to be changing at an unprecedented speed. New scientific insight accentuated the instability of conventional constructs for comprehending 'reality' and drew increased attention to the workings of the individual mind. The findings of Albert Einstein and other physicists, once popularized, helped to destabilize traditional notions of time and space (Einstein announced in 1919 that a prediction of his general theory of relativity was confirmed, and he received the Nobel Prize in 1921). Wilhelm Wundt's empirical psychology (his *Einführung in die Psychologie* was first published in 1911) investigated the small units and the rhythm in which consciousness worked, and Sigmund Freud's *fin-de-siècle* 'discovery' of the workings of the unconscious became widely known, at least in intellectual circles, where it also became fashionable to be analysed. Like the aestheticists before them, the modernists discovered the short story as a congenial form for pursuing a distinctly 'modern' art of fiction. Evoking the same *Zeitgeist* as Woolf's "Modern Fiction", Alfred C. Ward (1924, 17) specifically notes that "[t]he brief prose form lends itself readily to impressionistic effect; it affords a more suitable medium than the novel for excursions into the dim territory of the subconscious; it allows experimental glimpses into 'the otherworld', which is – how close? how far?"

[74] For a closer look at modernism, its cultural and intellectual climate and elements of style, see Bradbury and McFarlane (1976).

The distinguished place of the short story in modernist literature has been discussed in many critical studies. Clare Hanson (1985, 56f.) finds that in the modernist period "the short form came to have, for the first time in its history, a status almost equivalent to that of the novel. [...] the modernist short fiction is the paradigmatic form of early twentieth-century literature, best able to express a fragmented sensibility." To Dominic Head (1992, xi), the short story "ought to be seen as centrally involved in the modernist revolution in fictional practice". It "encapsulates the essence of literary modernism" and, through its "stress on literary artifice", "intensifies the modernist preoccupation with formal innovation". (*ibid.*, 1f.) Its brevity "demands oblique expression through image and symbol", and its artifice also "facilitates another modernist preoccupation: the analysis of personality, especially a consideration of the fragmented, dehumanized self". (*ibid.*, 7f.)

Virginia Woolf's "Modern Fiction" focusses on the novel, but there are indications that the kind of fiction she had in mind bears an affinity to the small form, for example when she writes: "Let us not take it for granted that life exists more fully in what is commonly thought big than in what is commonly thought small." Indeed, it has been noted that Woolf's novel *Mrs Dalloway* originated from a short story, and even when the novel was finished, Woolf continued writing stories about Mrs Dalloway and her party. **"Mrs Dalloway in Bond Street"** was originally intended as the beginning of *Mrs Dalloway*, but Woolf subsequently decided to publish the text separately in *The Dial* in 1923. The story's line of external action is trivial and distinctly plotless: Clarissa Dalloway goes shopping for gloves and in the end finds and buys a pair she likes. The story's focus is on Clarissa's mental life. The story has an external, 'authorial' narrator, who seems, however, almost completely withdrawn. The story's centre of perception is therefore the character, Mrs Dalloway, whose consciousness we share for most of the text: her perceptions and thoughts, as she walks through London streets and spends time in the shop. 'Atoms' which impress themselves on Clarissa's mind include details of street life and the weather as well as snatches of memories and other associations which her perceptions trigger in her mind: thoughts about her husband, daughter and acquaintances, her worries about middle age and death, lines from the literature she has read, the party she is planning, and so forth – everything presented in an exemplary 'stream' of consciousness. With its focus on the character's inner life, the use which the text makes of various modes for presenting consciousness in fiction (direct thought, free indirect discourse) is naturally extensive. Also typical of modernist texts, time and space are presented as subjectively rather than objectively given. In many modernist texts, this subjectivity is emphasized by the device of multiple perspective, a technique which is also to be found in "Mrs Dalloway in Bond Street". In the fourth paragraph Mrs Dalloway is seen by another character before the text returns to her point of view. The final sentence of the passage, with its phrase in parentheses, also illustrates how inner and external processes happen simultaneously so that an incident in the here and now is co-present with a memory:

> A charming woman, posed, eager, strangely white-haired for her pink cheeks, so Scope Purvis, C.B., saw her as he hurried to his office. She stiffened a little, waiting for Durtnall's van to pass. Big Ben struck the tenth; struck the eleventh stroke. The leaden circles dissolved in the air. Pride held her erect, inheriting, handing on, acquainted with discipline and with suffering. How people suffered, how they suffered, she thought, thinking of Mrs Foxcroft at the Embassy last night decked with jewels, eating her heart out, because that nice boy was dead, and now the old Manor House (Durtnall's van passed) must go to a cousin.

Since the story renders a snatch of ongoing experience, it is suitable that its beginning and ending are abrupt and 'open'. There is no explicit exposition to orientate the reader, and neither is there a tight ending. Significantly, the story's prime element of closure is not so much the completion of Mrs Dalloway's purchase as the completion of one of her lines of thought: she suddenly remembers who the other customer in the shop is. The story is thus formally closed to a certain extent, but it is also open in that it suggests ongoing life and continuous experience. The cause of the violent explosion mentioned in the last paragraph is unresolved, and one surmises that some encounter with the now identified Miss Anstruther will follow.

When Woolf published her stories, James Joyce's *Dubliners* had already appeared (they were published 1914 but completed earlier). This volume is often named as a shaping influence on the modernist story, with particular reference to their use of the 'epiphany'. In Joyce's adaptation of this religious notion, the epiphany[75] is a sudden revelation and illumination in which ordinary perception is momentarily transcended. It is thus another term for the "significant moment" (see p. 6) so frequently observed in relation to the short story of the twentieth century, a moment in which the world appears meaningful for at least a short glimpse. However, in her practice of the short story, Virginia Woolf was – at least sometimes – far more

[75] See Joyce's *Stephen Hero*: "By an epiphany he meant a sudden spiritual manifestation, whether in the vulgarity of speech or of gesture or in a memorable phase of the mind itself." (Joyce 1956, 216). Head (1992) devotes his second chapter to Joyce but goes for a 'non-epiphanic' reading.

radically experimental than Joyce in *Dubliners* or she herself in "Mrs Dalloway in Bond Street".

In "Modern Fiction", Woolf briefly discusses a short story by Chekhov, "Gusev", in which she locates her ideal of how fiction should be written. She emphasizes that a story like this transcends all traditional notions of genre: "But it is impossible to say 'this is comic', or 'that is tragic', nor are we certain, since short stories, we have been taught, should be brief and conclusive, whether this, which is vague and inconclusive, should be called a story at all." (Woolf 1994, 163) For some of her own stories, too, one can agree with Joanne Banks (1985, 81) that "only by enlarging the definition of the genre to the borders of poetry on the one hand and essays on the other can we include Woolf as a short-story writer at all". This is exemplified by two of Woolf's most famous stories, "Kew Gardens" and "The Mark on the Wall", even though both still are minimally narrative. "Kew Gardens" was first published in 1919 and later included in *Monday or Tuesday* (1921), the only collection of her stories which Woolf published herself. The title is that of a very short story (or sketch) also contained in the volume, which is linked with the programmatic phrase from "Modern Fiction" quoted above: "an incessant shower of innumerable atoms; and as they fall, as they shape themselves into the life of Monday or Tuesday." In "Kew Gardens", a narrator seems to have completely withdrawn, and the text cuts between various agents of perception. The text's main consciousness focusses on a flowerbed in London's botanical garden. A snail is slowly making its way there, while different couples pass the bed and snatches of their conversation are taken up. Again, there is no conventional conclusion to this kind of 'story'. Rather, the 'atoms' of conversations and relationships finally merge into a climactic wealth of impressions in which a momentary insight into the chaotic sensual richness of life is granted – although it is difficult to link this insight to a mind clearly traceable in the text:

> Yellow and black, pink and snow white, shapes of all these colours, men, women and children, were spotted for a second upon the horizon, and then, seeing the breadth of yellow that lay upon the grass, they wavered and sought shade beneath the trees, dissolving like drops of water in the yellow and green atmosphere, staining it faintly with red and blue. [...] Voices, yes, voices, wordless voices, breaking the silence suddenly with such depth of contentment, such passion of desire, or, in the voices of children, such freshness of surprise; breaking the silence? But there was no silence; all the time the motor omnibuses were turning their wheels and changing their gear; like a vast nest of Chinese boxes all of wrought steel turning ceaselessly one within another the city murmured; on the top of which the voices cried aloud and the petals of myriads of flowers flashed their colours into the air.

"Kew Gardens" thus ends as an impressionistic sketch – and at the same time a prose poem – with a pronounced synaesthesia of sight and sound impressions which blend into the complex, layered and deliberately non-linear structure of a "nest of chinese boxes".

"The Mark on the Wall" was originally published in 1917 and later also included in *Monday or Tuesday.* To Dominic Head (1992, 106), it is "perhaps the quintessential Woolf short story". The text's narrative is even less developed than in "Kew Gardens". It evolves over large stretches as an interior monologue composed of the central character's reflections and reminiscences, which are triggered by the perception of a mark on the wall. This initial incident is still narrated in an established manner ("Perhaps it was the middle of January in the present year that I first looked up and saw the mark on the wall."), but then a chain of sense impressions and associations is started:

> In order to fix a date it is necessary to remember what one saw. So now I think of the fire; the steady film of yellow light upon the page of my book; the three chrysanthemums in the round glass bowl on the mantelpiece. Yes, it must have been the winter time, and we had just finished our tea, for I remember that I was smoking a cigarette when I looked up and saw the mark on the wall for the first time. I looked up through the smoke of my cigarette and my eye lodged for a moment upon the burning coals, and that old fancy of the crimson flag flapping from the castle tower came into my mind, and I thought of the cavalcade of red knights riding up the side of the black rock. Rather to my relief the sight of the mark interrupted the fancy, for it is an old fancy, an automatic fancy, made as a child perhaps. The mark was a small round mark, black upon the white wall, about six or seven inches above the mantelpiece.

Throughout the text, the central subject's consciousness departs from the mark in all directions, but its rambling thoughts are then redirected to the material mark in the here and now. The mark thus also functions as a central structural element which holds the story together, and it is the element used to give the text a conclusion – the stream of associations is stopped rather abruptly and antithetically when the 'riddle' of the mark is revealed, by another character, to be a snail:

> I can't remember a thing. Everything's moving, falling, slipping, vanishing. ... There is a vast upheaval of matter. Someone is standing over me and saying –
>
> 'I'm going out to buy a newspaper.'
>
> 'Yes?'
>
> 'Though it's no good buying newspapers. ... Nothing ever happens. Curse

> this war; God damn this war! ... All the same, I don't see why we should have a snail on our wall.'
>
> Ah, the mark on the wall! It was a snail.

As Dominic Head (1992) points out, "The Mark on the Wall" plays with the pattern of the conventional mystery story, which is undermined by the puzzle's (and its solution's) banality. The exciting thing about this story is not a mystery in the external world, but the excitement which even a banal object may trigger in a subject's consciousness. A traditional story structure is thus invalidated, just as in two other Woolf stories, "An Unfinished Novel" (1920) and "Moments of Being: 'Slater's Pins Have No Points'" (1928). In both texts, the central subject imagines the life of another character in terms of traditional modes of fiction, and in both texts, these modes are devalidated when it is indicated that the persons may have led far more unconventional lives than those imagined according to the established patterns. To Head (1992, 26), modernist formal experiment relies generally on a tension with the narrative conventions from which it departs, and this formal departure coincides with ideological unconventionality: "for the modernists, [...] the disclosure of ideological context is often an integral part of their formal experimentation." The ending of "Moments of Being", for example, demonstrates "the inadequacy of a particular literary style" *and* the restrictiveness of conventional sexual morals when it suggests that the woman whose life has been imagined has remained unmarried because of a homosexual relationship. (*ibid.*, 83)

The same concurrence of modernist form and ideological dissent can be found in (some of) Katherine Mansfield's stories. In "Bliss" (1918), which gave its title to one of Mansfield's most famous collections, Head (1992, 109) observes "a dawning awareness on the protagonist's part of her latent homosexuality, a subtext partly suppressed by the social taboo it simultaneously criticizes". The story also illustrates the significance which the use of suggestive symbols had for the modernists, permitting plurisignation and the expression of mental content which is pre- or subconscious and thus pre-verbal. The female protagonist of "Bliss" has found herself in a state of inexplicable bliss throughout the day, which ends with a dinner she gives for a number of friends. These include a woman, Miss Fulton, by whom she has recently been fascinated. The protagonist is thrilled when she and Miss Fulton admire a flowering pear tree in the garden. This tree, with its flame-like beauty, appears to represent her state of bliss and the homoerotic relationship she seems – though yet unconsciously – to desire:

> Although it was so still it seemed, like the flame of a candle, to stretch up, to point, to quiver in the bright air, to grow taller and taller as they gazed – almost to touch the rim of the round, silver moon.

> How long did they stand there? Both, as it were, caught in that circle of unearthly light, understanding each other perfectly, creatures of another world, and wondering what they were to do in this one with all this blissful treasure that burned in their bosoms and dropped, in silver flowers, from their hair and hands?

After this experience of intimacy and enchantment, the protagonist suddenly discovers, in a more cruel 'significant moment', that her husband already has a relationship with Miss Fulton. The symbol of her secret desire, although outwardly unchanged, loses its significance to her: "'Oh, what is going to happen now?' she cried. But the pear tree was as lovely as ever and as full of flower and as still."

Compared with some of Woolf's short fiction, Mansfield's stories, which constitute the bulk of her oeuvre, are still more committed to external action. The stories written during Mansfield's mature period, however, are also centrally concerned with their characters' mental life.[76] Often, her main characters are children, and the texts convey through allusion and symbol thoughts which the children are yet unable to verbalize. "Prelude" (1917) and "At the Bay" (1922) are set in Mansfield's native New Zealand and present the Burnell family with its various adult and child characters. The first story is included in the collection *Bliss* (1920), the second in *The Garden Party* (1922). Both primarily develop the perceptions and thoughts of their characters, switching between their individual perspectives and thus fragmenting the narrative. A focus on characters' inner states during important moments in their lives also marks other well-known stories like "The Garden Party" (1922). Here a young girl experiences her first encounter with death when the party of her well-situated family is disturbed by the death of a lower-class character in the neighbourhood. She goes there to pay her condolences, thus instinctively rebelling against her family's conventionality and class consciousness. In another initiation story, "The Voyage" (1921), a young girl is taken on a voyage, not only into another part of New Zealand, but into a new phase of her life after her mother's death. "The Daughters of the Late Colonel" (1921) renders the present worries and memories of two elderly unmarried sisters who face a major reorientation in their lives when they lose their father's patriarchal guidance. In "Miss

[76] The early 'German stories', which satirize the German national character ("Germans at Meat") were collected as *In a German Pension* (1911). According to Banks (1985, 66), "Mansfield came to dislike her German stories. They represented in her mind clever but trivial juvenilia. As for the themes in her stories – particularly the relationship between men and women and the isolation of the young woman – these she would continue to write about, refining them as her sensibility matured."

Brill" (1920), another spinster whose only pleasure is her weekly visit to a park is hurt deeply by the insensitive remarks of a young couple.

The short fiction written by Jean Rhys during the 1920s is collected in *The Left Bank* (1927). The texts deal with bohemian life in Paris, the capital of modernist art, and we encounter again some of the key elements of modernist writing. Most of the pieces are very short, permitting only brief glimpses at life in the Left Bank milieu. Events and situations are presented as fragments, isolated from wider contexts; many pieces lack narrative altogether and throw a spotlight on places and character types. "Illusion", for example, sketches the tragic dilemma of an ugly woman painter who buys herself beautiful clothes but is afraid of wearing them; the artist has a strange reluctance to create for herself an illusion of beauty. From a strictly internal point of view, "Hunger" renders the dilemma of a person who lacks the money to buy food, and "A Night" is a stream-of-consciousness piece focussing on a mind troubled by insomnia.

With the exception of some of Woolf's short pieces and the even more radical formal and linguistic disruptions that mark the short fiction of the Irishman Samuel Beckett,[77] most writers of the short story associated with modernism in Britain are restrained as far as formal experiment is concerned. Some even use overtly conventional forms of story-telling to negotiate modernist thematic concerns. For Joseph Conrad, Daphna Erdinast-Vulcan (1999, 8) points out that his short fiction reflects the contemporary "crisis of metaphysics, the crisis of authority, and the crisis of subjectivity" but that only in part of his stories (like "The Lagoon", "An Outpost of Progress" or "The Secret Sharer") can we find traces of a modernist aesthetic such as the lack of a sense of an ending, layers of narrative that are left suspended or the "authorial position" that is "impossibly fluid or ambiguous". (*ibid.*, 2)

E.M. Forster shows his affinity with modernism primarily through a thematic occupation with myth or rather the loss of orientating myth in the modern world. In "The Road from Colonus" (1904), the worlds of Greece and contemporary England stand in stark contrast. The story evokes the myth of Oedipus; Colonus is the place near Athens where, according to Sophocles' play *Oedipus in Colonus*, the ancient king wished to die and *did* die, with the help of his daughter Antigone. Forster's story relates this situation to that of the ageing Mr Lucas who, with his daughter, is visiting Greece as a modern traveller. Mr Lucas adores Greece as a landscape of beauty and myth and would rather die there than in the grey, conventional England to which his daughter forces him to return. "Story of a Siren" (re-

[77] Beckett is discussed as an important influence on the later post-modernists by Hanson (1985, 143–153). His short piece "Ping" is included in Bradbury (1982).

jected by *The Temple Bar* in 1904 and not published until 1920) is set in an enchanting grotto in Italy, where an Italian tells an Englishman about another clash of ancient and modern civilization: the love between a siren woman and a man, which ends unhappily when the heathen siren is killed by a priest of the established Christian religion. Forster's "The Celestial Omnibus" (1908) takes up another form of traditional story. It is a parabolic fairy tale in which a vehicle of modern transport, driven by an English thinker of the seventeenth century, Sir Thomas Browne, takes a boy into the fantastic realm of the literary world. The child, with powers of the imagination that are still uncorrupted, discovers the beauties of literature. An adult, however, who repeats the journey, lacks this imagination and dies.

Dominic Head (1992, 34) excludes D.H. Lawrence from his study since he "stands in a difficult relation to mainstream modernism" and his stories are "predominantly conservative in structure and form". This applies both to Lawrence's parabolic stories, like "The Man Who Loved Islands" (1926), which traces a man's progressive alienation from all forms of human society, and the more 'realistic' ones, like "Odour of Chrysanthemums", "England, My England", "Tickets Please" or "The Horse-Dealer's Daughter". These stories frequently present their characters' consciousness and have a strong interest in their psychology, but there is still an explicit narrator-presence, and a clear line of external action. The stories are far more modern in the issues they discuss than in their form, especially Lawrence's provocative treatment of taboo subjects. "Odour of Chrysanthemums" (1911), for example, presents a collier's wife's reflections about her relationship with her husband, who has gone on the bottle. However, when he is brought home dead after a mine accident, she realizes that their marriage has turned out bad because she too has made mistakes and has had misconceptions. The following passage, which presents the pregnant woman's perception of her husband's naked corpse, is characteristic of Lawrence in its undisguised physicality and reference to sexual acts:

> The man's mouth was fallen back, slightly open under the cover of the moustache. The eyes, half shut, did not show glazed in the obscurity. Life with its smoky burning gone from him, had left him apart and utterly alien to her. And she knew what a stranger he was to her. In her womb was ice of fear, because of this separate stranger with whom she had been living as one flesh. Was this what it all meant – utter, intact separateness, obscured by heat of living? In dread she turned her face away. The fact was too deadly. There had been nothing between them, and yet they had come together, exchanging their nakedness repeatedly. Each time he had taken her, they had been isolated beings, far apart as now. He was no more responsible than she. The child was like ice in her womb.

In "The Horse-Dealer's Daughter" (1922), the protagonist is a young woman from an impoverished family. When she tries to commit suicide in a pond, she is rescued by a young doctor and they fall passionately in love with each other. The story exemplifies Lawrence's criticism of modern civilisation: in a world determined by industrialism and materialism, the horse-dealer's daughter and the doctor both live lives that are unsatisfactory and emotionally starved. The progress of industrialization has destroyed the rural environment and caused an agricultural crisis which destroys people's traditional way of life, their relationships and eventually drives them away to the cities. When the couple in the story find each other, this love relationship seems the only kind of redemption left in the modern world. "England, My England" (1915) centres on a less satisfactory relationship: a husband and wife have become estranged. Apart from discovering the unsatisfactory nature of conventional matrimony, the story explores what Englishness might still mean in the face of the First World War, an event which was perceived to have shaken all notions of a traditional English way of life. The male protagonist, Egbert, believes in an anti-modern, rural England epitomized in the country cottage and the garden which he devotedly cultivates and in which he first fell in love with his wife: "That was Crockham. The spear of modern invention had not passed through it, and it lay there secret, primitive, savage as when the Saxons first came." However, the old way of life and Egbert's pleasure in the garden are destroyed by the war in which he finally enlists although he does not believe in its cause: "He had no conception of Imperial England, and Rule Britannia was just a joke to him." Egbert dies in the trenches. "Tickets Please" (first publ. 1919 in the *Strand Magazine*) takes up the upheaval of gender roles in the wake of the First World War. The female protagonist works as a tram conductor, replacing a man who is fighting in the war. Having thus slipped into a 'masculine' role, she seems to feel empowered to take her revenge on the central male character, a notorious womanizer. Allied with other discarded girlfriends, she traps the man; the women beat and humiliate him in what has become a war of the sexes. As far as this story is concerned, satisfactory love relationships as a counterpoise to modernization seem to have become impossible.

Although the 'modernist' story features so prominently in short-story criticism, the British short story in the early decades of the twentieth century only rarely displays modernism in its most radical forms. Nevertheless, a moderate adoption of some features of modernism has become a staple even of 'mainstream' short-story writing during the further course of the twentieth century, in particular a focus on the presentation of character and the character's consciousness. Eileen Baldeshweiler (1994, 231) has therefore used the term 'lyric' short story[78] to designate what the more radical and more moderately modernist stories have in common: a concentration on "internal changes, moods, and feelings, utilizing a variety of structural patterns depending on the shape of the emotion itself", a tendency towards the 'open' ending and the "condensed, evocative, often figured language of the poem". Clare Hanson (1985, 112f.), by contrast, prefers to distinguish a 'free' story from the more narrowly modernist one: "The free story does not go beyond, but rather turns its back on, many of the barriers broken by the modernists." This shows, for example, in its conception of characters as "internally coherent and consistent in time". Free-story writers also tend to delineate character and locale in close detail, being "attracted to the particular rather than the general", and they "rarely use description for symbolic purposes: the emphasis is on the particular, concrete subject". Last but not least, the free story "also shows far more response to social pressures than does modernist short fiction". The stories of D.H. Lawrence can be subsumed under this label, as can many other stories written from the 1920s onwards. It seems fair to claim that – outside more specialized sub-genres like the detective, ghost or science fiction story – a new mainstream of short-story writing in the twentieth century is marked by a certain revaluation of outward action and situation (alongside the continued interest in the characters' inner lives) and a non-experimental orientation concerning language and structure. And in many examples one finds indeed an explicit commitment to people's life in a social context.

### *Modes of the 'Free' Mainstream*

Apart from the 'modernists', A.E. Coppard and H.E. Bates are the dominant names associated with the short story in Britain during the first half of the twentieth century. James Gindin (1985, 115) emphasizes that neither Coppard nor Bates "can accurately be called a 'modernist' writer" since "they generally wrote anecdotes or described situations, or defined characters or relationships, with directness and understatement, with no explicit sense that these represented or suggested anything further". Both are also designated as characteristically 'English' writers whose works are marked by a high degree of local colour. To Joseph M. Flora (1985, xix), they belong to "the solidly English, a conservative strain" and represent "an emphasis on the plain and ordinary that has persisted in British fiction at least since De-

[78] Baldeshweiler borrows it, in fact, from Elizabeth Bowen's preface to the *Faber Book of Modern Short Stories* (Bowen 1994).

foe". H.E. Bates (1965, 139) himself considered Coppard to be "as English and as sturdily beautiful as the Cotswold Hills and the Buckinghamshire beech-woods", a "poet" who "had taken up the short story, choosing as his backgrounds the countryside of middle England, the pubs, the provincial towns with their faded breweries and gloomy old-fashioned lawyers' offices". (*ibid.*, 136)

Against this background, which gains a highly visual quality through the detail with which external circumstances are described, Coppard develops stories that still have significant lines of action and are set in concrete situations; their characters are established both through their placement in the external world and the glimpses we are given into their thoughts and feelings. In "The Watercress Girl" (1925), for example, a young woman who has just had a miscarriage throws acid at another woman's face when she finds out that her lover wishes to get married to her rival. Although the 'watercress girl' has been punished with a spell in prison, her former lover, who has abandoned the disfigured woman, wants to disfigure her as well but then succumbs to her beauty again. The story ends with the possibility that their relationship will develop again. "The Higgler" (1925) also depicts an opportunity for love that is (almost) lost. A young veteran of the First World War earns his living as a higgler and thus gets acquainted with a prosperous farmer woman and her beautiful, educated daughter. The woman, a widow, offers her daughter to him since she wants her provided for before she dies. The higgler, however, although he has fallen in love with the girl, believes that she is above him and therefore does not return his feelings. He withdraws and gets married to a girl from his village instead. When he comes back to the farm after months, the widow has just died, and her daughter confesses her love to him. Regretting his marriage, the higgler decides that he will manage the daughter's farm for her and possibly enter a relationship with her after all. These are only few of Coppard's many stories, but they typically indicate his high esteem for personal freedom (including sexual freedom) which made him turn against many institutions of society – in particular the established church.

Like Coppard, H.E. Bates sets many of his stories in a country and provincial-town environment, and like Coppard, he often writes about sexual attraction or repression, as well as forms of emotional and social imprisonment. His stories also offer compact studies of character. **"For the Dead"** (first coll. 1934), for example, exposes the hypocrisy of two widowers who, for convention's sake, pretend in a cemetery that they still mourn the wives they have lost; their pose is clearly not 'for the dead', but for the living. In "The Waterfall" (first coll. 1934), a young woman who has spent an isolated life in the company of her clergyman father seems to have no perspective when the father dies. She marries her wealthy neighbour Abrahams, a widower who also leads a lonely life. Their relationship lacks passion until the couple engage an engineer, Phillips, to help with the blocked lake on their estate. The final release of water in the story is a symbol for hidden feelings and their liberation. The story sets in with the image of a lake half-frozen in winter, into which a waterfall empties itself with only a "thin glassy sound". It ends with the powerful release of water, which parallels the woman's final release of emotions, the outward sign of which is a 'waterfall' of tears:

> There was a sudden crash as the dam itself collapsed and then a roar, increasing rapidly, as the water tore down through the new channel, with Phillips and Abrahams running excitedly along the banks, to see the first leap of water into the lake, and then at last there was a sound of thunder as the water fell. The sound for a moment was terrific. She stood in suspense, startled. At her feet the water tore down the channel furiously, so that she went giddy from looking at it, and there was a shower of soft white spray as the torrent thundered into the lake. [...]
>
> The tears began to run down her cheeks. [...] Her tears kept on and behind her the torrent of water roared with soft thunder. She began to hurry, trying to dry her tears as she did so, but fresh tears filled her eyes as fast as she wiped them away and the sound of the waterfall followed her persistently. She hurried on as though afraid of it and long after she could hear it no more, the echo of it, like a remembered emotion, thundered through her mind.

The same focus on a decisive but undramatic moment of insight characterizes many stories of Rosamond Lehmann. "A Dream of Winter" (1941) has been frequently anthologized and is typical of her general approach to the genre. It is a story reflecting existential issues like illness, death and the will to live. These reflections are triggered by a situation in which a mother lies in her bedroom seriously ill with influenza, while the bee man removes a swarm of bees from the wall of her country house. The bees, producers of nourishing honey, are a reminder of summer and life in winter, and in the incident which closes the story, life and death are again set in a stark contrast when a bird accidentally gets burned in the fireplace where it was put by the protagonist's children to warm. Despite its severe burns, the bird still has a strong will to live. The story achieves its effect mainly through the evocation of a suggestive atmosphere and unobtrusive natural symbolism.

Graham Greene's career spanned from the late 1920s until the 1980s. Greene contributed to the 'exotic' story, for instance with "Across the Bridge" (1938), in which a criminal expatriate in South America, Mr Calloway, suffers human isolation on the Mexican-American border and longs for his English home before he dies tragically in an accident. However, Greene also cast a critical eye on society at home, especially its morals, which he tended to investigate from a Roman-Catholic stance. As John Bayley (1990, 93) observes, "Greene [...] hardly ever wrote a paragraph that did not contain a statement, or at least an implication, about Catholic Truth. And this is particularly true of his stories, where [...] a point can be made, a truth about society or human nature exhibited, with essential force and economy." The world which Greene repeatedly depicts is a morally derelict one; in the stories set in London during the immediate postwar decades, this decay of ethics is mirrored in external ruin. John Stinson (1985, 9) characterizes Greene's "best" stories as "lean and rock-hard; the lucid plot lines move with quickness and ease while allowing for an almost magical conjuring up of character and mood. Greene has distilled the essence of the thriller but turned it to his own religious/metaphysical ends." This is exemplified by one of Greene's best-known stories, a story of initiation. In "The Basement Room" (1935), a boy is left by his parents with their servant couple. The woman servant is extremely strict, both with the boy and her husband. The boy discovers that the man has a secret relationship with another woman, and the man bribes him with special treats to keep him quiet. The story reaches its climax when the wife is away for a day and the man brings his lover into the house. His suspicious wife returns earlier than expected, however, and husband and wife start to struggle. She accidentally falls over the banister of the stairwell and is killed. Deeply disturbed, the boy runs away, is brought home by the police and betrays what has happened while the husband is still trying to cover events up. The boy has to cope with guilt in two respects: the guilt of hiding the truth, and the guilt of betraying a friend. Another story with child protagonists, which was among Greene's own favourites (see Bayley 1990, 101), is "The Destructors" (1954). Here a gang of boys in London still marked by the devastation of the Blitz destroy the only house that is still intact in their neighbourhood. The house is an architectural beauty of times long before the war, and although he is perfectly aware of this, the boys' leader makes his friends destroy the building completely from within. The boys' anarchic impetus to cause complete destruction is, through its evocative setting, linked to the material damage and moral disorientation caused by the war, but also by post-World War II society with a new rebellious youth culture and a new social system, the Welfare State, which many perceived as destroying England from within.

V.S. Pritchett's long career as one of Britain's most prominent writers of short stories began during the war. Walter Allen (1981, 268) characterizes Pritchett as a "connoisseur of puritanism in its characteristically English manifestations, which, in social terms, have generally been lower-middle class". In "Handsome Is As Handsome Does" (first coll. 1938), Pritchett exposes the hypocrisy and chauvinism of an English couple, the Corams, during their first holiday abroad in France. They are both ugly and shabby people and a social mismatch. The wife comes from a family of the gentry, but her husband is a social climber who has made a career because scholarships gained him a good education: "He did not belong to the working class any more. He did not belong to her class. He did not belong to the class of the comfortable professional people he now met. He did not belong anywhere. He was lost, rough, unfinished, ugly, unshaped by the wise and harmonious hand of a good environment." Their holiday in a foreign environment proves highly disorientating for the Corams. While the husband, out of an inferiority complex, rejects and criticizes everything and especially the owner of their pension, Monsieur Pierre, his wife is fascinated by Alex, a young man who makes her regret that she has never had a child of her own and who awakens her sexual desire. The action climaxes when Alex, Pierre and the Corams go swimming. Pierre almost drowns and is rescued by Alex, while Mr Coram proves a coward and does nothing to help them. Back in the pension, Mrs Coram humiliates herself when she tries to seduce Alex, who does not desire her – and, to her surprise, neither does she desire him any more. Instead, she feels drawn to her husband again and believes that she has tried to debase herself to be on the same social level with him. They get reconciled and at night, in front of other English guests, she stylizes her husband into the rescuer of Monsieur Pierre, thus constructing a social lie.

Another well-known writer, William Sansom, also emerged during the war. His best-known stories are in fact based on his experiences of the London Blitz as a member of the National Fire Service; they are collected in *Fireman Flower* (1944). To Robert Gish (1985, 34), these stories "offer compelling evidence that the consciousness of modern man is inextricably associated with a kind of extended twentieth-century angst and paranoia", a characterization which applies to Sansom's stories generally. In "The Wall" (1941), a group of firemen are buried by the wall of a burning house; most of them survive because they happen to stand where an empty window frame comes down. This moment of heightened experience is rendered in a manner in which the first-person narrator's visual perception of the crashing wall is depicted in great detail, as if in slow motion.[79] This literal point of *view* foregrounds the personal experience of the moment rather than the incident itself. Other Sansom stories also present people in extremity and

[79] On the affinity between the visuality of Sansom's stories and photographic and cinematic techniques, see Hanson (1989, 136).

convey their experience with great intensity. In "The Vertical Ladder" (1944), a young man climbs a gasometer to impress his friends and in particular a girl among them. However, he suffers from fear of heights and gets into a desperate situation when parts of the upper ladder are missing and his friends abandon him, having removed the bottom part of the ladder. The story leaves the man literally hanging in the air and in panic; the open ending intensifies the sense of his desperate helplessness:

> Flegg, clutching his body close to the rust, made small weeping sounds through his mouth. Shivering, shuddering, he began to tread up again, working his knees and elbows outward like a frog, so that his stomach could feel the firm rungs. Were they firm? His ears filled with a hot roaring, he hurried himself, he began to scramble up, wrenching at his last strength, whispering urgent meaningless words to himself like the swift whispers that close in on a nightmare. A huge weight pulled at him, dragging him to drop. He climbed higher. He reached the top rung – and found his face staring still at a wall of red rust. He looked, wild with terror. It was the top rung! The ladder had ended! Yet – no platform ... the real top rungs were missing ... the platform jutted five impassable feet above ... Flegg stared dumbly, circling his head like a lost animal ... then he jammed his legs in the lower rungs and his arms past the elbows to the armpits in through the top rungs and there he hung shivering and past knowing what more he could ever do ...

Several writers mentioned in this section continued their careers well beyond the end of the 1940s and have remained household names of the short story in Britain, in particular Maugham, Bates, Greene and Pritchett. Another major influence during the 1940s and subsequent decades was the Anglo-Irish writer Elizabeth Bowen. These writers exemplify a wide range of approaches to the short story as far as theme, structure and narrative technique are concerned; the story with an explicit interest in social analysis and social satire appears as much as the story that has character and states of consciousness as its focus. However, none of the writers are marked by the spirit of deliberate innovation and experimentalism which characterized the more radical modernists. By the end of the Second World War, British literature had produced a number of prominent representatives who also enjoyed international acclaim. For the second half of the twentieth century, however, the short story in postwar Britain has often been observed to be on the decline. George Garrett (1981, 321), for instance, complains that "the years since World War II seem not to have been especially prosperous or productive ones for British short fiction. Certainly in vitality and influence they in no way match the years leading up to World War II."

*Postwar Stagnation?*

Dennis Vannatta (1985, xix) diagnoses that the short story in Britain stagnated after the Second World War and "it may be that the problem is rooted in a failure of growth, a failure of innovation". While the 1960s were "a period of great experimentation in America, the Continent, and Latin America [...] most stories of the same decade in Britain had an old-fashioned air in subject and technique".[80] A postwar malaise of the short story was even observed by its major representatives. V.S. Pritchett, for example, claimed in an essay on "The Short Story", published in *London Magazine* in 1966 that

> [t]he short story is one of the inextinguishable lost causes. It has always dismayed publishers. It is treated perfunctorily by the over-worked novel-reviewers – chiefly because it is very hard to make anything of an assortment. The financial rewards are disgracefully low in England, even for the well known, the top price for anything good which has taken weeks, perhaps months of work being about £60. It is difficult to get a story longer than 7,000 words published at all; after 10,000 words, impossible. The periodicals on which the writer can rely have almost all vanished, driven out by expensive printing, by television and the hundred and one new diversions of an extravert and leisured society. [...] Since the opportunities of publication are so few nowadays, short-story writers tend to become abstentionists, to wait for their moment. And the general weakness of short stories now is the lack of a distinctive, personal voice. Lacking that voice, the writer should become a novelist, however unusual his material. The great trap for the contemporary short-story writer is naturalism: to rely on that without the other ingredients of intensity and wit – meaning by wit trenchancy of mind, not witticism – simply means flat writing, the slice of life. (in Weber and Greiner 1977, 190 and 192)

For the *Kenyon Review*'s "International Symposium on the Short Story", H.E. Bates felt obliged to admit in 1970 that his earlier views about the development of the short story had been too optimistic:

> when I prophesied in *The Modern Short Story*, in 1941, that the inevitable distrust and dislocation of war's aftermath would surely lead new writers to find in the short story the essential medium for what they had to say, I felt certain I was right. Time has proved me wrong. It is true that a certain number of new short-story writers, notably Angus Wilson, Alan Sillitoe, John Wain, Roald Dahl, Elizabeth Taylor, and others have appeared, but the re-

[80] For similar comments, see Bergonzi (1979, 218) and Stinson (1985, 1).

> sults have, on the whole, been thinnish and disappointing. (in Weber and Greiner 1977, 209)

The alleged lack of productivity and innovation on the part of writers certainly coincided with a change of the short story's status in Britain's postwar literary system. As Pritchett notes, the literary market now provided significantly fewer outlets for short stories than during the preceding decades. Malcolm Bradbury (1971, 190) observes that during the years of the Second World War, magazines that sponsored new writers, like John Lehmann's *New Writing* or *Horizon*, still had a notable readership. After the war, however, "came a simultaneous drop in readership and rise in printing costs by which many small-circulation ventures were hit". Dean Baldwin (1985, 72f.), in his review of the fifties magazine scene, considers the end of *Penguin New Writing* (which continued Lehmann's series between 1940 and 1950) as "perhaps the most significant loss" in a publication landscape in Britain that was becoming increasingly unfavourable for the short story:

> In an attempt to fill the gap left by defunct periodicals, John Pudney in 1949 undertook to edit an annual collection, *The Pick of Today's Short Stories*. Pudney, himself an accomplished if not gifted author, annually sifted through hundreds of stories submitted by writers of all ages and talent, selecting twenty or so for inclusion. In nearly all cases, these were stories that had not been previously published, so these volumes can in no way be compared with Edward O'Brien's famous *Best Short Stories* series. [...] Another hardcover annual anthology was launched in 1955 by Macmillan with the intent of providing an outlet for longer stories that magazines could not publish. Called *Winter's Tales*, these volumes have continued to provide an important forum for that most neglected of all fictional forms, the long story. [...] Although commercial magazines were shrinking in number and in space available for fiction, by today's standards authors of the fifties perhaps should have felt themselves fortunate. Such traditional publishers of high-quality fiction as the *Listener, Argosy, Cornhill*, the *Spectator, Punch, Encounter*, and *Time and Tide* continued their commitment to the short story. Nevertheless, for many British writers, especially those more established and well known, it was American periodicals, particularly the *New Yorker*, that provided both the audience and the substantial check that writers need to survive.

The growing significance of American periodicals as a publication forum for British writers, with the *New Yorker* in the forefront, is also emphasized by George Garrett (1981, 313), who claims that without the *New Yorker*, "we should know even less than we do about the British and Irish story writers" and notes that this magazine, "through a system of contracts and bonuses, pays handsomely for its short fiction, making it at least possible for its regular authors to live off their writing alone". Alongside the magazines, opportunities for publishing short stories in anthologies and author collections also declined in Britain (Pickering 1985, 75), although there were important attempts to launch series like *Introduction: Stories by New Writers*, and *Penguin Modern Stories* (1969–1972).[81] In 1976, the Arts Council started its *New Stories* series (which ran until 1983), intended to replace vanished periodicals and compensate for publishers' reluctance to publish stories in book form: "It is hoped that the Arts Council anthology will fill a need, providing a market for the good, and encouragement for the new."[82]

This narrowed print market was only partially compensated for by new distribution opportunities in the radio. Stories read in the BBC's 'Third Programme' were subsequently published in the BBC's weekly magazine, the *Listener*, and the BBC's Women's Hour also regularly included story readings in its programme. T.O. Beachcroft (1968, 216f.) appreciates the significance of the radio for the short story: "Sound broadcasting has a special relationship to the short story – and various good comments have been written on the craft of radio stories, such as an article in the *Radio Times* of 4 May 1956 by James Langham, who was a most understanding producer of short stories of all types for the BBC for many years." He also notes, however, that the medium, with its commitment to mass entertainment, had a natural preference for more traditional kinds of story-telling: "typical Somerset Maugham stories, with a personal narrator, an easy talkative style, and a clearly pointed event, are naturally suited to radio as they stand."

The relative conventionality of literary story-writing after the Second World War, up to and including the 1960s and 70s, is apparent in any survey of prominent writers found in representative anthologies and some of their characteristic stories. The following writers, among others,[83] worked on a wide range of themes and styles and are, of course, idiosyncratic in

---

[81] *Penguin Modern Stories*, edited by Judith Burnley, with a total of twelve issues, published not only work by British writers. The introduction to the first volume (1969, 7) points out its important role at a time when publication opportunities were scarce: "There are today so few serious publications devoted to the short story that there is no need, in introducing *Penguin Modern Stories*, to say more than that we believe in the short story, know that a great many of the best contemporary writers are working in this form [...]."

[82] Thus the introduction to *New Stories 1* (1976, 7f.), which was edited by Margaret Drabble and Charles Osborne.

[83] Other writers who published stories during the 1950s and 1960s (and in some cases even into the 1980s and 1990s) cannot, for reasons of space, be considered here. They include Robert Graves, Joyce Cary, A.L. Barker, Olivia Manning, L.P. Hartley, T.F. Powys, Doris Lessing, Roald Dahl, Frank Tuohy as well as writers from Scotland like Eric Linklater.

their own right, but they all practised their art of short fiction within the framework of the 'mainstream' modes already identified above.

Sylvia Townsend Warner, for example, began writing before the Second World War but published stories until shortly before her death in 1979. "A Love Match" (first coll. 1961) tells the story of a brother and sister who discover their incestuous love for each other after the First World War and manage to hide this from the village in which they live until they are killed during an air-raid in the Second World War and found in bed together. The story discusses a taboo subject but is traditionally narrated. "A Widow's Quilt" (1977 in *The New Yorker*) is a psychological study with a surprise ending. An elderly woman feels trapped in an unsatisfactory marriage and makes herself a quilt traditionally used by widowed women; while working on it, she imagines how her life would be without her husband, but then, in an ironic twist, it is she who dies and not her husband to whom the quilt's significance remains hidden. Another major woman writer during the post-war decades was Elizabeth Taylor, whose stories frequently focus on relationships and women's lives. In "Hôtel du Commerce" (1965/6), a couple experience a depressing honeymoon in France; they seem not to be able to enjoy things together and at night witness a most disturbing quarrel between another couple next door. While the latter seem perfectly reconciled the next morning, the honeymooners, who do not seem to talk about their problems, leave the hotel unhappily. "The Devastating Boys" (first coll. 1972) centres on another unspectacular, unsatisfactory life which can, however, be remedied. A professor's wife in Oxfordshire feels lonely and depressed until she takes two London children into her home. The children make her live again and also put life back into her marriage. A highly successful writer from Scotland who emerged in the 1950s is Muriel Spark. "You Should Have Seen the Mess" (1958) is a monologue story in which a seventeen-year-old girl with a lower-class but 'proper' background finds everything she does not know and that is above her "messy"; she thus ruins her first love experience, apparently without being aware of it. "The Black Madonna" (1958) is a satire of religious bigotry especially targeted at Catholicism. A childless couple near Liverpool are members of a Catholic community in which they make friends with two Jamaicans and enjoy their generosity toward the colonials. The woman is outraged when she finds out that her sister, a widow with eight children, takes contraceptives, not least because she herself longs for a child. She prays to her community's Black Madonna and miraculously becomes pregnant. However, when the baby is black – because the woman has some black ancestry without having been aware of it – the couple behave in a most unchristian manner and reject the Black Madonna's gift. Since everybody believes that one of their Jamaican protégés has fathered the child, the couple move to London and have their baby adopted for the sake of a 'respectable' life.

Angus Wilson also devoted his satirical attention to postwar society. His short stories provide biting criticism of the Welfare State and its social consequences, often through a contrast with the pre-war world of the 1930s. "Realpolitik", one of the stories in Wilson's first collection, *The Wrong Set* (1949), exposes the recklessness of postwar Britain when a new administrator of a museum uses a meeting to drive the old and not very efficient staff away. The new values of business and efficiency have replaced the older values of liberalism and scholarship. The old-fashioned and soon-to-be extinct 'dodos' in "Such Darling Dodos" (1950) are an elderly academic couple in Oxford who have participated in all kinds of left and pacifist movements since the First World War but who cannot communicate their ideals to the young generation any more. The Welfare State, the story suggests, has created a new conservatism and egotism. "Higher Standards" (1953) portrays life in a lower-middle-class family of 'Chapel' people in which the father used to be a lay preacher and the mother still does charity work. The daughter, however, is an upwardly mobile young schoolteacher who despises her mother and feels alienated from the people with whom she went to school: "She was about to pass by with her usual self-conscious, majestic disregard, when her loneliness was shot through with an aching for those childhood days before awakening prudery and her scholarship to the 'County' had cut her off from the village Standard Four." Postwar society is again presented as a society in which material advantages are easier to gain than before the war, but at the cost of more human values and in particular human relationships.

Social criticism of the later 1950s and the 1960s is associated with the so-called 'angry young men' movement. Kingsley Amis's early stories, for example, "all concern the bureaucratization of life", as Dean Baldwin (1985, 58) points out, "though Amis also exposes remnants of the class war as it existed in postwar Britain". "A Court of Inquiry" (1956) is set in an army milieu after World War II; an officer loses a useless piece of equipment, and the matter is settled with a 'court martial' which everybody knows to be a farce without consequences; it is a mere act of bureaucracy. John Wain's "While the Sun Shines" (1967) depicts the conflict between a farm labourer and the farm's young owner. After he has been challenged by the Jaguar driver because he has driven with the tractor to a pub, the farm worker decides that he will mow a dangerous hill in order to win his personal war against his boss's class. Alan Sillitoe became famous with his collection *The Loneliness of the Long-Distance Runner* (1959), several stories of which have young protagonists who live in a world of poverty, who rebel against and are accordingly relegated by society. "Enoch's Two Letters" is from a later collection, *Men, Women and Children* (1986), but the story is rather similar in theme and setting to Sillitoe's earlier stories from the 'angry young men' phase: a young boy in Nottingham takes refuge at his grandmother's place when both his parents leave their desolate home, each believing that the other will stay and care for the boy. An 'angry young woman' of the 1960s was Nell Dunn, whose collection *Up the Junction* (1963), about cockney women's lower-class London life, sold half a million copies when it first appeared. Like **"Prison Visit"**, all of the sixteen stories in this volume are very short and consist of large dialogue sections, which, through Dunn's use of sociolect, significantly adds to the stories' documentary quality. Scottish writers of the period have also been noted for their social criticism. Fred Urquhart's "Maggie Logie and the National Health" (first coll. 1967), for instance, is a tragi-comic story about a modest widow living in a Scottish village whom the rising fees of the Welfare State tempt to ruin her health and happiness. Having to pay more and more for the stamps on her insurance card, Maggie is determined to get "her money's worth" and all the benefit she can from the system: medicine, false teeth and a wig which she does not need at all. Before she goes as far as sacrificing one of her legs in order to get an artificial one, she is killed in a road accident.

Even the attitude of protest of the 'angry' sixties writers added more to the thematics than the form of the British short story. They remained within the mainstream framework that followed after the brief spell of modernist experiment early in the twentieth century. However, the 1960s were also the decade when a new *post*-modernist experimentalism dawned – even in Britain.

### *Postmodernism and the Short Story in Britain: Another Delay?*

'Postmodernism' is a notoriously protean term and impossible to define in any satisfactory detail here. As Linda Hutcheon (2002, 1) notes: "Few words are more used and abused in discussions of contemporary culture than the word 'postmodernism'." What is of prime interest for the following discussion are the basic philosophical positions of postmodernism and their resulting narratological implications. Postmodernism's most pertinent ontological position, a radicalization of a position already held by the modernists, is that any sense of reality is only a construct. In Hutcheon's words, "it seems reasonable to say that the postmodern's initial concern is to denaturalize some of the dominant features of our way of life; to point out that those entities that we unthinkingly experience as 'natural' [...] are in fact 'cultural'; made by us, not given to us". (*ibid.*, 2) Essentially, reality is a construct arrived at through language and 'texts' in all kinds of media, and it is accessible to the subjects who experience it *only* through and as textualization. Any distinction between fiction and what we take for reality thus collapses, as does the notion that literature can represent the experience of 'reality' mimetically. (The modernists, by contrast, had still attempted to achieve a representation of how the mind processes reality.) Abandoning such notions, postmodernist literature typically draws attention to its own status as a linguistic and textual entity. Brian McHale (1987) identifies the following features of postmodernist fiction: a high use of meta-fictional devices (that is, self-reflexive elements which refer to the text's own constructedness and modes of construction),[84] a particular frequency of intertextuality and intermediality which locates a text in another textual (rather than 'natural') universe; 'metalepsis' or the violation of borderlines between conventional narrative – and implicitly ontological – levels, like the borderlines between 'author' and fictional characters; experiments with the external form and structure of the text; a foregrounding of the workings of language and its elements (grammar, vocabulary, punctuation etc.) which draws attention to textuality as such; an explicit deconstruction of the conventions of mimetic narrative, in particular the notion of plot, which is replaced by non-sequential text structures; where still in existence at all, narrative is fragmented and highly intermingled with non-narrative elements. An outwardly more traditional form of a-mimeticism is fabulation,[85] a mode which revels in the inventing of stories, exaggerating invention and using fantastic elements; it often implies a deliberate rediscovery of such old forms as fairy tales and myth, that is, again employs a form of intertextuality to emphasize the story-ness of the stories it tells.

During the later 1960s, 'postmodernism' thus brought experiment back into literature in general and the short story specifically, challenging writers to abandon modes of composition which had become conventional over the past decades. An anthology programmatically entitled *Anti-Story*, edited by the American Philip Stevick and published in 1971, assembles texts by international writers under chapter headings that indicate in what respects the new experimentalists departed from what had become a 'fatigued' form and, in Stevick's (1971, xii) words, "perhaps the most conservative art of mid-century". Instead, the anthology offers texts that are *against* mimesis,

[84] On metafiction, see Imhof (1986, 9): "A metafiction is a kind of self-reflexive narrative that narrates about narrating." For a standard study of metafiction, see also Waugh (1984).

[85] On fabulation, see Scholes (1967).

reality, event, subject, the middle range of experience, analysis, meaning and even scale (by reducing short fiction to the extreme of the 'minimal' story). The departure from notions of established narration can indeed be so strong that many texts can no longer be at all referred to as 'stories', as Stevick (xv) notes about his anthology:

> One hesitates to call most of the works in the collection [...] stories at all. They are 'short prose works', 'pieces', 'fictions', 'sketches', 'fables', anything but 'stories', since that word, the word that most easily and naturally names the classic genre of short fiction, inevitably carries connotations of narrative ease, facility, the arched shape, the climactic form, all of these being qualities generally avoided in the new experimental fiction. The works that follow are, in a sense, a reaction against 'story-ness' [...].

*Anti-Story*, however, includes only three texts by British writers (Ann Quin's "motherlogue", Nigel Dennis's "The Pukey" and Michael Goldstein's "The Self-Contained Compartment"), and it seems characteristic of the situation in Britain that quite a number of writers whom critics consider 'postmodernist' rejected the label for themselves, as Birgit Moosmüller (1993, 61) learnt when she interviewed British writers of short stories at the beginning of the 1990s for her groundbreaking study of the contemporary 'experimental' story.[86] According to Ulrich Broich (1990 and 1993), postmodernism in the British short story manifests itself only in a 'muted' form when compared with the American examples of John Barth, Robert Coover, Raymond Federman or Donald Barthelme. Once more, this may be attributed to the fact that publication outlets for experimental stories in Britain were relatively scarce. Only a few copies of an early 1960s collection of pieces by B.S. Johnson and Zulfikar Ghose (a Pakistani writer), *Statement against Corpses* (1964), are still available even in British libraries,[87] and in the major magazines and anthologies of the 1960s postmodernist short fiction is rarely found. Only in Malcolm Bradbury's landmark anthology, *The Penguin Book of Modern British Short Stories* (1987) is a fair number of such stories included – at a time when the high time of *radical* postmodernist experiment already belonged to the past.

Nevertheless, despite a reluctant beginning, postmodernism *did* affect the short story in Britain even in its more radical modes, and, in modes that

---

[86] Apart from Moosmüller, major surveys are still scarce, but see Hanson (1989, chapter 6).

[87] The preliminary 'statement' to the volume identifies the short story as currently practised as a 'corpse' (with a chance to be revived): "These short stories have been written in the knowledge that the form is in decline, but in the belief that this is due to no fault inherent in the form. [...] This book represents a joint attempt [...] to draw attention to a literary form which is quite undeservedly neglected." (n.p.)

are less extreme, features of postmodernism (like features of the modernist aesthetic before) have been incorporated into a new literary mainstream. Apart from US-American writers, major influences in postmodernist writing in Britain were European movements like the French *nouveau roman*, intellectual trends like structuralist and *post*structuralist thinking, and especially the short stories of the South American writer Jorge Luis Borges. The latter's function as a role model is openly acknowledged in a story by Russell Hoban, "The Man with the Dagger" (1989), which intertextually 'continues' Borges's "The South". The narrator in Hoban's story, a writer, sets out to talk to the central fictional character of Borges's story, so that within the story, narrative levels are metaleptically violated and the borderline between fiction and 'reality' is overstepped: "I thought the story would be the most likely place to look for Dahlmann, so I went there."

### *Metafictional 'Stories'*

Writers of short stories in Britain associated with overtly metafictional forms of postmodernism during the 1960s and 70s include Christine Brooke-Rose and Brigid Brophy, Giles Gordon and B.S. Johnson, John Fowles, Gabriel Josipovici, David Lodge and Malcolm Bradbury.[88] To Walter Evans (1985, 162), the "most relentlessly unconventional" writer of the 1960s was Giles Gordon, whose first collection is entitled *Pictures from an Exhibition* (1970). The piece which gave its title to this collection is an exercise in intermediality; it consists of five 'fragments', short texts of a length between one and four pages which convey an impression of pictures and sculptures. The fifth piece also refers to a Beatles song, "Eleanor Rigby", just like the title generally alludes to a famous (itself intermedial) piece of music: Modest Mussorgsky's piano piece *Pictures from an Exhibition* (1874, later orchestrated by Maurice Ravel). The components of Gordon's literary suite are inherently plotless, sketch- rather than story-like, and numbers 2 and 4 even cross over into concrete poetry. The typographic layout of number 2,

[88] Most of the pieces by these writers are discussed in greater detail by Moosmüller (1993). Moosmüller discusses Brophy for her use of intermedial elements, like musical notation (and hence music) in "Variations on Themes of Elgar and Brahms", or a graphic sketch in "A Classic Detective Story", which deconstructs all conventions of the detective story, even to the degree that no real crime is committed apart from consuming a traditionally meaty English breakfast. Brooke-Rose is discussed with the story "George and the Seraph", an example of fabulation. For more thorough treatments of some of the writers and stories referred to in this and the two following sections, see also the interpretations collected in *Anglistik und Englischunterricht*, 50 (1993) and Borgmeier (1999).

for instance, word-paints the face portrayed in the work of art which has inspired the text:

> You have her face, there you have her face. You look at it, draw it:
>
> forehead<br>
> eye eye<br>
> nose<br>
> cheek cheek<br>
> mouth<br>
> chin

Such reference to other forms of art and media is found, of course, in the aestheticist and modernist story. In the postmodernist stories, however, its prime function is not to make a statement about the relationship of life and art or the role of the artist in society, but to draw attention to the constructedness of art itself.

Gottfried Schröder (1993, 7) emphasizes that "B.S. Johnson, who realized that the term 'story' was inappropriate when story-telling (in the traditional sense of 'telling tales') had come to an end, deliberately avoided the term when he described his own writing". In Johnson's *Aren't You Rather Young to be Writing Your Memoirs* (1973), the texts, composed between 1960 and 1972, are arranged randomly. According to Schröder (*ibid.*, 13),

> [t]he 'pieces' are not homogeneous; many contain bits and pieces of narrative, but causality and closure are avoided. Narrative elements are rather anecdotal, sketchy, sometimes just extended (and obscene) jokes ('Instructions for the Use of Women'). Other devices to break up the flow of (traditional) narrative are: the montage of two independent narratives ('Mean Point of Impact'), which are centuries apart; the presentation of events or characters like forms filled out; catalogues of behavioural strategies; long lists, containing dozens of items each; descriptive parts are artificially broken up into separate categories. Dialogues are sometimes presented like parts of a police report. The overall tone of the narrator is conversational, witty, ironical, irreverent; the reader is often addressed directly, confronted with strange events or satirical comments.

In Johnson's **"A Few Selected Sentences"** (1973), the very title points to the text's fragmentation, its apparently random collection (or record-keeping, as far as the first and last sentence suggest) of single sentences and short pieces from an assortment of highly diverse sources (which are unidentified and possibly invented): one seems to be drawn from a Renaissance description of the cocoa plant and the drinking of chocolate, others are anecdotes, unelaborated mini-stories. One of these depicts the illegal killing of a stag by men who appear to belong to a Robin Hood club, another tells about a woman who commits suicide because she is pestered by her overly religious husband, yet another narrates how the members of an alcoholized wedding party run into a police control, and so forth. As the penultimate 'sentence' of the text indicates, all this may add up to an impression of *"Life"* – which is thus characterized as a random and episodic affair. There is no overall meaning to life; it resists the construction of an orderly plot. In a metafictional passage fairly close to the beginning, the text also points to its own strategy of composition, suggesting that this anti-narrative way of writing fiction might be the only one through which the randomness of life can be captured: "I love anecdotes. I fancy mankind may come in time to write all aphoristically, except in narrative; grow weary of preparation and connection and illustration, and all those arts by which a big book is made." Big books – like conventional novels – are no longer an adequate way of fiction writing, but neither is the modernist story in which the epiphany was offered as a way of glimpsing at least momentarily what the meaning of life might be.

In the critical literature, two stories with postmodernist elements have gained an almost canonical status: John Fowles's "The Enigma" (1972, coll. in *The Ebony Tower*, 1974) and Gabriel Josipovici's "Mobius the Stripper" (1972). The first exemplifies what Broich has termed 'muted' postmodernism. Fowles here encases postmodernist principles in a plot that seems fairly conventional and is derived, in fact, from the classical detective story. A Conservative Member of Parliament, John Marcus Fielding, "[f]ifty-seven years old, rich, happily married" has disappeared without a trace. A young sergeant of Scotland Yard, Michael Jennings, investigates the case but gets no useful clue until he speaks with the girlfriend of the disappeared man's son. Isobel Dodgson, with a degree in English Literature, works at a publisher's office and has already published a story book for children. (One might therefore link her with Charles Dodgson, that is, Lewis Carroll, one of the most successful fabulators in English literature – just as it might not be too far-fetched to associate Fielding with one of the fathers of the eighteenth-century realist novel.) It is through Isobel, a character with literary ambitions (and perhaps an intertextual name), that the story gets its metafictional touch. Isobel suggests that it is only through inventing fiction ("Nothing is real. All is fiction.") that the enigma of Fielding's disappearance can be solved: "I do have a private theory. About what happened. It's very wild. [...] Very literary." In this literary theory, the pretense is that "everything to do with the Fieldings, even you and me sitting here now, is in a novel. A detective story. Yes? Somewhere there's someone writing us, we're not real. He or she decides who we are, what we do, all about us."

Within this construct, in which the borderline between fact and fiction becomes blurred, the literary woman suggests the following solution: Fielding was a man tired of the life 'scripted' for him by society, that is, the 'author' that determined his boring, predictable, fossilizing life and "made him just a character in a book". In order to become memorable, Fielding had to do something really unpredictable and yet unscripted: become an enigma, a mystery. He has thus killed himself, Isobel suggests, in a manner that will make it impossible to find his body. Having thus freed himself, however, from all conventional plotting, he also transcends the norms of the detective story, and a story about him cannot have a conventional "decent ending" with a perfect solution:

> The sergeant smiled down. 'Except writers can write it any way they like.'
> 'You mean detective stories have to end with everything explained? Part of the rules?'
> 'The unreality.'
> 'Then if our story disobeys the unreal literary rules, that might mean it's actually truer to life?' She bit her lips again. 'Leaving aside the fact that it *has* all happened. So it must be true, anyway.'
> 'I'd almost forgotten that.'
> She set out her saucer as an ashtray.
> 'So all our writer could really do is find a convincing reason why this main character had forced him to commit the terrible literary crime of not sticking to the rules?' She said, 'Poor man.'

Whether the fiction here constructed by a character within a fictional story is 'true' in the sense that it matches what 'really' happened within the fictional world, is never revealed. The sergeant remains unable to solve his case (although he gets the girl). Fowles manages to pursue an intricate play with fact and fiction and genre conventions within a narrative framework that is at once conventional *and* undermines this conventionality.

Josipovici's "Mobius the Stripper" is structurally more radical. It works with a device for which postmodernist writers have developed a particular fancy: the Mobius strip, that is, a mathematical model of a surface with only one side, formed by joining the ends of a rectangular strip after twisting one end 180 degrees.

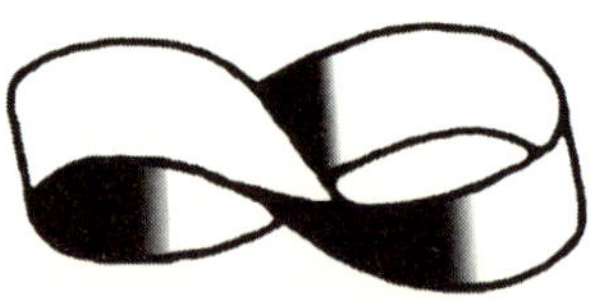

The American postmodernist John Barth uses the Mobius strip at the beginning of his book of short fiction, *Lost in the Funhouse* (1969). The 'frame-tale' at the beginning, composed of only one tell-tale sentence ("Once upon a time there was a story that began") comes with the instruction that it can be cut out and bent into a mobius strip, thus forming an infinite beginning. What intrigues postmodernist writers about the principle of the mobius strip is that it is an image of a non-linear structure and hence an ideal model for texts which aim to violate the convention that a narrative concludes and that a short story in particular should conclude effectively. The mobius-type text is typically inconclusive; it always returns to its own beginning in a manner which Brian McHale (1987, 119) calls the 'strange-loop' principle. Apart from this structural principle, Josipovici's Mobius story also takes up a preferred theme of postmodern literature: the idea that human identity is fragmented to an extent that the notion of a unified self has become redundant.

At first sight, "Mobius the Stripper" seems to consist of two stories. It violates typographical convention by presenting both stories simultaneously on two halves of the page, inviting us to read the text in a non-sequential manner. The upper text tells the story of Mobius, an enormously fat man who works as a stripper in a club in London's Notting Hill. He also strips an enormous amount of bananas which he constantly eats. Stripping can here be read as an expression of a desire, even a "metaphysical need", to come to the core of something. Mobius, through stripping, wants to get "to the centre of me", and find an identity which he lacks since he is completely unaware of his origins, his own personal beginning: "No one ever knew the origins and background of Mobius the Stripper. 'I'm not English', he would say, 'that's for certain.'" In the end, however, he kills himself since he will never be able to return to his own beginning and thus arrive at a core of his identity. The lower text has a metafictional theme, dealing with a writer who suffers from a creative block which is dissolved when the writer learns about Mobius and starts writing about him. The last sentence in the writer's story runs: "Then I sat down and began to write." Eventually, then, the upper half of the text emerges as what is being written in the lower half, and the Mobius strip is formed: the end of one side of the strip has joined the beginning of the other side. That the two halves of the story intersect is indicated several times: in the upper text Mobius hears voices which might be echos from the lower story where he is being talked about.

That metafiction marks the short fiction of Malcolm Bradbury and David Lodge is hardly surprising when one considers their other professional concern as professors of English literature with a strong interest in literary theory and in particular poststructuralism. Bradbury's "Composition" (first coll.

1976) embeds its postmodernist elements in what seems a fairly conventional story in the campus genre: the mishaps which a young British academic experiences at an American university. A prominent feature of the text, however, is its intertextuality, both to a key text of radical (post-)modernist experiment, Samuel Beckett's "Ping" (1967), and various forms of literary theory, including an important work about *The Sense of an Ending* by the critic Frank Kermode (1967). A metafictional element is also suggested through the fact that writing is the central purpose for which the story's protagonist has come to the university in a Middle Western Town. William Honeywell, well-versed in all sorts of literary theory, has to teach Freshman composition. Apart from that, he has various amorous encounters, and when he marks the essay of a girl too low is in a position to be easily blackmailed. As a solution to Honeywell's dilemma, the story offers three alternative endings, sections *Va* to *Vc*. These take the form of letters written by Honeywell himself, with varieties of how he might – or might not – extricate himself from the affair. Giving the reader a choice between endings is a metafictional device made famous in British literature through the multiple endings of John Fowles's novel *The French Lieutenant's Woman* (1969). It undermines the finiteness of the literary text and the authority traditionally attributed to its author. In a short story, the device is even more pertinent because the sense of an effective ending has become such an integral part of the genre's definition.

David Lodge's "Hotel des Boobs" (1986) makes prominent use of a structure related in effect to that of the 'strange loop' and metalepsis: the Chinese-box principle or *mise-en-abyme,* in which a story is embedded in a story which is embedded in a story and so forth. The effect evokes both an impression of infinity or resistance to closure and plays with the reality-fiction divide.[89] Lodge's story starts with a swimming-pool scene in which the protagonist enjoys the topless women sunbathing around him. It is then revealed, however, that this beginning is only a story within a story, composed by "the author" who is "seated at an umbrella-shaded table on the terrace overlooking the hotel pool". Then a mishap takes place: a powerful wind blows the sheets of his story away. When his wife returns from a shopping trip, the writer suggests that they had better leave the hotel since now certain hotel guests will be able to recognize themselves when they read fragments of the scattered story:

[89] See McHale (1987, chapter 8). While chinese boxes are used here as an image for a metafictional device that draws attention to the story-ness of reality, the image is used differently in the ending of Woolf's modernist "Kew Gardens" (see above, p. 130), namely as an image for the infinite richness of impressions with which the external world impinges itself on the subjective consciousness.

'I can't stand the thought of staying on here, on tenterhooks all the time in case one of the guests comes back from a walk in the woods with a compromising piece of fiction in their paws. What an extraordinary thing to happen.'

'You know,' said the author's wife. 'It's really a better story.'

'Yes,' said the author. 'I think I shall write it. I'll call it "Tit for Tat".'

'No, call it "Hotel des Boobs",' said the author's wife. 'Theirs and yours.'

[...]

The ending reveals, then, that the story we have just been reading is the one which the writer decided to write on the suggestion of his wife so that, by the end, we have been confronted with a triply-embedded story.

Adam Mars-Jones is another writer of the 1980s associated with postmodernism. His "Structural Anthropology", which closes Bradbury's anthology, illustrates once more the intertextual relationship which postmodernist literature enjoys with literary and cultural theory. The story proper is completely subordinated to critical analysis; criticism becomes more important than story-telling, and Mars-Jones here seems to satirize the self-importance of at least some critical vogues during the 1980s. The story component consists of a mere anecdote with urban-legend quality: a woman takes her revenge on her adulterous husband by glueing his hands to his penis. This act leads to intricate surgery and a long stay in hospital, during which the man is handled by women in the most unerotic, professional and humiliating intimacy. This mini-story is then analyzed mock-seriously in the mode of structural anthropology à la Claude Levi-Strauss, that is, in terms of rather obvious binary opposites like "Nature/Culture", "Limp/Stiff", "Food/Drug", "Private/Public", "Comedy/Tragedy". It concludes with a metanarrative comment:

> What remains of our original story? Certainly nothing of the sordid or trivial; these elements have been absorbed into their opposites. And simplicity too has yielded the complex, without losing its shape. For just below the surface of story, like the succulent separate threads beneath the skin of a perfectly cooked vegetable-spaghetti, lies the tangled richness of myth.

Mars-Jones came to fame with his collection *Lantern Lecture* (1981), which contains three longish stories. The volume dates one of these, "Hoosh-mi: A Farrago of Scurrilous Untruths", as 1977 – the year of Queen Elizabeth's Silver Jubilee, and Elizabeth II is also the story's protagonist. In Mars-Jones's fantasy, she has been infected with rabies (the illness against which the British have tried to isolate so vehemently until recently), and the event has to be hushed up in a machinery of media politics. This story exemplifies postmodernist fabulation rather than metafiction, the pleasure of inventing, of telling 'scurrilous untruths' because reality is an invention in the first place.

*Stories in the Fabulist Mode*

Clive Sinclair's "Genesis" (from his collection *Bedbugs*, 1982) combines fabulation and metafiction. The title is ambiguous, referring to various kinds of creation: in the Biblical context which the story evokes, but also the writing of fiction. In the story's version of the Genesis myth, God claims that the world he has created is only a fiction meant to entertain the heavenly creatures: "REMEMBER THAT WHAT YOU SEE IS NOT REAL. IT IS A FICTION." But in this fiction – which is of course a fiction within the fiction we are reading – a character who tries to write fiction suffers – once again – from writer's block. The narrator is an angel (a creature exempt, as he emphasizes, from the laws of fiction) whose brother has been thrown into hell because he has dared to criticize God's fiction: "Like creators everywhere, God felt that His critics misunderstood his intentions." The angel is given a chance to redeem his brother if he manages to "spend a year on earth without becoming involved in one of God's plots". Specifically, God demands that the angel, like Adam, "KEEP AWAY FROM WOMEN". However, like Adam, the angel is tempted. This happens in the city of angels, Los Angeles, where he gets acquainted with a Jewish couple; the husband is impotent and suffers from the creative block already mentioned while his wife longs for a child. She wants the angel to father the child, and when the required act is eventually committed, the angel has become a fallen angel and will have to spend the rest of his existence in the human world, that is, as a part of God's fiction. He is unable to redeem his brother, but at least the writer overcomes his block and begins to write "like an angel".

A Biblical theme is also taken up in a story of Julian Barnes's *A History of the World in 10 1/2 Chapters* (1989), a series of short texts (some narratives, others essays rather than stories) linked by the theme of shipwreck. The first is another ingenious piece of fabulation, "The Stowaway". This subversive rendering of the story of Noah's Ark is told from the perspective of a woodworm who, as a species dangerous to the wooden vessel, is on board only as an illegal passenger. He therefore feels not bound to the officially 'authorized' story of the Ark and gives his alternative (and allegedly true) version of the well-known tale:

> Now, I realize that accounts differ. Your species has its much repeated version, which still charms even sceptics; while the animals have a compendium of sentimental myths. But they're not going to rock the boat, are they?

> Not when they've been treated as heroes, not when it's become a matter of pride that each and every one of them can proudly trace its family tree straight back to the Ark. They were chosen, they endured, they survived: it's normal for them to gloss over the awkward episodes, to have convenient lapses of memory. But I am not constrained in that way. I was never chosen.[...] My account you can trust.

The postmodern leaning towards fabulation manifests itself most poignantly in retellings of such well-known stories, and it has unsurprisingly led to a new rediscovery of fairy tale and myth. Rüdiger Imhof (1986, 172) indicates why myths are so attractive for postmodernists or, in his terminology, metafictionists:

> A myth is an artefact, an artifice from a vanished world, and the re-telling of myths in the twentieth century in a fictional work that insists on its own fictionality is a fictionalization of a fiction and hence represents the creative procedure appropriate for self-reflexive fiction. Metafiction is a form of literature that totalises fiction. If the constituents of fiction are pushed to their utter limits, which they are if a totalization of fiction is intended, a writer can scarcely avoid the extremes of his artifice. In order to transcend the self-conscious flaunting of narrative conventions, in which he cannot remain if he wishes to eschew self-parody, he cannot adopt any other than the mythic mode. If he endeavours to stay consistent with his own artistic devices and design, he must develop into a teller of myths, or, more precisely, a supplier of variants to mythological formulae.

This statement can be easily extended to the fairy tale. Salman Rushdie's "The Prophet's Hair" (1981) is a fairy tale in the oriental mode but with an untypically unhappy ending even for the more likable of its protagonists. It tells how a precious relic, a hair of the prophet that has been stolen from a mosque, brings only unhappiness over those who come into contact with it. European traditions of fairy tale and myth have also been frequently reactivated by writers of the later twentieth century – in particular by a striking number by women writers.

Myths and fairy tales are narratives originally rooted in the patriarchal tradition and therefore pose a special challenge for feminist thinking and writing.[90] In fairy tale and myth the roles assigned to women are usually

[90] In an earlier phase in women's emancipation, Victorian women writers also (re-)wrote traditional fairy tales. See the anthology edited by Auerbach and Knoepflmacher (1992) which for the period from 1867 to 1879 includes, among others, work by Anne Thackeray Ritchie, Juliana Horatia Ewing, Christina Rossetti, Frances Hodgson Burnett and E. Nesbit. In their introduction, the editors suggest why the fairy tale offered women writers of that time greater freedom than other modes of writing stories: "Juvenile literature

predetermined, subordinate and passive – where they are not, the female characters tend to be demonized. At the same time, however, both kinds of stories also deal with transformations, with metamorphosis, and thus invite fabulation about the change of traditional gender concepts. Among the fairy-tale rewritings of the late twentieth century, the stories in Angela Carter's *The Bloody Chamber* (1979) are the most famous. The title story is a version of the Bluebeard tale, but also includes allusions to the popular myth of the Marquis de Sade, the tale about "The Beauty and the Beast" as well as LeFanu's vampire story "Carmilla". In "The Bloody Chamber" a young woman, a pianist, is brought home to her new husband's castle. As in the original fairy tale, the Marquis forbids his wife to enter a certain chamber in the house, and as in the ur-text, the woman disobeys. In her husband's absence, she enters the chamber and discovers its 'bloody' secret when she finds the remains of the Marquis's previous wives. They have been murdered in a most sadistic manner. Of course, the woman's disobedience is discovered; she too is about to be killed but is then rescued at the last minute. Although retaining the original's basic story, Carter's rewriting also departs from it in significant respects. In particular, her conception of the main characters is far more complex than in the classical fairy tale. The woman, for example, seems to take pleasure in her husband's sadistic sexual practices; she is not the stereotypical *ingénue* of the fairy tale; the Marquis is not simply evil but drawn as a disturbed personality. And Carter's story ends with a feminist flourish when the woman is saved not by her brothers but by a woman, her courageous mother. In "The Company of Wolves", Carter rewrites the tale of Little Red Ridinghood in a similar vein. Here again the female character feels attracted by the original tale's evil figure, the wolf. In Carter's version, the 'Little Red Ridinghood' falls in love with a werewolf who desires her, and she is unafraid, knowing that "she was nobody's meat". The story ends with and erotic image of her sleeping peacefully between the paws of the tender wolf.

When Sara Maitland wrote "The Wicked Stepmother's Tale" (1987), the feminist refashioning of fairy and other traditional tales had already become *en vogue*. This story retells the Cinderella tale; its beginning states explicitly that "[t]here's this thing going on at the moment where women tell all the

---

was produced in such volume that it could flourish uncensored. Since Victorian children were perceived as secure in their innocence, there was no felt need to expurgate anger, subversion, or literary experimentation from their reading." (2) Not included in this anthology is Elizabeth Gaskell's "Curious, if True" (first publ. in *The Cornhill Magazine* in 1860). The story imagines a meeting of well-known – though somewhat alienated – fairy-tale characters in a contemporary setting. For a general discussion of the fairy tale in late-twentieth-century English literature, see also Jacobmeyer (2000).

old stories again and turn them inside-out and back-to-front". The revisionist perspective chosen by Maitland is that of a traditionally wronged female character, Cinderella's allegedly evil stepmother, who rehabilitates herself as a well-meaning feminist whose cruelty was simply intended to instil the naive Cinderella with a sense of disobedience and independence: "All I wanted was for her to grow up, to grow up and realise that life was not a bed of roses and that she had to take some responsibility for her own life, to take some action on her own behalf, instead of waiting and waiting and waiting for something or someone to come shining out of the dark and force safety on her as I forced pain."

Classical myth is rewritten in Emma Tennant's "Philomela" (1975). Philomela, the sister of Prokne, is raped by her brother-in-law, Tereus, who subsequently has her imprisoned and her tongue cut out to hide his crime. Through the feminine art of weaving, however, the sisters manage to communicate, are reunited and get their revenge: they kill Tereus's son and serve him as a meal to his father. This is a story of women's solidarity and women's action; the sisters are not passive victims but know, if necessary, how to act as brutally as the man by whom they have been suppressed and harmed. Another myth, that of the woman transformed, is at the core of A.S. Byatt's "A Lamia in the Cevennes" (1996). Two stories of transformation are evoked here: that of the lamia, the serpent-woman (also treated in a famous poem by John Keats) and that of the fairy Melusine. In contrast to the examples discussed before, however, Byatt does not use these myths with a predominantly feminist intent. Rather, they become part of an artist story and are used to investigate the relationship between life and art. In the mid-1980s an English painter flies from a materialist Britain governed by Margaret Thatcher to live in the Cevennes and completely devote his life to art. When he discovers a beautiful snake-woman in his pool who wants to become his wife and thereby gain human shape, he ignores the creature's wish and uses her only as a source of inspiration. The disappointed snake-woman then attaches herself to the artist's friend who is less of an aesthete but capable of appreciating her femininity and giving her human life. The painter is left with the pursuit of another (and less sensual) object of beauty, a butterfly – apparently unaware of what he has given up.

With the attention it has directed to fairy tale and myth, fabulation engages with the past and old forms of story-telling. It also encourages speculation about the future, however, and a notable rejuvenation of science-fiction writing through the input of postmodernist elements. Science fiction, through its general interest in the consequences of scientific and technological 'progress', has an essential affinity with the upheaval of notions about the 'real' world that characterizes postmodernist ontology.[91] An overlap with postmodernist positions occurs most obviously where science-fiction stories of the late twentieth century emphasize the instability of time and space, that is, the categories through which we still experience our everyday world (despite the theory of relativity and quantum theory). "Memories of the Space Age" (1982), for example, written by the most prominent British representative of postmodernist science fiction, J.G. Ballard, is set in the future ruins of Cape Canaveral. The continuum of time has been destroyed as a consequence of an earlier space mission during which scientists, in order to conquer space, tampered with time. All characters in the story suffer from a false sense of time, which often seems to stand still for them. Events at Cape Canaveral, the centre of the disturbance, even appear to move in reverse. Ballard's "Dream Cargoes" (1990) adopts elements from Shakespeare's *The Tempest*. A young man – the story's Caliban character – takes over a ship, the *Prospero*, after the rest of the crew have abandoned the freighter which carries a load of highly poisonous chemical waste. This story deals with the perception of time, but also addresses other topical issues of the late twentieth century such as the pollution of the environment and interference with life's genetic material. The chemical waste 'magically' transforms a barren island in the Caribbean, where astonishing and beautiful new life is created. An American biologist discovers the man on the island and lets herself be impregnated by him to see how new human life will be affected by the transformations. However, the new life on the island turns out to be short-lived, and something has clearly gone wrong with time. 'Caliban' suffers from a distorted perception of time; his 'paradise' destroys itself since the natural biological clock is out of order: "Their cellular clocks seem to have stopped – instead of reproducing, they force-feed their own tissues [...]. The life of the individual becomes the entire life of the species. [...] That probably explains our friend's altered time sense – great blocks of memory were coalescing in his mind [...]."

The examples discussed in the last two sections establish that postmodernism *did* take hold in the short story in Britain despite the reservations of some critics and writers. In a moderate form, it has even affected writers who openly dissociate themselves from drastic formal experiment and return from a postmodernist concern with the textuality of 'reality' to texts about the morality of the contemporary world.

[91] On this approximation between science fiction and postmodernism, see also McHale (1987, 65–72).

*End-of-Millennium Moralists: Ian McEwan, Graham Swift and Martin Amis*

At the beginning of his career, Ian McEwan said in an interview in *The New Review* (1978) that "[e]xperimentation in its broadest and most viable sense should have less to do with formal factors like busting your syntax and scrambling your page order, and more to do with content – the representation of states of mind and the society that forms them". (quoted in Moosmüller 1993, 106) This is the programme of his first volume of stories, *First Love, Last Rites* (1975), his 'thesis' for a Master of Arts in Creative Writing taken at the University of East Anglia – and thus not quite exempt from the postmodernism fashionable at the time of its composition, as one can see in "Solid Geometry". This story uses elements of obvious sci-fi fabulation and metafiction, but certainly also represents a state of mind and the society by which it was formed. A writer who lives in an unsatisfactory marriage comes across a bizarre geometrical solution to this problem in his grandfather's papers: when a piece of paper is folded in a certain way, it becomes invisible for people who live in three-dimensional space because it then becomes part of another dimension. The writer perversely uses this folding technique to make his wife disappear during the act of love-making. He thereby makes come true what the woman has identified as the central problem of their relationship – he deals with everything as if it were fictional and not real: "'You talk like this was a fiction seminar,' Maisie said. [...] 'When you are talking,' she went on, 'I can feel myself, you know, being screwed up like a piece of paper.' 'Perhaps we *are* in a fiction seminar,' I said grimly." Apart from this metafictional dimension, "Solid Geometry" glimpses into a mind that has obviously lost its sense of the importance of relationships, that cannot make a marriage work any more but simply strives to rid itself of 'disturbing' influences.

Problems which people of the late twentieth century have in relating to each other are the dominant themes in McEwan's less obviously postmodernist short fiction. While more mimetic, these stories are also notoriously 'shocking'. Like other critics, Birgit Moosmüller (1993, 352) emphasizes McEwan's tendency to highlight extreme and grotesque aspects of so-called everyday reality and the fact that he does not hesitate to break taboos. Walter Evans (1985, 140) points out that "[d]espite his sometimes radical subject matter, McEwan for the most part refuses to concern himself with novelties of technique or with intellectual posturings. In his most striking stories he focuses on various kinds and degrees of monstrosity and perversion: physical, emotional, sexual, social, cultural". Violence against children is a drastic form of perverted relationships which is at the core of several stories in *First Love, Last Rites*. In "Homemade", a ten-year-old girl has sex with her brother. In "Butterflies", a disturbed first-person narrator causes a girl to drown after forcing her to have intercourse with him, but he is also a victim himself since his face is disfigured and he has become a lonely outsider. In "Conversations with a Cupboard Man", a young man, the first-person narrator, has been treated like a baby – restricted in both his mental and physical capacities – by his possessive mother until adolescence; when the mother finds a lover, however, she wants to get rid of her 'baby' as soon as possible. "First Love, Last Rites" deals with a problem of adolescence which the protagonists are eventually able to solve. A girl and a boy (who also narrates the story) have left school and now spend their first summer of love-making together. They enjoy sexuality but also experience the fears associated with it, especially the fear – but also fascination – of creating new life (the girl is careless about the use of the pill): "I had no wish to be a father, that was not in it at all. It was eggs, sperms, chromosomes, feathers, gills, claws, inches from my cock's end the unstoppable chemistry of a creature growing out of a dark red slime [...]." The animalism of their experience is emphasized through the story's animal imagery: eels (obvious in their phallic symbolism) and a rat which they hear scratching behind a wall of the room which they use for their love-making. When the rat finally comes through the wall, the couple panic and the boy kills the rat, which is then found to have been pregnant. When the protagonists bury the rat, "first love" and a "last rite", the initiation into the giving of life and the experience of death, go literally hand in glove.

Wrongs in contemporary relationships are also frequently addressed by Graham Swift, whose stories focus less on violence, though, but on isolation and problems of human communication. In "Seraglio" (1977), a married couple are on holiday in Istanbul. The place referred to in the title has symbolic significance, associating marriage with imprisonment and unequal power relationships between men and women. Istanbul is not only a place with historic harems, however, but also a place where the female tourist has just been molested by a man. The rift between husband and wife, by contrast, is the result not of a single act of emotional or physical violence, but of a mutual inability to discuss and thereby find a possible solution to relationship problems. Two people feel deeply hurt by each other; they in turn seek mutual revenge on each other. Their marriage has been marred by feelings of unacknowledged guilt: the man has betrayed his wife shortly after their marriage; as a consequence she has lost their baby; while he is aware of the sorrow he has caused, she feels guilty because she will not be able to become pregnant again. Since they cannot articulate their feelings, they deprive themselves of the only chance to make their relationship work again. Marital strife is also at the background of Swift's "Cliffedge" (1980).

The narrator of this story knows that his wife is having an affair because he has to care for his mentally retarded brother. Under this emotional stress, he does not prevent his brother's death through a fall from a cliff during a holiday on the coast. However, the brother's disappearance does not help the marriage anymore: his wife leaves the narrator for good, and he finds himself at the edge of a metaphorical cliff with his brother's death on his conscience for the rest of his life.

Another writer noted for the violence he diagnoses in the contemporary world is Martin Amis. The stories in *Einstein's Monsters* (1987) depict a world under the threat of nuclear warfare. As Amis states in his "Author's Note", the title of this collection "refers to nuclear weapons, but also to ourselves. We are Einstein's monsters, not fully human, not for now". It seems fitting that the volume closes with a piece of fabulation, a projection of what will become of a world in which people are not fully human. The final story of *Einstein's Monsters*, "The Immortals", has humanity exterminate itself. After a nuclear holocaust in the year 2045 AD, there will be only one survivor: an immortal who appeared on earth from another planet long before homo sapiens developed. He watches the final moments of human life in an apocalyptic scenario:

> We wail and dance and shake our heads. We crackle with cancers, we fizz with synergisms, under the furious and birdless sky. Shyly we peer at the heaven-filling target of the sun. Of course, I can take it, but this is suicide for the human beings. Wait, I want to say. Not yet. Be careful – you'll hurt yourselves. Please. Please try and stay a little longer.
>
> Soon you will all be gone and I will be alone for ever.
>
> I ... I am the Immortal.

Postmodernist elements, metafiction and fabulation, are not irreconcilable with an interest in the ethics of the contemporary world which some British writers of short stories have demonstrated since the 1970s. Generally, however, as Birgit Moosmüller (1993, 369) also observes, the short story in Britain has reverted to modes of writing more strongly orientated towards mimesis and *story*-telling in the sense of conveying at least a minimal plot. Arguably, it is this post-postmodern development which has helped the short story to become a more popular genre again. Radical postmodernism provided an important stimulus for formal innovation, but only in a 'tamed' version has this innovation become palatable for a wider audience. What may also have helped the short story on its way again is a willingness of writers to engage with topical themes such as the current refashionings of British society and culture.

*Tracing a Society in Change: Region, Ethnicity and Gender*

A survey of anthologies listed in the British Library catalogue which appeared between 1980 and 2000 identifies two thematic areas of which publishers apparently believed that books of short stories might sell. Apart from anthologies of stories in popular genres (detective, ghost/horror and science fiction), a significant number of collections have been devoted, firstly, to the issue of the regional and national identities in Britain and, secondly, issues of gender. More recently, there is also an increased number of collections with an interest in ethnicity, specifically, a new Black and Asian British identity.

We have seen already in chapter 1 (p. 17) that an increased interest in the internal cultural divisions and identities of Britain has been reflected in short-story production and collection since the 1980s. It was sparked by political devolution and cultural nationalism in Scotland and Wales, which eventually also led to a new interest in definitions of Britishness and Englishness. Scottish writers in particular have enjoyed major success over the last two decades. Some prominent names among them include Brian McCabe, Alasdair Gray, James Kelman, Bernard MacLaverty (who was born in Belfast but later moved to Scotland), Irvine Welsh, Philip Kerr, David McVey, Ronald Frame, Shena Mackay, Janice Galloway, Candia McWilliam, Ali Smith and A.L. Kennedy. 'Scottishness', however, is not their exclusive topic, nor is Scotland their exclusive setting. A.L. Kennedy's **"Awaiting an Adverse Reaction"** (1997), for example, is quite unaffected by a regional or national background: a woman gets injections for a trip abroad; the adverse reaction to which the title refers is not only a medical one, however, but also, as the woman suddenly notices, one against her partner. In a piece of fabulation by Irvine Welsh, "Catholic Guilt: You Know You Love It" (2000), the Scottishness of the first-person narrator is more prominent, but the story's dominant theme is sexual orientation, which Welsh treats in the taboo-breaking manner for which he has become notorious: the protagonist despises homosexuals but must do penance after his death during a heterosexual encounter by conducting same-sex intercourse. 'English' identity is explored, in turn, in Julian Barnes's collection *Cross Channel* (1996), through a contrast between England and France. The theme is particularly obvious in the volume's final story, "Tunnel", in which an "elderly Englishman" travels to Paris on the Eurostar train, reflecting on issues of personal and collective identities. The final sentence of the story reveals him to be the author of "the stories you have just read" – and thus also points to the narrative constructedness of identities *per se*.

Growing awareness of the diversification of British society and culture has made 'ethnicity' another prominent theme in recent British literature generally and in the short story. A number of Jewish British writers, for example, have explicitly addressed Jewishness in their short fiction since the 1980s, like Clive Sinclair, whose story "Genesis" was considered above (p. 158). Other representatives include Emanuel Litvinoff, Jonathan Wilson, Jonathan Treitel or Alan Isler.[92] Writers with a Black and Asian background have enjoyed a more spectacular breakthrough during the 1980s and particularly the 1990s with writers like Salman Rushdie, Hanif Kureishi, Romesh Gunesekera, Andrea Levy, or most recently Zadie Smith.

The Black and Asian *British* short story has developed out of the writing of migrants after the Second World War. A West Indian literature emerged in Britain already during the 1950s and 1960s. The stories of Sam Selvon, for instance, written in the first person and told by members of the migrant community, depict the racial discrimination which migrants from the Caribbean suffered in 1950s Britain, though in the humorous mood of the trickster story. "Obeah in the Grove" (1957), for example, goes back to West Indian traditions of folk narrative, telling how Caribbean tricks enabled migrants to take their revenge against the injustice they suffered from the whites:

> You want to know what them things doing up in that tree, eh? Well I will tell you. I mean, in the West Indies, from the time you see thing like that, you know right away that somebody in for something, because thing like that mean black magic and obeah. [...]
>
> Now, the latest rake when them English landlord and landlady want to sell house, is to get the tenants out, because the more empty room they have the more money they could ask for the place.

The story has a strong oral quality through its direct address of the reader and the use of some elements of Caribbean English. It imports a 'foreign' tradition of story-telling which reflects the foreignness of the migrant community in Britain.[93]

In the final decades of the twentieth century, however, migrant writing became Black and Asian *British* writing, a literature produced by writers born in Britain with African-Caribbean or African roots or a family background in the Indian subcontinent. Much of this literature expresses the

[92] For an anthology of Jewish writing in Britain which also includes short stories, see Cheyette (1998).

[93] A story about the migrant experience by a writer with a Caribbean, though European more than Black background is Jean Rhys's "Let Them Call It Jazz" (1962). This story also uses a voice that is unmistakably Black; it belongs to a narrator who is driven into mental illlness by harassment and racial abuse.

dilemma of living in a society that has only begun to understand itself as multiethnic and has not yet eliminated racism. But problems dealt with include such that also exist within the non-white communities, in particular intergenerational conflicts. In Hanif Kureishi's "My Son the Fanatic" (1995), for example, a young British-born Asian is driven to Muslim fundamentalism and thus gets into a severe conflict with his migrant father who, having always tried to adapt himself to British mainstream values, is appalled by his son's 'fanaticism'. A story by a Black woman writer with a Nigerian background also addresses intergenerational problems. Uchenna Izundu's **"It's a Hard-Knock Life"** (2000) renders the experience of a young black student who feels integrated in British society, believing that she is "liberated, living in this multicultural London". When her cousin has a love affair with a white man, however, she finds that she shares the belief of the older generation that this interracial relationship is wrong.

Writers with a Black and Asian background no longer write exclusively about topics involving 'their' communities. "Yorick", for instance, a story in Salman Rushdie's collection *East, West* (1994), is concerned with the jester figure in Shakespeare's *Hamlet*, and several of the stories in Hanif Kureishi's *Love in a Blue Time* (1997), which includes "My Son the Fanatic", are also ethnically non-distinctive.

The high attention given to matters of gender at the end of the twentieth century is rooted in 1960s feminism. The extent to which women writers have left their mark on the short story since the 1960s has already been noted, and much of their work has been inspired by feminist insight.[94] The writer most distinguished for a pronounced feminist interest, expressed both in her long and short fiction, is Fay Weldon. "Weekend" (1978) is a comico-tragic narrative told from the perspective of a harassed wife who has to manage an exhausting weekend at the family's country cottage with family and friends, playing cook and maid for everyone. When the weekend ends with her daughter's first period, the woman cannot withhold her tears, anticipating a similar fate for the girl. Weldon's "In the Great War" (1985) deals with the war of the sexes but foremostly a war between women. A young woman 'steals' another's husband, feeling pity and contempt for his first wife who did not manage the duties of her household very well. However, when the new wife is left to deal with the children of his first marriage, she goes downhill too and her husband returns to his first, less perfect wife. Eventually, the second wife becomes a devoted feminist. Apart from such realist and satirical work, feminist writers have also

[94] For influential anthologies of feminist stories, see Fairbairns (1978 and 1987).

produced science-fiction, fantasy and horror stories; Tanith Lee has been particularly successful in these modes. It should not have to be said that women writers are, of course, not necessarily feminists nor are they restricted to writing about women's lives or issues of gender in general. As anthologies of women's short stories[95] demonstrate, writers like Penelope Lively, Beryl Bainbridge, Margaret Drabble, Georgina Hammick, Michèle Roberts, A.S. Byatt, Rose Tremain, Penelope Gilliatt, Marina Warner or Jeanette Winterson have worked with a range of themes that is as broad as that of male writers. Tremain's "The Beauty of the Dawn Shift" (1996), for example, deals with a former soldier of the German Democratic Republic who cannot cope with German reunification. A growing interest in the construction of gender and sexual orientation emerges also from the increased number of gay and lesbian stories produced since the 1980s. Adam Mars-Jones's anthology of such stories, *Mae West Is Dead,* appeared in 1983; his stories "Remission" (1987) and "Baby Clutch" (1989), for example, deal with homosexual men suffering from AIDS-related diseases.[96]

The stories mentioned in this section illustrate that short stories written in Britain today address topics which 'concern' British society in fairly immediate terms. It would not be justified to subsume them under the 'submerged-population-group' formula. Rather, it is through their approach to major changes which British society and culture are currently undergoing that such stories have an appeal for a wider readership. And this appeal is, in turn, reflected in a market for and reputation of short-story writing that seems to have become more favourable again – at least as far as some writers and critics are concerned.

## *The Short Story Reinvigorated?*

In the 1990s, several critics found the short story notably revived when compared to its predicament in the preceding decades. To Charles May (1994, xi), it has enjoyed a "'renaissance' of interest". The publication platform for short stories had slightly improved already in the course of the 1980s; both anthologies and paperback magazines encouraged new writing in the shorter mode, as Gottfried Schröder (1993, 9) points out:

> Penguin made a very promising fresh start by launching the *Firebirds* (from 1982 onwards), full of by now famous names and innovative stories, unfortunately discontinued and now out of print. [...] Penguin tried again with

[95] See, among others, Hill (1991 and 1997) and Puschmann-Nalenz (2000).

[96] For other anthologies, see Reynolds (1993) and Leavitt and Mitchell (1994).

> *British Short Stories of Today* (edited by E. Jones), published in 1987; in the same year, Bradbury edited Penguin's most ambitious and representative collection: *The Penguin Book of Modern British Short Stories* [...]. The picture would of course be incomplete without at least a brief mentioning of *GRANTA*, Penguin's successful literary magazine. But if there was a revival of interest in short fiction during the 1980s, other publishers also contributed to bringing it about. *The New Review Anthology* was published by Heinemann in 1985 and the Heinemann group keeps track annually of the latest work with *The Best Stories*.[97] [...] The latest newcomer on the scene is *New Writing*, initiated by the British Council, which will be published annually as a 'shop window' for most recent British writing.
>
> [...] There is sufficient evidence that British short stories have been popular not only with readers, but with publishers, too; this is especially true when collections by individual authors are taken into account.

There are divergent opinions, however. *New Writing* contains an essay by the short-story writer Georgina Hammick – whose first collection, *People for Lunch*, appeared in 1987 – in which she complains that the genre still lacks support on the part of publishers, literary editors, booksellers and critics. According to Hammick (1994, 298),

> the traditional showcase for the story, the weekly or monthly literary/general magazine, has all but disappeared. (Since the demise of *The Listener* and Judy Cooke's *Fiction Magazine*, story writers seeking a first home have fared even worse than poets – *Stand, London Magazine, New Statesman & Society, Panurge* and *Critical Quarterly* being, I think, the only periodicals left which consistently publish new work of any length.)[98]

Remaining outlets for new short stories are the BBC's Radio 3 and 4 and, in particular, anthologies, which Hammick now considers the chief publication forum:

> One of the most useful and rewarding types of anthology must surely be the one, exemplified by *New Writing*, that in encouraging submissions from both established and unknown writers (on subjects and themes of the author's own, and written, in so far as is realistic, to his or her preferred length), acts as a forum for what is new and interesting in fiction and/or poetry. I wish there could be more of these. It's a solo collection, in hardcover or paper-

[97] *Best Short Stories*, edited by Giles Gordon and David Hughes, was begun in 1986; see the entry in the bibliography.

[98] The stories in Hammick's first collection originally appeared in some of the periodicals she mentions: *Stand, Fiction Magazine* and *Critical Quarterly*. For an anthology of *Stand* stories, see Tracy *et al.* (1988). *London Magazine* stories are collected in Rye (2001).

> back, that the story writer is hoping for, of course. But solo collections, on the whole (or unless you're Jeffrey Archer) don't sell and publishers, not unnaturally, are wary of them.[99]

That such collections do not sell particularly well is due to the fact that they are, "except in a very minor way, excluded from the award system". The major fiction prizes, Hammick (*ibid.*, 300f.) notes, like the Booker and the Whitbread, are for novels, while "[t]he prizes that do exist for story collections – the Macmillan Silver Pen Award, for example, [...] and the Geoffrey Faber Memorial Prize of £1000, awarded, in alternate years, for fiction and poetry [...] – although in themselves prestigious, are virtually unknown outside a tiny literary/book trade circle."

Despite such reservations, the short story seems to be comparatively well established in the British book market today and attracts the efforts of major talent. In the following section, a preliminary look at a few paperback anthologies of recent short fiction and the British Council's *New Writing* series – the annual publication launched in 1992 to promote contemporary work by known and new writers – will indicate which names have dominated the short story's genre landscape during the 1990s and what kinds of stories have been published in the hope of appealing to a general audience's

[99] This view is confirmed by a preliminary survey of the British Library catalogue for titles published between 1980 and 2000, as well as of the collections reviewed in the *Times Literary Supplement* and the *London Magazine* during the same period. There is a certain number of debut volumes, but the majority of solo collections and collected editions tend to be published for contemporary writers who are already 'established' and/or have proved more or less successful. The following list is in alphabetical order and far from complete, but the gist is clear: Kingsley Amis, Martin Amis, Beryl Bainbridge, J.G. Ballard, A.L. Barker, A.S. Byatt, Angela Carter, Roald Dahl, Elspeth Davie, Douglas Dunn, Penelope Fitzgerald, Ronald Frame, Janice Galloway, Penelope Gilliatt, Georgina Hammick, James Kelman, A.L. Kennedy, Doris Lessing, Eric Linklater, Penelope Lively, Ian McEwan, Shena Mackay, Bernard MacLaverty, Patrick McGrath, Candia McWilliam, Sara Maitland, V.S. Pritchett, Will Self, Alan Sillitoe, Helen Simpson, Clive Sinclair, Muriel Spark, Graham Swift, Elizabeth Taylor, Rose Tremain, Frank Tuohy, Sylvia Townsend Warner, Marina Warner, Fay Weldon, Irvine Welsh, Angus Wilson. Alongside these, there are collections of short stories by 'canonical' writers of the nineteenth and earlier twentieth century, including Sir Walter Scott, Charles Dickens, Anthony Trollope, Elizabeth Gaskell, Rudyard Kipling, Robert Louis Stevenson, Thomas Hardy, H.G. Wells, Oscar Wilde, Joseph Conrad, Virginia Woolf, Katherine Mansfield, E.M. Forster, D.H. Lawrence, Aldous Huxley, Evelyn Waugh, Walter de la Mare, W. Somerset Maugham and H.E. Bates, as well as writers who have enjoyed wide popularity in Britain since their first appearance, like Saki and P.G. Wodehouse, Hornung with his 'Raffles' stories, ghost-story writers like J.S. LeFanu, M.R. James, Algernon Blackwood and E.F. Benson, writers of classic detective stories like Conan Doyle, G.K. Chesterton, Agatha Christie and Dorothy Sayers, or science-fiction writers like Brian Aldiss and Arthur C. Clarke.

taste(s). Although the range of subject matters and styles is wide, this survey seems to confirm that radically experimental forms are still on the retreat, while certain postmodernist modes – in particular fabulation – have become part of the literary mainstream.

*Trends of the 1990s*

*The 'Time Out' Book of London Short Stories* (Lexton 1993) includes original fiction that focusses on London life and the plethora of possible approaches to this life. Writers represented here include Clive Barker, Robert Grossmith, Nick Hornby, Hilary Mantel, Lawrence Norfolk, Will Self and Adam Thorpe. Barker's "Pidgin and Theresa" is a fantasy depicting the confusions an angel causes on earth; Robert Grossmith's "S/he" takes current gender discourses to extremes in its portrayal of a disorientating world in which medicine makes all kinds of modish sex-manipulation operations possible; Nick Hornby's "Faith" deals with the unconventional behaviour of a football fan; Adam Thorpe's "Nothing But Bonfires" is an anti-utopian story set in a future in which books and the theatre have been banned and Shakespeare's works are read only by secret societies. *Shorts: New Writing from Granta Books* (1998) features writers such as Peter Ho Davies and Alan Isler, A.L. Kennedy, Livi Michael, Hanif Kureishi, Romesh Gunesekera and Louis de Bernières. Nick Hornby's anthology of original stories, *Speaking with the Angel* (2000) includes work by himself ("NippleJesus", about an artist whose provocative painting deeply touches the watchman who guards it in a gallery but which is then revealed to have been produced just for the sake of provocation and scandal), Irvine Welsh's "Catholic Guilt" (see above p. 166), or a story by Zadie Smith, "I'm the Only One".

The same names – alongside others – appear in *New Writing*, each volume of which contains a considerable number of short stories by new talent and the whole range of Britain's most prominent current writers of fiction: Julian Barnes, Simon Burt, Tibor Fischer, Philip Hensher, Adam Thorpe, Barry Unsworth, Jonathan Wilson, A.S. Byatt, Julia Darling, Penelope Fitzgerald, Georgina Hammick, Rose Tremain, Barbara Trapido, Helen Dunmore, Kathy Page, Marina Warner, Fay Weldon, A.L. Kennedy, Shena Mackay, Candia McWilliam, Alasdair Gray, Philip Kerr, David McVey, Hanif Kureishi, Andrea Levy, Romesh Gunesekera and Matthew Singh-Toor (one of the few writers included with formally more experimental texts). Rose Tremain's "The Crossing of Herald Montjoy" (1994) is a historical story about the Battle of Agincourt; Hilary Mantel's "Ties That Bind" (1996) depicts a friendship between two women that is based on a grotesque fight;

Philip Kerr's "Four Reviews in Search of a Biography" (1998) is a genre-bending 'story' composed entirely of (invented) reviews; Adam Thorpe's "Mercenary" (2000) unfolds the moral dilemma of a former mercenary soldier; in Helen Simpson's "The Tree" (2001), a middle-aged narrator faces problems with an ageing mother, and Louis de Bernières's "Rabbit" (2001) is a distinctly 'English' country story in which an incident during a bad-weather walk triggers war memories.

All these publications exemplify the great variety of stories that reflects the general diversity of Britain's present literary scene: women writers, 'ethnic' writers, writers from other parts of Britain than England leave a prominent mark on that scene; they write in modes that range from the fantastic to the mimetic, and about themes that range from angels to down-to-earth Englishness. As the publications reviewed also testify, print is still the prime medium through which the short story today is distributed. Our survey would be incomplete, however, without a look at how the short story fares in other media at a time when traditional print culture is (allegedly) being challenged.

### *The Short Story in Audio/Visual and Electronic Media*

In 1966, William Sansom wrote the following in an essay about "The Short Story" in *London Magazine*: "So stories may one day be written as fodder for ready-bugged ear-plugs or micro-discs, or whatever portends. But the stories will still be there with all their heart and art." (in Weber and Greiner 1977, 194) The story's standing in the current landscape of literary media seems to confirm this prophecy.

It has been mentioned already that the short story found a supportive non-print medium in the radio. Certain radio programmes (in particular the BBC's Radio 3 and Radio 4) still regularly feature readings of stories already published or stories that are written specially for radio. Even though the latter are often re-issued in the more permanent medium of print, short stories that are broadcast on the radio require a suitability for aural reception. As Duncan Minshull, a stories editor for BBC radio, notes in the introduction to his series of anthologies, *Telling Stories: The Best of BBC's Recent Short Fiction* (Minshull 1992, xi):

> Producing short fiction for radio always raises the question: what qualities do stories written for the ear share with those destined for the page? [...] Listen to a story and you are unable to go back and recoup your thoughts; no opportunity to ponder the convoluted plot or intricate description. [...] the radio story has to have even greater clarity and directness.

That reputed names can be won for contributing original fiction for radio is apparent from the writers included in *Telling Stories*: the volume published in 1992 features, among others, Angela Carter, Frederic Raphael, Maeve Binchy, Romesh Gunesekera and Michèle Roberts. An anthology celebrating BBC radio's programme *Woman's Hour* (Speirs 1996) and its regular short-story slot assembles work, among others, by Jeanette Winterson and Georgina Hammick. Winterson's "O'Brien's First Christmas" (1987) is a fantastical, bizarre story in which a Christmas fairy fulfils a wish for a sceptical saleswoman in a store's pet department, while Hammick's "High Teas" (1987) sketches the relationship between a High Church old lady and a young vicar who stands for reform measures in the Anglican Church. The short story's success in the radio is not surprising if one considers the affinity with oral narration which the short story has preserved until today (see chapter 1, p. 21). Short story audiobooks seem a natural consequence and provide a more stable medium for the story that is orally performed.

Film seems a less natural medium for the short story, in particular when one has the standard feature film in mind. Nevertheless, film and later television adaptations of stories have been attempted with a greater frequency than one might at first assume. Detective and horror stories, with their dense and climactic structure lend themselves to being filmed in the short format of a TV-series episode, but other types of stories have also been used as a basis for film – especially in times when films still tended to be considerably shorter than today.[100] The fidelity to the text of John Huston's version of Joyce's "The Dead" (UK 1987, 82 minutes), which is comparatively short for a modern feature film, has met with wide acclaim.[101] For full-length feature films, stories have often been only loosely adapted and considerably expanded in subject matter. Graham Greene's "The Basement Room", for instance, was the basis for *The Fallen Idol* (UK 1948, directed by Carol Reed, script by Greene),[102] Nicolas Roeg's *Don't Look Now* (USA/Italy,

[100] Smith (1973) and Emmens (1978) list films and the stories on which they are based. The majority of examples are American, but one finds a significant number of films based on British short stories. Many of these are detective, ghost and horror stories (by Chesterton, Christie, Conan Doyle, Dickens, W.W. Jacobs, M.R. James or Edgar Wallace), but there are also adaptations of P.G. Wodehouse, Robert Louis Stevenson, W.S. Maugham, D.H. Lawrence, Graham Greene and Aldous Huxley, to name only a few. For consideration of 'The Best Short Stories Ever Made into Film', see also Wheeler (1989). Marcus (1977) presents a detailed analysis of a selection of *short* films (all under thirty minutes) and their screenplays in comparison to the stories on which they are based, such as Saki's "The Open Window" or Katherine Mansfield's "The Garden Party".

[101] See, among others, Pilipp and Pederson (1993).

[102] For a comparison of the story and the film version, see Zambrano (1974).

1973) uses a story by Daphne Du Maurier, and Stanley Kubrick's *2001: A Space Odyssey* (USA 1968), with 141 epic minutes, is based on a story by Arthur C. Clarke, "The Sentinel".

None of these non-print media has seriously challenged the basic genre concept of the short story. A written story transfers comfortably into a reading, and a story can also be made into a short film or television play. In both cases, the original story retains what is perhaps its most definite genre feature: brevity. But what about the story as 'hypertext', the latest stage in the literature-media relationship? The term 'hypertext' today most usually refers to computer-based electronic texts (in the internet or on CD-ROM) which are both non-linear because they make use of links to other texts and other media representations (in sound and/or image) and interactive in that they require the recipient to select the links.[103] While the short story as we know it is defined by its limitation of scope and its focus on ending, one of the great advantages of hypertexts is that they can expand into a theoretically infinite web of levels and links. Hypertexts used for literary texts encourage non-linear reading and reader-authorship to an extent that even the most radical, print-based experiments of the postmodernists of the 1960s and 1970s could not achieve. The interconnectivity of hypertexts blurs the very notion of 'a' finite text. Furthermore, literary hypertexts have a high potential for transcending genres that developed in the print media. Hyperfiction easily integrates sound, still and moving images, links to purely informational databases, and so on. It may offer a choice not only between various developments of the action, but also such essential elements of transmission as narrative perspective. A piece of hyperfiction may abandon conventional story-ness entirely. Geoff Ryman's *253* (1996), for example, provides character sketches of passengers on the London underground rather than a distinctive 'action'. Nevertheless, in its subtitle this hypertext still identifies itself with a traditional genre label as *A Novel for the Internet about London Underground*. Similarly, there are also hypertexts declared as 'short stories', like Mark Weal's "A Major Hangover". This piece tells its story in blocks, offering readers a choice between various paths. It can also still be read linearly, however, revealing a fairly straightforward plot with a first-person narrator who finds himself in the aftermath of a party (including a sheep in his garden and a naked woman in his bathroom) when his girlfriend returns from a weekend trip.

---

[103] Some principles of electronic hypertexts have been anticipated in the print media, particularly by postmodernist writers. On hypertexts and literary hypertexts, see, among other publications, Landow (1992) and Rommel and Schnierer (2003), with further references.

The American writer Robert Coover speculated in the late 1990s that fiction in hyperspace, with its principle of 'linking', would be "ever lengthening". (Coover 1998, 138) Other features of the hypertext story also challenge a genre definition that evolved from the story in print: Is there still a special 'unity' and sense of structure where readers themselves determine the sequence in which the text is perused? Can hypertext stories still have a "pre-established" design as required by Edgar Allan Poe? Nevertheless, pieces like "A Major Hangover" demonstrate that a hypertext 'story' is significantly shorter than a hypertext 'novel' since it offers only a comparatively restricted number of links. The criterion of quantity at least has survived the short story's transfer into the newest medium, and it is still potentially possible to 'finish' this story, thanks to its 'pre-established' links, in the "half-hour to one or two hours" which Poe postulated as the ideal time for the story's perusal. The hypertext story is the final step – so far – of genre-bending; and even in this deliberately unstable medial form, something like a recognizably *short* story still manifests itself.

## Round-Up

This historical sketch has come a long way from medieval short narratives in verse to post-postmodernist varieties of short-story writing. Even if the short story did not acquire a distinct definition and status in the literary system until the second half of the nineteenth century, this kind of literature looks back to a distinguished pre-history – and as far as literature in English is concerned, it is in the cultural spaces of Britain that this early history of the genre took place. With its inherent tendency, because of its brevity, to depict moments rather than long-term developments, the short story may have a particular suitability for giving expression to the *condition moderne* (whether in modernist or more conventional form). However, short fiction in prose was put to effective use long before that condition arose, and long before the genre label 'short story' was coined and became part of readers' literary competence.

Both in its early and more recent manifestations, the short story in Britain has proved to be a highly flexible genre. It permits its practitioners to work on a wide range of themes in a wide variety of modes from the realist to the fantastic, the objective to the subjective. Short stories have been used for purposes as different as social criticism, aestheticism or (mass) entertainment. The short story has been deliberately commercial (once the appropriate market was established) and consciously artistic or even experimental.

It is thus impossible to see a single line or even uninterrupted lines of development. At any stage of production, the short story has participated in the major co-existing modes of the art of fiction generally (and thus has always also shared features with the novel). And like all genres, its history is marked by discontinuities as well as continuities (including the revival of older forms of narrative). It has been the prime purpose of this book, therefore, to present the short story as a many-flowered tree in the literary landscape of Britain, and to point out that some of the statements one often finds about this tree need to be qualified. One of these statements is that the short story in Britain has been overshadowed by the reputation of its American counterpart and that its appearance on the British literary scene was notably delayed. It is certainly true that the short story, during the Victorian period, suffered the strong competition of the three-decker novel and did not find an ideal publication platform until this competition ended in the mid-1890s. Nevertheless, as we have seen, a great number of stories *were* written even while the three-decker dominated the production of Victorian fiction, and the number of successful stories, especially in the Gothic mode, is too significant to disclaim such stories as having merely accidental success. In a similar manner, the view that the British short story has given a voice, above all, to 'submerged' experiences in the respective contemporary society and culture, seems too general. The examples surveyed include many stories that have indeed a potential of subversiveness or articulate what dominant cultural discourses at a given time have tried to exclude. Nevertheless, the short story in Britain has also been used as a vehicle to promote core cultural values or to openly satirize contemporary society.

Not least for this explicit engagement with society is it important to ask where the short story in Britain has developed in culturally most distinctive ways. Formally, Britain has participated in the genre's universal tendencies. Thematically, for instance, in a particular type of regional story, when it deals with class, or when it raises the issue of Britishness itself, the short story written in the various parts of Britain is obviously different from short stories produced elsewhere – whether in the United States or those parts of the English-speaking world that once were part of the British Empire.

# Part III:

## Anthology

ROBERT GREENE

## From: Third Part of Cony-Catching (1592)

*How a cunning knave got a trunk well-stuffed with linen and certain parcels of plate out of a citizen's house, and how the master of the house holp the deceiver to carry away his own goods.*

Within the City of London dwelleth a worthy man who hath very great dealing in his trade, and his shop very well frequented with customers, had such a shrewd mischance of late by a cony-catcher, as may well serve for an example to others lest they have the like.

A cunning villain, that had long time haunted this citizen's house, and gotten many a cheat which he carried away safely, made it his custom when he wanted money, to help himself ever where he had sped so often. Divers things he had which were never missed, especially such as appertained to the citizen's trade, but when any were found wanting, they could not devise which way they were gone, so politically this fellow always behaved himself. Well knew he what times of greatest business this citizen had in his trade, and when the shop is most stored with chapmen. Then would he step up the stairs (for there was and is another door to the house besides that which entereth into the shop), and what was next hand came ever away with. One time above the rest, in an evening about Candlemass, when daylight shuts in about six of the clock, he watched to do some feat in the house, and seeing the mistress go forth with her maid, the goodman and his folks very busy in the shop, up the stairs he goes as he was wont to do, and lifting up the latch of the hall portal door, saw nobody near to trouble him, when stepping into the next chamber, where the citizen and his wife usually lay, at the bed's feet there stood a handsome trunk, wherein was very good linen, a fair gilt salt, two silver French bowls for wine, two silver drinking pots, a stone jug covered with silver, and a dozen of silver spoons. This trunk he brings to the stairs' head, and, making fast the door again, draws it down the steps so softly as he could, for it was so big and heavy, as he could not easily carry it. Having it out at the door, unseen of any neighbour or anybody else, he stood struggling with it to lift it up on the stall, which by reason of the weight troubled him very much.

The goodman coming forth of his shop, to bid a customer or two farewell, made the fellow afraid he should now be taken for all together, but, calling his wits together to escape if he could, he stood gazing up at the sign belonging to the house, as though he were desirous to know what sign it was, which the citizen perceiving, came to him and asked him what he sought for.

'I look for the sign of the *Blue Bell*, sir,' quoth the fellow, 'where a gentleman having taken a chamber for this term-time hath sent me hither with this his trunk of apparel.'

Quoth the citizen, 'I know no such sign in this street, but in the next (naming it) there is such a one indeed, and there dwelleth one that letteth forth chambers to gentlemen.'

'Truly sir,' quoth the fellow, 'that's the house I should go to. I pray you, sir, lend me your hand but to help the trunk on my back, for I, thinking to ease me a while upon your stall, set it short, and now I can hardly get it up again.'

The citizen, not knowing his own trunk, but indeed never thinking on any such notable deceit, helps him up with the trunk, and so sends him away roundly with his own goods. When the trunk was missed, I leave to your conceits what household grief there was on all sides, especially the goodman himself, who, remembering how he helped the fellow up with a trunk, perceived that hereby he had beguiled himself, and lost more than in haste he should recover again. How this may admonish others I leave to the judgment of the indifferent opinion, that see when honest meaning is so craftily beleaguered as good foresight must be used to prevent such dangers.

Dr Samuel Johnson

## The History of Melissa (1750)

*Diligitur nemo, nisi cui Fortuna secunda est,*
*Quae, simul intonuit, proxima quaeque fugat.*
Ovid, EX PONTO, II.3.23–24.

When smiling fortune spreads her golden ray,
All crowd around to flatter and obey;
But when she thunders from an angry sky,
Our friends, our flatterers, our lovers fly.
Miss A.W.

TO THE RAMBLER.

SIR,

The diligence with which you endeavour to cultivate the knowledge of nature, manners, and life, will perhaps incline you to pay some regard to the observations of one who has been taught to know mankind by unwelcome information, and whose opinions are the result, not of solitary conjectures, but of practice and experience.

I was born to a large fortune, and bred to the knowledge of those arts which are supposed to accomplish the mind, and adorn the person of a woman. To these attainments which custom and education almost forced upon me, I added some voluntary acquisitions by the use of books, and the conversation of that species of men whom the ladies generally mention with terror and aversion under the name of scholars, but whom I have found a harmless and inoffensive order of beings, not so much wiser than ourselves, but that they may receive as well as communicate knowledge, and more inclined to degrade their own character by cowardly submission, than to overbear or oppress us with their learning or their wit.

From these men, however, if they are by kind treatment encouraged to talk, something may be gained, which embellished with elegance, and softened by modesty, will always add dignity and value to female conversation; and from my acquaintance with the bookish part of the world I derived many principles of judgment and maxims of prudence, by which I was enabled to draw upon myself the general regard in every place of concourse or pleasure. My opinion was the great rule of approbation, my remarks were remembered by those who desired the second degree of fame, my mien was studied, my dress was imitated, my letters were handed from one family to another, and read by those who copied them as sent to themselves, my visits were solicited as honours, and multitudes boasted of an intimacy with Melissa, who had only seen me by accident, and whose familiarity had never proceeded beyond the exchange of a compliment, or return of a courtesy.

I shall make no scruple of confessing that I was pleased with this universal veneration, because I always considered it as paid to my intrinsic qualities and inseparable merit, and very easily persuaded myself, that fortune had no part in my superiority. When I looked upon my glass I saw youth and beauty, with health that might give me reason to hope their continuance: when I examined my mind, I found some strength of judgment, and fertility of fancy; and was told that every action was grace, and that every accent was persuasion.

In this manner my life passed like a continual triumph amidst acclamations, and envy, and courtship, and caresses: to please Melissa was the general ambition, and every stratagem of artful flattery was practised upon me. To be flattered is grateful, even when we know that our praises are not believed by those who pronounce them; for they prove, at least, our power, and shew that our favour is valued, since it is purchased by the meanness of falshood. But, perhaps, the flatterer is not often detected, for an honest mind is not apt to suspect, and no one exerts the powers of discernment with much vigour when self-love favours the deceit.

The number of adorers, and the perpetual distraction of my thoughts by new schemes of pleasure, prevented me from listening to any of those who crowd in multitudes to give girls advice, and kept me unmarried and unengaged to my twenty-seventh year, when, as I was towering in all the pride of uncontested excellency, with a face yet little impaired, and a mind hourly improving, the failure of a fund, in which my money was placed, reduced me to a frugal competency, which allowed little beyond neatness and independence.

I bore the diminution of my riches without any outrages of sorrow, or pusillanimity of dejection. Indeed I did not know how much I had lost, for, having always heard and thought more of my wit and beauty, than of my fortune, it did not suddenly enter my imagination, that Melissa could sink beneath her established rank, while her form and her mind continued the same; that she could cease to raise admiration but by ceasing to deserve it, or feel any stroke but from the hand of time.

It was in my power to have concealed the loss, and to have married, by continuing the same appearance, with all the credit of my original fortune; but I was not so far sunk in my own esteem, as to submit to the baseness of fraud, or to desire any other recommendation than sense and virtue. I therefore dismissed my equipage, sold those ornaments which were become unsuitable to my new condition, and appeared among those with whom I used to converse with less glitter, but with equal spirit.

I found myself received at every visit, with sorrow beyond what is naturally felt for calamities in which we have no part, and was entertained with condolence and consolation, so frequently repeated, that my friends plainly consulted, rather their own gratification, than my relief. Some from that time refused my acquaintance, and forbore, without any provocation, to repay my visits; some visited me, but after a longer interval than usual, and every return was still with more delay; nor did any of my female acquaintances fail to introduce the mention of my misfortunes, to compare my present and former condition, to tell me how much it must trouble me to want the splendor which I became so well, to look at pleasures, which I had formerly enjoyed, and to sink to a level with those by whom I had been considered as moving in a higher sphere, and who had hitherto approached me with reverence and submission, which I was now no longer to expect.

Observations like these, are commonly nothing better than covert insults, which serve to give vent to the flatulence of pride, but they are now and then imprudently uttered by honesty and benevolence, and inflict pain where kindness is intended; I will, therefore, so far maintain my antiquated claim to politeness, as to venture the establishment of this rule, that no one ought to remind another of misfortunes of which the sufferer does not complain, and which there are no means proposed of alleviating. You have no right to excite thoughts which necessarily give pain whenever they return, and which perhaps might not have revived but by absurd and unseasonable compassion.

My endless train of lovers immediately withdrew, without raising any emotions. The greater part had indeed always professed to court, as it is termed, upon the square, had enquired my fortune, and offered settlements; these had undoubtedly a right to retire without censur, since they had openly treated for money, as necessary to their happiness, and who can tell how little they wanted any other portion? I have always thought the clamours of women unreasonable, who imagine themselves injured because the men who followed them upon the supposition of a greater fortune, reject them when they are discovered to have less. I have never known any lady, who did not think wealth a title to some stipulations in her favour; and surely what is claimed by the possession of money is justly forfeited by its loss. She that has once demanded a settlement has allowed the importance of fortune; and when she cannot shew pecuniary merit, why should she think her cheapener obliged to purchase?

My lovers were not all contented with silent desertion. Some of them revenged the neglect which they had formerly endured by wanton and superfluous insults, and endeavoured to mortify me by paying in my presence those civilities to other ladies, which were once devoted only to me. But, as it had been my rule to treat men according to the rank of their intellect, I had never suffered any one to waste his life in suspense, who could have employed it to better purpose, and had therefore no enemies but coxcombs, whose resentment and respect were equally below my consideration.

The only pain which I have felt from degradation, is the loss of that influence which I had always exerted on the side of virtue, in the defence of innocence, and the assertion of truth. I now find my opinions slighted, my sentiments criticised, and my arguments opposed by those that used to listen to me without reply, and struggle to be first in expressing their conviction. The female disputants have wholly thrown off my authority, and if I endeavour to enforce my reasons by an appeal to the scholars that happen to be present, the wretches are certain to pay their court by sacrificing me and my system to a finer gown, and I am every hour insulted with contradiction by cowards, who could never find till lately that Melissa was liable to error.

There are two persons only whom I cannot charge with having changed their conduct with my change of fortune. One is an old curate that has passed his life in the duties of his profession, with great reputation for his knowledge and piety; the other is a lieutenant of dragoons. The parson made no difficulty in the height of my elevation to check me when I was pert, and instruct me when I blundered; and if there is any alteration, he is now more timorous lest his freedom should be thought rudeness. The soldier never paid me any particular addresses, but very rigidly observed all the rules of politeness, which he is now so far from relaxing, that whenever he serves the tea, he obstinately carries me the first dish, in defiance of the frowns and whispers of the table.

This, Mr. Rambler, is ,"to see the world." It is impossible for those that have only known affluence and prosperity, to judge rightly of themselves or others. The rich and the powerful live in a perpetual masquerade, in which all about them wear borrowed characters; and we only discover in what estimation we are held, when we can no longer give hopes or fears.

I am, &c.

MELISSA.

'JUVENIS'

## Raymond: A Fragment (1799)

Night had diffused her darkness o'er the earth, and the moon darted her pale rays on the murmuring rivulet, which twined its narrow road through the fertile meads that surrounded the humble cottage of the unhappy Raymond, who was pensively reclining on a bench at the door of his cot. The melodious harmony of the nightingale, which at intervals floated with dulcet sweetness on the evening air; the universal silence which prevailed, and seemed (if I may so say) 'to waft the soul to realms unknown' together with his own melancholy thoughts, inspired Raymond with a degree of enthusiasm which he had never before experienced. When the sweet notes of the night-bird echoed along the dreary expanse he caught the harmonious sound, and when it died away expectantly waited for a repetition. His thoughts roved to the remembrance of past felicity, when he was blessed with the company of his much lamented and adored wife. His fancy represented her seated by him as she was wont, and at that delusive moment he forgot his miseries, and thought himself again blessed with his beloved companion: but when the visionary image had disappeared, and awful reality presented herself to his view, he exclaimed, with a voice half-stifled by the agitation of his soul –

'And are those truly happy days never to be repeated? Is she lost to me for ever! Oh, let me not indulge the heart-piercing thought!' Then suddenly recollecting himself – 'But what if she were to be restored to me – if I were once more to possess my lovely Miranda – and she to be bereft of that chastity, in the possession of which she was torn from me, tenfold unhappiness would be my portion! I should be miserable to eternity! The thought rends my very soul! Oh, God! why am I thus afflicted?' His agitated frame would not permit him to proceed, until after a short time, becoming more calm, he said, 'But what have I done? I have presumptuously questioned the great decree of Heaven, and thereby have justly merited its divine displeasure! Be calm; be calm, my soul! tear not my heart-strings thus with thy vague surmises; I *may* – Oh! the ecstatic thought adds fresh vigour to my nearly exhausted strength: it pours into my aching heart the sweet balsam of comfort! – I may once more possess my loved Miranda: I may press her panting bosom to mine own, chaste and unpolluted. But, oh! the thought seems almost impossible! – Yet, hold! there is an almighty being above, to whom nothing is impossible, although it appears so to my weak eye of mortality. To him I commit myself, and to his decree I patiently bow.'

Thus said Raymond: after which he seemed to have gained an ascendancy over despair, and sunk into a profound thoughtfulness.

He had not continued thus long before the air became tremulous, and the dull aspect of the heavens seemed to portend an approaching storm; thick clouds were rapidly collecting, and grew fast upon the horizon. The nightingale, affrighted, fled for shelter within her leafy nest; and the owlet, with dismal note, commenced her nightly wailing. Raymond was still buried in thought, when a distant and faint shriek assailed his ears. He started up; and, laying his hand on his sword, rushed into an adjoining mead, in the direction from whence he imagined the sound proceeded. He had not gone far before it was repeated in a more heart-rending sound, and seemed to be uttered by a person at the verge of despair. It almost froze the soul of Raymond.

Not until that moment did he notice the dreadful aspect of the elements; and, however regardless of the awful scene which he foresaw must infallibly ensue, he proceeded with eager inquiry, in order, if possible, to give succour to the person distressed. The voice seemed to be that of a female, and this discovery roused a sensation within him which again prompted him to proceed.

The thunder now began awfully to murmur from a distance, and the lightning streaked with fire the prominent clouds which rolled terrifically over the head of Raymond. The sky was so overshadowed with black vapours and impenetrable mists that they obscured every object, except when at intervals the moon-beams, darting between a cavity in the clouds, gave Raymond a melancholy opportunity of beholding the dreary prospect before him. He found himself to be entangled in an unknown path, and knew not how to proceed. He stopped to consider what he should do; and, after some conflict between his regard for his safety and his humanity, he determined to make the best way he could back to his mournful cottage, rather than still further bewilder himself in an unknown place.

He was turning round, in order to prosecute his intention, when a vivid flash of lightning, succeeded by a dreadful clap of thunder, burst over the spot on which he was standing, and seemed to rend the firmament. He stood appalled; never had dread seized him in so powerful a degree before; and he had scarcely recovered from the shock it had occasioned, when another shriek, much louder than either of the former, assailed his ears. The sound seemed to issue from a spot not far distant. He knew not which track to pursue, and was bewildered in a place, the labyrinths of which he was totally unacquainted with. His senses were confounded; and he, a second time, questioned himself whether it would be more advisable to proceed or return. He felt a peculiar *something* throb within his breast prompting him to the former: it was not merely a common sensation which he now experienced; a sensation which must naturally arise from the desire of dispensing succour to the unhappy; but a something, he knew not what, blended with that which rendered all return impracticable. He felt as if his own happiness were implicated with the present adventure; and, scarcely had he determined to proceed, when he perceived a light burst from a place at no great distance. He had not the least doubt but that the dreadful shrieks he had heard must have proceeded from thence. He grasped his sword, ejaculated a prayer to the director of all events, and rushed with alacrity to the place whence the light issued. The rain now poured from the swoln clouds with tremendous fury, and the hoarse thunder resounded reiteratedly along the perturbed vault of heaven. Raymond, undaunted by the rage of the storm, rushed on, totally occupied with the hope of giving his feeble aid to the piteous mourner.

It was not long ere his twinkling guide conducted him to the front of an ancient tower, whose walls were tottering under the decay of time. The light remained visible at the broken casement from whence he first observed it, and he traversed around the moss-covered walls in order to find an entrance. It was not long before he perceived one, to his great joy, open. As he was about to enter, a loud peal of thunder shook the hoary pile to its foundation; and he, ejaculating another prayer to Heaven, entered with a firm step the massy portal. He proceeded along a dark passage, which conveyed him into a spacious court-yard. The aspect of the place, although greatly decayed, still retained its native grandeur.

Whilst Raymond stood musing on the extraordinary adventure, which had drawn him thus far from his home, he perceived another light issue from a small casement, and almost instantly disappear. A violent crash now broke upon the prevailing silence, and seemed to convulse the earth. The sound indicated it to be the falling of armour. The dread it occasioned in the mind of Raymond can better be conceived than described: however, his ruffled spirit soon overcame the shock; and, by the assistance of a sudden flash of lightning, he perceived a small door situated at the extremity of the place in which he was. This was an entrance into the small turret from whence the light had before appeared and vanished. He advanced firmly towards it, and found it fast; but, on applying his strength, it flew open, and its harsh creaking hinges gave a doleful jar. He now found himself at the foot of a mouldering stair-case, and was ascending it when he distinctly heard foot-steps from above, and, almost instantly afterwards, two successive shrieks resounded through the tottering edifice. The sound, thrilling as it was, added fresh vigour to the soul of Raymond, since it confirmed the object of his solicitude to be in the turret in which he was; and, quickening his pace up the crazy steps, he soon arrived at a landing-place.

The first object that presented itself, was an old suit of armour lying on the ground, which had evidently just fallen down and occasioned the sound just mentioned. Raymond approached it: but judge his horror, his astonishment, when he, assisted by the rays of a glimmering lamp, perceived it still to confine within its rusty frame the skeleton of a human being. The sight sickened him; he recoiled with disgust, and proceeded onwards; muttering a prayer for the soul of the poor departed mortal.

In a few moments he arrived in a large Gothic chamber, in which a dreary lamp was suspended from the ceiling. But upon his entrance into this gloomy chamber, a tremendous clap of thunder burst over the edifice, and appalled him. A secret impulse directed his attention to a small door at the further end of the room. He distinctly heard footsteps from within, and a faint voice exclaim, 'Oh, spare me! spare me!' which was succeeded by a deep and convulsive groan. He sprang towards the door, which being only a-jar permitted him to enter; but oh, what a dreadful spectacle presented itself to the astonished Raymond. He beheld a man, brandishing, exultingly, a dagger, reeking with blood, over the body of a female, who had fallen a victim to his barbarity. His savage triumph was not long lived; for Raymond soon gave him that reward he so justly deserved, and thus, revenging the death of the murdered female, sent his loaded soul to expiate his mortal crimes in the regions of eternal misery.

He now approached the corpse of the unfortunate fair. On beholding her distorted countenance, a sudden shivering seized him, his strength failed him; he tottered a few paces back, and fell senseless to the floor. – It was Miranda.

Amelia Edwards

## The Phantom Coach (1864)

The circumstances I am about to relate to you have truth to recommend them. They happened to myself, and my recollection of them is as vivid as if they had taken place only yesterday. Twenty years, however, have gone by since that night. During those twenty years I have told the story to but one other person. I tell it now with a reluctance which I find it difficult to overcome. All I entreat, meanwhile, is that you will abstain from forcing your own conclusions upon me. I want nothing explained away. I desire no arguments. My mind on this subject is quite made up, and, having the testimony of my own senses to rely upon, I prefer to abide by it.

Well! It was just twenty years ago, and within a day or two of the end of the grouse season. I had been out all day with my gun, and had had no sport to speak of. The wind was due east; the month, December; the place, a bleak wide moor in the far north of England. And I had lost my way. It was not a pleasant place in which to lose one's way, with the first feathery flakes of a coming snowstorm just fluttering down upon the heather, and the leaden evening closing in all around. I shaded my eyes with my hand, and stared anxiously into the gathering darkness, where the purple moorland melted into a range of low hills, some ten or twelve miles distant. Not the faintest smoke-wreath, not the tiniest cultivated patch, or fence, or sheep-track, met my eyes in any direction. There was nothing for it but to walk on, and take my chance of finding what shelter I could, by the way. So I shouldered my gun again, and pushed wearily forward; for I had been on foot since an hour after daybreak, and had eaten nothing since breakfast.

Meanwhile, the snow began to come down with ominous steadiness, and the wind fell. After this, the cold became more intense, and the night came rapidly up. As for me, my prospects darkened with the darkening sky, and my heart grew heavy as I thought how my young wife was already watching for me through the window of our little inn parlour, and thought of all the suffering in store for her throughout this weary night. We had been married four months, and, having spent our autumn in the Highlands, were now lodging in a remote little village situated just on the verge of the great English moorlands. We were very much in love, and, of course, very happy. This morning, when we parted, she had implored me to return before dusk, and I had promised her that I would. What would I not have given to have kept my word!

Even now, weary as I was, I felt that with a supper, an hour's rest, and a guide, I might still get back to her before midnight, if only guide and shelter could be found.

And all this time, the snow fell and the night thickened. I stopped and shouted every now and then, but my shouts seemed only to make the silence deeper. Then a vague sense of uneasiness came upon me, and I began to remember stories of travellers who had walked on and on in the falling snow until, wearied out, they were fain to lie down and sleep their lives away. Would it be possible, I asked myself, to keep on thus through all the long dark night? Would there not come a time when my limbs must fail, and my resolution give way? When I, too, must sleep the sleep of death. Death! I shuddered. How hard to die just now, when life lay all so bright before me! How hard for my darling, whose whole loving heart – but that thought was not to be borne! To banish it, I shouted again, louder and longer, and then listened eagerly. Was my shout answered, or did I only fancy that I heard a far-off cry? I halloed again, and again the echo followed. Then a wavering speck of light came suddenly out of the dark, shifting, disappearing, growing momentarily nearer and brighter. Running towards it at full speed, I found myself, to my great joy, face to face with an old man and a lantern.

'Thank God!' was the exclamation that burst involuntarily from my lips.

Blinking and frowning, he lifted his lantern and peered into my face.

'What for?' growled he, sulkily.

'Well – for you. I began to fear I should be lost in the snow.'

'Eh, then, folks do get cast away hereabouts fra' time to time, an' what's to hinder you from bein' cast away likewise, if the Lord's so minded?'

'If the Lord is so minded that you and I shall be lost together, friend, we must submit,' I replied; 'but I don't mean to be lost without you. How far am I now from Dwolding?'

'A gude twenty mile, more or less.'

'And the nearest village?'

'The nearest village is Wyke, an' that's twelve mile t'other side.'

'Where do you live, then?'

'Out yonder,' said he, with a vague jerk of the lantern.

'You're going home, I presume?'

'Maybe I am.'

'Then I'm going with you.'

The old man shook his head, and rubbed his nose reflectively with the handle of the lantern.

'It ain't o' no use,' growled he. 'He 'ont let you in – not he.'

'We'll see about that,' I replied, briskly. 'Who is He?'

'The master.'

'Who is the master?'

'That's nowt to you,' was the unceremonious reply.

'Well, well; you lead the way, and I'll engage that the master shall give me shelter and a supper to-night.'

'Eh, you can try him!' muttered my reluctant guide; and, still shaking his head, he hobbled, gnome-like, away through the falling snow. A large mass loomed up presently out of the darkness, and a huge dog rushed out, barking furiously.

'Is this the house?' I asked.

'Ay, it's the house. Down, Bey!' And he fumbled in his pocket for the key.

I drew up close behind him, prepared to lose no chance of entrance, and saw in the little circle of light shed by the lantern that the door was heavily studded with iron nails, like the door of a prison. In another minute he had turned the key and I had pushed past him into the house.

Once inside, I looked round with curiosity, and found myself in a great raftered hall, which served, apparently, a variety of uses. One end was piled to the roof with corn, like a barn. The other was stored with flour-sacks, agricultural implements, casks, and all kinds of miscellaneous lumber; while from the beams overhead hung rows of hams, flitches, and bunches of dried herbs for winter use. In the centre of the floor stood some huge object gauntly dressed in a dingy wrapping-cloth, and reaching half way to the rafters. Lifting a corner of this cloth, I saw, to my surprise, a telescope of very considerable size, mounted on a rude movable platform, with four small wheels. The tube was made of painted wood, bound round with bands of metal rudely fashioned; the speculum, so far as I could estimate its size in the dim light, measured at least fifteen inches in diameter. While I was yet examining the instrument, and asking myself whether it was not the work of some self-taught optician, a bell rang sharply.

'That's for you,' said my guide, with a malicious grin. 'Yonder's his room.'

He pointed to a low black door at the opposite side of the hall. I crossed over, rapped somewhat loudly, and went in, without waiting for an invitation. A huge, white-haired old man rose from a table covered with books and papers, and confronted me sternly.

'Who are you?' said he. 'How came you here? What do you want?'

'James Murray, barrister-at-law. On foot across the moor. Meat, drink, and sleep.'

He bent his bushy brows into a portentous frown.

'Mine is not a house of entertainment,' he said, haughtily. 'Jacob, how dared you admit this stranger?'

'I didn't admit him,' grumbled the old man. 'He followed me over the muir, and shouldered his way in before me. I'm no match for six foot two.'

'And pray, sir, by what right have you forced an entrance into my house?'

'The same by which I should have clung to your boat, if I were drowning. The right of self-preservation.'

'Self-preservation?'

'There's an inch of snow on the ground already,' I replied, briefly; 'and it would be deep enough to cover my body before daybreak.'

He strode to the window, pulled aside a heavy black curtain, and looked out.

'It is true,' he said. 'You can stay, if you choose, till morning. Jacob, serve the supper.'

With this he waved me to a seat, resumed his own, and became at once absorbed in the studies from which I had disturbed him.

I placed my gun in a corner, drew a chair to the hearth, and examined my quarters at leisure. Smaller and less incongruous in its arrangements than the hall, this room contained, nevertheless, much to awaken my curiosity. The floor was carpetless. The whitewashed walls were in parts scrawled over with strange diagrams, and in others covered with shelves crowded with philosophical instruments, the uses of many of which were unknown to me. On one side of the fireplace, stood a bookcase filled with dingy folios; on the other, a small organ, fantastically decorated with painted carvings of medieval saints and devils. Through the half-opened door of a cupboard at the further end of the room, I saw a long array of geological specimens, surgical preparations, crucibles, retorts, and jars of chemicals; while on the mantelshelf beside me, amid a number of small objects, stood a model of the solar system, a small galvanic battery, and a microscope. Every chair had its burden. Every corner was heaped high with books. The very floor was littered over with maps, casts, papers, tracings, and learned lumber of all conceivable kinds.

I stared about me with an amazement increased by every fresh object upon which my eyes chanced to rest. So strange a room I had never seen; yet seemed it stranger still, to find such a room in a lone farmhouse amid those wild and solitary moors! Over and over again, I looked from my host to his surroundings, and from his surroundings back to my host, asking myself who and what he could be? His head was singularly fine; but it was more the head of a poet than of a philosopher. Broad in the temples, prominent over the eyes, and clothed with a rough profusion of perfectly white hair, it had all the ideality and much of the ruggedness that characterises the head of Louis von Beethoven. There were the same deep lines about the mouth, and the same stern furrows in the brow. There was the same concentration of expression. While I was yet observing him, the door opened, and Jacob brought in the supper. His master then closed his book, rose, and with more courtesy of manner than he had yet shown, invited me to the table.

A dish of ham and eggs, a loaf of brown bread, and a bottle of admirable sherry, were placed before me.

'I have but the homeliest farmhouse fare to offer you, sir,' said my entertainer. 'Your appetite, I trust, will make up for the deficiencies of our larder.'

I had already fallen upon the viands, and now protested, with the enthusiasm of a starving sportsman, that I had never eaten anything so delicious.

He bowed stiffly, and sat down to his own supper, which consisted, primitively, of a jug of milk and a basin of porridge. We ate in silence, and, when we had done, Jacob removed the tray. I then drew my chair back to the fireside. My host, somewhat to my surprise, did the same, and turning abruptly towards me, said:

'Sir, I have lived here in strict retirement for three-and-twenty years. During that time, I have not seen as many strange faces, and I have not read a single newspaper. You are the first stranger who has crossed my threshold for more than four years. Will you favour me with a few words of information respecting that outer world from which I have parted company so long?'

'Pray interrogate me,' I replied. 'I am heartily at your service.'

He bent his head in acknowledgement; leaned forward, with his elbows resting on his knees and his chin supported in the palms of his hands; stared fixedly into the fire; and proceeded to question me.

His inquiries related chiefly to scientific matters, with the later progress of which, as applied to the practical purposes of life, he was almost wholly unacquainted. No student of science myself, I replied as well as my slight information permitted; but the task was far from easy, and I was much relieved when, passing from interrogation to discussion, he began pouring forth his own conclusions upon the facts which I had been attempting to place before him. He talked, and I listened spellbound. He talked till I believe he almost forgot my presence, and only thought aloud. I had never heard anything like it then; I have never heard anything like it since. Familiar with all systems of all philosophies, subtle in analysis, bold in generalisation, he poured forth his thoughts in an uninterrupted stream, and, still leaning forward in the same moody attitude with his eyes fixed upon the fire, wandered from topic to topic, from speculation to speculation, like an inspired dreamer. From practical science to mental philosophy; from electricity in the wire to electricity in the nerve; from Watts to Mesmer, from Mesmer to Reichenbach, from Reichenbach to Swedenborg, Spinoza, Condillac, Descartes, Berkeley, Aristotle, Plato, and the Magi and mystics of the East, were transitions which, however bewildering in their variety and scope, seemed easy and harmonious upon his lips as sequences in music. By-and-by – I forget now by what link of conjecture or illustration – he passed on to that field which lies beyond the boundary line of even conjectural philosophy, and reaches no man knows whither. He spoke of the soul and its aspirations; of the spirit and its powers; of second sight; of prophecy; of those phenomena which, under the names of ghosts, spectres, and supernatural appearances, have been denied by the sceptics and attested by the credulous, of all ages.

'The world,' he said, 'grows hourly more and more sceptical of all that lies beyond its own narrow radius; and our men of science foster the fatal tendency. They condemn as fable all that resists experiment. They reject as false all that cannot be brought to the test of the laboratory or the dissecting-room. Against what superstition have they waged so long and obstinate a war, as against the belief in apparitions? And yet what superstition has maintained its hold upon the minds of men so long and so firmly? Show me any fact in physics, in history, in archaeology, which is supported by testimony so wide and so various. Attested by all races of men, in all ages, and in all climates, by the soberest sages of antiquity, by the rudest savage of today, by the Christian, the Pagan, the Pantheist, the Materialist, this phenomenon is treated as a nursery tale by the philosophers of our century. Circumstantial evidence weighs with them as a feather in the balance. The comparison of causes with effects, however valuable in physical science, is put aside as worthless and unreliable. The evidence of competent witnesses, however conclusive in a court of justice, counts for nothing. He who pauses before he pronounces, is condemned as a trifler. He who believes, is a dreamer or a fool.'

He spoke with bitterness, and, having said thus, relapsed for some minutes into silence. Presently he raised his head from his hands, and added, with an altered voice and manner,

'I, sir, paused, investigated, believed, and was not ashamed to state my convictions to the world. I, too, was branded as a visionary, held up to ridicule by my contemporaries, and hooted from that field of science in which I had laboured with honour during all the best years of my life. These things happened just three-and-twenty years ago. Since then, I have lived as you see me living now, and the world has forgotten me, as I have forgotten the world. You have my history.'

'It is a very sad one,' I murmured, scarcely knowing what to answer.

'It is a very common one,' he replied. 'I have only suffered for the truth, as many a better and wiser man has suffered before me.'

He rose, as if desirous of ending the conversation, and went over to the window.

'It has ceased snowing,' he observed, as he dropped the curtain, and came back to the fireside.

'Ceased!' I exclaimed, starting eagerly to my feet. 'Oh, if it were only possible – but no! it is hopeless. Even if I could find my way across the moor, I could not walk twenty miles tonight.'

'Walk twenty miles tonight!' repeated my host. 'What are you thinking of?'

'Of my wife,' I replied, impatiently. 'Of my young wife, who does not know that I have lost my way, and who is at this moment breaking her heart with suspense and terror.'

'Where is she?'

'At Dwolding, twenty miles away.'

'At Dwolding,' he echoed, thoughtfully. 'Yes, the distance, it is true, is twenty miles; but – are you so very anxious to save the next six or eight hours?'

'So very, very anxious, that I would give ten guineas at this moment for a guide and a horse.'

'Your wish can be gratified at a less costly rate,' said he, smiling. 'The night mail from the north, which changes horses at Dwolding, passes within five miles of this spot, and will be due at a certain cross-road in about an hour and a quarter. If Jacob were to go with you across the moor, and put you into the old coach-road, you could find your way, I suppose, to where it joins the new one?'

'Easily – gladly.'

He smiled again, rang the bell, gave the old servant his directions, and, taking a bottle of whisky and a wineglass from the cupboard in which he kept his chemicals, said:

'The snow lies deep, and it will be difficult walking tonight on the moor. A glass of usquebaugh before you start?'

I would have declined the spirit, but he pressed it on me, and I drank it. It went down my throat like liquid flame, and almost took my breath away.

'It is strong,' he said; 'but it will help to keep out the cold. And now you have no moments to spare. Good night!'

I thanked him for his hospitality, and would have shaken hands, but that he had turned away before I could finish my sentence. In another minute I had traversed the hall, Jacob had locked the outer door behind me, and we were out on the wide white moor.

Although the wind had fallen, it was still bitterly cold. Not a star glimmered in the black vault overhead. Not a sound, save the rapid crunching of the snow beneath our feet, disturbed the heavy stillness of the night. Jacob, not too well pleased with his mission, shambled on before in sullen silence, his lantern in his hand, and his shadow at his feet. I followed, with my gun over my shoulder, as little inclined for conversation as himself. My thoughts were full of my late host. His voice yet rang in my ears. His eloquence yet held my imagination captive. I remember to this day, with surprise, how my over-excited brain retained whole sentences and parts of sentences, troops of brilliant images, and fragments of splendid reasoning, in the very words in which he had uttered them. Musing thus over what I had heard, and striving to recall a lost link here and there, I strode on at the heels of my guide, absorbed and unobservant. Presently – at the end, as it seemed to me, of only a few minutes – he came to a sudden halt, and said:

'Yon's your road. Keep the stone fence to your right hand, and you can't fail of the way.'

'This, then, is the old coach-road?'

'Ay, 'tis the old coach-road.'

'And how far do I go, before I reach the cross-roads?'

'Nigh upon three mile.'

I pulled out my purse, and he became more communicative.

'The road's a fair road enough,' said he, 'for foot passengers; but 'twas over-steep and narrow for the northern traffic. You'll mind where the parapet's broken away, close again the sign-post. It's never been mended since the accident.'

'What accident?'

'Eh, the night mail pitched right over into the valley below – a gude fifty feet an' more – just at the worst bit o' road in the whole county.'

'Horrible! Were many lives lost?'

'All. Four were found dead, and t'other two died next morning.'

'How long is it since this happened?'

'Just nine year.'

'Near the sign-post, you say? I will bear it in mind. Good night.'

'Gude night, sir, and thankee.' Jacob pocketed his half-crown, made a faint pretence of touching his hat, and trudged back by the way he had come.

I watched the light of his lantern till it quite disappeared, and then turned to pursue my way alone. This was no longer matter of the slightest difficulty, for, despite the dead darkness overhead, the line of stone fence showed distinctly enough against the pale gleam of the snow. How silent it seemed now, with only my footsteps to listen to; how silent and how solitary! A strange disagreeable sense of loneliness stole over me. I walked faster. I hummed a fragment of a tune. I cast up enormous sums in my head, and accumulated them at compound interest. I did my best, in short, to forget the startling speculations to which I had but just been listening, and, to some extent, I succeeded.

Meanwhile the night air seemed to become colder and colder, and though I walked fast I found it impossible to keep myself warm. My feet were like ice. I lost sensation in my hands, and grasped my gun mechanically. I even breathed with difficulty, as though, instead of traversing a quiet north country highway, I were scaling the uppermost heights of some gigantic Alp. This last symptom became presently so distressing, that I was forced to stop for a few minutes, and lean against the stone fence. As I did so, I chanced to look back up the road, and there, to my infinite relief, I saw a distant point of light, like the gleam of an approaching lantern. I at first concluded that Jacob had retraced his steps and followed me; but even as the conjecture presented itself, a second light flashed into sight – a light evidently parallel with the first, and approaching at the same rate of motion. It needed no second thought to show me that these must be the carriage-lamps of some private vehicle, though it seemed strange that any private vehicle should take a road professedly disused and dangerous.

There could be no doubt, however, of the fact, for the lamps grew larger and brighter every moment, and I even fancied I could already see the dark outline of the carriage between them. It was coming up very fast, and quite noiselessly, the snow being nearly a foot deep under the wheels.

And now the body of the vehicle became distinctly visible behind the lamps. It looked strangely lofty. A sudden suspicion flashed upon me. Was it possible that I had passed the cross-roads in the dark without observing the sign-post, and could this be the very coach which I had come to meet?

No need to ask myself that question a second time, for here it came round the bend of the road, guard and driver, one outside passenger, and four steaming greys, all wrapped in a soft haze of light, through which the lamps blazed out, like a pair of fiery meteors.

I jumped forward, waved my hat, and shouted. The mail came down at full speed, and passed me. For a moment I feared that I had not been seen or heard, but it was only for a moment. The coachman pulled up; the guard, muffled to the eyes in capes and comforters, and apparently sound asleep in the rumble, neither answered my hail nor made the slightest effort to dismount; the outside passenger did not even turn his head. I opened the door for myself, and looked in. There were but three travellers inside, so I stepped in, shut the door, slipped into the vacant corner, and congratulated myself on my good fortune.

The atmosphere of the coach seemed, if possible, colder than that of the outer air, and was pervaded by a singularly damp and disagreeable smell. I looked round at my fellow-passengers. They were all three, men, and all silent. They did not seem to be asleep, but each leaned back in his corner of the vehicle, as if absorbed in his own reflections. I attempted to open a conversation.

'How intensely cold it is tonight,' I said, addressing my opposite neighbour.

He lifted his head, looked at me, but made no reply.

'The winter,' I added, 'seems to have begun in earnest.'

Although the corner in which he sat was so dim that I could distinguish none of his features very clearly, I saw that his eyes were still turned full upon me. And yet he answered never a word.

At any other time I should have felt, and perhaps expressed, some annoyance, but at the moment I felt too ill to do either. The icy coldness of the night air had struck a chill to my very marrow, and the strange smell inside the coach was affecting me with an intolerable nausea. I shivered from head to foot, and, turning to my left-hand neighbour, asked if he had any objection to an open window?

He neither spoke nor stirred.

I repeated the question somewhat more loudly, but with the same result. Then I lost patience, and let the sash down. As I did so, the leather strap broke in my hand, and I observed that the glass was covered with a thick coat of mildew, the accumulation, apparently, of years. My attention being thus drawn to the condition of the coach, I examined it more narrowly, and saw by the uncertain light of the outer lamps that it was in the last stage of dilapidation. Every part of it was not only out of repair, but in a condition of decay. The sashes splintered at a touch. The leather fittings were crusted over with mould, and literally rotting from the woodwork. The floor was almost breaking away beneath my feet. The whole machine, in short, was foul with damp, and had evidently been dragged from some outhouse in which it had been mouldering away for years, to do another day or two of duty on the road.

I turned to the third passenger, whom I had not yet addressed, and hazarded one more remark.

'This coach,' I said, 'is in a deplorable condition. The regular mail, I suppose, is under repair?'

He moved his head slowly, and looked me in the face, without speaking a word. I shall never forget that look while I live. I turned cold at heart under it. I turn cold at heart even now when I recall it. His eyes glowed with a fiery unnatural lustre. His face was livid as the face of a corpse. His bloodless lips were drawn back as if in the agony of death, and showed the gleaming teeth between.

The words that I was about to utter died upon my lips, and a strange horror – a dreadful horror – came upon me. My sight had by this time become used to the gloom of the coach, and I could see with tolerable distinctness. I turned to my opposite neighbour. He, too, was looking at me, with the same startling pallor in his face, and the same stony glitter in his eyes. I passed my hand across my brow. I turned to the passenger on the seat beside my own, and saw – oh Heaven! how shall I describe what I saw? I saw that he was no living man – that none of them were living men, like myself! A pale phosphorescent light – the light of putrefaction – played upon their awful faces; upon their hair, dank with the dews of the grave; upon their clothes, earth-stained and dropping to pieces; upon their hands, which were as the hands of corpses long buried. Only their eyes, their terrible eyes, were living; and those eyes were all turned menacingly upon me!

A shriek of terror, a wild unintelligible cry for help and mercy; burst from my lips as I flung myself against the door, and strove in vain to open it.

In that single instant, brief and vivid as a landscape beheld in the flash of summer lightning, I saw the moon shining down through a rift of stormy cloud – the ghastly sign-post rearing its warning finger by the wayside – the broken parapet – the plunging horses – the black gulf below. Then, the coach reeled like a ship at sea. Then, came a mighty crash – a sense of crushing pain – and then, darkness.

It seemed as if years had gone by when I awoke one morning from a deep sleep, and found my wife watching by my bedside I will pass over the scene that ensued, and give you, in half a dozen words, the tale she told me with tears of thanksgiving. I had fallen over a precipice, close against the junction of the old coach-road and the new, and had only been saved from certain death by lighting upon a deep snowdrift that had accumulated at the foot of the rock beneath. In this snowdrift I was discovered at daybreak, by a couple of shepherds, who carried me to the nearest shelter, and brought a surgeon to my aid. The surgeon found me in a state of raving delirium, with a broken arm and a compound fracture of the skull. The letters in my pocket-book showed my name and address; my wife was summoned to nurse me; and, thanks to youth and a fine constitution, I came out of danger at last. The place of my fall, I need scarcely say, was precisely that at which a frightful accident had happened to the north mail nine years before.

I never told my wife the fearful events which I have just related to you. I told the surgeon who attended me; but he treated the whole adventure as a mere dream born of the fever in my brain. We discussed the question over and over again, until we found that we could discuss it with temper no longer, and then we dropped it. Others may form what conclusions they please – I *know* that twenty years ago I was the fourth inside passenger in that Phantom Coach.

RUDYARD KIPLING

## Beyond the Pale (1888)

> Love heeds not caste nor sleep a broken bed. I went in search of love and lost myself. – Hindu Proverb.

A man should, whatever happens, keep to his own caste, race and breed. Let the White go to the White and the Black to the Black. Then whatever trouble falls is in the ordinary course of things – neither sudden, alien, nor unexpected.

This is the story of a man who wilfully stepped beyond the safe limits of decent everyday society, and paid for it heavily.

He knew too much in the first instance; and he saw too much in the second. He took too deep an interest in native life; but he will never do so again.

Deep away in the heart of the City, behind Jitha Megji's bustee, lies Amir Nath's Gully, which ends in a dead-wall pierced by one grated window. At the head of the Gully is a big cow-byre, and the walls on either side of the Gully are without windows. Neither Suchet Singh nor Gaur Chand approve of their women-folk looking into the world. If Durga Charan had been of their opinion he would have been a happier man to-day, and little Bisesa would have been able to knead her own bread. Her room looked out through the grated window into the narrow dark Gully where the sun never came and where the buffaloes wallowed in the blue slime. She was a widow, about fifteen years old, and she prayed the Gods, day and night, to send her a lover; for she did not approve of living alone.

One day, the man – Trejago his name was – came into Amir Nath's Gully on an aimless wandering; and, after he had passed the buffaloes, stumbled over a big heap of cattle-food.

Then he saw that the Gully ended in a trap, and heard a little laugh from behind the grated window. It was a pretty little laugh, and Trejago, knowing that, for all practical purposes, the old *Arabian Nights* are good guides, went forward to the window, and whispered that verse of 'The Love Song of Har Dyal' which begins:

> Can a man stand upright in the face of the naked Sun; or a Lover in the Presence of his Beloved?
> If my feet fail me, O Heart of my Heart, am I to blame, being blinded by the glimpse of your beauty? –

There came the faint *tchink* of a woman's bracelets from behind the grating, and a little voice went on with the song at the fifth verse:

> Alas! alas! Can the Moon tell the Lotus of her love when the Gate of Heaven is shut and the clouds gather for the rains?
> They have taken my Beloved, and driven her with the pack-horses to the North.
> There are iron chains on the feet that were set on my heart.
> Call to the bowmen to make ready –

The voice stopped suddenly, and Trejago walked out of Amir Nath's Gully, wondering who in the world could have capped 'The Love Song of Har Dyal' so neatly.

Next morning, as he was driving to office, an old woman threw a packet into his dogcart. In the packet was the half of a broken glass-bangle, one flower of the blood-red *dhak*, a pinch of *bhusa* or cattle-food, and eleven cardamoms. That packet was a letter – not a clumsy compromising letter, but an innocent unintelligible lover's epistle.

Trejago knew far too much about these things, as I have said. No Englishman should be able to translate object-letters. But Trejago spread all the trifles on the lid of his office-box and began to puzzle them out.

A broken glass-bangle stands for a Hindu widow all India over; because, when her husband dies, a woman's bracelets are broken on her wrists. Trejago saw the meaning of the little bit of glass. The flower of the *dhak* means diversely 'desire', 'come', 'write', or 'danger', according to the other things with it. One cardamom means 'jealousy'; but when any article is duplicated in an object-letter, it loses its symbolic meaning and stands merely for one of a number indicating time, or, if incense, curds, or saffron be sent also, place. The message ran then: 'A widow – *dhak* flower and *bhusa* – at eleven o'clock.' The pinch of *bhusa* enlightened Trejago. He saw – this kind of letter leaves much to instinctive knowledge – that the *bhusa* referred to the big heap of cattle-food over which he had fallen in Amir Nath's Gully, and that the message must come from the person behind the grating; she being a widow. So the message ran then: 'A widow, in the Gully in which is the heap of *bhusa*, desires you to come at eleven o'clock.'

Trejago threw all the rubbish into the fireplace and laughed. He knew that men in the East do not make love under windows at eleven in the forenoon, nor do women fix appointments a week in advance. So he went, that very night at eleven, into Amir Nath's Gully, clad in a *boorka*, which cloaks a man as well as a woman. Directly the gongs of the City made the hour, the little voice behind the grating took up 'The Love Song of Har Dyal' at the verse where the Pathan girl calls upon Har Dyal to return. The song is really pretty in the vernacular. In English you miss the wail of it. It runs something like this:

Alone upon the housetops, to the North
I turn and watch the lightning in the sky, –
The glamour of thy footsteps in the North,
*Come back to me, Beloved, or I die!*

Below my feet the still bazar is laid,
Far, far below the weary camels lie, –
The camels and the captives of thy raid.
*Come back to me, Beloved, or I die!*

My father's wife is old and harsh with years,
And drudge of all my father's house am I. –
My bread is sorrow and my drink is tears,
*Come back to me, Beloved, or I die!*

As the song stopped, Trejago stepped up under the grating and whispered, 'I am here.'

Bisesa was good to look upon.

That night was the beginning of many strange things, and of a double life so wild that Trejago to-day sometimes wonders if it were not all a dream. Bisesa, or her old handmaiden who had thrown the object-letter, had detached the heavy grating from the brick-work of the wall; so that the window slid inside, leaving only a square of raw masonry into which an active man might climb.

In the daytime, Trejago drove through his routine of office-work, or put on his calling-clothes and called on the ladies of the Station, wondering how long they would know him if they knew of poor little Bisesa. At night, when all the City was still, came the walk under the evil-smelling *boorka*, the patrol through Jitha Megji's *bustee*, the quick turn into Amir Nath's Gully between the sleeping cattle and the dead walls, and then, last of all, Bisesa, and the deep, even breathing of the old woman who slept outside the door of the bare little room that Durga Charan allotted to his sister's daughter. Who or what Durga Charan was, Trejago never inquired; and why in the world he was not discovered and knifed never occurred to him till his madness was over, and Bisesa... But this comes later.

Bisesa was an endless delight to Trejago. She was as ignorant as a bird; and her distorted versions of the rumours from the outside world that had reached her in her room, amused Trejago almost as much as her lisping attempts to pronounce his name – 'Christopher.' The first syllable was always more than she could manage, and she made funny little gestures with her roseleaf hands, as one throwing the name away, and then, kneeling before Trejago asked him, exactly as an Englishwoman would do, if he were sure he loved her. Trejago swore that he loved her more than any one else in the world. Which was true.

After a month of this folly, the exigencies of his other life compelled Trejago to be especially attentive to a lady of his acquaintance. You may take it for a fact that anything of this kind is not only noticed and discussed by a man's own race but by some hundred and fifty natives as well. Trejago had to walk with this lady and talk to her at the Bandstand, and once or twice to drive with her; never for an instant dreaming this would affect his dearer, out-of-the-way life. But the news flew, in the usual mysterious fashion, from mouth to mouth, till Bisesa's duenna heard of it and told Bisesa. The child was so troubled that she did the household work evilly, and was beaten by Durga Charan's wife in consequence.

A week later, Bisesa taxed Trejago with the flirtation. She understood no gradations and spoke openly. Trejago laughed, and Bisesa stamped her little feet – little feet, light as marigold flowers, that could lie in the palm of a man's one hand.

Much that is written about Oriental passion and impulsiveness is exaggerated and compiled at second hand, but a little of it is true, and when an Englishman finds that little, it is quite as startling as any passion in his own proper life. Bisesa raged and stormed, and finally threatened to kill herself if Trejago did not at once drop the alien Memsahib who had come between them. Trejago tried to explain, and to show her that she did not understand these things from a Western standpoint. Bisesa drew herself up, and said simply:

'I do not. I know only this – it is not good that I should have made you dearer than my own heart to me, Sahib. You are an Englishman. I am only a black girl' – she was fairer than bar-gold in the Mint, – 'and the widow of a black man.'

Then she sobbed and said – 'But on my soul and my Mother's soul, I love you. There shall no harm come to you, whatever happens to me.'

Trejago argued with the child, and tried to soothe her, but she seemed quite unreasonably disturbed. Nothing would satisfy her save that all relations between them should end. He was to go away at once. And he went. As he dropped out of the window, she kissed his forehead twice, and he walked home wondering.

A week, and then three weeks, passed without a sign from Bisesa. Trejago, thinking that the rupture had lasted quite long enough, went down to Amir Nath's Gully for the fifth time in the three weeks, hoping that his rap at the sill of the shifting grating would be answered. He was not disappointed.

There was a young moon, and one stream of light fell down into Amir Nath's Gully, and struck the grating, which was drawn away as he knocked. From the black dark, Bisesa held out her arms into the moonlight. Both hands had been cut off at the wrists, and the stumps were nearly healed.

Then, as Bisesa bowed her head between her arms and sobbed, some one in the room grunted like a wild beast, and something sharp – knife, sword, or spear – thrust at Trejago in his *boorka*. The stroke missed his body, but cut into one of the muscles of the groin, and he limped slightly from the wound for the rest of his days.

The grating went into its place. There was no sign whatever from inside the house – nothing but the moonlight strip on the high wall, and the blackness of Amir Nath's Gully behind.

The next thing Trejago remembers, after raging and shouting like a madman between those pitiless walls, is that he found himself near the river as the dawn was breaking, threw away his *boorka* and went home bareheaded.

What was the tragedy – whether Bisesa had, in a fit of causeless despair, told everything, or the intrigue had been discovered and she tortured to tell; whether Durga Charan knew his name, and what became of Bisesa – Trejago does not know to this day. Something horrible had happened, and the thought of what it must have been comes upon Trejago in the night now and again, and keeps him company till the morning. One special feature of the case is that he does not know where lies the front of Durga Charan's house. It may open on to a courtyard common to two or more houses, or it may lie behind any one of the gates of Jitha Megji's *bustee*. Trejago cannot tell. He cannot get Bisesa – poor little Bisesa – back again. He has lost her in the City where each man's house is as guarded and as unknowable as the grave; and the grating that opens into Amir Nath's Gully has been walled up.

But Trejago pays his calls regularly, and is reckoned a very decent sort of man.

There is nothing peculiar about him, except a slight stiffness, caused by a riding-strain, in the right leg.

George Egerton

## A Lost Masterpiece
## A City Mood, Aug. '93 (1893)

I regret it, but what am I to do? It was not my fault – I can only regret it. It was thus it happened to me.

I had come to town straight from a hillside cottage in a lonely plough land, with the smell of the turf in my nostrils, and the swish of the scythes in my ears; the scythes that flashed in the meadows where the upland hay, drought-parched, stretched thirstily up to the clouds that mustered upon the mountain-tops, and marched mockingly away, and held no rain.

The desire to mix with the crowd, to lay my ear once more to the heart of the world and listen to its life-throbs, had grown too strong for me; and so I had come back – but the sights and sounds of my late life clung to me – it is singular how the most opposite things often fill one with associative memory.

That *gamin* of the bird-tribe, the Cockney sparrow, recalled the swallows that built in the tumble-down shed; and I could almost see the gleam of their white bellies, as they circled in ever narrowing sweeps and clove the air with forked wings, uttering a shrill note, with a querulous grace-note in front of it.

The freshness of the country still lurked in me, unconsciously influencing my attitude towards the city.

One forenoon business drove me citywards, and following an inclination that always impels me to water-ways rather than road-ways, I elected to go by river steamer.

I left home in a glad mood, disposed to view the whole world with kindly eyes. I was filled with a happy-go-lucky *insouciance* that made walking the pavements a loafing in Elysian fields. The coarser touches of street-life, the oddities of accent, the idiosyncrasies of that most eccentric of city-dwellers, the Londoner, did not jar as at other times – rather added a zest to enjoyment; impressions crowded in too quickly to admit of analysis, I was simply an interested spectator of a varied panorama.

I was conscious, too, of a peculiar dual action of brain and senses, for, though keenly alive to every unimportant detail of the life about me, I was yet able to follow a process by which delicate inner threads were being spun into a fanciful web that had nothing to do with my outer self.

At Chelsea I boarded a river steamer bound for London Bridge. The river was wrapped in a delicate grey haze with a golden subtone, like a beautiful bright thought struggling for utterance through a mist of obscure words. It glowed through the turbid waters under the arches, so that I feared to see a face or a hand wave through its dull amber – for I always think of drowned creatures washing wearily in its murky depths – it lit up the great warehouses, and warmed the brick-work of the monster chimneys in the background. No detail escaped my outer eyes – not the hideous green of the velveteen in the sleeves of the woman on my left, nor the supercilious giggle of the young ladies on my right, who made audible re-marks about my personal appearance.

But what cared I? Was I not happy, absurdly happy? – because all the while my inner eyes saw undercurrents of beauty and pathos, quaint contrasts, whimsical de-tails that tickled my sense of humour deliciously. The elf that lurks in some inner cell was very busy, now throwing out tender mimosa-like threads of creative fancy, now recording fleeting impressions with delicate sure brushwork for future use; touch-ing a hundred vagrant things with the magic of imagination, making a running comment on the scenes we passed.

The warehouses told a tale of an up-to-date Soll and Haben, one of my very own, one that would thrust old Freytag out of the book-mart. The tall chimneys ceased to be giraffic throats belching soot and smoke over the blackening city. They were obelisks rearing granite heads heavenwards! Joints in the bricks, weather-stains? You are mistaken; they were hieroglyphics, setting down for posterity a tragic epic of man the conqueror, and fire his slave; and how they strangled beauty in the grip of gain. A theme for a Whitman!

And so it talks and I listen with my inner ear – and yet nothing outward escapes me – the slackening of the boat – the stepping on and off of folk – the lowering of the funnel – the name 'Stanley' on the little tug, with its self-sufficient puff-puff, fussing by with a line of grimy barges in tow; freight-laden, for the water washes over them – and on the last a woman sits suckling her baby, and a terrier with bad-ly cropped ears yaps at us as we pass .... .

And as this English river scene flashes by, limes of association form angles in my brain; and the point of each is a dot of light that expands into a background for for-gotten canal scenes, with green-grey water, and leaning balconies, and strange crafts – Canaletti and Guadi seen long ago in picture galleries .... .

A delicate-featured youth with gold-laced cap, scrapes a prelude on a thin-toned violin, and his companion thrums an accompaniment on a harp.

I don't know what they play, some tuneful thing with an undernote of sadness and sentiment running through its commonplace – likely a music-hall ditty; for a lad with a cheap silk hat, and the hateful expression of knowingness that makes him a type of his kind, grins appreciatively and hums the words.

I turn from him to the harp. It is the wreck of a handsome instrument, its gold is tarnished, its white is smirched, its stucco rose-wreaths sadly battered. It has the air of an antique beauty in dirty ball finery; and is it fancy, or does not a shamed wail lurk in the tone of its strings?

The whimsical idea occurs to me that it has once belonged to a lady with drooping ringlets and an embroidered spencer; and that she touched its chords to the words of a song by Thomas Haynes Baily, and that Miss La Creevy transferred them both to ivory.

The youth played mechanically, without a trace of emotion; whilst the harpist, whose nose is a study in purples and whose bloodshot eyes have the glassy brightness of drink, felt every touch of beauty in the poor little tune, and drew it tenderly forth.

They added the musical note to my joyous mood; the poetry of the city dovetailed harmoniously with country scenes too recent to be treated as memories – and I stepped off the boat with the melody vibrating through the city sounds.

I swung from place to place in happy, lightsome mood, glad as a fairy prince in quest of adventures. The air of the city was exhilarating ether – and all mankind my brethren – in fact I felt effusively affectionate.

I smiled at a pretty, anaemic city girl, and only remembered that she was a stranger when she flashed back an indignant look of affected affront.

But what cared I? Not a jot! I could afford to say pityingly: 'Go thy way, little city maid, get thee to thy typing.'

And all the while that these outward insignificant things occupied me, I knew that a precious little pearl of a thought was evolving slowly out of the inner chaos.

It was such an unique little gem, with the lustre of a tear, and the light of moonlight and streamlight and love smiles reflected in its pure sheen – and, best of all, it was all my own – a priceless possession, not to be bartered for the Jagersfontein diamond – a city childling with the prepotency of the country working in it – and I revelled in its fresh charm and dainty strength; it seemed original, it was so frankly natural.

And as I dodged through the great waggons laden with wares from outer continents, I listened and watched it forming inside, until my soul became filled with the light of its brightness; and a wild elation possessed me at the thought of this darling brain-child, this offspring of my fancy, this rare little creation, perhaps embryo of genius that was my very own.

I smiled benevolently at the passersby, with their harassed business faces, and shiny black bags bulging with the weight of common everyday documents, as I thought of the treat I would give them later on; the delicate feast I held in store for them, when I would transfer this dainty elusive birthling of my brain to paper for their benefit.

It would make them dream of moonlit lanes and sweethearting; reveal to them the golden threads in the sober city woof; creep in close and whisper good cheer, and smooth out tired creases in heart and brain; a draught front the fountain of Jouvence could work no greater miracle than the tale I had to unfold.

Aye, they might pass me by now, not even give me the inside of the pavement, I would not blame them for it! – but later on, later on, they would flock to thank me. They just didn't realise, poor money-grubbers! How could they? But later on ... I grew perfectly radiant at the thought of what I would do for poor humanity, and absurdly self-satisfied as the conviction grew upon me that this would prove a work of genius – no mere glimmer of the spiritual afflatus – but a solid chunk of genius.

Meanwhile I took a 'bus and paid my penny. I leant back and chuckled to myself as each fresh thought-atom added to the precious quality of my pearl. Pearl? Not one any longer – a whole quarrelet of pearls, Oriental pearls of the greatest price! Ah, how happy I was as I fondled my conceit!

It was near Chancery Lane that a foreign element cropped up and disturbed the rich flow of my fancy.

I happened to glance at the sidewalk. A woman, a little woman, was hurrying along in a most remarkable way. It annoyed me, for I could not help wondering why she was in such a desperate hurry. Bother the jade! what business had she to thrust herself on my observation like that, and tangle the threads of a web of genius, undoubted genius?

I closed my eyes to avoid seeing her; I could see her through the lids. She had square shoulders and a high bust, and a white gauze tie, like a snowy feather in the breast of a pouter pigeon.

We stop – I look again – aye, there she is! Her black eyes stare boldly through her kohl-tinted lids, her face has a violet tint. She grips her gloves in one hand, her white-handled umbrella in the other, handle up, like a knobkerrie.

She has great feet, too, in pointed shoes, and the heels are under her insteps; and as we outdistance her I fancy I can hear their decisive tap-tap above the thousand sounds of the street.

I breathe a sigh of relief as I return to my pearl – my pearl that is to bring *me* kudos and make countless thousands rejoice. It is dimmed a little, I must nurse it tenderly.

Jerk, jerk, jangle – stop. – Bother the bell! We pull up to drop some passengers, the idiots! and, as I live, she overtakes us! How the men and women cede her the middle of the pavement! How her figure dominates it, and her great feet emphasise her ridiculous haste! Why should she disturb me? My nerves are quivering pitifully; the sweet inner light is waning, I am in mortal dread of losing my little masterpiece. Thank heaven, we are off again ... .

'Charing Cross, Army and Navy, V'toria!' – Stop!

Of course, naturally! Here she comes, elbows out, umbrella waving! How the steel in her bonnet glistens! She recalls something, what is it? – what is it? A-ah! I have it! – a strident voice, on the deck of a steamer in the glorious bay of Rio, singing:

'Je suis le vr-r-rai pompier,
Le seul pompier ...'

and *la mióla* snaps her fingers gaily and trills her *r's*; and the Corcovado is outlined clearly on the purple background as if bending to listen; and the palms and the mosque-like buildings, and the fair islets bathed in the witchery of moonlight, and the star-gems twinned in the lap of the bay, intoxicate as a dream of the East.

'Je suis le vr-r-rai pompier,
Le seul pompier ...'

What in the world is a *pompier*? What connection has the word with this creature who is murdering, deliberately murdering, a delicate creation of my brain, begotten by the fusion of country and town?

'Je suis le vr-r-rai pompier ...'

I am convinced *pompier* expresses her in some subtle way – absurd word! I look back at her, I criticise her, I anathematise her, I *hate* her!

What is she hurrying for? We can't escape her – always we stop and let her overtake us with her elbowing gait, and tight skirt shortened to show her great splay feet – ugh!

My brain is void, all is dark within; the flowers are faded, the music stilled; the lovely illusive little being has flown, and yet she pounds along untiringly.

Is she a feminine presentment of the wandering Jew, a living embodiment of the ghoul-like spirit that haunts the city and murders fancy?

What business had she, I ask, to come and thrust her white-handled umbrella into the delicate network of my nerves and untune their harmony?

Does she realise what she has done? She has trampled a rare little mind-being unto death, destroyed a precious literary gem. Aye, one that, for ought I know, might have worked a revolution in modern thought; added a new human document to the archives of man; been the keystone to psychic investigations; solved problems that lurk in the depths of our natures and tantalise us with elusive gleams of truth; heralded in, perchance, the new era; when such simple problems as Home Rule, Bimetallism, or the Woman Question will be mere themes for schoolboard compositions – who can tell?

Well, it was not my fault. – No one regrets it more, no one – but what could I do?

Blame her, woman of the great feet and dominating gait, and
waving umbrella-handle! – blame her! I can only regret it – regret it!

H.G. WELLS

## The Stolen Bacillus (1894)

'This again,' said the Bacteriologist, slipping a glass slide under the microscope, 'is a preparation of the celebrated Bacillus of cholera – the cholera germ.'

The pale-faced man peered down the microscope. He was evidently not accustomed to that kind of thing, and held a limp white hand over his disengaged eye. 'I see very little,' he said.

'Touch this screw,' said the Bacteriologist; 'perhaps the microscope is out of focus for you. Eyes vary so much. Just the fraction of a turn this way or that.'

'Ah! now I see,' said the visitor. 'Not so very much to see after all. Little streaks and shreds of pink. And yet those little particles, those mere atomies, might multiply and devastate a city! Wonderful!'

He stood up, and releasing the glass slip from the microscope, held it in his hand towards the window. 'Scarcely visible,' he said, scrutinising the preparation. He hesitated. 'Are these – alive? Are they dangerous now?'

'Those have been stained and killed,' said the Bacteriologist. 'I wish, for my own part, we could kill and stain every one of them in the universe.'

'I suppose,' the pale man said with a slight smile, 'that you scarcely care to have such things about you in the living – in the active state?'

'On the contrary, we are obliged to,' said the Bacteriologist. 'Here, for instance – –' He walked across the room and took up one of several sealed tubes. 'Here is the living thing. This is a cultivation of the actual living disease bacteria.' He hesitated. 'Bottled cholera, so to speak.'

A slight gleam of satisfaction appeared momentarily in the face of the pale man. 'It's a deadly thing to have in your possession,' he said, devouring the little tube with his eyes. The Bacteriologist watched the morbid pleasure in his visitor's expression. This man, who had visited him that afternoon with a note of introduction from an old friend, interested him from the very contrast of their dispositions. The lank black hair and deep grey eyes, the haggard expression and nervous manner, the fitful yet keen interest of his visitor were a novel change from the phlegmatic deliberations of the ordinary scientific worker with whom the Bacteriologist chiefly associated. It was perhaps natural, with a hearer evidently so impressionable to the lethal nature of his topic, to take the most effective aspect of the matter.

He held the tube in his hand thoughtfully. 'Yes, here is the pestilence imprisoned. Only break such a little tube as this into a supply of drinking-water, say to these minute particles of life that one must needs stain and examine with the highest powers of the microscope even to see, and that one can neither smell nor taste – say to them, "Go forth, increase and multiply, and replenish the cisterns," and death – mysterious, untraceable death, death swift and terrible, death full of pain and indignity – would be released upon this city, and go hither and thither seeking his victims. Here he would take the husband from the wife, here the child from its mother, here the statesman from his duty, and here the toiler from his trouble. He would follow the water-mains, creeping along streets, picking out and punishing a house here and a house there where they did not boil their drinking-water, creeping into the wells of the mineral-water makers, getting washed into salad, and lying dormant in ices. He would wait ready to be drunk in the horse-troughs, and by unwary children in the public fountains. He would soak into the soil, to reappear in springs and wells at a thousand unexpected places. Once start him at the water supply, and before we could ring him in, and catch him again, he would have decimated the metropolis.'

He stopped abruptly. He had been told rhetoric was his weakness.

'But he is quite safe here, you know – quite safe.'

The pale-faced man nodded. His eyes shone. He cleared his throat. 'These Anarchist-rascals,' said he, 'are fools, blind fools – to use bombs when this kind of thing is attainable. I think – '

A gentle rap, a mere light touch of the finger-nails was heard at the door. The Bacteriologist opened it. 'Just a minute, dear,' whispered his wife.

When he re-entered the laboratory his visitor was looking at his watch. 'I had no idea I had wasted an hour of your time,' he said. 'Twelve minutes to four. I ought to have left here by half-past three. But your things were really too interesting. No, positively I cannot stop a moment longer. I have an engagement at four.'

He passed out of the room reiterating his thanks, and the Bacteriologist accompanied him to the door, and then returned thoughtfully along the passage to his laboratory. He was musing on the ethnology of his visitor. Certainly the man was not a Teutonic type nor a common Latin one. 'A morbid product, anyhow, I am afraid,' said the Bacteriologist to himself. 'How he gloated on those cultivations of disease-germs!' A disturbing thought struck him. He turned to the bench by the vapour-bath, and then very quickly to his writing-table. Then he felt hastily in his pockets, and then rushed to the door. 'I may have put it down on the hall table,' he said.

'Minnie!' he shouted hoarsely in the hall.

'Yes, dear,' came a remote voice.

'Had I anything in my hand when I spoke to you, dear, just now?'

Pause.

'Nothing, dear, because I remember – –'

'Blue ruin!' cried the Bacteriologist, and incontinently ran to the front door and down the steps of his house to the street.

Minnie, hearing the door slam violently, ran in alarm to the window. Down the street a slender man was getting into a cab. The Bacteriologist, hatless, and in his carpet slippers, was running and gesticulating wildly towards this group. One slipper came off, but he did not wait for it. 'He has gone *mad*!' said Minnie; 'it's that horrid science of his'; and, opening the window, would have called after him. The slender man, suddenly glancing round, seemed struck with the same idea of mental disorder. He pointed hastily to the Bacteriologist, said something to the cabman, the apron of the cab slammed, the whip swished, the horse's feet clattered, and in a moment the cab, and Bacteriologist hotly in pursuit, had receded up the vista of the roadway and disappeared round the corner.

Minnie remained straining out of the window for a minute. Then she drew her head back into the room again. She was dumbfounded. 'Of course he is eccentric,' she meditated. 'But running about London – in the height of the season, too – in his socks!' A happy thought struck her. She hastily put her bonnet on, seized his shoes, went into the hall, took down his hat and light overcoat from the pegs, emerged upon the doorstep, and hailed a cab that opportunely crawled by. 'Drive me up the road and round Havelock Crescent, and see if we can find a gentleman running about in a velveteen coat and no hat.'

'Velveteen coat, ma'am, and no 'at. Very good, ma'am.' And the cabman whipped up at once in the most matter-of-fact way, as if he drove to this address every day in his life.

Some few minutes later the little group of cabmen and loafers that collects round the cabmen's shelter at Haverstock Hill were startled by the passing of a cab with a ginger-coloured screw of a horse, driven furiously.

They were silent as it went by, and then as it receded – 'That's 'Arry 'Icks. Wot's *he* got?' said the stout gentleman known as Old Tootles.

'He's a-using his whip, he is, *to* rights,' said the ostler boy.

'Hullo!' said poor old Tommy Byles; 'here's another bloomin' loonatic. Blowed if there ain't.'

'It's old George,' said old Tootles, 'and he's drivin' a loonatic, *as* you say. Ain't he a-clawin' out of the keb? Wonder if he's after 'Arry 'Icks?'

The group round the cabmen's shelter became animated. Chorus: 'Go it, George!' 'It's a race!' 'You'll ketch 'em!' 'Whip up!'

'She's a goer, she is!' said the ostler boy.

'Strike me giddy!' cried old Tootles. 'Here! *I'm* a-goin' to begin in a minute. Here's another comin'. If all the kebs in Hampstead ain't gone mad this morning!'

'It's a fieldmale this time,' said the ostler boy.

'She's a followin' *him*,' said old Tootles. 'Usually the other way about.'

'What's she got in her 'and?'

'Looks like a 'igh 'at.'

'What a bloomin' lark it is! Three to one on old George,' said the ostler boy. 'Nexst!'

Minnie went by in a perfect roar of applause. She did not like it but she felt that she was doing her duty, and whirled on down Haverstock Hill and Camden Town High Street with her eyes ever intent on the animated back view of old George, who was driving her vagrant husband so incomprehensively away from her.

The man in the foremost cab sat crouched in the corner, his arms tightly folded, and the little tube that contained such vast possibilities of destruction gripped in his hand. His mood was a singular mixture of fear and exultation. Chiefly he was afraid of being caught before he could accomplish his purpose, but behind this was a vaguer but larger fear of the awfulness of his crime. But his exultation far exceeded his fear. No Anarchist before him had ever approached this conception of his. Ravachol, Vaillant, all those distinguished persons whose fame he had envied, dwindled into insignificance beside him. He had only to make sure of the water supply, and break the little tube into a reservoir. How brilliantly he had planned it, forged the letter of introduction and got into the laboratory, and how brilliantly he had seized his opportunity! The world should hear of him at last. All those people who had sneered at him, neglected him, preferred other people to him, found his company undesirable, should consider him at last. Death, death, death! They had always treated him as a man of no importance. All the world had been in a conspiracy to keep him under. He would teach them yet what it is to isolate a man. What was this familiar street? Great Saint Andrew's Street, of course! How fared the chase? He craned out of the cab. The Bacteriologist was scarcely fifty yards behind. That was bad. He would be caught and stopped yet. He felt in his pocket for money, and found half-a-sovereign. This he thrust up through the trap in the top of the cab into the man's face. 'More,' he shouted, 'if only we get away.'

The money was snatched out of his hand. 'Right you are,' said the cabman, and the trap slammed, and the lash lay along the glistening side of the horse. The cab swayed, and the Anarchist, half-standing under the trap, put the hand containing the little glass tube upon the apron to preserve his balance. He felt the brittle thing crack, and the broken half of it rang upon the floor of the cab. He fell back into the seat with a curse, and stared dismally at the two or three drops of moisture on the apron.

He shuddered.

'Well! I suppose I shall be the first. *Phew*! Anyhow, I shall be a Martyr. That's something. But it is a filthy death, nevertheless. I wonder if it hurts as much as they say.'

Presently a thought occurred to him – he groped between his feet. A little drop was still in the broken end of the tube, and he drank that to make sure. It was better to make sure. At any rate, he would not fail.

Then it dawned upon him that there was no further need to escape the Bacteriologist. In Wellington Street he told the cabman to stop and got out. He slipped on the step, and his head felt queer. It was rapid stuff this cholera poison. He waved his cabman out of existence, so to speak, and stood on the pavement with his arm folded upon his breast awaiting the arrival of the Bacteriologist. There was something tragic in his pose. The sense of imminent death gave him a certain dignity. He greeted his pursuer with a defiant laugh.

'*Vive l'Anarchie!* You are too late, my friend. I have drunk it. The cholera is abroad!'

The Bacteriologist from his cab beamed curiously at him through his spectacles. 'You have drunk it! An Anarchist! I see now.' He was about to say something more, and then checked himself. A smile hung in the corner of his mouth. He opened the apron of his cab as if to descend, at which the Anarchist waved him a dramatic farewell and strode off towards Waterloo Bridge, carefully jostling his infected body against as many people as possible. The Bacteriologist was so preoccupied with the vision of him that he scarcely manifested the slightest surprise at the appearance of Minnie upon the pavement with his hat and shoes and overcoat. 'Very good of you to bring my things,' he said, and remained lost in contemplation of the receding figure of the Anarchist.

'You had better get in,' he said, still staring. Minnie felt absolutely convinced now that he was mad, and directed the cabman home on her own responsibility. 'Put on my shoes? Certainly, dear,' said he, as the cab began to turn, and hid the strutting black figure, now small in the distance, from his eyes. Then suddenly something grotesque struck him, and he laughed. Then he remarked, 'It is really very serious, though.'

'You see, that man came to my house to see me, and he is an Anarchist. No – don't faint, or I cannot possibly tell you the rest. And I wanted to astonish him, not knowing he was an Anarchist, and took up a cultivation of that new species of Bacterium I was telling you of, that infest, and I think cause, the blue patches upon various monkeys; and like a fool, I said it was Asiatic cholera. And he ran away with it to poison the water of London, and he certainly might have made things look blue for this civilized city. And now he has swallowed it. Of course, I cannot say what will happen, but you know it turned that kitten blue, and the three puppies – in patches, and the sparrow – bright blue. But the bother is, I shall have all the trouble and expense of preparing some more.

'Put on my coat on this hot day! Why? Because we might meet Mrs. Jabber. My dear, Mrs. Jabber is not a draught. But why should I wear a coat on a hot day because of Mrs. – –? Oh! *very* well.'

Baroness Emma Orczy

## The Mysterious Death on the Underground Railway (1905)

DRAMATIS PERSONAE
The Man
*who explains each mystery to*
The Lady Journalist
*whilst at lunch at an A.B.C.*
Mr. Hazeldene
*(shipping agent).*
Mrs. Hazeldene
*(his wife, found dead on the Underground Railway).*
Frank Errington
*(suspected of her murder).*
Mr. Andrew Campbell Mr. James Verner
*(witnesses before the Magistrates at Bow Street).*

I

'Will you be good enough to give me a description of the man who sat next to you just now, while you were having your cup of coffee and scone?' said the man in the corner to me that day.

He had been sitting in his accustomed place when I came into the A.B.C. shop, but had made no remark all the time that I was partaking of my modest luncheon. I was just in the act of thinking how rude he was not to have said 'Good morning,' when his abrupt remark caused me to look up.

'Do you know at all if he was tall! or short, dark or fair?' he insisted, seemingly not the least disconcerted by my somewhat rude survey of his eccentric personality, 'Can you tell me at all what he was like?'

'Of course I can,' I rejoined impatiently, 'but I don't see that my description of one of the customers of an A.B.C. shop can have the slightest importance.'

He was silent for a minute, while his nervous fingers fumbled about in his capacious pockets in search of the inevitable piece of string. When he had found this necessary 'adjunct to thought,' he viewed me again through his half-closed lids, and added maliciously:

'But supposing it were of paramount importance that you should give an accurate description of a man who sat next to you for half-an-hour today, how would you proceed?'

'I should say that he was of medium height – –'

'Five foot eight, nine, or ten?' he interrupted quietly.

'How can one tell to an inch or two?' I rejoined crossly. 'He was between colours.'

'What's that?' he inquired blandly.

'Neither fair nor dark – his nose – –'

'Well, what was his nose like? Will you sketch it?'

'I am not an artist. His nose was fairly straight – his eyes – –'

'Were neither dark nor light – his hair had the same striking peculiarity – he was neither short nor tall – his nose was neither aquiline nor snub – –' he recapitulated sarcastically.

'No,' I retorted; 'he was just ordinary-looking.'

'Would you know him again – say tomorrow, and among a number of other men who were "neither tall nor short, dark nor fair, aquiline nor snub-nosed," etc?'

'I don't know – I might – he was certainly not striking enough to be specially remembered.'

'Exactly,' he said, while he leant forward excitedly, for all the world like a jack-in-the-box let loose.

'Precisely; and you are a novelist – call yourself one, at least – and it should be part of your business to notice and describe people. I don't mean only the wonderful personage with the clear Saxon features, the fine blue eyes, the noble brow and classic face, but the ordinary person – the person who represents ninety out of every hundred of his own kind – the average Englishman, say, of the middle classes, who is neither very tall nor very short, who wears a moustache which is neither fair nor dark, but which masks his mouth, and a top hat which hides the shape of his head and brow, a man, in fact, who dresses like hundreds of his fellow creatures, moves like them, speaks like them, has no peculiarity.

'Try to describe *him*, to recognise him, say a week hence, among his other eighty-nine doubles; worse still, to swear his life away, if he happened to be implicated in some crime, wherein *your* recognition of him would place the halter round his neck.

'Try that, I say, and having utterly failed you will more readily understand how one of the greatest scoundrels unhung is still at large, and why the mystery on the Underground Railway was never cleared up.

'I think it was the only time in my life that I was seriously tempted to give the police the benefit of my own views upon the matter. You see, though I admire the brute for his cleverness, I did not see that his being unpunished could possibly benefit anyone.

'The Central London Railway had just been opened a few days, and the old Underground was being deserted for the time being for the sake of the novelty of the other line. Anyway, when that particular train steamed into Aldgate at about 4 P.M. on June 18th last, the first-class carriages were all but empty.

'The guard marched up and down the platform looking into all the carriages to see if anyone had left a halfpenny evening paper behind for him, and opening the door of one of the first class compartments, he noticed a lady sitting in the further corner, with her head turned away towards the window evidently oblivious of the fact that on this line, Aldgate is the terminal station.

'"Where are you for, lady?" he said.

'The lady did not move, and the guard stepped into the carriage, thinking that perhaps the lady was asleep. He touched her arm lightly and looked into her face. In his own poetic language he was "struck all of a 'eap." In the glassy eyes, the ashen colour of the cheeks, the rigidity of the head, there was the unmistakable look of death.

'Hastily the guard, having carefully locked the carriage door, summoned a couple of porters, and sent one of them off to the police station, and the other in search of the stationmaster.

'Fortunately at this time of day the up platform is not very crowded, all the traffic tending westward in the afternoon. It was only when an inspector and two police constables, accompanied by a detective in plain clothes and a medical officer, appeared upon the scene, and stood round a first-class railway compartment, that a few idlers realised that something unusual had occurred, and crowded round, eager and curious.

'Thus it was that the later editions of the evening papers, under the sensational heading, "Mysterious Suicide on the Underground Railway," had already an account of the extraordinary event. The medical officer had very soon come to the decision that the guard had not been mistaken, and that life was indeed extinct.

'The lady was young, and must have been very pretty, before the look of fright and horror had so terribly distorted her features. She was very elegantly dressed, and the more frivolous papers were able to give their feminine readers a detailed account of the unfortunate woman's gown, her shoes, hat, and gloves.

'It appears that one of the latter, the one on the right hand, was partly off, leaving the thumb and wrist bare. That hand held a small satchel, which the police opened, with a view to the possible identification of the deceased, but which was found to contain only a little loose silver, some smelling salts, and a small empty bottle which was handed over to the medical officer for purposes of analysis.

'It was the presence of that small bottle which had caused the report to circulate freely that the mysterious case on the Underground Railway was one of suicide. Certain it was that neither about the lady's person, nor in the appearance of the railway carriage, was there the slightest sign of struggle or even of resistance. Only the look in the poor woman's eyes spoke of sudden terror, of the rapid vision of an unexpected and violent death, which probably only lasted an infinitesimal fraction of a second, but which had left its indelible mark upon the face, otherwise so placid and so still.'

## II

'The body of the deceased was conveyed to the mortuary. So far, of course, not a soul had been able to identify her, or to throw the slightest light upon the mystery which hung around her death.

'Against that, quite a crowd of idlers – genuinely interested or not – obtained admission to view the body, on the pretext of having lost or mislaid a relative or a friend. At about 8:30 P.M. a young man, very well dressed, drove up to the station in a hansom, and sent in his card to the superintendent. It was Mr. Hazeldene, shipping agent, of 11, Crown Lane, E.C., and No. 19, Addison Row, Kensington.

'The young man looked in a pitiable state of mental distress; his hand clutched nervously a copy of the *St. James's Gazette*, which contained the fatal news. He said very little to the superintendent except that a person who was very dear to him had not returned home that evening.

'He had not felt really anxious until half-an-hour ago, when suddenly he thought of looking at his paper. The description of the deceased lady, though vague, had terribly alarmed him. He had jumped into a hansom, and now begged permission to view the body, in order that his worst fears might be allayed.

'You know what followed, of course,' continued the man in the corner, 'the grief of the young man was truly pitiable. In the woman lying there in a public mortuary before him, Mr. Hazeldene had recognised his wife.

'I am waxing melodramatic,' said the man in the corner who looked up at me with a mild and gentle smile, while his nervous fingers vainly endeavoured to add another knot on the scrappy bit of string with which he was continually playing, 'and I fear that your story will savour this time of the penny novelette, but you must admit, and no doubt you remember, that it was an intensely pathetic and truly dramatic moment.

'The unfortunate young husband of the deceased lady was not much worried with questions that night. As a matter of fact he was not in a fit condition to make any coherent statement. It was at the coroner's inquest on the following day, that certain facts came to light, which for the time being seemed to clear up the mystery surrounding Mrs. Hazeldene's death, only to plunge that same mystery, later on, into denser gloom than before.

'The first witness at the inquest was, of course, Mr. Hazeldene himself. I think everyone's sympathy went out to the young man, as he stood before the coroner and tried to throw what light he could upon the mystery. He was well dressed as he had been the day before, but he looked terribly ill and worried, and no doubt the fact that he had not shaved gave his face a careworn and neglected air.

'It appears that he and the deceased had been married some six years or so, and that they had always been happy in their married life. They had no children. Mrs. Hazeldene seemed to enjoy the best of health till lately, when she had had a slight attack of influenza, in which Dr. Arthur Jones had attended her. The doctor was present at this moment and would no doubt explain to the coroner and the jury whether he thought that Mrs. Hazeldene had the slightest tendency to heart disease, which might have had a sudden and fatal ending.

'The coroner was, of course, very considerate to the bereaved husband. He tried by circumlocution to get at the point he wanted, namely, Mrs. Hazeldene's mental condition lately. Mr. Hazeldene seemed loth to talk about this. No doubt he had been warned as to the existence of the small bottle found in his wife's satchel.

'"It certainly did seem to me at times," he at last reluctantly admitted, "that my wife did not seem quite herself. She used to be very gay and bright, and lately, I often saw her in the evening sitting, as if brooding over some matters, which evidently she did not care to communicate to me."

'Still the coroner insisted, and suggested the small bottle.

'"I know, I know," replied the young man with a short, heavy sigh. "You mean – the question of suicide – I cannot understand it at all – it seems so sudden and so terrible – she certainly had seemed listless and troubled lately – but only at times – and yesterday morning, when I went to business, she appeared quite herself again, and I suggested that we should go to the opera in the evening. She was delighted, I know, and told me she would do some shopping, and pay a few calls in the afternoon."

'"Do you know at all where she intended to go when she got into the Underground Railway?"

'"Well, not with certainty. You see she may have meant to get out at Baker Street, and go down to Bond Street to do her shopping. Then again, she sometimes goes to a shop in St. Paul's Churchyard, in which case, she would take a ticket to Aldersgate Street; but I cannot say."

'"Now, Mr. Hazeldene,' said the coroner at last very kindly, "will you try to tell me if there was anything in Mrs. Hazeldene's life which you know of, and which might in some measure explain the cause of the distressed state of mind, which you yourself had noticed? Did there exist any financial difficulty which might have preyed upon Mrs. Hazeldene's mind; was there any friend – to whose intercourse with Mrs. Hazeldene – you – er – at any time took exception to. In fact," added the coroner, as if thankful that he had got over an unpleasant moment, "can you give me the slightest indication which would tend to confirm the suspicion that the unfortunate lady, in a moment of mental anxiety or derangement, may have wished to take her own life."

'There was silence in the court for a few moments. Mr. Hazeldene seemed to everyone there present to be labouring under some terrible moral doubt. He looked very pale and wretched, and twice attempted to speak, before he at last said in scarcely audible tones.

'"No; there were no financial difficulties of any sort. My wife had an independent fortune of her own – she had no extravagant tastes – –"

'"Nor any friend you at any time objected to?" insisted the coroner.

'"Nor any friend, I – at any time objected to," stammered the unfortunate young man, evidently speaking with an effort.

'I was present at the inquest,' resumed the man in the corner, after he had drunk a glass of milk, and ordered another, 'and I can assure you that the most obtuse person there plainly realized that Mr. Hazeldene was telling a lie. It was pretty plain to the meanest intelligence that the unfortunate lady had not fallen into a state of morbid dejection for nothing, and that perhaps there existed a third person who could throw more light on her strange and sudden death than the unhappy, bereaved young widower.

'That the death was more mysterious even than it had at first appeared, became very soon apparent. You read the case at the time, no doubt, and must remember the excitement in the public mind caused by the evidence of the two doctors. Dr. Arthur Jones, the lady's usual medical man, who had not attended her in a last very slight illness, but who had seen her in a professional capacity fairly recently, declared most emphatically that Mrs. Hazeldene suffered from no organic complaint which could possibly have been the cause of sudden death. Moreover, he had assisted Mr. Andrew Thorton, the district medical officer, in making a postmortem examination, and together they had come to the conclusion that death was due to the action of prussic acid, which had caused instantaneous failure of the heart, but how the drug had been administered neither he nor his colleague were at present able to state.

'"Do I understand, then, Dr. Jones, that the deceased died, poisoned with prussic acid?"

'"Such is my opinion," replied the doctor.

'"Did the bottle found in her satchel contain prussic acid?"

'"It had contained some at one time, certainly."

'"In your opinion, then, the lady caused her own death by taking a dose of that drug?"

'"Pardon me, I never suggested such a thing; the lady died poisoned by the drug, but how the drug was administered we cannot say. By injection of some sort, certainly. The drug certainly was not swallowed; there was not a vestige of it in the stomach.

'"Yes," added the doctor in reply to another question from the coroner, "death had probably followed the injection in this case almost immediately; say within a couple of minutes, or perhaps three. It was quite possible, that the body would not have more than one quick and sudden convulsion, perhaps not that; death in such cases is absolutely sudden and crushing."

'I don't think that at the time anyone in the room realised how important the doctor's statement was, a statement which, by the way, was confirmed in all its details by the district medical officer, who had conducted the postmortem. Mrs. Hazeldene had died suddenly from an injection of prussic acid, administered no one knew how or when. She had been travelling in a first-class railway carriage, in a busy time of the day. That young and elegant woman must have had singular nerve and coolness to go through the process of a self-inflicted injection of a deadly poison in the presence of perhaps two or three other persons.

'Mind you, when I say that no one there realised the importance of the doctor's statement at that moment, I am wrong; there were three persons, who fully understood at once the gravity of the situation, and the astounding development which the case was beginning to assume.

'Of course, I should have put myself out of the question,' added my strange interlocutor, with that inimitable self-conceit peculiar to himself. 'I guessed then and there in a moment where the police were going wrong, and where they would go on going wrong until the mysterious death on the Underground Railway had sunk into oblivion, together with the other cases which they mismanage from time to time.

'I said there were three persons who understood the gravity of the two doctors' statements – the other two were, firstly, the detective who had originally examined the railway carriage, a young man of energy and plenty of misguided intelligence, the other was Mr. Hazeldene.

'At this point the interesting element of the whole story was first introduced into the proceedings, and this was done through the humble channel of Emma Funnel, Mrs. Hazeldene's maid, who, as far as was known then, was the last person who had seen the unfortunate lady alive and had spoken to her.

'"Mrs. Hazeldene lunched at home," explained Emma, who was shy, and spoke almost in a whisper, "she seemed well and cheerful. She went out at about half-past three, and told me she was going to Spence's in St. Paul's Churchyard, to try on her new tailor-made gown. Mrs. Hazeldene had meant to go there in the morning, but was prevented as Mr. Errington called."

'"Mr Errington?" asked the coroner casually. "Who is Mr. Errington?"

'But this, Emma found difficult to explain. "Mr. Errington was – Mr. Errington, that's all."

'"Mr. Errington was a friend of the family. He lived in a flat in the Albert Mansions. He very often came to Addison Crescent, and generally stayed late."

'Pressed still further with questions, Emma at last stated that latterly Mrs. Hazeldene had been to the theatre several times with Mr. Errington, and that on those nights the master looked very gloomy, and was very cross.

'Recalled, the young widower was strangely reticent. He gave forth his answers very grudgingly, and the coroner was evidently absolutely satisfied with himself at the marvellous way in which, after a quarter of an hour of firm, yet very kind questionings, he had elicited from the witness what information he wanted.

'Mr. Errington was a friend of his wife. He was a gentleman of means, and seemed to have a great deal of time at his command. He himself did not particularly care about Mr. Errington, but he certainly had never made any observations to his wife on the subject.

'"But who is Mr. Errington?" repeated the coroner once more. "What does he do? What is his business or profession?"

'"He has no business or profession."

'"What is his occupation, then?"

'"He has no special occupation. He has ample private means. But he has a great and very absorbing hobby."

'"What is that?"

'"He spends all his time in chemical experiments, and is, I believe, as an amateur, a very distinguished toxicologist."'

III

'Did you ever see Mr. Errington, the gentleman so closely connected with the mysterious death on the Underground Railway?' asked the man in the corner as he placed one or two of his little snapshot photos before me. 'There he is, to the very life. Fairly good-looking, a pleasant face enough, but ordinary, absolutely ordinary.

'It was this absence of any peculiarity which very nearly, but not quite, placed the halter round Mr. Errington's neck. But I am going too fast, and you will lose the thread.

'The public, of course, never heard how it actually came about that Mr. Errington, the wealthy bachelor of Albert Mansions, of the Grosvenor, and other young dandies' clubs, one fine day found himself before the magistrates at Bow Street charged with being concerned in the death of Mary Beatrice Hazeldene, late of No. 19, Addison Row.

'I can assure you both press and public were literally flabbergasted. You see Mr. Errington was a well-known and very popular member of a certain smart section of London society. He was a constant visitor at the opera, the racecourse, the Park, and the Carlton, he had a great many friends, and there was consequently quite a large attendance at the police court that morning.

'What had transpired was this:

'After the very scrappy bits of evidence which came to light at the inquest, two gentlemen bethought themselves that perhaps they had some duty to perform towards the State and the public generally. Accordingly, they had come forward in order to offer to throw what light they could upon the mysterious affair on the Underground Railway.

'The police naturally felt that their information, such as it was, came rather late in the day, but as it proved of paramount importance, and the two gentlemen, moreover, were of undoubtedly good position in the world, they were thankful for what they could get, and acted accordingly; they accordingly brought Mr. Errington up before the Magistrate on a charge of murder.

'The accused looked pale and worried when I first caught sight of him in the Court that day, which was not to be wondered at, considering the terrible position in which he found himself.

'He had been arrested at Marseilles, where he was preparing to start for Colombo.

'I don't think he realised how terrible his position really was, until later in the proceedings when all the evidence relating to the arrest had been heard, and Emma Funnel had repeated her statement as to Mr. Errington's call at l9, Addison Row in the morning, and Mrs. Hazeldene starting off for St. Paul's Churchyard at 3:30 in the afternoon.

'Mr. Hazeldene had nothing to add to the statements he had made at the coroner's inquest. He had last seen his wife alive on the morning of the fatal day. She had seemed very well and cheerful. I think everyone present understood that he was trying to say as little as possible that could in any way couple his deceased wife's name with that of the accused.

'And yet, from the servant's evidence, it undoubtedly leaked out that Mrs. Hazeldene, who was young, pretty, and evidently fond of admiration, had once or twice annoyed her husband by somewhat open, yet perfectly innocent, flirtations with Mr. Errington.

'I think everyone was most agreeably impressed by the widower's moderate and dignified attitude. You will see his photo there, among this bundle. That is just how he appeared in court. In deep black, of course, but without any sign of ostentation in his mourning. He had allowed his beard to grow lately. and wore it closely cut in a point. After his evidence, the sensation of the day occurred. A tall dark-haired man with the word "City" written metaphorically all over him, had kissed the book, and was waiting to tell the truth, and nothing but the truth.

'He gave his name as Andrew Campbell, head of the firm of Campbell & Co., brokers, of Throgmorton Street.

'In the afternoon of June l8th Mr. Campbell, travelling on the Underground Railway, had noticed a very pretty woman in the same carriage as himself. She had asked him if she was in the right train for Aldersgate. Mr. Campbell replied in the affirmative, and then buried himself in the Stock Exchange quotations of his evening paper. At Gower Street, a gentleman in a tweed suit and bowler hat got into the carriage, and took a seat opposite the lady.

'She seemed very much astonished at seeing him, but Mr. Andrew Campbell did not recollect the exact words she said.

'The two talked to one another a good deal, and certainly the lady appeared animated and cheerful. Witness took no notice of them; he was very much engrossed in some calculations, and finally got out at Farringdon Street. He noticed that the man in the tweed suit also got out close behind him, having shaken hands with the lady, and said in a pleasant way: "*Au revoir*! Don't be late tonight." Mr. Campbell did not hear the lady's reply, and soon lost sight of the man in the crowd.

'Everyone was on tenterhooks, and eagerly waiting for the palpitating moment when witness would describe and identify the man who last had seen and spoken to the unfortunate woman, within five minutes probably of her strange and unaccountable death. Personally, I knew what was coming before the Scotch stockbroker spoke. I could have jotted down the graphic and lifelike description he would give of a probable murderer. It would have fitted equally well the man who sat and had luncheon at this table just now; it would certainly have described five out of every ten young Englishmen you know.

'The individual was of medium height, he wore a moustache which was not very fair nor yet very dark, his hair was between colours. He wore a bowler hat, and a tweed suit, and – and – that was all – Mr. Campbell might perhaps know him again, but then again, he might not – be was not paying much attention – the gentleman was sitting on the same side of the carriage as himself – and he had his hat on all the time. He himself was busy with his newspaper – yes – he might know him but he really could not say – –

'Mr. Andrew Campbell's evidence was not worth very much, you will say. No. It was not in itself, and would not have justified any arrest were it not for the additional statements made by Mr. James Verner, manager of Messrs. Rodney & Co., colour printers.

'Mr. Verner is a personal friend of Mr. Andrew Campbell, and it appears that at Farringdon Street, where he was waiting for his train, he saw Mr. Campbell get out of a first-class railway carriage. Mr. Verner spoke to him for a second, and then, just as the train was moving off, he stepped into the same compartment which had just been vacated by the stockbroker, and the man in the tweed suit. He vaguely recollects a lady sitting in the opposite corner to his own with her face turned away from him, apparently asleep, but he paid no special attention to her. He was like nearly all business men when they are travelling – engrossed in his paper. Presently a special quotation interested him; he wished to make a note of it, took out a pencil from his waistcoat pocket, and seeing a clean piece of paste-board on the floor, he picked it up, and scribbled on it the memoranda he wished to keep. He then slipped the card into his pocketbook.

'"It was only two or three days later," added Mr. Verner in the midst of breathless silence, 'that I had occasion to refer to these same notes again. In the meanwhile the papers had been full of the mysterious death on the Underground Railway, and the names of those connected with it were pretty familiar to me. It was, therefore, with much astonishment that on looking at the pasteboard which I had casually picked up in the railway carriage I saw the name on it "Frank Errington."'

'There was no doubt that the sensation in Court was almost unprecedented. Never since the days of the Fenchurch Street mystery, and the trial of Smethurst had I seen so much excitement. Mind you, I was not excited – I knew by now every detail of that crime as if I had committed it myself. In fact, I could not have done it better, although I have been a student of crime for many years now. Many people there – his friends, mostly – believed that Errington was doomed. I think he thought so too, for I could see that his face was terribly white, and he now and then passed his tongue over his lips, as if they were parched.

'You see he was in the awful dilemma – a perfectly natural one, by the way – of being absolutely incapable of *proving* an alibi. The crime – if crime there was – had been committed three weeks ago. A man about town like Mr. Frank Errington might remember that he spent certain hours of a special afternoon at his club, or in the Park, but it is very doubtful in nine cases out of ten if he can find a friend who could positively swear as to having seen him there. No! no! Mr. Errington was in a tight corner and he knew it. You see, there were – besides the evidence – two or three circumstances which did not improve matters for him. His hobby in the direction of toxicology, to begin with. The police had found in his room every description of poisonous substances, including prussic acid.

'Then, again, that journey to Marseilles, the start for Colombo, was, though perfectly innocent, a very unfortunate one. Mr. Errington had gone on an aimless voyage, but the public thought that he had fled terrified at his own crime. Sir Arthur Inglewood, however, here again displayed his marvellous skill on behalf of his client by the masterly way in which he literally turned all the witnesses for the Crown inside out.

'Having first got Mr. Andrew Campbell to state positively that in the accused he certainly did *not* recognise the man in the tweed suit, the eminent lawyer, after twenty minutes' cross-examination, had so completely upset the stockbroker's equanimity that it is very likely he would not have recognised his own office boy.

'But through all his flurry and all his annoyance Mr. Andrew Campbell remained very sure of one thing; namely, that the lady was alive and cheerful, and talking pleasantly with the man in the tweed suit up to the moment when the latter, having shaken hands with her, left her with a pleasant "*Au revoir*! Don't be late tonight." He had heard neither scream nor struggle, and in his opinion, if the individual in the tweed suit had administered a dose of poison to his companion, it must have been with her own knowledge and free will; and the lady in the train most emphatically neither looked nor spoke like a woman prepared for a sudden and violent death.

'Mr. James Verner, against that, swore equally positively that he had stood in full view of the carriage door, from the moment that Mr. Campbell got out until he himself stepped into the compartment, that there was no one else in that carriage between Farringdon Street and Aldgate, and that the lady, to the best of his belief, had made no movement during the whole of that journey.

IV

'No; Frank Errington was *not* committed for trial on the capital charge,' said the man in the corner with one of his sardonic smiles, 'thanks to the cleverness of Sir Arthur Inglewood, his lawyer. He absolutely denied his identity with the man in the tweed suit, and swore he had not seen Mrs. Hazeldene since eleven o'clock in the morning of that fatal day. There was no *proof* that he had; moreover, according to Mr. Campbell's opinion, the man in the tweed suit was in all probability not the murderer. Common sense would not admit that a woman could have a deadly poison injected into her without her knowledge, while chatting pleasantly to her murderer.

'Mr. Errington lives abroad now. He is about to marry. I don't think any of his real friends for a moment believed that he committed the bastardly crime.The police think they know better. They do know this much, that it could not have been a case of suicide, that if the man who undoubtedly travelled with Mrs. Hazeldene on that fatal afternoon had no crime upon his conscience he would long ago have come forward and thrown what light he could upon the mystery.

'As to who that man was, the police in their blindness have not the faintest doubt. Under the unshakable belief that Errington is guilty they have spent the last few months in unceasing labour to try and find further and strong proofs of his guilt. But they won't find them, because there are none. There are no positive proofs against the actual murderer, for he was one of those clever blackguards who think of everything, foresee every eventuality, who know human nature well, and can foretell exactly what evidence will he brought against them, and act accordingly.

'This blackguard from the first kept the figure, the personality, of Frank Errington before his mind. Frank Errington was the dust which the scoundrel threw metaphorically in the eyes of the police, and you must admit that he succeeded in blinding them – to the extent even of making them entirely forget the one simple little sentence, overheard by Mr. Andrew Campbell, and which was, of course, the clue to the whole thing – the only slip the cunning rogue made – "*Au revoir*! Don't be late tonight." Mrs. Hazeldene was going that night to the opera with her husband – –

'You are astonished?' he added with a shrug of the shoulders, 'you do not see the tragedy yet, as I have seen it before me all along. The frivolous young wife, the flirtation with the friend? – all a blind, all pretence. I took the trouble which the police should have taken immediately, of finding out something about the finances of the Hazeldene *ménage*. Money is in nine cases out of ten the keynote to a crime. I found that the will of Mary Beatrice Hazeldene had been proved by the husband, her sole executor, the estate being sworn at £l5,000. I found out, moreover, that Mr. Edward Sholto Hazeldene was a poor shipper's clerk when he married the daughter of a wealthy builder in Kensington – and then I made note of the fact that the disconsolate widower had allowed his beard to grow since the death of his wife.

'There's no doubt that he was a clever rogue,' added the strange creature leaning excitedly over the table, and peering into my face. 'Do you know how that deadly poison was injected into the poor woman's system? By the simplest of all means, one known to every scoundrel in Southern Europe. A ring – yes! a ring, which has a tiny hollow needle capable of bolding a sufficient quantity of prussic acid to have killed two persons instead of one. The man in the tweed suit shook bands with his fair companion – probably she hardly felt the prick, not sufficiently in any case to make her utter a scream. And, mind you, the scoundrel had every facility, through his friendsbip with Mr. Errington, of procuring what poison he required, not to mention his friend's visiting card. We cannot gauge how many months ago he began to try and copy Frank Errington in his style of dress, the cut of his moustache, his general appearance, making the change probably so gradual, that no one in his own *entourage* would notice it. He selected for his model a man his own height and build, with the same coloured hair.'

'But there was the terrible risk of being identified by his fellow-traveller in the Underground,' I suggested.

'Yes, there certainly was that risk; he chose to take it, and he was wise. Re reckoned that several days would in any case elapse before that person, who, by the way, was a business man absorbed in his newspaper, would actually see him again. The great secret of successful crime is to study human nature,' added the man in the corner, as he began looking for his hat and coat. 'Edward Hazeldene knew it well.'

'But the ring?' I said.

'He may have bought that when he was on his honeymoon,' he suggested with a grim chuckle, 'the tragedy was not planned in a week; it may have taken years to mature. But you will own that there goes a frightful scoundrel unhung. I have left you his photograph as he was a year ago, and as he is now. You will see he has shaved his beard again, but also his moustache. I fancy he is a friend now of Mr. Andrew Campbell.'

He left me wondering. I don't know what I did believe; his whole story sounded so farfetched and strange. Was he really giving me the results of continued thought, or was he experimenting as to exactly how far the credulity of a lady novelist could go?

SAKI

## Esmé (1911)

'All hunting stories are the same,' said Clovis; 'just as all Turf stories are the same, and all –'

'My hunting story isn't a bit like any you've ever heard,' said the Baroness. 'It happened quite a while ago, when I was about twenty-three. I wasn't living apart from my husband then; you see, neither of us could afford to make the other a separate allowance. In spite of everything that proverbs may say, poverty keeps together more homes than it breaks up. But we always hunted with different packs. All this has nothing to do with the story.'

'We haven't arrived at the meet yet. I suppose there was a meet,' said Clovis.

'Of course there was a meet,' said the Baroness; 'all the usual crowd were there, especially Constance Broddle. Constance is one of those strapping florid girls that go so well with autumn scenery or Christmas decorations in church. "I feel a presentiment that something dreadful is going to happen," she said to me; "am I looking pale?"

'She was looking about as pale as a beetroot that has suddenly heard bad news.

'"You're looking nicer than usual," I said, "but that's so easy for you." Before she had got the right bearings of this remark we had settled down to business; hounds had found a fox lying out in some gorse-bushes.'

'I knew it,' said Clovis; 'in every fox-hunting story that I've ever heard there's been a fox and some gorse-bushes.'

'Constance and I were well mounted,' continued the Baroness serenely, 'and we had no difficulty in keeping ourselves in the first flight, though it was a fairly stiff run. Towards the finish, however, we must have held rather too independent a line, for we lost the hounds, and found ourselves plodding aimlessly along miles away from anywhere. It was fairly exasperating, and my temper was beginning to let itself go by inches, when on pushing our way through an accommodating hedge we were gladdened by the sight of hounds in full cry in a hollow just beneath us.

'"There they go," cried Constance, and then added in a gasp, "In Heaven's name, what are they hunting?"

'It was certainly no mortal fox. It stood more than twice as high, had a short, ugly head, and an enormous thick neck.

'"It's a hyæna," I cried; "it must have escaped from Lord Pabham's Park."

'At that moment the hunted beast turned and faced its pursuers, and the hounds (there were only about six couple of them) stood round in a half-circle and looked foolish. Evidently they had broken away from the rest of the pack on the trail of this alien scent, and were not quite sure how to treat their quarry now they had got him.

'The hyæna hailed our approach with unmistakable relief and demonstrations of friendliness. It had probably been accustomed to uniform kindness from humans, while its first experience of a pack of hounds had left a bad impression. The hounds looked more than ever embarrassed as their quarry paraded its sudden intimacy with us, and the faint toot of a horn in the distance was seized on as a welcome signal for unobtrusive departure. Constance and I and the hyæna were left alone in the gathering twilight.

'"What are we to do?" asked Constance.

'"What a person you are for questions," I said.

'"Well, we can't stay here all night with a hyæna," she retorted.

'"I don't know what your ideas of comfort are," I said; "but I shouldn't think of staying here all night even without a hyæna. My home may be an unhappy one, but at least it has hot and cold water laid on, and domestic service, and other conveniences which we shouldn't find here. We had better make for that ridge of trees to the right; I imagine the Crowley road is just beyond."

'We trotted off slowly along a faintly marked cart-track, with the beast following cheerfully at our heels.

'"What on earth are we to do with the hyæna?" came the inevitable question.

'"What does one generally do with hyænas?" I asked crossly.

'"I've never had anything to do with one before," said Constance.

'"Well, neither have I. If we even knew its sex we might give it a name. Perhaps we might call it Esmé. That would do in either case."

'There was still sufficient daylight for us to distinguish wayside objects, and our listless spirits gave an upward perk as we came upon a small half-naked gipsy brat picking blackberries from a low-growing bush. The sudden apparition of two horsewomen and a hyæna set it off crying, and in any case we should scarcely have gleaned any useful geographical information from that source; but there was a probability that we might strike a gipsy encampment somewhere along our route. We rode on hopefully but uneventfully for another mile or so.

'"I wonder what that child was doing there," said Constance presently.

'"Picking blackberries. Obviously."

'"I don't like the way it cried," pursued Constance; "somehow its wail keeps ringing in my ears."

'I did not chide Constance for her morbid fancies; as a matter of fact the same sensation, of being pursued by a persistent fretful wail, had been forcing itself on my rather over-tired nerves. For company's sake I hulloed to Esmé, who had lagged somewhat behind. With a few springy bounds he drew up level, and then shot past us.

'The wailing accompaniment was explained. The gipsy child was firmly, and I expect painfully, held in his jaws.

'"Merciful Heaven!" screamed Constance, "what on earth shall we do? What are we to do?"

'I am perfectly certain that at the Last Judgment Constance will ask more questions than any of the examining Seraphs.

'"Can't we do something?" she persisted tearfully, as Esmé cantered easily along in front of our tired horses.

'Personally I was doing everything that occurred to me at the moment. I stormed and scolded and coaxed in English and French and gamekeeper language; I made absurd, ineffectual cuts in the air with my thongless hunting-crop; I hurled my sandwich case at the brute; in fact, I really don't know what more I could have done. And still we lumbered on through the deepening dusk, with that dark uncouth shape lumbering ahead of us, and a drone of lugubrious music floating in our ears. Suddenly Esmé bounded aside into some thick bushes, where we could not follow; the wail rose to a shriek and then stopped altogether. This part of the story I always hurry over, because it is really rather horrible. When the beast joined us again, after an absence of a few minutes, there was an air of patient understanding about him, as though he knew that he had done something of which we disapproved, but which he felt to be thoroughly justifiable.

'"How can you let that ravening beast trot by your side?" asked Constance. She was looking more than ever like an albino beetroot.

'"In the first place, I can't prevent it," I said; "and in the second place, whatever else he may be, I doubt if he's ravening at the present moment."

'Constance shuddered. "Do you think the poor little thing suffered much?" came another of her futile questions.

'"The indications were all that way," I said; "on the other hand, of course, it may have been crying from sheer temper. Children sometimes do."

'It was nearly pitch-dark when we emerged suddenly into the high road. A flash of lights and the whir of a motor went past us at the same moment at uncomfortably close quarters. A thud and a sharp screeching yell followed a second later. The car drew up, and when I had ridden back to the spot I found a young man bending over a dark motionless mass lying by the roadside.

'"You have killed my Esmé," I exclaimed bitterly.

'"I'm so awfully sorry," said the young man; "I keep dogs myself, so I know what you must feel about it. I'll do anything I can in reparation."

'"Please bury him at once," I said; "that much I think I may ask of you."

'"Bring the spade, William," he called to the chauffeur. Evidently hasty roadside internments were contingencies that had been provided against.

'The digging of a sufficiently large grave took some little time. "I say, what a magnificent fellow," said the motorist as the corpse was rolled over into the trench. "I'm afraid he must have been rather a valuable animal."

'"He took second in the puppy class at Birmingham last year," I said resolutely.

'Constance snorted loudly.

'"Don't cry, dear," I said brokenly; "it was all over in a moment. He couldn't have suffered much."

'"Look here," said the young fellow desperately, "you simply must let me do something by way of reparation."

'I refused sweetly, but as he persisted I let him have my address.

'Of course, we kept our own counsel as to the earlier episodes of the evening. Lord Pabham never advertised the loss of his hyæna; when a strictly fruit-eating animal strayed from his park a year or two previously he was called upon to give compensation in eleven cases of sheep-worrying and practically to re-stock his neighbours' poultry-yards, and an escaped hyæna would have mounted up to something on the scale of a Government grant. The gipsies were equally unobtrusive over their missing offspring; I don't suppose in large encampments they really know to a child or two how many they've got.'

The Baroness paused reflectively, and then continued:

'There was a sequel to the adventure, though. I got through the post a charming little diamond brooch, with the name Esmé set in a sprig of rosemary. Incidentally, too, I lost the friendship of Constance Broddle. You see, when I sold the brooch I quite properly refused to give her any share of the proceeds. I pointed out that the Esmé part of the affair was my own invention, and the hyæna part of it belonged to Lord Pabham, if it really was his hyæna, of which, of course, I've no proof.'

VIRGINIA WOOLF

## Mrs Dalloway in Bond Street (1923)

Mrs Dalloway said she would buy the gloves herself. Big Ben was striking as she stepped out into the street. It was eleven o'clock and the unused hour was fresh as if issued to children on a beach. But there was something solemn in the deliberate swing of the repeated strokes; something stirring in the murmur of wheels and the shuffle of footsteps.

No doubt they were not all bound on errands of happiness. There is much more to be said about us than that we walk the streets of Westminster. Big Ben too is nothing but steel rods consumed by rust were it not for the care of H.M's Office of Works. Only for Mrs Dalloway the moment was complete; for Mrs Dalloway June was fresh. A happy childhood – and it was not to his daughters only that Justin Parry had seemed a fine fellow (weak of course on the Bench); flowers at evening, smoke rising; the caw of rooks falling from ever so high, down down through the October air – there is nothing to take the place of childhood. A leaf of mint brings it back: or a cup with a blue ring.

Poor little wretches, she sighed, and pressed forward. Oh, right under the horses' noses, you little demon! and there she was left on the kerb stretching her hand out, while Jimmy Dawes grinned on the further side.

A charming woman, posed, eager, strangely white-haired for her pink cheeks, so Scope Purvis, C.B., saw her as he hurried to his office. She stiffened a little, waiting for Durtnall's van to pass. Big Ben struck the tenth; struck the eleventh stroke. The leaden circles dissolved in the air. Pride held her erect, inheriting, handing on, acquainted with discipline and with suffering. How people suffered, how they suffered, she thought, thinking of Mrs Foxcroft at the Embassy last night decked with jewels, eating her heart out, because that nice boy was dead, and now the old Manor House (Durtnall's van passed) must go to a cousin.

'Good morning to you,' said Hugh Whitbread raising his hat rather extravagantly by the china shop, for they had known each other as children. 'Where are you off to?'

'I love walking in London,' said Mrs Dalloway. 'Really it's better than walking in the country!'

'We've just come up,' said Hugh Whitbread. 'Unfortunately to see doctors.'

'Milly?' said Mrs Dalloway, instantly compassionate.

'Out of sorts,' said Hugh Whitbread. 'That sort of thing. Dick all right?'

'First rate!' said Clarissa.

Of course, she thought, walking on, Milly is about my age – fifty – fifty-two. So it is probably *that* Hugh's manner had said so, said it perfectly – dear old Hugh, thought Mrs Dalloway, remembering with amusement, with gratitude, with emotion, how shy, like a brother – one would rather die than speak to one's brother – Hugh had always been, when he was at Oxford, and came over, and perhaps one of them (drat the thing!) couldn't ride. How then could women sit in Parliament? How could they do things with men? For there is this extraordinarily deep instinct, something inside one; you can't get over it; it's no use trying; and men like Hugh respect it without our saying it, which is what one loves, thought Clarissa, in dear old Hugh.

She had passed through the Admiralty Arch and saw at the end of the empty road with its thin trees Victoria's white mound, Victoria's billowing motherliness, amplitude and homeliness, always ridiculous, yet how sublime, thought Mrs Dalloway, remembering Kensington Gardens and the old lady in horn spectacles and being told by Nanny to stop dead still and bow to the Queen. The flag flew above the Palace. The King and Queen were back then. Dick had met her at lunch the other day – a thoroughly nice woman. It matters so much to the poor, thought Clarissa, and to the soldiers. A man in bronze stood heroically on a pedestal with a gun on her left hand side – the South African war. It matters, thought Mrs Dalloway walking towards Buckingham Palace. There it stood four-square, in the broad sunshine, uncompromising, plain. But it was character she thought; something inborn in the race; what Indians respected. The Queen went to hospitals, opened bazaars – the Queen of England, thought Clarissa, looking at the Palace. Already at this hour a motor car passed out at the gates; soldiers saluted; the gates were shut. And Clarissa, crossing the road, entered the Park, holding herself upright.

June had drawn out every leaf on the trees. The mothers of Westminster with mottled breasts gave suck to their young. Quite respectable girls lay stretched on the grass. An elderly man, stooping very stiffly, picked up a crumpled paper, spread it out flat and flung it away. How horrible! Last night at the Embassy Sir Dighton had said, 'If I want a fellow to hold my horse, I have only to put up my hand.' But the religious question is far more serious than the economic, Sir Dighton had said, which she thought extraordinarily interesting, from a man like Sir Dighton. 'Oh, the country will never know what it has lost,' he had said, talking, of his own accord, about dear Jack Stewart.

She mounted the little hill lightly. The air stirred with energy. Messages were passing from the Fleet to the Admiralty. Piccadilly and Arlington Street and the Mall seemed to chafe the very air in the Park and lift its leaves hotly, brilliantly, upon waves of that divine vitality which Clarissa loved. To ride; to dance; she had adored all that. Or going long walks in the country, talking, about books, what to do with one's life, for young people were amazingly priggish – oh, the things one had said! But one had conviction. Middle age is the devil. People like Jack'll never know that, she thought; for he never once thought of death, never, they said, knew he was dying. And now can never mourn – how did it go? – a head grown grey. ... From the contagion of the world's slow stain. ... Have drunk their cup a round or two before. ... From the contagion of the world's slow stain! She held herself upright.

But how Jack would have shouted! Quoting Shelley, in Piccadilly! 'You want a pin,' he would have said. He hated frumps. 'My God Clarissa! My God Clarissa!' – she could hear him now at the Devonshire House party, about poor Sylvia Hunt in her amber necklace and that dowdy old silk. Clarissa held herself upright for she had spoken aloud and now she was in Piccadilly, passing the house with the slender green columns, and the balconies; passing club windows full of newspapers; passing old Lady Burdett Coutt's house where the glazed white parrot used to hang; and Devonshire House, without its gilt leopards; and Claridge's, where she must remember Dick wanted her to leave a card on Mrs Jepson or she would be gone. Rich Americans can be very charming. There was St James's Palace; like a child's game with bricks; and now – she had passed Bond Street – she was by Hatchard's book shop. The stream was endless – endless – endless. Lords, Ascot, Hurlingham – what was it? What a duck, she thought, looking at the frontispiece of some book of memoirs spread wide in the bow window, Sir Joshua perhaps or Romney; arch, bright, demure; the sort of girl – like her own Elizabeth – the only *real* sort of girl. And there was that absurd book, *Soapy Sponge*, which Jim used to quote by the yard; and Shakespeare's Sonnets. She knew them by heart. Phil and she had argued all day about the Dark Lady, and Dick had said straight out at dinner that night that he had never heard of her. Really, she had married him for that! He had never read Shakespeare! There must be some little cheap book she could buy for Milly – *Cranford* of course! Was there ever anything so enchanting as the cow in petticoats? If only people had that sort of humour, that sort of self-respect now, thought Clarissa, for she remembered the broad pages; the sentences ending; the characters – how one talked about them as if they were real. For all the great things one must go to the past, she thought. From the contagion of the world's slow stain. ... Fear no more the heat o' the sun. ... And now can never mourn, can never mourn, she repeated, her eyes straying over the window; for it ran in her head; the test of great poetry; the moderns had never written anything one wanted to read about death, she thought; and turned.

Omnibuses joined motor cars; motor cars vans; vans taxicabs; taxicabs motor cars – here was an open motor car with a girl, alone. Up till four, her feet tingling, I know, thought Clarissa, for the girl looked washed out, half asleep, in the corner of the car after the dance. And another car came; and another. No! No! No! Clarissa smiled good-naturedly. The fat lady had taken every sort of trouble, but diamonds! orchids! at this hour of the morning! No! No! No! The excellent policeman would, when the time came, hold up his hand. Another motor car passed. How utterly unattractive! Why should a girl of that age paint black round her eyes? And a young man with a girl, at this hour, when the country – The admirable policeman raised his hand and Clarissa acknowledging his sway, taking her time, crossed, walked towards Bond Street; saw the narrow crooked street, the yellow banners; the thick notched telegraph wires stretched across the sky.

A hundred years ago her great-great-grandfather, Seymour Parry, who ran away with Conway's daughter, had walked down Bond Street. Down Bond Street the Parrys had walked for a hundred years, and might have met the Dalloways (Leighs on the mother's side) going up. Her father got his clothes from Hill's. There was a roll of cloth in the window, and here just one jar on a black table, incredibly expensive; like the thick pink salmon on the ice block at the fishmonger's. The jewels were exquisite – pink and orange stars, paste, Spanish, she thought, and chains of old gold; starry buckles, little brooches which had been worn on sea-green satin by ladies with high head-dresses. But no looking! One must economise. She must go on past the picture dealer's where one of the odd French pictures hung, as if people had thrown confetti – pink and blue – for a joke. If you had lived with pictures (and it's the same with books and music) thought Clarissa, passing the Aeolian Hall, you can't be taken in by a joke.

The river of Bond Street was clogged. There, like a queen at a tournament, raised, regal, was Lady Bexborough. She sat in her carriage, upright, alone, looking through her glasses. The white glove was loose at her wrist. She was in black, quite shabby, yet, thought Clarissa, how extraordinarily it tells, breeding, self-respect, never saying a word too much or letting people gossip; an astonishing friend; no one can pick a hole in her after all these years, and now, there she is, thought Clarissa, passing the Countess who waited powdered, perfectly still, and Clarissa would have given anything to be like that, the mistress of Clarefield, talking politics, like a man. But she never goes anywhere, thought Clarissa, and it's quite useless to ask her, and the carriage went on and Lady Bexborough was borne past like a queen at a tournament, though she had nothing to live for and the old man is failing and they say she is sick of it all, thought Clarissa and the tears actually rose to her eyes as she entered the shop.

'Good morning,' said Clarissa in her charming voice. 'Gloves,' she said with her exquisite friendliness and putting her bag on the counter began, very slowly, to undo the buttons. 'White gloves', she said. 'Above the elbow,' and she looked straight into the shopwoman's face – but this was not the girl she remembered? She looked quite old. 'These really don't fit,' said Clarissa. The shop-girl looked at them. 'Madame wears bracelets?' Clarissa spread out her fingers. 'Perhaps it's my rings,' And the girl took the grey gloves with her to the end of the counter.

Yes, thought Clarissa, it's the girl I remember, she's twenty years older. ... There was only one other customer, sitting sideways at the counter, her elbow poised, her bare hand drooping, vacant; like a figure on a Japanese fan, thought Clarissa, too vacant perhaps, yet some men would adore her. The lady shook her head sadly.

Again the gloves were too large. She turned round the glass. 'Above the wrist,' she reproached the grey-headed woman who looked and agreed.

They waited; a clock ticked; Bond Street hummed, dulled, distant; the woman went away holding gloves. 'Above the wrist,' said the lady, mournfully, raising her voice. And she would have to order chairs, ices, flowers, and cloak-room tickets, thought Clarissa. The people she didn't want would come; the others wouldn't. She would stand by the door. They sold stockings – silk stockings. A lady is known by her gloves and her shoes, old Uncle William used to say. And through the hanging silk stockings' quivering silver she looked at the lady, sloping shouldered, her hand drooping, her bag slipping, her eyes vacantly on the floor. It would be intolerable if dowdy women came to her party! Would one have liked Keats if he had worn red socks? Oh, at last – she drew into the counter and it flashed into her mind:

'Do you remember before the war you had gloves with pearl buttons?'

'French gloves, Madame?'

'Yes, they were French,' said Clarissa. The other lady rose very sadly and took her bag, and looked at the gloves on the counter. But they were all too large – always too large at the wrist. 'With pearl buttons,' said the shop-girl, who looked ever so much older. She split the lengths of tissue paper apart on the counter.

With pearl buttons, thought Clarissa, perfectly simple – how French!

'Madame's hands are so slender,' said the shop-girl, drawing the glove firmly, smoothly, down over her rings. And Clarissa looked at her arm in the looking-glass. The glove hardly came to the elbow. Were there others half an inch longer? Still it seemed tiresome to bother her – perhaps the one day in the month, thought Clarissa, when it's an agony to stand. 'Oh, don't bother,' she said. But the gloves were brought.

'Don't you get fearfully tired,' she said in her charming voice, 'standing? When d'you get your holiday?'

'In September, Madame, when we're not so busy.'

When we're in the country thought Clarissa. Or shooting. She has a fortnight at Brighton. In some stuffy lodging. The landlady takes the sugar. Nothing would be easier than to send her to Mrs Lumley's right in the country (and it was on the tip of her tongue). But then she remembered how on their honeymoon Dick had shown her the folly of giving impulsively. It was much more important, he said, to get trade with China. Of course he was right. And she could feel the girl wouldn't like to be given things. There she was in her place. So was Dick. Selling gloves was her job. She had her own sorrows quite separate, 'and now can never mourn, can never mourn', the words ran in her head. 'From the contagion of the world's slow stain,' thought Clarissa holding her arm stiff, for there are moments when it seems utterly futile (the glove was drawn off leaving her arm flecked with powder) – simply one doesn't believe, thought Clarissa, any more in God.

The traffic suddenly roared; the silk stockings brightened. A customer came in.

'White gloves,' she said, with some ring in her voice that Clarissa remembered.

It used, thought Clarissa, to be so simple. Down, down through the air came the caw of the rooks. When Sylvia died, hundreds of years ago, the yew hedges looked so lovely with the diamond webs in the mist before early church. But if Dick were to die to-morrow, As for believing in God – no, she would let the children choose, but for herself, like Lady Bexborough, who opened the bazaar, they say, with the telegram in her hand – Roden, her favourite, killed – she would go on. But why, if one doesn't believe? For the sake of others, she thought taking the glove in her hand. The girl would be much more unhappy if she didn't believe.

'Thirty shillings,' said the shop-woman. 'No, pardon me Madame, thirty-five. The French gloves are more.'

For one doesn't live for oneself, thought Clarissa.

And then the other customer took a glove, tugged it, and it split.

'There!' she exclaimed.

'A fault of the skin,' said the grey-headed woman hurriedly. 'Sometimes a drop of acid in tanning. Try this pair, Madame.'

'But it's an awful swindle to ask two pound ten!'

Clarissa looked at the lady; the lady looked at Clarissa.

'Gloves have never been quite so reliable since the war,' said the shop-girl, apologising, to Clarissa.

But where had she seen the other lady? – elderly, with a frill under her chin; wearing a black ribbon for gold eyeglasses; sensual, clever, like a Sargent drawing. How one can tell from a voice when people are in the habit, thought Clarissa, of making other people – 'It's a shade too tight,' she said – obey. The shop-woman went off again. Clarissa was left waiting. Fear no more she repeated, playing her finger on the counter. Fear no more the heat o' the sun. Fear no more she repeated. There were little brown spots on her arm. And the girl crawled like a snail. Thou thy worldly task hast done. Thousands of young men had died that things might go on. At last! Half an inch above the elbow; pearl buttons; five and a quarter. My dear slow coach, thought Clarissa, do you think I can sit here the whole morning? Now you'll take twenty-five minutes to bring me my change!

There was a violent explosion in the street outside. The shop-women cowered behind the counters. But Clarissa, sitting very upright, smiled at the other lady. 'Miss Anstruther!' she exclaimed.

H.E. Bates

## For the Dead (1934)

A LITTLE pink-faced man, wearing a bowler hat and a mackintosh over a black suit, was hurrying towards the cemetery carrying a bunch of white chrysanthemums wrapped in newspaper and smoking a stump of cigarette that was half hidden by his greyish yellow moustache. A gentle rain was falling, a drizzling misty November rain that dung like dew to the chrysanthemums and like tiniest beads of quicksilver to the man's moustache and his bowler hat. The afternoon would be dark early. The sky was a single vast leaden cloud; the rain was coming a little faster each moment. As the rain came faster the man increased his pace. He carried the chrysanthemums dose to his side, furtively, flowers downward, uneasily conscious of them.

The cemetery was deserted. In the distance the rain made a faint vapour, dissolving the white tombstones. The cypress trees drooped heavily and the branches of the leafless almond trees stood black against the sky, delicately laced with odd jewels of rain.

Hurrying, the man went past the public water-tap and the watering-cans and along the wet devious paths among the graves. He walked as though it were all very distasteful to him – the rain, the deserted cemetery, the very thought of placing the flowers on the grave of his dead wife. Yet there was a kind of indifference also in his very irritation, as though he hardly cared whether the flowers were put there or not. He began to walk even faster, anxious to have done with it all.

He came at last to his wife's grave, a rectangle of white marble enclosing a mound of neglected grass, and without taking off his hat and still sucking the cigarette through his wet moustache he took the chrysanthemums from their wrapping of newspaper, shook them and dropped them carelessly on the wet grass. On the grass, in a half-rusty green tin vase, stood the chrysanthemums he had put there a fortnight before. Once white, they were now shrivelled and blackened by frost and rain. Straddling the grave he seized the tin, wrenched out the old flowers and dropped them too on the wet grass.

Picking up the new chrysanthemums, he hesitated. The tin was empty of water. He stood for a moment wondering if he should walk back across the cemetery to the water-tap. And then, impatiently, he decided against it. It was a long way in the rain. What did it matter? A lot of trouble, a lot of trouble for nothing. The flowers would die in any case. He wanted to get it over.

He hastily picked up the new white bunch of chrysanthemums. But stooping with them he again hesitated.

Down the path, also at a grave, was another man. He was a thin stooping figure and with his black bowler hat and his black overcoat he had the almost ascetic respectability of a tired shopwalker. Like the small man he was middle-aged, and like him also he was arranging a bunch of white chrysanthemums hastily, as though it were distasteful and he wanted to escape from the cemetery and the rain.

They noticed each other simultaneously and could not avoid speaking.

'Good afternoon.'

'Ah, good afternoon.'

They were slightly acquainted and they spoke deferentially, their voices a little embarrassed, and they stood for a moment hesitant, not knowing what to do or what also to say.

Then casually the smaller man glanced up at the sky. 'I shouldn't wonder if it rained all night,' he remarked.

Then, as he lowered his eyes, he saw that the other man had removed his hat and was staring dismally at the rain, as though in thought.

'Ah!' he said heavily. 'I shouldn't wonder.' The small man glanced at the other man with secret annoyance for having removed his hat.

There was a silence, then, after a moment, the small man unobtrusively took off his hat also. His head, very bald, like a bladder of pink lard, seemed to stand out strangely large in the colourless rainy air. Then, as he stood with his head half-bowed, the little man remembered his cigarette. It seemed suddenly disrespectful and he let it fall from his mouth and it dropped on the wet grass, hissing faintly until he put his foot on it.

They stood there with their hats in their hands and with the rain drizzling on their bare heads until the tall man spoke again.

'You haven't a drop of water to spare,' he said, 'have you?'

The little man shook his head. 'But I was just going to the tap,' he said. 'I'll bring a can.'

'Oh no, I was going myself.'

'It seems a pity for us both to go.'

The tall man smiled and shook his head with a heavy and deliberate pretence of mournfulness.

'One day we shall have to go,' he said.

The little man nodded. 'I suppose so,' he said, heavily also.

Almost before they were aware of it they were walking down the path together, leaving their flowers on the wet grass. They walked at a slow almost solemn pace, with their hats still in their hands, as though to a funeral. Now and then they shot furtive glances of secret impatience at each other, each irritably wondering when the other would put on his hat. But neither made a sign, and they walked to the water-tap and back to the graves again without a change of pace, each with a can of water in one hand and his hat still in the other.

Stooping over the graves they arranged their flowers with a kind of deliberate reverence, filling the tin vases carefully, touching the flower petals with a perceptible show of tenderness. At intervals they half glanced up at each other, each as though wondering if the other were looking and what he were thinking.

At last they were finished and they stood upright. The thin man had been kneeling and he brushed his hands across his wet knees. The little man could feel the rain falling in larger drops on his bald head and collecting into even larger drops that rolled suddenly, like little balls of ice, down his neck.

They stood in silence, a pace or two back from the graves, their heads a trifle bowed in a pretence of grief. They stood there for what seemed to both of them a long time, secretly impatient, staring heavily into space, as though reflecting regretfully on the past and the dead. They had no longer any need to pretend wretchedness. The rain was coming down each moment faster and colder, dripping swiftly down from the wintry branches to the glistening marble tombs and the yellowish muddy paths. Once or twice the tall man ran his hand in concern across his damp knees and the other shook his head slightly, shivering miserably under the cold rain.

At last the tall man gave a sigh as though reluctant to depart, and picked up his watering-can.

'Well, it's no use standing here,' he said mournfully.

He shook his head as he spoke. 'No use standing here.' The little man shook his head in melancholy agreement, sighing also.

A moment later, with secret relief, they were walking away together down the path. Unobtrusively the tall man put on his hat and then the small man put on his too. They walked deferentially, in silence, until they reached the water-tap, where they left their watering-cans.

At the gates they stood for a moment and then parted. The rain was falling heavily, the mist and the darkness together hid the farthest tombs and trees from sight, and the two men hurried away from each other with angry relief and impatience, as though they never wished to see each other again.

W. Somerset Maugham

## Louise (1936)

I could never understand why Louise bothered with me. She disliked me and I knew that behind my back, in that gentle way of hers, she seldom lost the opportunity of saying a disagreeable thing about me. She had too much delicacy ever to make a direct statement, but with a hint and a sigh and a little flutter of her beautiful hands she was able to make her meaning plain. She was a mistress of cold praise. It was true that we had known one another almost intimately, for five-and-twenty years, but it was impossible for me to believe that she could be affected by the claims of old association. She thought me a coarse, brutal, cynical and vulgar fellow. I was puzzled at her not taking the obvious course and dropping me. She did nothing of the kind; indeed, she would not leave me alone; she was constantly asking me to lunch and dine with her and once or twice a year invited me to spend a week-end at her house in the country. At last I thought that I had discovered her motive. She had an uneasy suspicion that I did not believe in her; and if that was why she did not like me, it was also why she sought my acquaintance: it galled her that I alone should look upon her as a comic figure and she could not rest till I acknowledged myself mistaken and defeated. Perhaps she had an inkling that I saw the face behind the mask and because I alone held out was determined that sooner or later I too should take the mask for the face. I was never quite certain that she was a complete humbug. I wondered whether she fooled herself as thoroughly as she fooled the world or whether there was some spark of humour at the bottom of her heart. If there was it might be that she was attracted to me, as a pair of crooks might be attracted to one another, by the knowledge that we shared a secret that was hidden from everybody else.

I knew Louise before she married. She was then a frail, delicate girl with large and melancholy eyes. Her father and mother worshipped her with an anxious adoration, for some illness, scarlet fever I think, had left her with a weak heart and she had to take the greatest care of herself. When Tom Maitland proposed to her they were dismayed, for they were convinced that she was much too delicate for the strenuous state of marriage. But they were not too well off and Tom Maitland was rich. He promised to do everything in the world for Louise and finally they entrusted her to him as a sacred charge. Tom Maitland was a big, husky fellow, very good-looking, and a fine athlete. He doted on Louise. With her weak heart he could not hope to keep her with him long and he made up his mind to do everything he could to make her few years on earth happy. He gave up the games he excelled in, not because she wished him to, she was glad that he should play golf and hunt, but because by a coincidence she had a heart attack whenever he proposed to leave her for a day. If they had a difference of opinion she gave in to him at once, for she was the most submissive wife a man could have, but her heart failed her and she would be laid up, sweet and uncomplaining, for a week. He could not be such a brute as to cross her. Then they would have quite a little tussle about which should yield and it was only with difficulty that at last he persuaded her to have her own way. On one occasion seeing her walk eight miles on an expedition that she particularly wanted to make, I suggested to Tom Maitland that she was stronger than one would have thought. He shook his head and sighed.

'No, no, she's dreadfully delicate. She's been to all the best heart specialists in the world, and they all say that her life hangs on a thread. But she has an unconquerable spirit.'

He told her that I had remarked on her endurance.

'I shall pay for it to-morrow,' she said to me in her plaintive way. 'I shall be at death's door.'

'I sometimes think that you 're quite strong enough to do the things you want to,' I murmured.

I had noticed that if a party was amusing she could dance till five in the morning, but if it was dull she felt very poorly and Tom had to take her home early. I am afraid she did not like my reply, for though she gave me a pathetic little smile I saw no amusement in her large blue eyes.

'You can't very well expect me to fall down dead just to please you,' she answered.

Louise outlived her husband. He caught his death of cold one day when they were sailing and Louise needed all the rugs there were to keep her warm. He left her a comfortable fortune and a daughter. Louise was inconsolable. It was wonderful that she managed to survive the shock. Her friends expected her speedily to follow poor Tom Maitland to the grave. Indeed they already felt dreadfully sorry for Iris, her daughter, who would be left an orphan. They redoubled their attentions towards Louise. They would not let her stir a finger; they insisted on doing everything in the world to save her trouble. They had to, because if she was called upon to do anything tiresome or inconvenient her heart went back on her and there she was at death's door. She was entirely lost without a man to take care of her, she said, and she did not know how, with her delicate health, she was going to bring up her dear Iris. Her friends asked why she did not marry again. Oh, with her heart it was out of the question, though of course she knew that dear Tom would have wished her to, and perhaps it would be the best thing for Iris if she did; but who would want to be bothered with a wretched invalid like herself? Oddly enough more than one young man showed himself quite ready to undertake the charge and a year after Tom's death she allowed George Hobhouse to lead her to the altar. He was a fine, upstanding fellow, and he was not at all badly off. I never saw any one so grateful as he for the privilege of being allowed to take care of this frail little thing.

'I shan't live to trouble you long,' she said.

He was a soldier and an ambitious one, but he resigned his commission. Louise's health forced her to spend the winter at Monte Carlo and the summer at Deauville. He hesitated a little at throwing up his career, and Louise at first would not hear of it; but at last she yielded as she always yielded, and he prepared to make his wife's last few years as happy as might be.

'It can't be very long now,' she said. 'I'll try not to be troublesome.'

For the next two or three years Louise managed, notwithstanding her weak heart, to go beautifully dressed to all the most lively parties, to gamble very heavily, to dance and even to flirt with tall, slim young men. But George Hobhouse had not the stamina of Louise's first husband and he had to brace himself now and then with a stiff drink for his day's work as Louise's second husband. It is possible that the habit would have grown on him, which Louise would not have liked at all, but very fortunately (for her) the war broke out. He rejoined his regiment and three months later was killed. It was a great shock to Louise. She felt, however, that in such a crisis she must not give way to a private grief; and if she had a heart attack nobody heard of it. In order to distract her mind, she turned her villa at Monte Carlo into a hospital for convalescent officers. Her friends told her that she would never survive the strain.

'Of course it will kill me,' she said, 'I know that. But what does it matter? I must do my bit.'

It didn't kill her. She had the time of her life. There was no convalescent home in France that was more popular. I met her by chance in Paris. She was lunching at the Ritz with a tall and very handsome young Frenchman. She explained that she was there on business connected with the hospital. She told me that the officers were too charming to her. They knew how delicate she was and they wouldn't let her do a single thing. They took care of her, well – as though they were all her husbands. She sighed.

'Poor George, who would ever have thought that I with my heart should survive him?'

'And poor Tom!' I said.

I don't know why she didn't like my saying that. She gave me her plaintive smile and her beautiful eyes filled with tears.

'You always speak as though you grudged me the few years that I can expect to live.'

'By the way, your heart's much better, isn't it?'

'It'll never be better. I saw a specialist this morning and he said I must be prepared for the worst.'

'Oh, well, you've been prepared for that for nearly twenty years now, haven't you?'

When the war came to an end Louise settled in London. She was now a woman of over forty, thin and frail still, with large eyes and pale cheeks, but she did not look a day more than twenty-five. Iris, who had been at school and was now grown up, came to live with her.

'She'll take care of me,' said Louise. 'Of course it'll be hard on her to live with such a great invalid as I am, but it can only be for such a little while, I'm sure she won't mind.'

Iris was a nice girl. She had been brought up with the knowledge that her mother's health was precarious. As a child she had never been allowed to make a noise. She had always realized that her mother must on no account be upset. And though Louise told her now that she would not hear of her sacrificing herself for a tiresome old woman the girl simply would not listen. It wasn't a question of sacrificing herself, it was a happiness to do what she could for her poor dear mother. With a sigh her mother let her do a great deal.

'It pleases the child to think she's making herself useful,' she said.

'Don't you think she ought to go out and about more?' I asked.

'That's what I'm always telling her. I can't get her to enjoy herself. Heaven knows, I never want any one to put themselves out on my account.'

And Iris, when I remonstrated with her, said: 'Poor dear mother, she wants me to go and stay with friends and go to parties, but the moment I start off anywhere she has one of her heart attacks, so I much prefer to stay at home.'

But presently she fell in love. A young friend of mine, a very good lad, asked her to marry him and she consented. I liked the child and was glad that she was to be given at last the chance to lead a life of her own. She had never seemed to suspect that such a thing was possible. But one day the young man came to me in great distress and told me that his marriage was indefinitely postponed. Iris felt that she could not desert her mother. Of course it was really no business of mine, but I made the opportunity to go and see Louise. She was always glad to receive her friends at tea-time and now that she was older she cultivated the society of painters and writers.

'Well, I hear that Iris isn't going to be married,' I said after a little.

'I don't know about that. She's not going to be married quite as soon as I could have wished. I've begged her on my bended knees not to consider me, but she absolutely refuses to leave me.'

'Don't you think it's rather hard on her?'

'Dreadfully. Of course it can only be for a few months, but I hate the thought of any one sacrificing themselves for me.'

'My dear Louise, you've buried two husbands, I can't see the least reason why you shouldn't bury at least two more.'

'Do you think that's funny?' she asked me in a tone that she made as offensive as she could.

'I suppose it's never struck you as strange that you're always strong enough to do anything you want to and that your weak heart only prevents you from doing things that bore you?'

'Oh, I know, I know what you've always thought of me. You've never believed that I had anything the matter with me, have you?'

I looked at her full and square.

'Never. I think you've carried out for twenty-five years a stupendous bluff. I think you're the most selfish and monstrous woman I have ever known. You ruined the lives of those two wretched men you married and now you're going to ruin the life of your daughter.'

I should not have been surprised if Louise had had a heart attack then. I fully expected her to fly into a passion. She merely gave me a gentle smile.

'My poor friend, one of these days you'll be so dreadfully sorry you said this to me.'

'Have you quite determined that Iris shall not marry this boy?'

'I've begged her to marry him. I know it'll kill me, but I don't mind. Nobody cares for me. I'm just a burden to everybody.'

'Did you tell her it would kill you?'

'She made me.'

'As if any one ever made you do anything that you were not yourself quite determined to do.'

'She can marry her young man to-morrow if she likes. If it kills me, it kills me.'

'Well, let's risk it, shall we?'

'Haven't you got any compassion for me?'

'One can't pity any one who amuses one as much as you amuse me,' I answered.

A faint spot of colour appeared on Louise's pale cheeks and though she smiled still her eyes were hard and angry.

'Iris shall marry in a month's time,' she said, 'and if anything happens to me I hope you and she will be able to forgive yourselves.'

Louise was as good as her word. A date was fixed, a trousseau of great magnificence was ordered, and invitations were issued. Iris and the very good lad were radiant. On the wedding-day, at ten o'clock in the morning, Louise, that devilish woman, had one of her heart attacks – and died. She died gently forgiving Iris for having killed her.

Nell Dunn

## Prison Visit (1963)

Snow blew up in white sheets low across the black road and wind blew through the castle gates. We sat in rows on wooden benches, feet cold on the green lino. Rube and I sat close together talking in whispers.

'There'll be a crowd of them standing outside Jock's in the Arcade and a girl'll go by and one of them'll say, "I fancy that!" and another will say, "You won't get nothing out of her. She's no good." But if it's some slag what's bin with everyone he'll say, "Yeah, she's a good girl, you can get the lot out of her."'

An old girl with a henna rinse chatted to her daughter:

'She liked the fur – got it up Brixton Market – it was a good fur, nice colour and all, but it turned out too short after she'd 'ad her operation up the hospital; she's taller than ever.'

'Oh, he was awfully sociable – he talked to everyone, even the women.'

'Here,' said Rube, 'a man in my work asked me out today. Brian would be wild if he found out. This fella asked me to go for a drink and then go back to his house – said his mum would be out. He's a handsome fella, short with wavy black hair – he works in front of me and he stares at me all day.'

'The trouble with Dave is he's too bloody vain. He used to twist me arm and say, "Who's the best-looking boy in the road?" and I'd say Fred Hewar and he'd twist it further till I shrieked and I had to say David Macarthy, then he'd let me go...'

The names were read out briefly and the visitors filed across the prison yard strung out, the young woman carrying her baby, followed by two little girls in fur coats and white bonnets trotting over the icy concrete yard and into the Nissen hut.

'They look good, them stockings – seams are very provocative,' said Rube.

Dave come in, his hair cut short, wearing a blue serge battledress. 'I'm writing a book. It's going to be called *In Out In.*'

We sit on tin chairs around a tin table and two prisoners serve cups of grey tea and little threepenny packets of biscuits.

'So what's going on with you?' Dave smokes aggressively.

'Oh, yeah – we went to help with the spring-cleaning in Michael Wilding's flat. You should have seen the place. The bath was all pink and sunken. Directly I saw it I had to have a bath. Off come me clothes and there I am lounging back like Elizabeth Taylor, ton of perfume rising up with the steam. The bed had a satin coverlet and lemon blankets with satin binding, and a bamboo bar with every sort of drink, the walls covered with thick green paper and green satin curtains ... Ooh, mate.'

At the next table a sleek young man was entertaining his friend. 'Have you got all you want, Alfred?'

'See this skirt?' The fat woman at the next table bunched her brown skirt between her hands. 'A month ago this skirt was too tight for me and look at it now – I can get whole handfuls of it. That's dieting, that is.'

'I had to evict me father-in-law. He was sixty-five and his wife died and he began bringin' in old women and misbehavin' with them in his room. We had a terrible law-case, me standing in one box yelling me head off and him in another yelling back. The names he called me ...'

Two warders walked around the room past the black notices saying what we mustn't do.

'Give us a quid, Rube.'

'Here, you'll get me nicked.'

'You can stick it under the table with yer chewing gum and then fetch another cup of tea, and I'll take it.'

Rube went to get the tea. Dave stretched out his hands on the table. 'They say Borstal's all right – sort of university for them what can't afford Oxford.'

He touched my cheek with his finger. 'Is it too late to get meself a decent education?'

A warder leant against the wall, above his head a notice: VISITORS PASSING ANYTHING TO PRISONERS WILL BE PROSECUTED.

'A bloke in the next cell done himself in – stood on a chair in a pot of piss and plugged himself into the light socket. He got a Dear John – a letter from his bird saying she didn't want to know any more.'

Rube came back with the tea. It spilt over the edge of the white mug and made a little pool on the tin table. Dave dipped his fingertip in and drew a ship. Outside the snow fluttered past, clean in the dirty air, and then fell grey in the concrete yard. A bell went and visitors got up to go. For a moment men clung to their wives. A girl ground painted lips against her boy's teeth and a tongue stretched out for a last feel.

And then it was all quiet. No one said good-bye, but the men lined up through the door and straggled out of the hut, and the visitors straggled towards the giant gate and stopped in a bunch.

'Hey,' said Rube, 'look at them blacks.'

Just inside the gates two Coloured men were arguing excitedly with the warders. 'Have you ever seen anything like the state of their tarts?'

Suddenly the two warders catch hold of one of the women and drag her down the passage – the other is hauled by the arm. Someone unlocks the huge door and first one and then the other is flung out into the road. Their men hurry after them.

The Irish blonde staggers to her feet, her eye cut, both her hands bleeding and her stockings torn, opens her mouth and pours forth abuse. The Coloureds talk fast in unintelligible language. The other woman with frizzed red-rinsed hair and a scar across her forehead shouts. 'Dirty, bleeding cowards – you didn't dare touch our men.' She is about forty and wears a low-cut dress, no stockings and high suede shoes. Her feet bulge over; her legs are mottled.

Muttering threats, the oddly assorted foursome hobble down the road.

'Cor,' says Rube. 'I couldn't fancy that roasted!'

B.S. Johnson

## A Few Selected Sentences (1973)

Someone has to keep the records ...

The Cacao is a fruite little lesse then Almonds, yet more fat, the which being roasted hath no ill taste. The chief use of this Cacao is in a drinke which they call Chocholate, whereof they make great accompt in that Country, foolishly, and without reason; for it is loathsome to such as are not acquainted with it, having a skum or froth that is very unpleasant to taste, if they be not very well conceited thereof. Yet it is a drinke very much esteemed among the Indians, wherewith they feast Noble men as they passe through their Country.

What are hands for, if not to hide the eyes?

Le Soixante-neuf est Interdit dans les Couloirs.

*Eight years' penal servitude.*

As a lorry driven by Croxley left the scene, the sound of a hunting horn was heard. Was it a warning? The police found the body of a stag in the bracken, still warm. Later, police came across Croxley, Ryman and Straker standing by the lorry at the place where the stag had been. Croxley said he was birdwatching, Ryman said his hobby was photography, and Straker, who was carrying a crossbow, said: 'I am interested in all forms of medieval weaponry.' In the lorry police found a quiver full of arrows, a pair of binoculars, two pairs of Sherwood Green tights, and five sheath knives. A broken arrowshaft corresponded to an arrowhead embedded in the dead stag. All three men said they were committee members of Bowmen for Britain, had been out seeking small vermin, and had been on a public footpath. Straker said: 'I saw a squirrel and fired at it but the stag which I did not know was there ran into it.'

A child left to himself bringeth his mother to shame.

I love anecdotes. I fancy mankind may come in time to write all aphoristically, except in narrative; grow weary of preparation and connection and illustration, and all those arts by which a big book is made.

The man had long white hands, which he clasped tightly behind his back when not using them to eat several helpings of jellied eels. Most customers looked thoughtful.

*One year, suspended.*

All afternoon the girl threatened to jump. She said her husband had become converted to a religious sect which forbade her the use of her television. When she had wished to listen to the Queen's Xmas broadcast she had had to go into the bathroom. It was her radio. Because she used makeup her husband likened her to Jezebel, the painted woman of the Scriptures. It was accepted that he was sincere. As soon as they brought a priest to talk to her, she jumped.

Permission to laugh?

Have you heard what Cynon sang?
Beware of drunkards –
Drink unlocks the human heart.

The father appealed for witnesses to his son's death to come forward, not expecting to be overwhelmed by numbers. What had happened as far as they knew was that on Furse Bend he had crossed the inner edge on to the central reserve and in the resulting spill (which was not particularly dangerous in itself) the point of the clutch lever had entered his brain by way of the base of his skull. The father wished to know how designers of safety helmets had not taken this possibility into account. His colleagues said he should have had a ball on it.

But I am trying to be benign.

A rusty charlatan stated dogmatically that a discussion was an argument in which no one was particularly interested. He was reminded that every good deed is followed by the punishment of God. But, he insisted, one must have a proper regard for the ordinary.

The continuous process of recognizing that what is possible is not achievable.

A man taking pictures of a man taking pictures: there must be something in that.

At a wedding reception everyone was drunk, including the children.
Indeed, one of the children became so affected as to seem ill, and it was considered advisable to take him to a hospital to have him seen to, stomach-pumped if neces-

sary. They chose the receptor who seemed least drunk to drive the child, quickly. On the way the car was stopped by a policeman on a horse, who invited the driver to puff breath into a plastic bag. Crystals in the tube attached to this bag turned a certain colour which convinced the policeman that the driver was under the influence of alcohol and he informed him that he would be charged with an offence. 'Oh no,' said the driver, 'Your bags must be faulty. Perhaps indeed you have a batch of faulty bags. Why don't we test them by trying one out on this innocent child?'

A bard's land shall be free. He shall have a horse when he follows the king and a gold ring from the queen and the harp he shall never part with.

Do I want that to be the truth?

The Vice-Chancellor was killed when inspecting the progress of the building of Senate House. A technician was pushing a loaded wheelbarrow across a plank spanning a liftshaft. He saved himself, but the wheelbarrow was lost. The Vice-Chancellor was standing at the bottom of the liftshaft. Accommodate that mess.

Most of the time they look for things to want, schoolfriends.

Miceal and I would play snooker. He would generally win. His was always the same remark when he sank the green or the brown which would put him beyond being caught unless he gave away an unlikely number of penalty points: 'Now you haven't got enough balls. You'll have to put your own up.' I cannot say I laughed more than the first and second times, despite tradition. And 'No points for hard luck' was another saying of his that stuck.

– Who was there?
– The usual mess, of course. Baldies, hairies, collapsed faces, fallen women, who would you think?

*Life.*

—

Someone has to keep the records. I may even be thanked, in time.

A.L. Kennedy

## Awaiting an Adverse Reaction (1997)

It's unmistakable, organic, the flavour of something live.

'Oh that's dreadful.'

She shifts in her chair while the doctor pads across to his fridge.

'Dreadful?'

'The taste. I don't get a sweetie for after?'

'No.' He turns back with a blur of smile. 'No sugar lump to go with it and no sweetie for afterwards.' Quietly teasing between the slim and softly shining shelves. 'Sugar is bad for you and here we don't ever dispense what is bad for you.'

'A small piece of fruit, then?'

'This is a surgery, not a restaurant.' He coughs out a small laugh and decides to risk, 'And that's a Scottish medicine – if it tastes bad, it must be working,' before glancing to check if she takes him in good part.

She grimaces back, not entirety unhappily, and swims the flavour round her tongue, hoping it will weaken. Under the tickle of spreading salt, the cold initial weight of the vaccine, there is something familiar about the taste. She knows that if she concentrates, identification will come.

Her doctor advances, hands benevolently folded round a stack of suitably chilled inoculations: the start of any truly happy holiday.

'I'll need the use of both your arms.' Laying out his packages and snapping the first needle free, 'Diphtheria and tetanus this side ...' he grins curatively, 'typhoid and malaria that.'

Something about his casual enumeration of plagues is strangely enjoyable, a comfort to her. She is being made safe; a part of her bloodstream is welcoming something foreign, so that none of her will go wrong when she takes all her body abroad.

She swallows and briefly considers the matter of Gordon. Gordon will not be made safe, because he will not go with her, because he does not like abroad. He does like her, but not abroad. She does like abroad. The thought of abroad is something she likes very much.

'I won't hurt.' The doctor draws a careful epidemic up inside his syringe.

'I know you won't. I will.'

She rolls up her sleeves, hoping that she can offer him flesh high enough on her arms. She would rather not take off her blouse. In the past, her doctor's acts of examination have been both medical and polite; a nurse discreetly attending, should any extensive explorations be required. Even so, undressing is always more awkward than being undressed – stumbling her clothes off while the doctor slips outside and the nurse presses breaths through the disinfected silence and shifts tinily on white crêpe soles, observing. Nothing to enjoy. But that won't happen today.

He nods, 'Good,' then pushes a pinching kind of pain inside her skin; holds it, dabs around it, withdraws and dabs again. 'Terribly bad?'

'Not bad at all.'

'Mm. I am actually quite good at giving injections. I still practise, you see. Others I could mention do not. How's the polio doing?'

'I can still taste it. In fact, I think it's getting worse. It reminds me of, I don't know what.' He slips in another needle, while she thinks. 'That wasn't fair.'

'Some people would rather not know what's going on.'

'It's my arm, I like to keep tabs on it.'

'I quite understand. Other side now and then we're done. We lust ask you to wait for a few minutes more, in case there's an adverse reaction.'

As soon as he says this, she feels a rush in her circulation, a burst of strangeness, but nothing she would call adverse. Her flesh is being fortified like wine, science defending her against nature more deeply with every prick.

'You're getting tense – this will be painful if you don't relax.'

'Sorry.'

'Not to worry. You've been a very patient patient. And. Last one. There. Will you be going away for long?'

'A month.' A month away from Gordon, during which time she will try to phone him and will certainly write him postcards and may nevertheless experience increasing bouts of what she might well call relief. She has already suffered from immanent release.

'Terrific. A month.'

One whole month of release.

They probably will fire her when she gets back home. She has calculated the likelihood of summary dismissal. She finds that it doesn't scare her – not in the way that disease might, or a month staying here with Gordon and his list of things they shouldn't talk about.

'Yes, I've saved up my holiday time,' pausing, recalling the polio taste and where she met it once before, knowing it, making a smile, 'And I'm taking four days off sick.'

'Really?' He pauses to look quintessentially medical: phial held high, a glimmer at his needle and obviously chill but steady hands. 'What will be wrong, in your professional opinion?' His voice relaxes into a type of wink – his eyes being unable to do the same, for reasons of professional distance and confidence.

'Wrong? Oh, probably flu. Probably not typhoid, or cholera, or –'

'Or tetanus, or diphtheria, or polio. Yes, I think that flu would probably be best. In my professional opinion.'

Or polio. She licked against her teeth and smiled again. On their second anniversary, last spring, when Gordon had asked her to do it and she'd finally agreed, when he'd got his way – this is how he'd tasted. The gagging nudge in her throat, repeating, and then warmed polio vaccine. It's just like him.

'As you're away so long ...' The doctor ponders, above her notes. 'I could write out your next prescription for Trinovum.'

'For?'

'Your contraceptive.'

Her passport for Gordon to travel, pregnancy free.

'Oh yes, thank you.'

'No problems, periods normal?'

'No problems at alt.' She can say this because it will be true soon and might as well be now.

She waits as he checks the pressure of her altering blood, not minding the hard fit of the cuff, and taking – for the sake of politeness – the prescription for an oral contraceptive she intends never to use.

'Thank you.'

'We aim to please.' He opens the door so she can start to go away. 'Do have a nice holiday.'

'I will.'

She is aware that, when she speaks, her breath is vaguely coloured with the taste of something not unlike seminal fluid. She is aware of something not unlike the cloy and tang of spunk. She is aware that her husband has the flavour of a tentatively sweetened disease.

UCHENNA IZUNDU

## It's a Hard-Knock Life (2000)

I've just learned that I'm even more African than my parents are. Up till now, I've always denied it.

Don't laugh, it's not funny.

Self-realization is a very scary thing indeed. I thought I was liberated, living in this multicultural London, and that it was my parents who needed to 'fix up and get with it'. But I've just had Nkem, my cousin, tell me to $!"* and die to my face. I was proper insulted. Koro-koro.

Is it because I've had bad experiences with relationships that I can't be happy for her?

I DON'T think so.

Yeah, I've been through bastards one, two, three and four, and all of them messed with my money and with my head. I'm persecuted in my own society with guys who do the run-around in *real style.* Take my *word* for it.

So, there are nice ones out there. Those of you who have them, good for you.

I'm jealous.

So what? I ain't denying it. When I too am in the land of milk and honey with fine man, then my tone will probably change, but at this moment I'm not, so there.

I'm all for watching interracial love on the TV screen, on the likes of Rikki and Jerry and what not. I was part of the crowd that would be, 'Nuh, man, that's out of order ... Let them be ... Love knows no colour, no boundaries ... You can't help who you fall in love with ... The kids will be enriched, having the best of both worlds ...' Blah blah blah.

'All grammar,' my dad would say. Because when interracial love came knocking on my door, I just went ´Er no' and immediately slammed it shut.

Nkem, my cousin, is like the sister I never had and never wanted. Stunning, super-clever and popular. But I love her to bits, even though I was sick and tired of hearing comparisons being drawn between the pair of us by *mes parents.* If there's one thing African parents never learn while in this land of the living is that doing so, like, lowers one's self-esteem. It's amazing how the Western style of parenting just never penetrates.

This incident then just seems all the weirder, because it was only ten minutes prior to meeting Nkem at the library that I'd been chatting to Trisha, my best friend, abut getting married and having babies and stuff. Anyhow, Nkem was lending me her notes to photocopy and all rushing-rushing me, saying how she had to go meet Paul.

'What's up with this Paul, man?' I was moaning. 'I never see you these days. Ain't you ever hear that men will always come and go but family stays around for ever?'

She laughed. 'Get a life and give me my notes.' Biting her lips and looking at her watch anxiously, she murmured, 'I don't want to be late.'

I looked at her closely. 'It's true, you know. You've never said much about him except that he's a friend of a friend and that he's safe.'

Nkem nodded vaguely, and the bright light of the humming machine distracted her for a second. Suddenly she became focused. 'Have you finished? Good,' she said, before I had a chance to talk, grabbing her sheets out of my hands.

'Is this the real deal?' I asked, panting. She was walking so fast, almost military-style, to go see her 'precious Paul'.

She paused. 'Why do you ask that?'

'Coz of the way you talk about him, and both of you are literally up each other's cracks, man. God knows, I never see you these days.'

'Sometimes you can be so coarse.'

I grinned. 'I try. So spill. I wanna hear all the nasty details.'

I was bitterly disappointed. All Nkem rewarded me with was a goofy, mysterious smile. 'I feel very strongly about him.'

'And? You've told me jack. What does that mean?'

'Precisely that,' she retorted. Glancing at her watch again, she squealed, 'Oh, darn, I'm going to be late!'

And with that she ran off into the sunset to spend quality time with her man.

The hall lights were off when I arrived home, and the whole place appeared to be deserted. It had been a hard day's work at the library. I'd intended to stay late and do some reading for tomorrow's criminology class but, of course, being sociable, talkative, popular and the like, I ended up cracking jokes with my brethren and checking some nice man left, right and centre who I had not seen before. My life is long, it's hard being me, what can I say?

Okonkwo, my younger brother, was in the kitchen making cereal, in other words 'dinner' for himself.

'Where's Mum and Dad?' I shouted, dumping my bag next to the staircase, which I knew annoyed the hell out of him, because I never carried it upstairs, as I couldn't be arsed. He was a neat freak.

'You missed some action,' he mumbled, Frosties in his mouth. 'Mum and Dad just jumped the car round to Ngozi's place. Ngozi's having babies, man.' Ngozi was Nkem's mum, and in any other household she must be addressed as 'Da Ngozi', as this is the respectful thing to do for someone older than you in Igbo culture, but she allowed it with us. I saw Ngozi as my older sister; she was pretty cool, easier to deal with than my own mum.

'Why, what happened?' I asked, switching on the kettle to make gari. Mum had left my share of the okro soup in the microwave. Okonkwo started sniggering. 'Nkem brought Paul home.'

'Yeah and?' Sometimes he could be sooo tiresome in relaying information.

'And he's white.'

I screamed.

It took me twenty minutes to make food which normally took two minutes, as I was in what they call 'deep shock'. Okonkwo thought the whole issue was pure joke. 'I dunno why you're so surprised,' he said, washing up his bowl immediately after eating. 'Nkem has problems, boy. I've always said she's white, and now she's with her own.'

'Shut up,' I snapped.

'It's true though,' he insisted. 'She listens to her whale music' – this is what he called Nkem's love for panpipe tunes – 'she can't dress, speaks like a dictionary, dances like a mark ...' He shrugged. 'She needs to fix up, bwoy, fix up big-time. I've always said it, wigger in reverse.'

'What happened?' I asked desperately, trying to ignore his cussing, because I actually agreed with him, hut I was also extremely protective of Nkem when Okonkwo went into one.

'Nkem said to Ngozi that she may possibly bring Paul, and Ngozi was all for it, really up to meeting him. Then Paul, blond hair, blue eyes, steps through the front door all holding Nkem's band, and Ngozi and Uncle David' – this was Ngozi's husband, who insisted on being addressed formally – 'almost died there and then.' Okonkwo at this point bust up laughing. 'Then, once he's gone, Nkem chats fart about how she's in love and she wants to marry him coz they've been talking about it. Ngozi just got straight on the phone to Mum and Dad. They both splurted over there to see if the gal has gone mad.'

He began stacking the dishes. 'I've got to give it to her though. She's dread bringing home White man, saying she's gonna marry him.'

'She's serious?'

Okonkwo looked at me. 'When have you ever known Nkem to joke?'

'But this is like her first man! No wonder she never told me nothing! I tried milking her today for some info, and she was all there saying how she feels very strongly about him.' I swallowed some soup, feeling hurt that she hadn't confided in me. 'I don't even know what to say.'

At that moment the front door was unlocked and our parents came in, talking hurriedly in Igbo. I called greetings to them. Both were tall, stately people, well respected in the community. My friends were amazed at the beauty of my mum. She made a great effort to look good all the time.

'So what did Nkem say?' Okonkwo barked the minute mum came into the kitchen.

She sighed. 'Only God knows where we've gone wrong.' My father took out a couple of glasses and poured them both some drink.

'How's Ngozi?' I asked.

'Distraught. What else do you expect?' Dad answered.

'Is it that bad?'

'Nkem is wholly serious. She claims that she's in love and she'll marry Paul regardless of what any of us say.'

'I don't really get what the big deal is,' I said. *Ma bouche* had this bad habit of saying one thing while my heart is really thinking another.

'What's that supposed to mean? You were the one who screamed when I told you now,' Okonkwo snarled.

I gave him a cool, condescending look. 'That's because I was so shocked to hear first that she's talking about getting married and second because Paul is white.'

'You lie.'

'Whatever.'

'Can both of you shut up with your nonsense?' Mum snapped. She began pacing the kitchen anxiously. 'I don't understand. I just don't understand. We've really tried to practise our culture here for you so that you understand who you are and where you come from. When did white people ever become part of the picture?' She suddenly looked at me. 'I hope you have no intention of pulling this same kind of stupidity that Nkem is talking about and expecting all of us to tolerate it.'

'Oh, so for once Nkem's actually in the wrong. Wow, that sure makes a change!'

Dad kissed his teeth. Mum lectured. 'That's all you learn, disrespecting your elders and opening your mouth to talk anyhow. Try going back to Nigeria, let's see how far that attitude will take you. *I di iberibe';* in other words, 'You stupid one': Igbo style, straight off the boat.

'Well, we're not in Nigeria now, Mum, are we? We're in London, different attitudes, different lifestyles. Nkem wants to shack up with some white man. She loves him, good for her. It's you lot that's making life difficult, not her!'

Okonkwo laughed as he made his exit. 'You're in for it now, boy.'

'Are any of our relations married to white people?' Dad asked. He always tried to take the rationalistic approach whereas mum and I went for blows.

'No.'

'Precisely. We believe in marrying amongst our own, and Ibos who don't, we look down on them. They haven't done themselves or their families justice. White people and us, we don't share the same culture, it's not workable, practical or viable. Just tell me how on earth Paul is going to feel comfortable or understand what is going on when we do things the traditional way.'

Sipping some of her juice, Mum said, 'The best bit of this entire farce is that Nkem believes that since Paul grew up in Nigeria while he was young, that suddenly makes things seem so much better.'

'Don't it? At least he has some idea where we're coming from.'

Dad sighed. 'When are you going to understand that we're not the same? They don't speak or think like us. Nkem is disgracing her parents – and the children, chi! They're going to be the most confused of all.'

'I don't believe that.' Dad also has this tendency to make sweeping generalizations, which really gets on my nerves. 'The way you're talking no one would guess that you've been living here for the past twenty years and that you see this kind of thing all the time.'

'And we see them break up all the time,' Mum murmured. 'There's statistics to prove it.' She put down her glass. 'Udo, I'm going to bed.'

I decided to try talking some sense to Nkem the moment Dad upped and went to bed too. I could *not* see the attraction. Yeah, so one can admire Brad Pitt and them from afar, but for me to get it on with one of them? Uh-uh, no sirree. I like my chocolate and I like it dark. I shuddered. Damn, how far had Nkem gone? She had never seemed too attracted to our own hut I'd always thought that had been due to her never finding the right one. Okonkwo attributed it to the fact that their family had grown up in Edinburgh and the air up north had messed up Nkem's head severely.

'Ngozi?'

'Oh, hello!' She was breathless. 'I'm so happy that you called.' The explosion erupted. 'I hope that you're going to talk to your sister and get her to think aright.' My blood pressure is up. Nkem wants to destroy me! 'You speak to a child, they don't want to listen. Only God knows where she got this nonsense from.'

'I'll try.'

Nkem came to the phone several minutes later. Her greeting was tentative.

'Are you OK?' I asked.

'I've been better. Dad is refusing to talk to me, and every time I open my mouth Mum goes into a rant that never seems to stop.' She started sniffling. 'I never realized that it would be this hard. I thought ... I thought ... I just thought ...'

'Hey, it's OK. They're hardcore Africans. What else do you expect?"

She giggled. 'Koro-koro. You always cheer me up. Thank goodness you support me.'

Silence.

'You do support me, don't you?'

Longer silence. 'Talk now, you're making me nervous.'

'Nkem, have you thought this through properly?'

'What kind of stupid question is that? Do I go around saying that I'm going to marry everyone these days?'

'No, but I don't think you know what you're doing. C'mon Nkem, White boy, Black girl. White boy, Black girl. T'ink about it and t'ink hard.'

'Your point being?'

'Didn't you hear me? He's White, you're Black. You're not the same. It's weird.'

'Do you say that when you see Black men and White girls together?'

That one I had to think about. I responded in the negative.

The next thing I heard was a tirade of abuse.

'You should he ashamed of yourself' was her ending note. 'You've grown up with White people, you adopt those parts of the culture that suit you and to hell with anything else. You know what's the worst? At least our parents say they're African and stick to it. You deny it when in suits you and fluctuate whenever you like because you have no clue whatsoever of who you are! It's the insecurity that makes you try to be even *more* African than them. It doesn't come over at all. You're a hypocrite, because then you try to dispute it!'

The line went dead.

Koro-koro.

## Sources

In the text, stories are, where possible, quoted from author collections or the periodical in which they first appeared. In addition to these sources, the following listing notes selected anthologies in which a story can also be found. For bibliographical details of these anthologies, see the bibliography (pp. 275–293).

Addison, Joseph. "Alnaschar" [*The Spectator*, no. 535]. In: *The Spectator in Four Volumes*, ed. Gregory Smith. London: Dent, 1958, vol. 4, 185–188.

—. "A Story of an Heir" [*The Spectator*, no. 123]. In: *The Spectator in Four Volumes*, vol. 1, 373–377. Also in: Wilson (1921), 64–67.

—. "The Vision of Mirzah" [*The Spectator*, no. 159]. In: *The Spectator in Four Volumes*, vol. 1, 478–482. Also in: Melville and Hargreaves (1931), 35–39.

Aikin, Anna Laetitia [later Barbauld]. "Sir Bertrand: A Fragment." In: Baldick (1992), 3–6. Also in: Haining (1973), 44–48; Jump (1998), 37–40.

Amis, Kingsley. "Court of Inquiry." In: Kingsley Amis, *Collected Short Stories*. London: Hutchinson, 1980, 35–42. Also in: Oeser (1992), 68–83.

Amis, Martin. "The Immortals." In: Martin Amis, *Einstein's Monsters*. London: Cape, 1987, 117–127.

Aumonier, Stacy. "The Match." In: *Ups and Downs: A Collection of Stories by Stacy Aumonier*. London: Heinemann, 1929, 239–251. Also in: Lewin (1949), 190–200.

Ballard, J.G. "Dream Cargo." In: J.G. Ballard, *The Complete Short Stories*. London: Flamingo, 2001, 1161–1172. Also in: Byatt (1998), 381–395.

—. "Memories of the Space Age." In: *The Complete Short Stories*, 1037–1060. Also in: Bradbury (1988), 234–261.

Barker, Clive. "Pidgin and Theresa." In: Lexton (1993), 1–12.

Barnes, Julian. "The Stowaway." In: Julian Barnes, *A History of the World in 10 1/2 Chapters*. London: Picador 1990 [1989], 1–30.

—. "Tunnel." In: Julian Barnes, *Cross Channel*. London: Cape, 1996, 191–211.

Barth, John. *Lost in the Funhouse: Fiction for Print, Tape, Live Voice*. New York: Grosset and Dunlap, 1969.

Bates, H.E. "For the Dead." In: *The Woman Who Had Imagination and Other Stories by H.E. Bates*. Bath: Lythway Press 1974 [1934], 147–152.

—. "The Waterfall." In: *The Woman Who Had Imagination*, 169–202. Also in: Byatt (1998), 325–344.

Behn, Aphra. "The Unfortunate Happy Lady: A True History." In: *The Works of Aphra Behn*, ed. Janet Todd. London: Pickering, 1995, vol. 3, 361–387. Also in: *An Anthology of Seventeenth-Century Fiction*, ed. Paul Salzmann. Oxford: Oxford University Press, 1991, 529–553.

Bennett, Arnold. "Mimi." In: Arnold Bennett, *The Matador of the Five Towns and Other Stories*. Leipzig: Tauchnitz, 1912, 52–73.

Bowen, Elizabeth. "Mysterious Kôr." In: *The Collected Stories of Elizabeth Bowen*. London: Cape, 1980, 728–740. Also in: Bradbury (1988), 32–45.

Bradbury, Malcolm. "Composition." In: Malcolm Bradbury, *Who Do You Think You Are? Stories and Parodies*. London: Secker and Warburg, 1976, 107–133. Also in: Bradbury (1988), 286–308.

Braddon, Mary Elizabeth. "The Shadow in the Corner." In: Cox and Gilbert (1986), 51–68.

Brown, John. "Rab and His Friends." Edinburgh: John Douglas, 1885 [individual edition]. Also in: Walker (1914), 217–231; Melville and Hargreaves (1931), 449–459.

Bulwer-Lytton, Edward George. "The Haunted and the Haunters: Or, The House and the Brain." In: Melville and Hargreaves (1931), 287–309. Also in: Search (1959), 107–138.

Byatt, A.S. "A Lamia in the Cevennes." In: *New Writing 5*, ed. Christopher Hope and Peter Porter. London: Vintage and The British Council, 1996, 1–17. Also in: Puschmann-Nalenz (2000), 163–194.

—. *The Matisse Stories*. London: Chatto and Windus, 1993.

Carter, Angela. "The Bloody Chamber." In: Angela Carter, *Burning Your Boots: Collected Short Stories*. London: Vintage, 1996 [1995], 111–143.

—. "The Company of Wolves." In: *Burning Your Boots*, 212–220. Also in: Puschmann-Nalenz (2000), 35–56.

Clarke, Arthur C. "Nightfall." In: Arthur C. Clarke, *The Collected Stories*. London: Gollancz, 2000, 89–91. Also in: Jones (1987), 26–28 [under the title "The Curse"].

Collins, Wilkie. "A Stolen Letter." In: Wilkie Collins, *Tales of Terror and the Supernatural*. New York: Dover, 1972, 171–186.

—. "A Terribly Strange Bed." In: *Tales of Terror and the Supernatural*, 24–39. Also in: Melville and Hargreaves (1931), 592–605.

Conan Doyle, Sir Arthur. *The Complete Sherlock Holmes*. London: Secker and Warburg, 1981.

—. "The Ring of Thoth." In: *The Conan Doyle Stories*. London: John Murray, 1929, 782–802.

Conrad, Joseph. "An Outpost of Progress." In: Joseph Conrad, *Tales of Unrest*. (The Medallion Edition of the Works of Joseph Conrad, vol. 1.) London: Gresham, 1925, 86–117. Also in: Dolley (1967), 56–81.

Coppard, A.E. "The Higgler." In: *The Collected Tales of A.E. Coppard*. New York: Knopf, 1951, 3–30.

—. "The Watercress Girl." In: *The Collected Tales*, 504–517.

Crackanthorpe, Hubert. "Embers." In: *Collected Stories (1893–1897) of Hubert Crackanthorpe*. Gainesville, FL: Scholar's Facsimiles and Reprints, 1969, 215–232.

Cross, Victoria [Vivian Cory]. "Theodora: A Fragment." In: *Yellow Book*, 4 (January 1895), 156–188. Also in: Showalter (1993), 6–37.

D'Arcy, Ella. "Irremediable." In: *Yellow Book*, 1 (April 1894), 87–108. Also in: Orel (1990), 99–115.

—. "A Marriage." In: *Yellow Book,* 11 (October 1896), 309–342.
de Bernières, Louis. "Rabbit." In: *New Writing 10,* ed. Penelope Lively and George Szirtes. London: Picador and The British Council, 2001, 223–229.
Defoe, Daniel. "In Defence of His Right." In: Daniel Defoe, *An Essay on the History and Reality of Apparitions.* London: J. Roberts, 1727, 152–166. Also in: Wilson (1921), 54–63.
—. "The True Relation of the Apparition of one Mrs Veal." In: *Selected Writings of Daniel Defoe,* ed. James T. Boulton. Cambridge: Cambridge University Press, 1975 [1965], 134–141. Also in: Melville and Hargreaves (1931), 26–33; Search (1959), 21–24.
De la Mare, Walter. "The Creatures." In: *The Collected Tales of Walter de la Mare.* New York: Knopf, 1950, 423–434. Also in: Wilson (1921), 311–320.
—. "Seaton's Aunt." In: *The Collected Tales,* 112–142. Also in: Davin (1990), 181–209.
Dickens, Charles. "The Signal-Man." In: Charles Dickens, *Christmas Stories and Other Stories.* (Works, vol. 13.) London: Chapman and Hall, 1911, 312–322. Also in: Dolley (1967), 11–24.
Dowson, Ernest. "The Dying of Frances Donne: A Study." In: Gerber (1967), 82–91.
Dunn, Nell. "Prison Visit." In: Nell Dunn, *Up the Junction.* Philadelphia: Lippincott, 1966 [1963], 99–103.
Edgeworth, Maria. *Moral Tales: In Two Volumes.* (Tales and Novels by Maria Edgeworth in Eighteen Volumes, vols. 2 and 3.) London: Baldwin and Cradock, 1832.
—. *Popular Tales in Two Volumes.* (Tales and Novels by Maria Edgeworth in Eighteen Volumes, vols. 4 and 5.) London: Baldwin and Cradock, 1832.
Edwards, Amelia. "The Phantom Coach." In: Cox and Gilbert (1986), 13–24.
Egerton, George [Mary Chavelita Dunne Bright]. "A Lost Masterpiece: A City Mood, Aug. '93." In: *Yellow Book,* 1 (April 1894). Also in: Gerber (1967), 131–138.
Forster, E.M. "The Celestial Omnibus." In: *Collected Short Stories of E.M. Forster.* London: Sidgwick and Jackson, 1947, 38–58. Also in: Dolley (1972), 113–125.
—. "The Road from Colonus." In: *Collected Short Stories,* 100–114. Also in: Dolley (1972), 113–125.
—. "The Story of a Siren." In: *Collected Short Stories,* 196–206. Also in: Oeser (1984), 35–47.
Fowles, John. "The Enigma." In: John Fowles, *The Ebony Tower.* London: Granada, 1975 [1974], 189–244. Also in: Bradbury (1988), 189–233.
Galsworthy, John. *Caravan: The Assembled Tales of John Galsworthy.* London: Heinemann, 1925.
—. "Told by the Schoolmaster." In: Oeser (1985), 102–119.
Gaskell, Elizabeth. "Curious, if True." In: Elizabeth Gaskell, *Gothic Tales,* ed. Laura Kranzler. Harmondsworth: Penguin, 2000, 271–286. Also in: Melville and Hargreaves (1931), 460–473.
—. "The Manchester Marriage." In: Jump (1998), 93–113. Also in: Orel (1990), 158–184.

—. "The Old Nurse's Story." In: *Gothic Tales,* 11–32.

*Gesta Romanorum: A Record of Auncient Histories Newly Perused by Richard Robinson (1595).* A Facsimile Reproduction with an Introduction by John Weld. Delmar, NY: Scholars' Facsimiles and Reprints, 1973.

Gissing, George. "The House of Cobwebs." In: George Gissing, *The House of Cobwebs and Other Stories.* London: Constable, 1906, 1–27. Also in: Gerber (1967), 219–237.

Goldsmith, Oliver. "Character of the Man in Black" [*The Citizen of the World,* Letter XXVI]. In: *The Citizen of the World.* (Collected Works of Oliver Goldsmith, vol. 2.) Oxford: Clarendon Press, 1966, 108–112.

—. "On the Distresses of the Poor, Exemplified in the Life of a Private Centinel" [*The Citizen of the World,* Letter CXIX]. In: *The Citizen of the World,* 458–465. Also in: Wilson (1921), 96–100 [under the title "The Disabled Soldier"].

—. "The Proceedings of Providence Vindicated: An Eastern Tale." In: *Essays.* (Collected Works of Oliver Goldsmith, vol. 3.) Oxford: Clarendon Press, 1966, 58–55. Also in: Melville and Hargreaves (1931), 61–66 [under the title "Asem: An Eastern Tale"].

Gordon, Giles. "Pictures from an Exhibition." In: *Pictures from an Exhibition.* London: Allison and Busby, 1970, 9–21.

Grahame, Kenneth. "The Reluctant Dragon." In: Kenneth Grahame, *Dream Days.* London: Bodley Head, 1973, 109–150.

Greene, Graham. "Across the Bridge." In: Graham Greene, *Collected Stories.* (The Collected Edition, vol. 8.) London: Heinemann, 1972, 420–432. Also in: Dolley (1967), 302–312; Oeser (1987), 149–165.

—. "The Basement Room." In: *Collected Stories,* 457–489. Also in: Hudson (1972), 133–166.

—. "The Destructors." In: *Collected Stories,* 327–346. Also in: Dolley (1972) and Byatt (1998), 311–324.

Greene, Robert. "How a Cunning Knave Got a Trunk ..." from *The Third Part of Cony-Catching.* In: *The Elizabethan Underworld,* ed. A.V. Judges. London: Routledge and Kegan Paul, 1930, 199–201.

Grossmith, Robert. "Company." In: *The Minverva Book of Short Stories 3,* ed. Giles Gordon and David Hughes. London: Minerva, 1991, 70–80.

—. "S/he." In: Lexton (1993), 103–115.

Hammick, Georgina. "High Teas." In: Georgina Hammick, *Spoilt.* London: Chatto and Windus, 1992, 159–169. Also in: *The Minverva Book of Short Stories 1,* ed. Giles Gordon and David Hughes. London: Minerva, 1990, 89–97; Speirs (1996), 122–130.

Hardy, Thomas. "For Conscience' Sake." In: Thomas Hardy, *Life's Little Ironies: A Set of Tales.* (Thomas Hardy's Works, vol. 14.) London: Macmillan, 1923, 25–50. Also in: Oeser (1985), 13–43.

—. "The Three Strangers." In: Thomas Hardy, *Wessex Tales.* (Thomas Hardy's Works, vol. 13.) London: Macmillan, 1923, 35–61. Also in: Wilson (1921), 339–359; Jones (1973), 1–30.

Haywood, Eliza. *Selected Fiction and Drama of Elizabeth Haywood,* ed. Paula R. Backscheider. Oxford: Oxford University Press, 1999.

Hawkesworth, John. "The History of Melissa." In: *The Adventurer in Two Volumes.* A new edition, revised and corrected. Dublin: John Millekin, 1771, vol. 1, 30–44. Also in: Wilson (1921), 84–95.

Hoban, Russell. "The Man with the Dagger." In: *The Minverva Book of Short Stories 3*, ed. Giles Gordon and David Hughes. London: Minerva, 1991, 81–93.

Hornby, Nick. "Faith." In: Lexton (1993), 126–133.

—. "NippleJesus." In: Hornby (2000), 91–114.

*A Hundred Merry Tales and Other English Jestbooks of the Fifteenth and Sixteenth Centuries*, ed. P.M. Zall. Lincoln: University of Nebraska Press, 1977.

Hunt, Leigh. "A Tale for a Chimney Corner." In: Leigh Hunt, *Selected Essays*. London: Dent, 1929, 281–288. Also in: Haining (1973), 350–359.

Huxley, Aldous. "Fard." In: Aldous Huxley, *Little Mexican: Six Stories*. London: Chatto and Windus, 1948, 236–246. Also in: Oeser (1984), 87–96.

—. "The Gioconda Smile." In: Aldous Huxley, *Moral Coils*. London: Chatto and Windus, 1949, 1–62. Also in: Dolley (1967), 251–282.

Izundu, Uchenna. "It's a Hard-Knock Life." In: Newland and Sesay (2000), 369–375.

Jacobs, W.W. "The Monkey's Paw." In: Cox and Gilbert (1986), 180–189.

Johnson, B.S. "A Few Selected Sentences." In: Bradbury (1988), 282–285.

— and Zulfikar Ghose. *Statement against Corpses: Short Stories by B.S. Johnson and Zulfikar Ghose*. London: Constable, 1964.

Johnson, Samuel. "The History of Melissa." In: *The Rambler*, ed. W.J. Bate and Albrecht B. Strauss. (The Yale Edition of the Works of Samuel Johnson.) New Haven: Yale University Press, vol. 4, 28–33.

Josipovici, Gabriel. "Mobius the Stripper: A Topological Exercise." In: Gabriel Josipovici, *Mobius the Stripper: Stories and Short Plays*. London: Gollancz, 1974, 64–85. Also in: Gabriel Josipovici, *Steps: Selected Fiction and Drama*. Manchester: Carcanet, 1990, 133–152.

Juvenis. "Raymond." In: Baldick (1992), 23–26.

Kennedy, A.L. "Awaiting an Adverse Reaction." In: *New Writing 6*, ed. A.S. Byatt and Peter Porter. London: Vintage and The British Council, 1997, 43–46. Reprint with kind permission of Antony Harwood Ltd.

Kerr, Philip. "Four Reviews in Search of a Biography." In: *New Writing 7*, ed. Carmen Callil and Craig Raine. London: Vintage and The British Council, 1998, 299–313.

Kipling, Rudyard. "The Man Who Would Be King." In: Rudyard Kipling, *The Writings in Prose and Verse of Rudyard Kipling. Vol. V: The Phantom Rickshaw and Other Stories*. New York: Scribner, 1911, 39–97.

—. "Mary Postgate." In: Rudyard Kipling, *War Stories and Poems*, ed. Andrew Rutherford. Oxford: Oxford University Press, 1987, 235–249.

—. "A Matter of Fact." In: *Writings in Prose and Verse of Rudyard Kipling. Vol. V*, 192–213.

—. "Mrs. Bathurst." In: *Writings in Prose and Verse of Rudyard Kipling. Vol. XXII: Traffics and Discoveries*. New York: Scribner, 1911, 379–408.

—. "The Phantom Rickshaw." In: *Writings in Prose and Verse of Rudyard Kipling. Vol. V*, 1–38.

—. *The Writings in Prose and Verse of Rudyard Kipling. Vol. I: Plain Tales from the Hills*, New York: Scribner, 1911.
—. "Wireless." In: *Writings in Prose and Verse of Rudyard Kipling. Vol. XXII.* New York: Scribner, 1911, 239–269. Also in: Byatt (1998), 110–126.
Kureishi, Hanif. "My Son the Fanatic." In: Hanif Kureishi, *Love in a Blue Time*. London: Faber, 1997, 119–131. Also in: Korte and Sternberg (1997), 147–165.
Lamb, Charles [and Mary Lamb]. *Mrs Leicester's School and Other Writings in Prose and Verse*. London: Macmillan, 1885.
Lawrence, D.H. "England, My England." In: *The Complete Short Stories of D.H. Lawrence in Three Volumes*. London: Heinemann, 1955, vol. 2, 303–333.
—. "The Horse-Dealer's Daughter." In: *The Complete Short Stories*, vol. 2, 441–457. Also in: Dolley (1972), 150–167.
—. "The Man Who Loved Islands." In: *The Complete Short Stories*, vol. 3, 722–746.
—. "Odour of Chrysanthemums." In: *The Complete Short Stories*, vol. 2, 283–302.
—. "The Rocking-Horse Winner." In: *The Complete Short Stories*, vol. 3, 790–804.
—. "Tickets Please." In: *The Complete Short Stories*, vol. 2, 334–346. Also in: Oeser (1984), 63–86.
Lee, Harriet and Sophia. *The Canterbury Tales*, ed. Harriet Gilbert. London: Pandora, 1989.
Lee, Tanith. *Women as Demons: The Male Perception of Women through Space and Time*. London: The Women's Press, 1989.
LeFanu, Joseph Sheridan. "Green Tea." In: *Best Ghost Stories of J.S. LeFanu*, ed. E.F. Bleiler. New York: Dover, 1964, 178–207.
Lehmann, Rosamond. "A Dream of Winter." In: Rosamond Lehmann, *The Gipsy's Baby and Other Stories*. London: Collins, 1946, 99–112. Also in: Hudson (1972), 349–362; Lewin (1949), 46–55; Byatt (1998), 286–294.
Lewis, Matthew Gregory. "My Uncle's Garret Window." In: Matthew Gregory Lewis, *Romantic Tales*. London: Longman, 1808, vol. 4, 1–91. Also in: Melville and Hargreaves (1931), 87–117; Search (1959), 40–67.
Linklater, Eric. "Sealskin Trousers." In: Hudson (1972), 84–104. Also in: Hendry (1970), 155–171.
Lodge, David. "Hotel des Boobs." In: David Lodge, *The Man Who Wouldn't Get Up and Other Stories*. London: Bridgewater, 1998, 67–78. Also in: Bradbury (1988), 326–333.
Machen, Arthur. "The Bowmen." In: *The Collected Arthur Machen*, ed. Christopher Palmer. London: Duckworth, 1988, 295–302.
Mackenzie, Henry. "Story of Louisa Venoni." In: *The Works of Henry Mackenzie*. London: Routledge and Thoemmes, 1996, vol. 5, 55–77.
Maitland, Sara. "The Wicked Stepmother's Tale." In: Fairbairns (1987), 157–163. Also in: Puschmann-Nalenz (2000), 81–92.
Mansfield, Katherine. "At the Bay." In: *The Stories of Katherine Mansfield*, ed. Antony Alpers. Auckland: Oxford University Press, 1984, 441–469.
—. "Bliss." In: *The Stories of Katherine Mansfield*, 305–315.
—. "The Daughters of the Late Colonel." In: *The Stories of Katherine Mansfield*, 386–402.

—. "The Garden Party." In: *The Stories of Katherine Mansfield*, 487–499.
—. "Miss Brill." In: *The Stories of Katherine Mansfield*, 373–377.
—. "Prelude." In: *The Stories of Katherine Mansfield*, 223–259.
—. "The Voyage." In: *The Stories of Katherine Mansfield*, 470–476. Also in: Dolley (1967), 224–232.
Mantel, Hilary. "Ties That Bind." In: *New Writing 5*, ed. Christopher Hope and Peter Porter. London: Vintage and The British Council, 1996, 487–493.
Mars-Jones, Adam. "Baby Clutch." In: *The Minverva Book of Short Stories 3*, ed. Giles Gordon and David Hughes. London: Minerva, 1991, 198–223.
—. "Hoosh-mi: A Farrago of Scurrilous Untruths." In: Adam Mars-Jones, *Lantern Lecture*. London: Faber, 1981, 29–100.
—. "Remission." In: *The Minverva Book of Short Stories 1*, ed. Giles Gordon and David Hughes. London: Minerva, 1990, 119–142.
—. "Structural Anthropology." In: Bradbury (1988), 443–448.
Maugham, W. Somerset. "The Facts of Life." In: *The Complete Short Stories of W. Somerset Maugham*. London: Heinemann, 1963, vol. 1, 198–215.
—. "The Force of Circumstance." In: *The Complete Short Stories*, vol. 1, 481–505. Also in: Dolley (1967), 129–156.
—. "Louise." In: *The Complete Short Stories*, vol. 1, 438–443.
—. "Rain." In: *The Complete Short Stories*, vol. 1, 1–38.
McEwan, Ian. "First Love, Last Rites." In: Ian McEwan, *First Love, Last Rites*. London: Cape, 1975, 115–129. Also in: Oeser (1992), 117–137.
—. "Solid Geometry." In: *First Love, Last Rites*, 31–52. Also in: Byatt (1998), 420–434.
Meredith, George. "The Punishment of Shahpesh, the Persian, on Khipil, the Builder." In: Walker (1914), 283–288.
Mew, Charlotte. "A White Night." In: Byatt (1998), 139–154. Also in: Showalter (1993), 118–138.
Mitford, Mary Russell. "The Fresh Water Fisherman." In: Wilson (1921), 137–152.
—. "The Village Schoolmistress." In: Melville and Hargreaves (1931), 143–151.
More, Hannah. *Tales for the Common People*. (The Works of Hannah More in Eight Volumes, vol. 5.) London: T. Cadell and W. Davies, 1801.
Morris, William. "The Story of the Unknown Church." In: Walker (1914), 301–310.
Morrison, Arthur. *Martin Hewitt, Investigator*. London: Remploy, 1978.
—. *Tales of Mean Streets*. Woodbridge: Bookmaster [by Boydell], 1983. ["Behind the Shade" also in: Byatt (1998), 105–109; "A Street" and "Lizerunt" also in: Gerber (1967), 182–201; Keating (1971), 1–7 and 29–41.]
Mudford, William. "The Iron Shroud." In: Haining (1973), 507–522.
Oliphant, Margaret. *The Doctor's Family and Other Stories*. Oxford: Oxford University Press, 1986.
—. *Selected Stories of the Supernatural*, ed. Margaret K. Gray. Edinburgh: Scottish Academic Press, 1985.
Orczy, Baroness Emma. "The Mysterious Death on the Underground Railway." In: Baroness Orczy, *The Old Man in the Corner: Twelve Mysteries*. New York: Dover, 1980, 15–28.

Painter, William. "The Duchess of Malfy." In: *An Elizabethan Story-Book: Famous Tales from the 'Palace of Pleasure'*, ed. Peter Haworth. London: Longman's, Green, 1928, 98–153.

Pater, Walter. "The Child in the House." In: *Selected Writings of Walter Pater*, ed. Harold Bloom. New York: Columbia University Press, 1982 [1974], 1–16. Also in: Gerber (1967), 21–34.

Polidori, John. "The Vampyre." In: Haining (1973), 286–307.

Powys, T.F. "Mr Pim and the Holy Crumb." In: T.F. Powys, *Fables*. London: Chatto and Windus, 1929, 17–25.

Pritchett, V.S. "Handsome Is as Handsome Does." In: V.S. Pritchett, *The Complete Short Stories*. London: Chatto and Windus, 1990, 38–73. Also in: Dolley (1972), 215–253.

—. "The Voice." In: *The Complete Short Stories*, 243–248. Also in: Hudson (1972), 105–112; Oeser (1984), 117–127.

Rhys, Jean. "Hunger." In: Jean Rhys, *The Collected Short Stories*. New York: Norton, 1992, 42–44.

—. "Illusion." In: *The Collected Short Stories*, 1–5.

—. "Let Them Call It Jazz." In: *The Collected Short Stories*, 158–175. Also in: Korte and Sternberg (1997), 65–92.

—. "A Night." In: *The Collected Short Stories*, 47–49.

Rossetti, Dante Gabriel. "Hand and Soul." In: *The Collected Works of Dante Gabriel Rossetti in Two Volumes*, ed. William M. Rossetti. London: Ellis, 1906, vol. 1, 383–398. Also in: Wilson (1921), 195–207.

Rushdie, Salman. "The Prophet's Hair." In: Salman Rushdie, *East, West*. London: Cape, 1994, 33–58. Also in: Bradbury (1988), 389–399.

—. "Yorick." In: *East, West*, 61–83.

Saki. "Esmé." In: *The Short Stories of Saki (H.H. Munro)*. London: John Lane and Bodley Head, 1930, 119–124.

—. "Reginald." In: *The Short Stories of Saki*, 15–18.

—. "Sredni Vashtar." In: *The Short Stories of Saki*, 159–163. Also in: Oeser (1985), 120–129; McDougall (1989), 141–146.

—. "Tobermory." In: *The Short Stories of Saki*, 127–134.

Sansom, William. "The Vertical Ladder." In: *The Stories of William Sansom*. Second ed. London: Hogarth Press, 1969, 34–45. Also in: Hudson (1972), 250–265.

—. "The Wall." In: *The Stories of William Sansom*, 13–16.

Scott, Sir Walter. "The Tapestried Chamber." In: Walter Scott, *The Talisman: A Tale of the Crusades and The Chronicles of the Canongate*. (The Waverley Novels, 20.) London: Adam and Charles Black, 1897, 387–401. Also in: Melville and Hargreaves (1931), 70–82; Wilson (1921), 101–113.

—. "The Two Drovers." In: *The Talisman: A Tale of the Crusades and The Chronicles of the Canongate*, 324–349. Also in: Walker (1914), 1–29; Bergner (1969), 53–78; Dunn (1995), 31–50.

Selvon, Sam. "Obeah in the Grove." In: Sam Selvon, *Ways of Sunlight*. Harlow: Longman, 1979 [1958], 167–174. Also in: Korte and Sternberg (1997), 52–64.

Shelley, Mary. "Transformation." In: *Mary Shelley: Collected Tales and Stories*, ed.

Charles E. Robinson. Baltimore: Johns Hopkins University Press, 1976, 121–135.
Sillitoe, Alan. "Enoch's Two Letters." In: Alan Sillitoe, *Men, Women and Children.* London: W.H. Allen, 1974, 93–105. Also in: Byatt (1998), 372–380.
—. *The Loneliness of the Long-Distance Runner*. Third ed. London: W.H. Allen, 1963.
Simpson, Helen. "The Tree." In: *New Writing 10*, ed. Penelope Lively and George Szirtes. London: Picador and The British Council, 2001, 159–165.
Sinclair, Clive. "Genesis." In: Clive Sinclair, *Bedbugs*. Harmondsworth: Penguin, 1983 [1982], 22–35.
Spark, Muriel. "The Black Madonna." In: Muriel Spark, *The Complete Short Stories*. London: Viking, 2001, 371–89. Also in: McDougall (1989), 598–618; Hill (1991), 108–129.
—. "You Should Have Seen the Mess." In: *The Complete Short Stories*, 216–221. Also in: Dolley (1972), 301–307.
Steel, Flora Annie. "The Doll-Maker." In: Cowasjee (1998), 19–26.
Steele, Richard. "Marriage of Jenny Distaff." In: *The Tatler*, ed. Lewis Gibbs. London: Dent, 1953, 108–112. Also in: Wilson (1921), 68–71 [under the title "The Wedding of Jenny Distaff"].
Stevenson, Robert Louis. "Markheim." In: Robert Louis Stevenson, *The Collected Shorter Fiction*, ed. Peter Stoneley. London: Robinson, 1991, 425–438. Also in: Walker (1914), 382–399; Wilson (1921), 230–245; Search (1959), 235–248.
—. "Thrawn Janet." In: *The Collected Shorter Fiction*, 315–323. Also in: Walker (1914), 400–410; Bergner (1969), 422–434; Dunn (1995), 110–117.
Swift, Graham. "Cliffedge." In: Graham Swift, *Learning to Swim and Other Stories*. London: Heinemann, 1985 [1982], 114–120. Also in: Oeser (1992), 138–152.
—. "Seraglio." In: *Learning to Swim*, 1–9. Also in: Bradbury (1988), 425–433.
Symons, Arthur. "Christian Trevalga." In: *The Collected Works of Arthur Symons*. London: Secker, 1924, vol. 5, 57–75. Also in: Gerber (1967), 36–49.
Taylor, Elizabeth. "The Devastating Boys." In: *Dangerous Calm: The Selected Stories of Elizabeth Taylor*. London: Virago, 1995, 195–216. Also in: Hill (1991), 1–21.
—. "Hôtel du Commerce." In: *Dangerous Calm*, 246–257. Also in: Oeser (1992), 24–40.
Thorpe, Adam. "Mercenary." In: *New Writing 9*, ed. A.L. Kennedy and John Fowles. London: Vintage and The British Council, 2000, 267–272.
—. "Nothing But Bonfires." In: Lexton (1993), 109–218.
Tennant, Emma. "Philomela." In: Bradbury (1988), 407–413. Also in: Puschmann-Nalenz (2000), 20–34.
Tremain, Rose. "The Beauty of the Dawn Shift." *New Writing 5*, ed. Christopher Hope and Peter Porter. London: Vintage and The British Council, 1996, 151–171. Also in: Byatt (1998), 403–419; Puschmann-Nalenz (2000), 112–144.
—. "The Crossing of Herald Montjoy." In: *New Writing 3*, ed. Andrew Motion and Candice Rodd. London: Minerva and The British Council, 1994, 256–270.

Trollope, Anthony. "Malachi's Cove." In: Anthony Trollope, *The Collected Shorter Fiction*, ed. Julian Thompson. London: Robinson, 1992, 421–436. Also in: Walker (1914), 261–282; Flint (1997), 52–70.

—. "Relics of General Chassé: A Tale of Antwerp." In: *The Collected Shorter Fiction*, 1–16. Also in: Byatt (1998), 44–62.

—. "The Spotted Dog." In: *The Collected Shorter Fiction*, 603–638.

—. "An Unprotected Female at the Pyramids." In: *The Collected Shorter Fiction*, 81–103.

Urquhart, Fred. "Maggie Logie and the National Health." In: *Modern Scottish Short Stories*, ed. Fred Urquhart and Giles Gordon. London: Faber, 1978, 126–133.

Wain, John. "While the Sun Shines." In: John Wain, *The Life Guard: Stories*. London: Macmillan, 1971, 42–55. Also in: Oeser (1992), 84–102.

Warner, Sylvia Townsend. "A Love Match." In: *Selected Stories of Sylvia Townsend Warner*. London: Chatto and Windus, 1989, 1–20. Also in: Hill (1991), 186–209.

—. "A Widow's Quilt." In: *Selected Stories*, 132–139. Also in: Byatt (1998), 243–249.

Waugh, Evelyn. "An Englishman's Home." In: Evelyn Waugh, *Work Suspended and Other Short Stories Written Before the Second World War*. London: Chapman and Hall, 1949, 59–80. Also in: Byatt (1998), 295–310.

—. "Mr Loveday's Little Outing." In: *Work Suspended*, 7–17. Also in: Dolley (1967), 293–301.

Weal, Mark. "A Major Hangover." 21 May 2003 <http://www.equator.ecs.soton.ac.uk/~mjw/creative/hypertext/>.

Weldon, Fay. "In the Great War." In: Fay Weldon, *Polaris and Other Stories*. London: Hodder and Stoughton, 1985, 129–143. Also in: Puschmann-Nalenz (2000), 57–80.

—. "Weekend." In: Fay Weldon, *Watching Me, Watching You: A Collection of Short Stories*. London: Hodder and Stoughton, 1981, 189–208. Also in: Bradbury (1988), 309–325; Hill (1991), 352–371.

Welsh, Irvine. "Catholic Guilt: You Know You Love It." In: Hornby (2000), 169–188.

Wells, H.G. "The Country of the Blind." In: *The Complete Short Stories of H.G. Wells*. London: Ernest Benn, 1927, 167–192. Also in: Dolley (1967), 103–128.

—. "The Door in the Wall." In: *The Complete Short Stories*, 144–161.

—. "The Lord of the Dynamos." In: *The Complete Short Stories*, 284–293.

—. "The Plattner Story." In: *The Complete Short Stories*, 325–345.

—. "A Slip Under the Microscope." In: *The Complete Short Stories*, 529–548. Also in: Jones (1973), 57–81.

—. "The Stolen Bacillus." In: *The Complete Short Stories*, 195–202. Also in: Melville and Hargreaves (1931), 817–822.

White, T.H. "The Troll." In: T.H. White, *The Maharajah and Other Stories*. London: Macdonald, 1981, 85–97. Also in: Byatt (1998), 345–354.

Wilde, Oscar. "The Happy Prince." In: *The Annotated Oscar Wilde*, ed. H. Montgomery Hyde. London: Orbis, 1982, 105–111.

Williams, Helen Maria. "History of Perourou, or the Bellows-Mender, Written by Himself." In: Helen Maria Williams, *Sketches of the State of Manners and Opinions in the French Republic Towards the Close of the Eighteenth Century in a Series of Letters*. London: G.G. and J. Robinson, 1801, vol. 1, 248–298.

Wilson, Angus. "Higher Standards." In: *The Collected Stories of Angus Wilson*. London: Secker and Warburg, 1980, 374–379. Also in: Oeser (1992), 41–51.

—. "Realpolitik." In: *The Collected Stories*, 40–46.

—. "Such Darling Dodos." In: *The Collected Stories*, 196–211.

Winterson, Jeanette. "O'Brien's First Christmas." In: Jeanette Winterson, *The World and Other Places*. London: Cape, 1998, 87–100. Also in: Speirs (1996), 138–144.

Wollstonecraft, Mary. "The Story of Crazy Robin." In: Mary Wollstonecraft, *Original Stories from Real Life*. Otley and Washington D.C.: Woodstock, 2001, 19–28. Also in: Melville and Hargreaves (1931), 67–69.

Woolf, Virginia. "Kew Gardens." In: *The Complete Shorter Fiction of Virginia Woolf*, ed. Susan Dick. London: Hogarth Press, 1985, 84–89. Also in: Dolley (1967), 201–207.

—. "The Mark on the Wall." In: *The Complete Shorter Fiction*, 77–83. Also in: Dolley (1972), 142–149.

—. "Moments of Being." In: *The Complete Shorter Fiction*, 209–214.

—. "Mrs. Dalloway in Bond Street." In: *Mrs Dalloway's Party: A Short Story Sequence*, ed. Stella McNichol. London: Hogarth Press, 1973, 19–28.

Zangwill, Israel. "A Rose of the Ghetto." In: Gerber (1967), 204–216.

## Bibliography

*I. Selected Anthologies*

Adrian, Jack (ed.). *Detective Stories from 'The Strand'*. Oxford: Oxford University Press, 1991.

— (ed.). *Strange Tales from 'The Strand'*. Oxford: Oxford University Press, 1991.

— (ed.). *Twelve Mystery Stories*. Oxford: Oxford University Press, 1998.

Ashley, Leonard R.N. and Stuart L. Astor (eds). *British Short Stories: Classics and Criticism*. Englewood Cliffs, NJ: Prentice-Hall, 1968.

Ashwood, Sheila (ed.). *Shorts from Nottinghamshire and Derbyshire*. Peterborough: New Fiction, 1992.

Ashwood has also edited several other volumes in the *Shorts from* ... series.

Auerbach, Nina and U.C. Knoepflmacher (eds). *Forbidden Journeys: Fairy Tales and Fantasies by Victorian Women Writers*. Chicago: University of Chicago Press, 1992.

Backscheider, Paula R. and John Richetti (eds). *Popular Fiction by Women 1660–1730: An Anthology*. Oxford: Clarendon Press, 1996.

Baldick, Chris (ed.). *The Oxford Book of Gothic Tales*. Oxford: Oxford University Press, 1992.

Beare, Geraldine (ed.). *Short Stories from the 'Strand'*. London: The Folio Society, 1992.

Bell, Julia and Jackie Gay (eds). *England Calling: 24 Stories for the 21st Century*. London: Phoenix, 2002 [2001].

Bennett, Bridget (ed.). *Ripples of Dissent: Women's Stories of Marriage in the 1890s*. London: Dent, 1996.

Bergner, Heinz (ed.). *English Short Stories of the Nineteenth Century*. Hildesheim: Olms, 1969.

Blair, Suzi (ed.). *Forty Shades of Green: Short Stories by Writers from Northern Ireland*. Peterborough: New Fiction, 1993.

— (ed.). *Paper Clips, Eastern England: Short Stories by Writers from Eastern England*. Peterborough: New Fiction, 1993.

Blair has also published several other volumes in the *Paper Clips* ... series.

— (ed.). *Shorts from Lancashire*. Peterborough: New Fiction, 1993.

Blair has also edited several other volumes in the *Shorts from* ... series.

Booth, Bradford Allen (ed.). *A Cabinet of Gems: Short Stories from the English Annuals*. Berkeley: University of California Press, 1938.

Bradbury, Malcolm (ed.). *The Penguin Book of Modern British Short Stories*. Harmondsworth: Penguin, 1988 [1987].

Byatt, Antonia (ed.). *The Oxford Book of English Short Stories.* Oxford: Oxford University Press, 1998.

Cheyette, Bryan (ed.). *Contemporary Jewish Writing in Britain and Ireland: An Anthology.* London: Peter Halban, 1998.

Cowasjee, Saros (ed.). *The Oxford Anthology of Raj Stories.* Delhi: Oxford University Press, 1998.

Cox, Michael and Jack Adrian (eds). *The Oxford Book of Historical Stories.* Oxford: Oxford University Press, 1994.

— and R.A. Gilbert (eds). *The Oxford Book of English Ghost Stories.* Oxford: Oxford University Press, 1986.

Craig, Patricia (ed.). *The Oxford Book of English Detective Stories.* Oxford: Oxford University Press, 1990.

— (ed.). *The Penguin Book of British Comic Stories.* London: Viking, 1990.

Davin, Dan (ed.). *The Oxford Library of Classic English Short Stories. Vol. I: 1900–1956.* Oxford: Oxford University Press, 1990.

Companion volume to Dorsch and Sharrock (1990). First published as *English Short Stories of Today, Second Series* (1958).

Dolley, Christopher (ed.). *The Penguin Book of English Short Stories.* Harmondsworth: Penguin, 1967.

— (ed.). *The Second Penguin Book of English Short Stories.* Harmondsworth: Penguin, 1972.

Dorsch, T.S. and Roger Sharock (eds). *The Oxford Library of Classic English Short Stories. Vol. II: 1956–1975.* Oxford: Oxford University Press, 1990.

Companion volume to Davin (1990). First published as *English Short Stories of Today, Third Series* (1965).

Dunn, Douglas (ed.). *The Oxford Book of Scottish Short Stories.* Oxford: Oxford University Press, 1995.

Fairbairns, Zoë (ed.). *Tales I Tell My Mother: Feminist Short Stories.* London: Journeyman, 1978.

— (ed.). *More Tales I Tell My Mother: Feminist Short Stories.* London: Journeyman, 1987.

Finn, F.E.S. (ed.). *Telling Tales: An Anthology of Short Stories in Verse.* London: John Murray, 1982.

Flint, Kate (ed.). *Victorian Love Stories: An Oxford Anthology.* Oxford: Oxford University Press, 1997 [1996].

Forkner, Ben (ed.). *Modern Irish Short Stories.* Harmondsworth: Penguin, 1982.

Gerber, Helmut E. (ed.). *The English Short Story in Transition 1880–1920.* New York: Pegasus, 1967.

Gordon, Giles (ed.). *English Short Stories: 1900 to the Present.* London: Dent, 1988.

— and David Hughes (eds). *Best Short Stories.* London: Heinemann, 1986–1995.

The series published new work by new and established writers; it appeared in paperback as *The Minerva Book of Short Stories.*

— and David Hughes (eds). *The Best of Best Short Stories 1986–1995.* London: Minerva, 1995.

Haining, Peter (ed.). *Great British Tales of Terror: Gothic Stories of Horror and Romance 1765–1840.* Harmondsworth: Penguin, 1973 [1972].

Hendry, J.F. (ed.). *The Penguin Book of Scottish Short Stories*. Harmondsworth: Penguin, 1970.
Hill, Susan (ed.). *The Penguin Book of Modern Women's Short Stories*. Harmondsworth: Penguin, 1991.
First published as *The Parchment Moon* (1990).
— (ed.). *The Second Penguin Book of Modern Women's Short Stories*. Harmondsworth: Penguin, 1998 [1997].
Hornby, Nick (ed.). *Speaking with the Angel*. London: Penguin, 2000.
Hudson, Derek (ed.). *Classic English Short Stories 1930–1955*. Oxford: Oxford University Press, 1972.
First published as *Modern English Short Stories, Second Series* (1956).
Hunt, Leigh (ed.). *Classic Tales: Serious and Lively. With Critical Essays on the Merits and Reputation of the Authors*. 5 vols. London: John Hunt and Carew Reynell, 1806.
Jones, Esmor (ed.). *British Short Stories of Today*. Harmondsworth: Penguin, 1987.
Jones, Gwyn and Islwyn Ffowc Elis (eds). *Classic Welsh Short Stories*. Oxford: Oxford University Press, 1992 [1971].
Jones, Phyllis M. (ed.). *English Short Stories 1888–1937*. Oxford: Oxford University Press, 1973.
First published as *Modern English Short Stories* (1939).
Jump, Harriet Devine (ed.). *Nineteenth-Century Short Stories by Women*. London: Routledge, 1998.
Keating, P.J. (ed.). *Working-Class Stories of the 1890s*. London: Routledge and Kegan Paul, 1971.
Kiely, Benedict (ed.). *The Penguin Book of Irish Short Stories*. Harmondsworth: Penguin, 1981.
Korte, Barbara and Claudia Sternberg (eds). *Many Voices – Many Cultures: Multicultural British Short Stories*. Stuttgart: Reclam, 1997.
Leavitt, David and Mark Mitchell (eds). *The Penguin Book of Gay Short Stories*. London: Viking, 1994.
Lewin, Ronald (ed.). *English Country Short Stories*. London: Paul Elek, 1949.
Lexton, Maria (ed.). *The 'Time Out' Book of London Short Stories*. London: Penguin, 1993.
McDougall, Carl (ed.). *The Devil and the Giro: Two Centuries of Scottish Stories*. Edinburgh: Canongate, 1989.
Mars-Jones, Adam (ed.). *Mae West Is Dead: Recent Lesbian and Gay Fiction*. London: Faber, 1983.
Melville, Lewis and Reginald Hargreaves (eds). *Great English Short Stories*. London: Harrap, 1931.
*The Minerva Book of Short Stories*. London: Minerva.
Paperback edition of Gordon and Hughes (1986–1995).
Minshull, Duncan (ed.). *Telling Stories: The Best of BBC Radio's Recent Short Fiction*. London: Coronet, 1992.
Mish, Charles C. (ed.). *Short Fiction of the Seventeenth Century*. New York: New York University Press, 1963.
Murray, Ian (ed.). *The New Penguin Book of Scottish Short Stories*. Harmondsworth: Penguin, 1983.

*New Stories*. London: The Arts Council, 1976ff.

*New Writing*. London: The British Council in association with Minerva, Vintage, Picador, 1982ff.

Newland, Courttia and Kadija Sesay (eds). *IC3: The Penguin Book of New Black Writing in Britain*. London: Hamish Hamilton, 2000.

O'Connor, Frank (ed.). *Classic Irish Short Stories*. Oxford: Oxford University Press, 1986.

First published as *Modern Irish Short Stories* (1957).

Oeser, Hans-Christian (ed.). *Modern English Short Stories II: From Coppard to Greene*. Stuttgart: Reclam, 1984.

– (cd.). *Modern English Short Stories I: From Hardy to Maugham*. Stuttgart: Reclam, 1985.

— (ed.). *Contemporary Irish Short Stories*. Stuttgart: Reclam, 1989.

— (ed.). *Modern English Short Stories III: From Bates to Swift*. Stuttgart: Reclam, 1992.

Orel, Harold (ed.). *Victorian Short Stories: An Anthology*. London: Dent, 1987.

— (ed.). *Victorian Short Stories 2: The Trials of Love*. London: Dent, 1990.

Parker, Michael (ed.). *The Hurt World: Short Stories of the Troubles*. Belfast: The Blackstaff Press, 1995.

*Penguin Modern Stories*, ed. Judith Burnley. Harmondsworth: Penguin, 1969ff.

Pritchett, V.S. (ed.). *The Oxford Book of Short Stories*. Oxford: Oxford University Press, 1981.

Puschmann-Nalenz, Barbara (ed.). *Ten British Women Writers: Contemporary Short Stories*. Stuttgart: Reclam, 2000.

Rabb, Jane M. (ed.). *The Short Story and Photography 1880's–1980's: A Critical Anthology*. Albuquerque: University of New Mexico Press, 1998.

Reid, Christopher (ed.). *Not to Speak of the Dog: 101 Short Stories in Verse*. London: Faber, 2000.

Reynolds, Margaret (ed.). *The Penguin Book of Lesbian Short Stories*. London: Viking, 1993.

Richards, Alun (ed.). *The Penguin Book of Welsh Short Stories*. Harmondsworth: Penguin, 1976.

— (ed.). *The Second Penguin Book of Welsh Short Stories*. Harmondsworth: Penguin, 1994 [1993].

Richardson, Angelique (ed.). *Women Who Did: Stories by Men and Women, 1890–1914*. London: Penguin, 2002.

Rye, Jane (ed.). *Signals-3: Thirty London Magazine Stories*. London: London Magazine, 2001.

Search, Pamela (ed.). *The Supernatural in the English Short Story*. London: Bernard Hanison, 1959.

Shippey, Tom (ed.). *The Oxford Book of Science Fiction Stories*. Oxford: Oxford University Press, 1992.

*Shorts: New Writing from Granta Books*. London: Granta, 1998.

Showalter, Elaine (ed.). *Daughters of Decadence: Women Writers of the Fin de Siècle*. London: Virago, 1993.

Speirs, Di (ed.). *Woman's Hour 50th Anniversary Short Story Collection*. London: Penguin Books and BBC Worldwide, 1996.
Stanford, Derek (ed.). *Short Stories of the 'Nineties: A Biographical Anthology*. London: John Baker, 1968.
Stevick, Philip (ed.). *Anti-Story: An Anthology of Experimental Fiction*. New York: The Free Press, 1971.
Tracy, Lorna, Jon Silkin and John Wardle (eds). *Best Short Stories from Stand Magazine*. London: Methuen, 1988.
Trevor, William (ed.). *The Oxford Book of Irish Short Stories*. Oxford: Oxford University Press, 1989.
Walker, Hugh (ed.). *Selected English Short Stories: XIX Century*. London: Oxford University Press, 1914.
Walton, Tracey (ed.). *Shorts from Cornwall*. Peterborough: New Fiction, 1992.
Walton has also edited several other volumes in the *Shorts from ...* series.
Wilson, Richard (ed.). *English Short Stories: An Anthology*. London: Dent, 1921.

*Electronic Text Databases*

http://www.bibliomania.com
http://www.short-stories.co.uk

*II. Reference Works*

Baldwin, Dean and Gregory L. Morris. *The Short Story in English: Britain and North America. An Annotated Bibliography*. (Magill Bibliographies.) Metuchen, NJ and London: The Scarecrow Press/Pasadena, CA and Englewood Cliffs, NJ: Salem Press, 1994.
Intended as a guide for student users. Individual sections with Reference Works, Histories of the Short Story, Short Story Theory, followed by entries for individual writers. The latter include well-known British representatives usually found in anthologies.
Block, Andrew. *The English Novel 1740–1850: A Catalogue Including Prose Romances, Short Stories, and Translations of Foreign Fiction*. London: Dawsons of Pall Mall, 1961 [1931].
Lists works by author (where known) and has a title index, but does not separate pieces of long and short fiction.
Cook, Dorothy E. and Isabel S. Monro. *Short Story Index: An Index to 60,000 Stories in 4,320 Collections*. New York: H.W. Wilson, 1953.
Useful for tracing stories; with author, title and subject entries. This edition had a number of supplement volumes.
Davis, Gwenn and Beverly A. Joyce. *Short Fiction by Women to 1900: A Bibliography of American and British Writers*. London and New York: Mansell, 1999.
Illustrates the impressive number of short fiction written by women in the nineteenth century.
*Dictionary of Literary Biography* (*DLB*). Detroit: Gale Research.
Five volumes on *British Short-Fiction Writers*. Each entry lists a writer's book and pe-

riodical publications, comprises an essay on the writer's short fiction and provides further bibliographic references.

*British Short-Fiction Writers, 1800–1880*, ed. John R. Greenfield – *DLB*, vol. 159 (1996).

*British Short-Fiction Writers, 1880–1914: The Romantic Tradition*, ed. William F. Naufftus – *DLB*, vol. 156 (1996).

*British Short-Fiction Writers, 1880–1914: The Realist Tradition*, ed. William B. Thesing – *DLB*, vol. 135 (1994).

*British Short-Fiction Writers, 1915–1945*, ed. John R. Rogers – *DLB*, vol. 162 (1996).

*British Short-Fiction Writers, 1945–1980*, ed. Dean Baldwin – *DLB*, vol. 139 (1994).

Fallon, Erin *et al.* (eds). *A Reader's Companion to the Short Story in English*. London: Fitzroy Dearborn, 2001.

Essays on selected writers of short stories from the English-speaking countries.

Gordon, Giles. *The Twentieth-Century Short Story in English: A Bibliography*. London: The British Council, 1989.

A useful listing of anthologies and author collections.

Riggs, Thomas (ed.). *Reference Guide to Short Fiction*. Detroit and London: St. James Press, 1999 [1994].

The second edition covers 376 writers of short stories and novellas (in English and other languages), almost all born after 1740, including authors of the 1990s. About twenty per cent are listed as British, English, Scottish, Welsh or Irish. Section 1 has entries on writers (biographical and bibliographical data, major studies) and includes critical survey essays on the entrants' short fiction. Section 2 comprises essays which discuss individual stories, at least one per entrant.

*Short Story Criticism: Excerpts from Criticism of the Works of Short Fiction Writers*. Detroit: Gale Research, 1988ff.

The volumes in this series present "significant passages from criticism of the greatest short story writers of all time and provide supplementary materials – biographical and bibliographical – to guide the interested student to a greater understanding of short fiction". ("Preface", 7) Each volume covers ten to fifteen writers and provides easy access to important criticism of their work. The selection of British writers ranges from nineteenth-century and early twentieth-century 'classic' authors to more recent ones, such as J.G. Ballard.

Thurston, Jarvis *et al. Short Fiction Criticism: A Checklist of Interpretation since 1925 of Stories and Novelettes (American, British, Continental) 1800–1958*. Denver: Alan Swallow, 1960.

Useful for tracing interpretations of individual stories; use to supplement Walker (1977).

Walker, Warren S. *Twentieth-Century Short Story Explication: Interpretations 1900–1975, of Short Fiction Since 1800*. Hamden, CT: Shoe String Press, 1977 [1966].

The third edition lists more than 850 writers from 45 countries and provides the bibliographical data of interpretations of their short stories. Five supplement volumes until 1992, and a new series (ed. Wendell M. Aycock) starting with vol. 1 for 1989/90 (1993); vol. 4 for 1995/96 was published 1999.

Watson, Noelle (ed.). *Reference Guide to Short Fiction*. Detroit: St. James Press, 1994.

Contains entries on international writers and individual works. Author entries provide brief information on the writer's biography, main publications, a short bibliography and include one short article. For works, the entries give an overview of the critical reception and interpretations.

*III. Collections of Interpretations*

*Anglistik und Englischunterricht,* 18 (1982) and 23 (1984). Thematic issues devoted to *The Very Short Story.*

Includes discussions of very short stories from Britain.

*Anglistik und Englischunterricht,* 50 (1993). Thematic issue devoted to *Recent British Short Story Writing.*

Following a survey article (see Schröder 1993 below), the essays are devoted to the work of individual writers, often focussing on selected stories that are discussed in greater detail. Writers treated include Doris Lessing, Fay Weldon, Malcolm Bradbury, Ian McEwan, Angela Carter, Gabriel Josipovici and Graham Swift.

Borgmeier, Raimund (ed.). *Interpretationen: Englische Short Stories von Thomas Hardy bis Graham Swift.* Stuttgart: Reclam, 1999.

A welcome complement to previous collections of interpretations such as Göller and Hoffmann (1973) and Lubbers (1990), since it also covers more recent writers.

Göller, Karl Heinz and Gerhard Hoffmann (eds). *Die englische Kurzgeschichte.* Düsseldorf: Bagel, 1973.

A collection of interpretations of British and Irish short stories ranging from the late nineteenth century to the 1970s.

Lubbers, Klaus (ed.). *Die englische und amerikanische Kurzgeschichte.* Darmstadt: Wissenschaftliche Buchgesellschaft, 1990.

A collection of interpretations of stories the majority of which are by US-American writers; British writers discussed include Kipling, Maugham, Lawrence, Mansfield, Greene and Sillitoe.

*IV. History, Theory and Criticism of the Short Story, with a Special Focus on the Short Story in Britain*

Ahrends, Günter. "Ästhetizismus und Realismus in der englischen Kurzgeschichte der Nineties." In: *Die 'Nineties: Das Englische Fin de siècle zwischen Dekadenz und Sozialkritik,* ed. Manfred Pfister and Bernd Schulte-Middelich. München: Francke, 1983, 248–274.

Allen, Walter. *The Short Story in English.* Oxford: Clarendon Press, 1981.

A broad survey of the short story since the nineteenth century, in all English-speaking countries; Allen focusses on a selection of representative writers and discusses a number of their stories in greater detail.

Allingham, Philip V. "Dickens's Aesthetic of the Short Story." *The Dickensian,* 95.448 (Summer 1999), 144–153.

Annen, Ulrich. *George Gissing und die Kurzgeschichte.* Bern: Francke, 1973.

Archer, Stanley. *W. Somerset Maugham: A Study of the Short Fiction.* (Twayne's Studies in Short Fiction.) New York: Twayne, 1993.

A basic introduction to the author and his work, including the views of major critics. All volumes in this Twayne series, more of which are listed in this bibliography, follow this basic scheme.

Averill, Deborah M. *The Irish Short Story from George Moore to Frank O'Connor.* Lanham and New York: University Press of America, 1982.

Aycock, Wendell M. (ed.). *The Teller and the Tale: Aspects of the Short Story.* Lubbock: Texas Tech Press, 1982.

Baldeshwiler, Eileen. "The Lyric Short Story: The Sketch of a History." In: May (1994), 231–241 [first in *Studies in Short Fiction*, 6 (1969), 443–453].

Baldwin, Dean. "The English Short Story in the Fifties." In: Vannatta (1985), 34–74.

—. *Virginia Woolf: A Study of the Short Fiction.* (Twayne's Studies in Short Fiction.) Boston: Twayne, 1989.

—. "The Tardy Evolution of the British Short Story." *Studies in Short Fiction*, 30 (1993), 23–33.

Banks, Joanne Trautmann. "Virginia Woolf and Katherine Mansfield." In: Flora (1985), 57–82.

Bardolph, Jacqueline (ed.). *Short Fiction in the New Literatures in English: Proceedings of the Nice Conference of the European Association for Commonwealth Literature and Language Studies.* Aarhus: EACLALS, 1989.

Bates, H.E. *The Modern Short Story: A Critical Survey.* Boston: The Writer, Inc., 1965 [1941].

Written by a short-story writer himself, this is a survey with strong judgements. Bates discusses a relatively small selection of writers from Britain, the United States and Ireland as well as European (French, Russian) influences: "the present book [...] sets out to be a study of certain established writers from Poe and Gogol to the present-day who have practised the short story as a craft separate from that of the novel." (10)

Bauer, Helen Pike. *Rudyard Kipling: A Study of the Short Fiction.* (Twayne's Studies in Short Fiction.) New York: Twayne, 1994.

Bayley, John. *The Short Story: Henry James to Elizabeth Bowen.* Brighton: Harvester, 1988.

A useful survey for the period covered.

—. "Graham Greene: The Short Stories." In: *Graham Greene: A Revaluation*, ed. Jeffrey Meyers. Basingstoke: Macmillan, 1990, 93–103.

Beachcroft, Thomas O. *The English Short Story.* (Writers and Their Works, 168, 169.) 2 vols. London: Longman's, Green, 1964 (for the British Council and The National Book League).

Two booklets which portray a selection of important representatives of the short story in Britain and Ireland.

—. *The Modest Art: A Survey of the Short Story in English.* London: Oxford University Press, 1968.

This survey includes the ancestry of the modern short story but focusses on 'canonical' writers from the nineteenth century onwards.

Bergonzi, Bernard. "An Appendix on the Short Story." In: Bernard Bergonzi, *The Situation of the Novel.* Basingstoke: Macmillan, 1970, 214–218.

Bonheim, Helmut. *The Narrative Modes: Techniques of the Short Story*. Cambridge: Brewer, 1982.

Bowen, Elizabeth. "Preface to *The Faber Book of Modern Short Stories*." In: May (1994), 256–262.

Boyce, Benjamin. "English Short Fiction in the Eighteenth Century: A Preliminary View." *Studies in Short Fiction*, 5 (1968), 95–112.

Brady, Kristin. *The Short Stories of Thomas Hardy*. New York: St. Martin's Press, 1982.

Briggs, Julia. *Night Visitors: The Rise and Fall of the English Ghost Story*. London: Faber, 1977.

Broich, Ulrich. "John Fowles, 'The Enigma' and the Contemporary British Short Story." In: *Modes of Narrative: Approaches to American, Canadian and British Fiction*, ed. Reingard M. Nischik and Barbara Korte. Würzburg: Königshausen und Neumann, 1990, 179–189.

—. "Muted Postmodernism: The Contemporary British Short Story." *Zeitschrift für Anglistik und Amerikanistik*, 41 (1993), 31–39.

Brown, Suzanne Hunter. "The Chronotope of the Short Story: Time, Character, and Brevity." In: Kaylor (1997), 181–213.

Bungert, Hans (ed.). *Die amerikanische Short Story: Theorie und Entwicklung*. Darmstadt: Wissenschaftliche Buchgesellschaft, 1972.

A collection of important texts related to the history and poetics of the short story.

Canby, Henry Seidel. *The Short Story in English*. New York: Henry Holt, 1909.

This early study sees the short story 'proper' as emerging with Poe but nevertheless gives an outline of its pre-history beginning with the middle ages.

Cochran, Robert. *Samuel Beckett: A Study of the Short Fiction*. (Twayne's Studies in Short Fiction.) New York: Twayne, 1991.

Coover, Robert. "Storying in Hyperspace: 'Linkages'." In: Lounsberry, Lohafer *et al.* (1998), 133–138.

Current-García, Eugene and Walton R. Patrick (eds). *What Is the Short Story?* Glenville, IL: Scott, Foresman, 1974 [1961].

The first part is a collection of critical statements on the short story, most of them by writers themselves. The second part is an anthology, including stories by writers from Britain.

Duncan, Edgar Hill. "Short Fiction in Medieval English: A Survey." *Studies in Short Fiction*, 9 (1972), 1–28.

— . "Short Fiction in Medieval English: II. The Middle English Period." *Studies in Short Fiction*, 11 (1974), 227–241.

Dunn, Maggie and Ann Morris. *The Composite Novel: The Short Story Cycle in Transition*. New York: Twayne, 1995.

Emmens, Carol A. *Short Stories on Film*. Littleton, CO: Libraries Unlimited, 1978.

Erdinast-Vulcan, Daphna. *The Strange Short Fiction of Joseph Conrad: Writing, Culture, and Subjectivity*. Oxford: Oxford University Press, 1999.

Evans, Walter. "Short Fiction: 1800–1840." In: Magill (1981), vol. 1, 153–172.

—. "The English Short Story in the Seventies." In: Vannatta (1985), 120–172.

Ferguson, Suzanne C. "The Rise of the Short Story in the Hierarchy of Genres." In: Lohafer and Clarey (1989), 176–192.

—. "Defining the Short Story: Impressionism and Form." In: May (1994), 218–230 [first in *Modern Fiction Studies*, 28 (1982), 13–24].

—. "Local Color and the Function of Setting in the English Short Story." In: Kaylor (1997), 1–33.

Flora, Joseph M. (ed.). *The English Short Story 1880–1945: A Critical History*. (Twayne's Critical History of the Short Story.) Boston: Twayne, 1985.

A companion volume to Vannatta (1985), this is a collection of introductory essays of uneven quality addressed primarily at an American readership. It is useful for a first survey and the materials provided (lists of anthologies, collections, secondary materials); however, some of the chapters are strongly evaluative.

Fogle, Richard Harter. "Saki and Wodehouse." In: Flora (1985), 83–111.

Friedman, Norman."What Makes a Short Story Short." In: Bungert (1972), 280–297 [first in *Modern Fiction Studies*, 4 (1958), 103–117].

Ganzmann, Jochen. *Vorbereitung der Moderne: Aspekte erzählerischer Gestaltung in den Kurzgeschichten von James Joyce und Katherine Mansfield*. Frankfurt am Main: Lang, 1986.

Garrett, George. "Short Fiction Since 1950." In: Magill (1981), vol. 1, 278–322.

Gilbert, Elliott L. *The Good Kipling: Studies in the Short Story*. Manchester: Manchester University Press, 1972.

Gindin, James. "A.E. Coppard and H.E. Bates." In: Flora (1985), 113–141.

Gish, Robert. "The Exotic Short Story: Kipling and Others." In: Flora (1985), 1–37.

Goetsch, Paul. *Literarische und soziale Bedingungen erzählerischer Kurzformen: Die Short Story*. Tübingen: Deutsches Institut für Fernstudien, 1978a.

A helpful compact introduction which stresses the short story's flexibility and emphasizes the relevance of literary sociology for an understanding of the genre.

— (ed.). *Studien und Materialien zur Short Story*. Frankfurt am Main: Diesterweg, 1978b [1971].

A collection of essays about techniques of the short story, with a focus on American examples.

Grove, Allen W. "To Make a Long Story Short: Gothic Fragments and the Gender Politics of Incompleteness." *Studies in Short Fiction*, 34 (1997), 1–10.

Hammick, Georgina. "In Defense of the Short Story." In: *New Writing 3*, ed. Andrew Motion and Candice Rodd, 1994, 297–302.

Hammond, J.R. *H.G. Wells and the Short Story*. Basingstoke: Macmillan, 1992.

Hanson, Clare. *Short Stories and Short Fictions, 1880–1980*. Basingstoke: Macmillan, 1985.

A recommendable survey of the short story in the twentieth century, including major developments after the Second World War.

— (ed.). *Re-Reading the Short Story*. Basingstoke: Macmillan, 1989.

Hardy, Sarah. "A Poetics of Immediacy: Oral Narrative and the Short Story." *Style*, 27 (1993), 352–368.

Harris, Wendell V. "Beginnings of and for the True Short Story in England." *English Literature in Transition*, 15 (1972), 269–276.

—. *British Short Fiction in the Nineteenth Century: A Literary and Bibliographic Guide*. Detroit: Wayne State University Press, 1979.

A helpful survey of well-known and now-forgotten writers of short fiction in nineteenth-century Britain. The 'true' short story is not seen to have emerged until the 1880s and 1890s, but Harris identifies important earlier developments. The "Bibliographic Appendix" is useful especially for tracing primary sources.

—. "Vision and Form: The English Novel and the Emergence of the Short Story." In: May (1994), 182–191.

Head, Dominic. *The Modernist Short Story: A Study in Theory and Practice*. Cambridge: Cambridge University Press, 1992.

A standard study of the modernist story.

Hönig, Hans G. *Studien zur englischen Short Story am Ende des 19. Jahrhunderts: Stevenson, Hardy, Kipling und Wells*. Göppingen: Alfred Kümmerle, 1971.

Hofheinz, Ellen. *Die Kurzgeschichten von D.H. Lawrence: Struktur – Sprache – Tradition*. Frankfurt am Main: Lang, 1991.

Hubbard Harris, Janice. *The Short Fiction of D.H. Lawrence*. New Brunswick, NJ: Rutgers University Press, 1984.

Jolles, André. *Einfache Formen: Legende, Sage, Mythe, Rätsel, Spruch, Kasus, Memorabile, Märchen, Witz*. Tübingen: Niemeyer, 1982 [1930].

Kay, Donald. *Short Fiction in 'The Spectator'*. University: University of Alabama Press, 1975.

Kaylor, Noel Harold Jr. (ed.). *Creative and Critical Approaches to the Short Story*. Lewiston: Edwin Mellen, 1997.

Kearney, Martin F. *Major Short Stories of D.H. Lawrence: A Handbook*. New York: Garland Publishing, 1998.

Kelly, Richard. *Graham Greene: A Study of the Short Fiction*. (Twayne's Studies in Short Fiction.) New York: Twayne, 1992.

*Kenyon Review International Symposium on the Short Story*. Part I, 30.4 (1968) to Part IV, 32.1 (1970).

Statements by writers on the short story's form, its status and other questions. Writers from Britain include John Wain, Elizabeth Taylor and H.E. Bates.

Kilchenmann, Ruth J. *Die Kurzgeschichte: Formen und Entwicklung*. Stuttgart: Kohlhammer, 1967.

Kilroy, James F. (ed.). *The Irish Short Story: A Critical History*. (Twayne's Critical History of the Short Story.) Boston: Twayne, 1984.

Kobler, J.F. *Katherine Mansfield: A Study of the Short Fiction*. (Twayne's Studies in Short Fiction.) New York: Twayne, 1990.

Link, Franz. "'Tale', 'Sketch', 'Essay' und 'Short Story'." In: Bungert (1972), 211–221 [first in *Die Neueren Sprachen*, 56 (1957), 345–352].

Lohafer, Susan. *Coming to Terms with the Short Story*. Baton Rouge: Louisiana State University Press, 1983.

—. "Interdisciplinary Thoughts on Cognitive Science and Short Fiction Studies." In: Lounsberry, Lohafer *et al.* (1998), 147–150.

— and Jo Ellyn Clarey (eds). *Short Story Theory at a Crossroads*. Baton Rouge: Louisiana State University Press, 1989.

An important collection of essays on the state of the art of short-story theory and short-story definition, by leading American scholars.

— and Charles E. May (eds). *Studies in Short Fiction*, 33.4 (1996): "A Special Number of Short Story Theory."

Lounsberry, Barbara, Susan Lohafer *et al.* (eds). *The Tales We Tell: Perspectives on the Short Story.* Westport, CT: Greenwood Press, 1998.

Lubbers, Klaus. *Typologie der Short Story.* Darmstadt: Wissenschaftliche Buchgesellschaft, 1977.

MacAndrew, Elizabeth. "The Gothic Influence on Short Fiction." In: Magill (1981), vol. 2, 469–482.

Magill, Frank N. (ed.). *Critical Survey of Short Fiction.* Englewood Cliffs, NJ: Salem Press, 1981.

This compilation provides a survey of short fiction from antiquity to postmodernism, from an international perspective but with a particular focus on the United States. The overviews offered in the two volumes of essays (vols 1 and 2) are cursory but provide summaries of the most important studies extant, on such areas as: definition of the short story, terms and techniques, criticism, short fiction in special regions and periods, genres and subgenres. Vol. 1 also contains a helpful annotated bibliography of "Short-Fiction Criticism" by Charles May (pp. 68–94). Vols 3 to 7 consist of brief author entries, giving biographical and bibliographical data, "influences" and "story characteristics". A revised edition appeared in 1993.

Malcolm, Cheryl Alexander and David Malcolm. *Jean Rhys: A Study of the Short Fiction.* (Twayne's Studies in Short Fiction.) New York: Twayne, 1996.

Mann, Susan Garland. *The Short Story Cycle: A Genre Companion and Reference Guide.* Westport, CT: Greenwood Press, 1989.

Manz-Kunz, Marie-Antoinette. "The European Sensibility in Short Fiction." In: Magill (1981), vol. 2, 457–468.

Marcus, Fred H. *Short Story/Short Film.* New Jersey: Prentice-Hall, 1977.

Martin, Peter A. "The Short Story in England: 1930s Fiction Magazines." *Studies in Short Fiction*, 14 (1977), 233–240.

Matthews, Brander. *The Philosophy of the Short-story.* New York: Longman's, Green, 1901.

Maugham, William Somerset. "The Short Story." In: W. Somerset Maugham, *Points of View.* London: Heinemann, 1958, 142–188.

—. *Selected Prefaces and Introductions of W. Somerset Maugham.* London: Heinemann, 1963.

May, Charles E. "Short Fiction: 1840–1880." In: Magill (1981), vol. 1, 173–217.

—. "The Nature of Knowledge in Short Fiction." In: May (1994), 131–143 [first in *Studies in Short Fiction*, 21 (1984), 327–338].

—. *The Short Story: The Reality of Artifice.* New York: Twayne, 1995.

A survey of the genre from renaissance beginnings to postmodernism, but with a strong focus on American authors, especially for the twentieth century. A bibliographic essay reviews important work in the area.

—. "Prolegomenon to a Generic Study of the Short Story." In: Lohafer and May (1996), 461–473.

— (ed.). *The New Short Story Theories.* Athens: Ohio University Press, 1994.

A highly recommendable, completely new edition of May's important collection *Short Story Theories* (1976), with many additional texts. It includes 'classics' of short-story research as well as new narratological and cognitive approaches. The annotated bibliography is very useful.

Mayo, Robert D. *The English Novel in the Magazines 1740–1815: With a Catalogue of 1375 Magazine Novels and Novelettes.* Evanston: Northwestern University Press and London: Oxford University Press, 1962.

Mertner, Edgar. "Zur Theorie der Short Story in England und Amerika." In: Bungert (1972), 103–120 [first in *Anglia,* 53 (1941), 188–205].

Mish, Charles C. "English Short Fiction in the Seventeenth Century." *Studies in Short Fiction,* 6 (1968/69), 233–330.

*Modern Fiction Studies,* 28.1 (Spring 1982): Thematic Issue devoted to *The Modern Short Story.*

Moosmüller, Birgit. *Die experimentelle englische Kurzgeschichte der Gegenwart.* München: Fink, 1993.

This is still the only and a recommendable major study on more recent developments of short-story writing in Britain.

Myszor, Frank. *The Modern Short Story.* Cambridge: Cambridge University Press, 2001.

Written for student readers, this booklet offers a very basic survey of the American and British short story from the nineteenth century to postmodernism.

Nischik, Reingard M. "Nachwort: Die Macht der Winzigkeit." In: *Short Short Stories Universal,* ed. Reingard M. Nischik. Stuttgart: Reclam, 1993, 191–229.

O'Connor, Frank. *The Lonely Voice: A Study of the Short Story.* London: Macmillan, 1963.

This is a frequently cited and hence influential survey by a major Irish writer of short stories. O'Connor is outspoken in his judgements of individual writers and their work.

O'Faoláin, Seán. *The Short Story.* London: Collins, 1948.

Orel, Harold. *The Victorian Short Story: Development and Triumph of a Literary Genre.* Cambridge: Cambridge University Press, 1986.

A useful study which discusses selected (major) nineteenth-century writers from England, Ireland and Scotland like Carleton, LeFanu, Dickens, Trollope, Hardy, Stevenson, Kipling, Conrad and Wells. Individual stories which can be considered representative of (a stage of) a writer's work are analyzed in detail. Orel emphasizes the relationship between Victorian short-story writing and the contemporary publishing system.

Pache, Walter. "Towards the Modern English Short Story." In: *Modes of Narrative: Approaches to American, Canadian and British Fiction,* ed. Reingard M. Nischik and Barbara Korte. Würzburg: Königshausen und Neumann, 1990, 218–233.

Pasco, Allan H. "On Defining Short Stories." In: May (1994), 114–129.

Peden, William. "Realism and Anti-Realism in the Modern Short Story." In: Aycock (1982), 47–62.

—. "V.S. Pritchett." In: Flora (1985), 143–151.

Penn, W.S. "The Tale as Genre in Short Fiction." In: May (1994), 44–55 [first in *Southern Humanities Review,* 15 (1981), 231–241].

Pickering, Jean. "The English Short Story in the Sixties." In: Vannatta (1985), 75–119.
—. "Time and the Short Story." In: Hanson (1989), 45–54.
Pickering, Sam. "*The Cheap Repository Tracts* and the Short Story." *Studies in Short Fiction*, 12 (1975), 15–21.
Pilipp, Frank and Ann Pederson. "Narrative Devices and Aesthetic Perception in Joyce's and Huston's 'The Dead'/Uncovering 'The Dead': A Study of Adaptation." *Literature/Film Quarterly*, 21 (1993), 61–70.
Pitcher, Edward W. "On the Conventions of Eighteenth-Century British Short Fiction." *Studies in Short Fiction*, 12 (1975a), 199–212.
—. "On the Conventions of Eighteenth-Century British Short Fiction: Part II: 1760–1785." *Studies in Short Fiction*, 12 (1975b), 327–341.
—. "Changes in Short Fiction in Britain 1785–1810: Philosophic Tales, Gothic Tales, and Fragments and Visions." *Studies in Short Fiction*, 13 (1976), 331–354.
—. "The Short Story in Anthology and Miscellany 1750–1800: A Response to Robert Mayo." *Studies in Short Fiction*, 14 (1977), 1–11.
—. "Eighteenth-Century Gothic Fragments and the Paradigm of Violation and Repair." *Studies in Short Fiction*, 33 (1996), 35–42.
Poe, Edgar Allan. "How to Write a Blackwood's Article." In: *The Short Fiction of Edgar Allan Poe*, ed. Stuart and Susan Levine. Indianapolis: Bobbs-Merrill, 1976, 357–363.
—. "[Review of] Twice-Told Tales [May 1842]." In: Edgar Allan Poe, *Essays and Reviews*, ed. G.R. Thompson. New York: Literary Classics of the U.S., 1984, 569–577.
Polsgrove, Carol. "They Made It Pay: British Short-Fiction Writers, 1820–1840." *Studies in Short Fiction*, 11 (1974), 417–421.
Pratt, Mary Louise. "The Short Story: The Long and the Short of It." In: May (1994), 91–113.
Quadflieg, Helga. *Die Short Story der Nineties: Narrative Kurzprosa im Spannungsfeld zwischen Ästhetizismus und Naturalismus*. Frankfurt am Main: Lang, 1988.
Rafroidi, Patrick and Terence Brown (eds). *The Irish Short Story*. Gerrards Cross: Colin Smythe, 1979.
Reid, Ian. *The Short Story*. London: Methuen, 1977.
A brief and basic introduction from the Critical Idiom series, taking its examples also from other than literatures in English.
Salzman, Paul. *English Prose Fiction 1558–1700: A Critical History*. Oxford: Clarendon Press, 1986 [1985].
Schlauch, Margaret. "English Short Fiction in the 15th and 16th Centuries." *Studies in Short Fiction*, 3 (1966), 393–434.
Schröder, Gottfried. "Recent British Short Stories." *Anglistik und Englischunterricht*, 50 (1993), 7–31.
Schulz, Volker. *Das kurzepische Werk Graham Greenes: Gesamtdarstellung und Einzelinterpretationen*. Trier: Wissenschaftlicher Verlag Trier, 1987.
Seiler-Franklin, Andreas. *Dekadenz und Avantgarde: Erzählerische Experimente im England der Jahrhundertwende*. PhD thesis, Zurich, 1977.

Shaw, Valerie. *The Short Story: A Critical Introduction*. London: Longman, 1983.

Though not convincingly structured, this is a useful study discussing the short story as genre, addressing historical developments and treating selected stories in greater detail. It draws on examples from Britain but also other cultural contexts, in particular the United States, France and Russia.

Shelston, Alan. "The Supernatural in the Stories of Elizabeth Gaskell." In: *Exhibited by Candlelight: Sources and Developments in the Gothic Tradition*, ed. Valeria Tinkler-Villani and Peter Davidson. Amsterdam: Rodopi, 1995, 137–146.

Smith, Julian. "Short Fiction on Film: A Selected Filmography." *Studies in Short Fiction*, 10 (1973), 397–409.

Sodowsky, Roland. "The Minimalist Short Story: Its Definition, Writers, and (Small) Heyday." *Studies in Short Fiction*, 33 (1996), 529–540.

Stevenson, Lionel. "The Short Story in Embryo." *English Literature in Transition*, 15 (1972), 261–268.

Stilz, Gerhard. *Die anglo-indische Short Story: Geschichte einer Kolonialliteratur*. Tübingen: Niemeyer, 1980.

Stinson, John J. "The English Short Story, 1945–1950." In: Vannatta (1985), 1–33.

—. *V.S. Pritchett: A Study of the Short Fiction*. (Twayne's Studies in Short Fiction.) New York: Twayne, 1992.

Stummer, Peter O. (ed.). *The Story Must Be Told: Short Narrative Prose in the New English Literatures*. Würzburg: Königshausen und Neumann, 1986.

Sullivan, Jack. *Elegant Nightmares: The English Ghost Story from LeFanu to Blackwood*. Athens: Ohio University Press, 1978.

Symons, Julian. *Bloody Murder: From the Detective Story to the Crime Novel. A History*. London: Faber, 1972.

Thomas, Deborah A. *Dickens and the Short Story*. Philadelphia: University of Pennsylvania Press, 1982.

Thompson, Richard J. *Everlasting Voices: Aspects of the Modern Irish Short Story*. Troy, NY: Whitston Publishing, 1989.

Thornton, Weldon. "D.H. Lawrence." In: Flora (1985), 39–56.

Vannatta, Dennis (ed.). *The English Short Story 1945–1980: A Critical History*. (Twayne's Critical History of the Short Story.) Boston: Twayne, 1985.

This is a companion volume to Flora (1985). The essays proceed by decades and discuss author collections mostly.

Walker, Warren S. "From Raconteur to Writer: Oral Roots and Printed Leaves of Short Fiction." In: Aycock (1982), 13–26.

Waller, Gary F. "British Short Fiction in the Sixteenth and Seventeenth Centuries." In: Magill (1981), vol. 2, 483–504.

Ward, Alfred C. *Aspects of the Modern Short Story: English and American*. London: University of London Press, 1924.

Focusses on individual writers and their work; still useful because Ward discusses a number of writers now rarely considered in historical surveys.

Watson, J.R. "'Round the Sofa': Elizabeth Gaskell Tells Stories." *Yearbook of English Studies*, 26 (1996), 89–99.

Weber, Alfred and Walter F. Greiner. *Short-Story-Theorien (1573–1973): Eine Sammlung und Bibliographie englischer und amerikanischer Quellen*. Kronberg: Athenäum, 1977.

A useful collection of comments (excerpts from reviews, prefaces, books etc.) on the short story as genre by its British and American practitioners. Also includes a bibliography of further sources.

Wheeler, David (ed.). *No, But I Saw the Movie: The Best Short Stories Ever Made Into Film*. New York: Penguin, 1989.

Windholz, Anne M. "The American Short Story and Its British Critics: *Athenaeum* Reviews, 1880–1900." *Victorian Periodicals Review*, 23.4 (1990), 156–166.

Wolpers, Theodor. "Kürze im Erzählen." *Anglia*, 89 (1971), 48–86.

Zambrano, A.L. "Greene's Visions of Childhood: 'The Basement Room' and 'The Fallen Idol'." *Literature/Film Quarterly*, 2 (1974), 324–331.

*V. Other Materials*

Altick, Richard D. *The English Common Reader: A Social History of the Mass Reading Public 1800–1900*. Chicago: University of Chicago Press, 1957.

—. *Victorian Studies in Scarlet*. London: Dent, 1972.

Ascham, Roger. *The Schoolmaster (1570)*, ed. Lawrence V. Ryan. Ithaca, NY: Cornell University Press for The Folger Shakespeare Library, 1967.

Bradbury, Malcolm. *The Social Context of Modern English Literature*. Oxford: Blackwell, 1971.

— and James McFarlane (eds). *Modernism 1890–1930*. Harmondsworth: Penguin, 1976.

Benson, Eugene and L.W. Conolly (eds). *Encyclopaedia of Post-Colonial Literatures in English*. London: Routledge, 1994, entry "Short Fiction" in vol. 2, 1451–1488.

— and William Toye (eds). *The Oxford Companion to Canadian Literature*. Oxford: Oxford University Press, 1997.

Congreve, William. "The Preface to the Reader [to *Incognita*]." In: William Congreve, *Incognita and The Way of the World* , ed. A. Norman Jeffares. London: Arnold, 1966, 32–34.

Cooper, Pat and Ken Dancyger. *Writing the Short Film*. Boston: Focal Press, 1994.

Crackanthorpe, Hubert. "Reticence in Literature: Some Roundabout Remarks." *Yellow Book*, 2 (July 1894), 259–269.

Culler, Jonathan. *Structuralist Poetics: Structuralism, Linguistics and the Study of Literature*. London: Routledge and Kegan Paul, 1975.

Easthope, Antony. *Englishness and National Culture*. London: Routledge, 1999.

Eigner, Edwin M. and George J. Worth (eds). *Victorian Criticism of the Novel*. Cambridge: Cambridge University Press, 1985.

Fishelov, David. "Genre Theory and Family Resemblance – Revisited." *Poetics*, 20 (1991), 123–138.

—. *Metaphors of Genre: The Role of Analogies in Genre Theory*. University Park: Pennsylvania State University Press, 1993.

—. "The Structure of Generic Categories: Some Cognitive Aspects." *Journal of Literary Semantics*, 24 (1995), 117–126.

Fowler, Alastair. *Kinds of Literature: An Introduction to the Theory of Genres and Modes*. Oxford: Clarendon Press, 1982.

—. *A History of English Literature: Forms and Kinds from the Middle Ages to the Present.* Oxford: Blackwell, 1987.

—. "The Future of Genre Theory: Functions and Constructional Types." In: *The Future of Literary Theory*, ed. Ralph Cohen. New York: Routledge, 1989, 291–303.

Hawkesworth, John. "Of the Different Kinds of Narrative, and Why They are Universally Read" [essay no. 4, 18 November 1752]. In: *The Adventurer in Two Volumes*. A new edition, revised and corrected. Dublin: John Millekin, 1771, 15–18.

Heinrich, Katrin. *Der Kurzfilm: Geschichte, Gattungen, Narrativik*. Alfeld: Coppi-Verlag, 1997.

Hernadi, Paul. *Beyond Genre: New Directions in Literary Classification*. Ithaca: Cornell University Press, 1972.

Horstmann, Johannes (ed.). *Sprache des Kurzfilms*. Paderborn: Schöningh, 1981.

Houghton, Walter E. "Periodical Literature and the Articulate Classes." In: Shattock and Wolff (1982), 3–27.

Hunter, J. Paul. *Before Novels: The Cultural Contexts of Eighteenth-Century English Fiction*. New York and London: Norton, 1990.

Hutcheon, Linda. *The Politics of Postmodernism*. London: Routledge, 2002 [1989].

Imhof, Rüdiger. *Contemporary Metafiction: A Poetological Study of Metafiction in English since 1939*. Heidelberg: Winter, 1986.

Jacobmeyer, Hannah. *Märchen und Romanzen in der zeitgenössischen englischen Literatur: Fallstudien zu intertextuellen Relationen zwischen Prämoderne und Postmoderne*. Münster: LIT-Verlag, 2000.

Joyce, James. *Stephen Hero*, ed. Theodore Spencer. London: Cape, 1956.

Kipling, Rudyard. "The Three Decker." In: *The Writings in Prose and Verse of Rudyard Kipling. Vol. 9: Verses 1889–1896*. New York: Scribner, 1911, 284–287.

Kosok, Heinz. "Das Kurzdrama." In: *Drama und Theater im England des 20. Jahrhunderts*, ed. Heinz Kosok. Düsseldorf: Bagel, 1980, 80–90.

Landow, George P. *Hypertext: The Convergence of Contemporary Critical Theory and Technology*. Baltimore: Johns Hopkins University Press, 1992.

László, János and Reinhold Viehoff. "Literarische Gattungen als kognitive Schemata." *SPIEL*, 12 (1993), 230–251.

McHale, Brian. *Postmodernist Fiction*. London: Methuen, 1987.

Mergenthal, Silvia. *A Fast-Forward Version of England*. Heidelberg: Winter, 2002.

Mighall, Robert. *A Geography of Victorian Gothic Fiction: Mapping History's Nightmares*. Oxford: Oxford University Press, 1999.

Olmsted, John Charles (ed.). *A Victorian Art of Fiction: Essays on the Novel in British Periodicals 1870–1900*. New York: Garland, 1979.

Olson, Gary M. *et al.* "Cognitive Aspects of Genre." *Poetics*, 10 (1981), 283–315.

Ong, Walter J. *Orality and Literacy: The Technologizing of the Word*. London: Methuen, 1982.

Pater, Walter. "Conclusion." In: *Studies in the History of the Renaissance: Selected Writings of Walter Pater*, ed. Harold Bloom. New York: Columbia University Press, 1982, 58–63.

Punter, David. *The Literature of Terror: A History of Gothic Fiction from 1765 to the Present Day*. London: Longman, 1980.

Raskin, Richard. *The Art of the Short Fiction Film: A Shot by Shot Study of Nine Modern Classics*. London: McFarland, 2002.

Robbins, Keith. *Great Britain: Identities, Institutions and the Idea of Britishness*. London: Longman, 1998.

Rommel, Thomas and Peter Paul Schnierer (eds). *Literarische Hypertexte*. Tübingen: Niemeyer, 2003 [forthcoming].

Rosmarin, Adena. *The Power of Genre*. Minneapolis: University of Minneapolis Press, 1985.

Schmidt, Siegfried J. *Foundations for the Empirical Study of Literature: The Components of a Basic Theory*. Hamburg: Buske, 1982 [translation by Robert de Beaugrande of *Grundriss der Empirischen Literaturwissenschaft*].

Scholes, Robert. *The Fabulators*. New York: Oxford University Press, 1967.

Shattock, Joanne and Michael Wolff (eds). *The Victorian Periodical Press: Samplings and Soundings*. Leicester: Leicester University Press, 1982.

Stierstorfer, Klaus. *Konstruktion literarischer Vergangenheit: Die englische Literaturgeschichte von Warton bis Courthope und Ward*. Heidelberg: Winter, 2001.

Stratmann, Gerd (ed.). *Journal for the Study of British Culture*, 5.1 (1998). Thematic Issue on "National Identities".

Sullivan, Alvin (ed.). *British Literary Magazines: The Augustan Age and the Age of Johnson, 1698–1788*. Westport, CT: Greenwood Press, 1983a.

— (ed.). *British Literary Magazines: The Romantic Age, 1786–1836*. Westport, CT: Greenwood Press, 1983b.

— (ed.). *British Literary Magazines: The Victorian and Edwardian Age, 1837–1913*. Westport, CT: Greenwood Press, 1984.

— (ed.). *British Literary Magazines: The Modern Age, 1914–1984*. Westport, CT: Greenwood Press, 1986.

Todorov, Tzvetan. "Literary Genres." In: *Current Trends in Linguistics*, ed. Thomas A. Sebeok. The Hague: Mouton, 1974, 957–962.

Vosskamp, Wilhelm. "Gattungen als literarisch-soziale Institutionen." In: *Textsortenlehre – Gattungsgeschichte*. Heidelberg: Quelle und Meyer, 1977, 27–42.

Wagner, Peter. *A Short History of English and American Literature*. Stuttgart: Klett, 1988.

Waugh, Arthur. "Reticence in Literature." *Yellow Book*, 1 (April 1894), 201–219.

Waugh, Patricia. *Metafiction: The Theory and Practice of Self-Conscious Fiction*. London: Methuen, 1984.

Wells, H.G. "The Contemporary Novel." In: *A Modern Utopia and Other Discussions*. (The Works of H.G. Wells. Atlantic Edition, vol. 9.) New York: Scribner's, 1925, 357–380.

Wenzel, Peter. "Gattung, literarische", "Gattungsgeschichte", "Gattungstheorie und Gattungspoetik." In: *Metzler Lexikon Literatur- und Kulturtheorie*, ed. Ansgar Nünning. Stuttgart: Metzler, 2001, 204–209.

Wilde, Oscar. "The Decay of Lying: An Observation." In: *The Complete Works of Oscar Wilde*, ed. J.B. Foreman. London: Collins, 1948, 970–992.

Woolf, Virginia. "Modern Fiction." In: *The Essays of Virginia Woolf. Vol. IV: 1925–1928*, ed. Andrew McNeillie. London: Hogarth Press, 1994, 157–165.

# Index